THE CLAIM TO COMMUNITY

THE CLAIM TO COMMUNITY

Essays on Stanley Cavell and Political Philosophy

Edited by Andrew Norris

STANFORD UNIVERSITY PRESS

STANFORD, CALIFORNIA

2006

Stanford University Press
Stanford, California

A slightly different version of Andrew Norris's "Political Revisions: Stanley Cavell
and Political Philosophy" was originally published in *Political Theory* 30, no. 6
©2002, SAGE Publications. Reprinted with permission.

Printed in the United States of America on acid-free, archival-quality paper

Library of Congress Cataloging-in-Publication Data

The claim to community : essays on Stanley Cavell and political philosophy /
edited by Andrew Norris.

p. cm.--

Includes bibliographical references and index.

ISBN-13: 978-0-8047-5129-2 (cloth : alk. paper)

ISBN-13: 978-0-8047-5132-2 (pbk. : alk. paper)

1. Cavell, Stanley, 1926---Political and social views. 2. Political science--Philoso-
phy. 3. Community. I. Norris, Andrew John.

JC251.C38C5313 2006

320.092--dc22   2006006601

Contents

Acknowledgments

This volume grew out of a panel on Stanley Cavell and political philosophy that Tom Dumm and I put together at the 2001 Annual Convention of the American Political Science Association with Hans Sluga, Tracy Strong, and Cavell himself. In the years since then, Tom helped me assemble the rest of the outstanding group of contributors and has always been there to help me sort through the various issues raised by their essays. I am happy to have a chance to publicly acknowledge the extent of my debt to him. Stanley Cavell's own active and generous engagement in this project has been a tremendous privilege for me, as well as a great pleasure. The other contributors to this volume have been exceptionally conscientious and helpful, and I am grateful to them all. I should particularly like to thank Dick Flathman and David Owen for coming up with such fine pieces on such short notice, Tracy Strong for well-timed hints and suggestions, and Hans Sluga for more than ten years of instruction and friendship. Thanks are also due to my editors, Norris Pope and Angie Michaelis, my brothers and sisters, William E. Abraham, Jane Bennett, Richard Eldridge, Jeremy Elkins, Kurt Rudolf Fischer, Lisa Gottreich, Christian Jurlando, Deborah Lowry, James Wallenstein, Eric Wilson, the directors of the Max Planck Institute for European Legal History, and my colleagues at the Department of Political Science at the University of Pennsylvania. My greatest debts, however, are to my daughters and my wife. It is an especial theme of Cavell's that humanity is a learned way of being, and that it is learned in the company of an exemplary friend. I am indebted to Cecilia Meral and Stephanie Zeynep for their demanding pedagogy, and to Yasemin for showing me again and again how to go on.

All of the essays in this collection appear here for the first time, with the exception of my own pieces, "Stanley Cavell and the Claim to Community" and "Political Revisions: Stanley Cavell and Political Philosophy," slightly different versions of which were published in *Theory and Event* 8, no. 1 (Winter 2005) and *Political Theory* 30, no. 6 (December 2002), respectively. I am grateful to the editors for their kind permission to reprint.

THE CLAIM TO COMMUNITY

CHAPTER ONE

Stanley Cavell and the Claim to Community

Andrew Norris

The philosophical appeal to what we say, and the search for our criteria
on the basis of which we say what we say, are claims to community. And
the claim to community is always a search for the basis upon which
it can or has been established. I have nothing more to go on than my
conviction, my sense that I make sense. It may prove to be the case
that I am wrong, that my conviction isolates me, from all others, from
myself. That will not be the same as a discovery that I am dogmatic or
egomaniacal. The wish and the search for community are the wish and
search for reason.

—STANLEY CAVELL, *The Claim of Reason*

To many, the very idea that Stanley Cavell's work contributes anything significant to political theory might seem odd.[1] The Walter M.
Cabot Emeritus Professor of Aesthetics and the General Theory of Value
at Harvard University and a philosopher centrally concerned with the significance of modern philosophical skepticism, Cavell is more easily and
commonly seen as being engaged with aesthetic, ethical, and epistemological questions than he is with political ones. In Richard Eldridge's fine recent collection of essays on Cavell, for instance, there are essays on Cavell's

contributions to ethics, aesthetics, the theory of action, the philosophy of language, film, Shakespeare, the reception of German Romanticism, and American philosophy—but not one directly devoted to politics or political philosophy.[2] And of the 214 records under his name in *The Philosopher's Index*, only nine center on political features or implications of his work.[3] This is, however, somewhat peculiar. As the quotation above reminds us, the claim of reason that is Cavell's central theme and the title of his magnum opus is itself a claim to *community*. What counts as reasonable for us, as a fitting explanation or motivation, shows who and where we are, which community we are a part of, and how we stand with that community. Conversely, our claims to community—specifically, our uses of the first person plural—make that community present in the world. Who *we* are and what beliefs and actions *we* are committed to is something only you and I and others joining us can say. Our common identity is articulated in conversations in which we as individuals give and weigh our reasons, our sense of what should count for us, and why. The public community exists in its representation by us—a representation that is always vulnerable to your or my repudiation. Such repudiation and the alienation that it bespeaks is not a simple matter, as a claim to what is *common* is an appeal to both a sharing that attracts us and an ordinary that uncannily resists or even repels us.

These are eminently political themes: as Sheldon Wolin observes, "the words 'public,' 'common,' and 'general' have a long tradition of usage which has made them synonyms for what is political."[4] Leo Strauss goes further, and writes in connection with the question of the style of Plato's dialogues, "Communication may be a means for living together; in its highest form, communication *is* living together."[5] No doubt, the claims canvassed above come under regular attack in the history of political thought, and have most recently been vehemently dismissed by an administration apparently influenced by some strains of Strauss's own thought.[6] From this perspective, *community* is only a fancy name for *unity*. The unified identity of the group is one that might be definitively identified and enunciated by a founding father or a chief executive, and it is one that citizens and members question or reinterpret only at the risk of its fracturing. Hence Attorney General John Ashcroft's claim that any criticism of the administration's decisions or its handling of "the war on terror" only serves to "aid terrorists [and] erode our national unity and diminish our resolve."[7] Mr. Bush put the same point yet more bluntly when he announced, "Either you are with us, or you are with the terrorists." Such claims hearken back to Hobbes's *Leviathan*, the frontispiece to which shows the individuals who compose the body of the sovereign turned away from the reader and from one another, toward the sovereign who speaks for them and brings them together, depicting a silent and closed unity in which individuals, like the cells of the body, are utterly dependent upon the whole.[8] Silence and obedience are the cost of escape from the war of all against all. As Hobbes famously puts it:

The only way to erect such a Common Power, as may be able to defend them from the invasion of Forraigners, and the injuries of one another . . . is, to conferre all their power and strength upon one Man, or one Assembly of men, that may reduce all their Wills, . . . unto one Will: which is as much to say, to appoint one man, or Assembly of men, to beare their Person; and every one to . . . submit their Wills, every one to his Will, and their Judgements, to his Judgement. This is more than Consent, or Concord; it is a real Unitie of them all, in one and the same Person.[9]

Cavell's pairing of the claim to reason and the claim to community and his suggestion that each is inherently tentative and exploratory—that "the claim to community is always a *search* for the basis upon which it can or has been established"—are dismissed here: the nation is unified by force, not by reason or the desire for it, and it is represented by its chief executive and revealed in its self-assertion in the international arena, not in the conversation of its citizens.

But if this contests Cavell's claims, that serves only to remind us that they, like those of Ashcroft, Bush, and Hobbes, are political in nature as well as topic. Given that we are discussing different conceptions of community, and hence different understandings of politics, this will mean different things in different cases: each statement will self-reflexively define the conditions of its own enunciation. In Hobbes's case, his extreme skepticism regarding the ability of common sense and private judgment to cohere makes his own claims either superhuman, or else partial and hence potentially polemical.[10] (His greatest modern follower will radicalize this and claim that, of necessity, "all political concepts, images, and terms have a polemical meaning . . . focused on a specific conflict and bound to a concrete situation."[11]) Cavell reverses this: his self-reflexive claims on public-ity, community, and deliberation are themselves of necessity deliberative and open-ended, addressed to interlocutors who will question, reinterpret, and possibly reject them—and who will do so on the basis of a shared de-sire for a community whose basis they too *seek*. A "patriotic" communi-ty in which a sovereign executive claims a monopoly upon the ability to speak for the community is one in which the claim to community is left unaddressed, not one in which it is irrelevant: and a community in which the claim to community is never raised because it is taken as being defini-tively addressed is, for Cavell, no community at all. *The Claim of Reason* is just that, a claim of reason—one that eschews polemics, as Cavell does not follow Hobbes in picturing an ultimate agreement as a prerequisite of a successful or peaceful common life. This goes some way toward explain-ing why Cavell takes the pains he does to introduce himself in its opening pages: what might look like a self-indulgent exercise is an attempt to estab-lish an "intellectual community" with the reader (*CR*, pp. xix–xx, 3, and xxii).[12] In what he describes as one of his most explicit attempts to demon-strate the political purchase of Emerson's work, Cavell argues that "sharing the Emersonian text creates a kind of community," a "democratic" one. We should understand his own texts in similar terms, as both describing and depicting the distinctively democratic community their conversation requires and makes possible.[13]

If this finds a place for Cavell in the seemingly omnipresent strug-gle in political theory for a (conception of) community that escapes the smothering demands of unity, it must nonetheless be granted that he did not begin working on these themes in an explicitly political context, but in an engagement with J. L. Austin's ordinary language philosophy and, perhaps more decisively, Wittgenstein's *Philosophical Investigations*.[14] Witt-genstein's suggestion that "if language is to be a means of communica-tion there must be agreement not only in definitions but also (queer as this sounds) in judgments"[15] is one that highlights the social aspect of both the epistemological and the personal. For our language to function, a great number of my personal judgments must agree with yours: you and I must be mutually attuned to one another.[16] This attunement or com-munity reveals itself in our language: "It is what human beings *say* that is true and false; and they agree in the *language* they use. This is not agreement in opinions but in form of life" (*PI*, I:241). Such *Lebensformen* are, as the phrase suggests, living things, negotiated achievements that are always subject to change:

There are *countless* kinds . . . of use of what we call "symbols," "words," "sentences." And this multiplicity is not something fixed, given once and for all; but new types of language, new language-games, as we may say, come into existence, and others become obsolete and get forgotten. . . . Here the term "language-*game*" is meant to bring into prominence the fact that the speaking of language is part of an activity, or of a form of life. (*PI*, I:23)

For many Wittgensteinians, Wittgenstein's analogy here with games also brings into prominence the idea that forms of life are properly understood as systems of rules and their applications—an interpretation that appears to receive support in Wittgenstein's hugely influential discussion of rule-following.[17] Students of politics will be familiar with this reading of Wittgenstein from Peter Winch's *The Idea of a Social Science and Its Relation to Philosophy*, where Winch states baldly, "all behavior which is meaningful (therefore all specifically human behavior) is *ipso facto* rule-governed."[18] This is a view the adequacy of which Cavell has contested from at least as far back as his 1962 "The Availability of Wittgenstein's Later Philosophy."[19] Living a common life requires not merely that we follow rules (of grammar, etiquette, law, and so on), but that we agree in *how* to do so—that, as in the passage from Wittgenstein in the first paragraph above, we agree *in our judgments*. A rule, like a sign, does not dictate its own application. Hence it may seem that rules require our interpretation. But any given interpretation is just another rule, another statement that in turn needs to be applied. Such a potentially infinite regress, as described in *Philosophical Investigations* (pp. 198–202), is cut off when we see rule-following as a *practice* of judgment.[20] As Cavell puts it, "In the sense in which 'playing chess' has rules, 'obeying a rule' has none . . . and yet it can be done correctly or incorrectly—which just means that it can be done or not done. . . . It is a matter of . . . 'forms of life.' That is always the ultimate appeal for Wittgenstein—not rules, not decisions."[21] "Not decisions," because Cavell is anxious not to fall into the positivist assumption—which he attacks in his critique of David Pole's book on Wittgenstein—that when rules give out all that is left is an unregulated *decision* (AWLP, p. 54). But to say that there is no decision (as celebrated, in different settings and in different ways, by

Hobbes, Bush, Jaspers, Sartre, Weber, and the early Schmitt) does not imply that there is no need for *judgment*. Indeed, even in those cases where a rule is at hand to guide us, it can do so only insofar as we can agree upon the criteria that define it and identify behavior that falls under it. Such criteria are not themselves defined by another rule, but defined by *us*.

We learn and teach words in certain contexts, and then we are expected, and expect others, to be able to project them into further contexts. Nothing ensures that this projection will take place (in particular, not the grasping of universals nor the grasping of books of rules), just as nothing insures that we will make, and understand, the same projections. That on the whole we do is a matter of our sharing routes of interest and feeling, senses of humor and of significance and of fulfillment, of what is outrageous, of what is similar to what else, what a rebuke, what forgiveness, of when an utterance is an assertion, when an appeal, when an explanation—all the whirl of organism Wittgenstein calls "forms of life." Human speech and activity, sanity and community, rest on nothing more, but nothing less, than this. It is a vision as simple as it is difficult, and as difficult as it is (and because it is) terrifying (AWLP, p. 52).

The terror of this—well described by John McDowell as "a sort of vertigo"—is one to which Cavell remains attuned throughout his writings.[22] Cavell consistently emphasizes both the ways our common form of life is held together by individual commitments and the manner in which that community can break down into skepticism and confusion, and in which we can find ourselves out of tune with one another, unable to make sense of one another—in which, as he puts it, we can fall into "intellectual tragedy" (*CR*, p. 19). When he speaks of "the truth of skepticism" he refers to fact that the possibility of such tragedy is always present, and no appeal to rules or practices can (permanently) dispel it, or provide a foundation for our responses that is independent of those responses. If Wittgenstein offers a therapy for this, it is a therapy without an obvious or predetermined end, one that ends only provisionally. "Nothing is deeper than the fact, or extent, of agreement itself" (*CR*, p. 32). It is on the basis of our agreement that we make sense to one another; hence agreement is prior to proof, not wrung out of it. (One might follow the respective etymologies here and say that such test or proof there is will be what pleases us.) In holding fast to this Cavell distinguishes himself from prominent Wittgensteinians like P. M. S. Hacker, who in his influential *Insight and Illusion: Themes in the Phi-*

losophy of Wittgenstein dismisses skepticism as nonsensical and confidently explains that the "explanation of concepts . . . ends in good judgment," as if what constitutes good judgment were not itself a matter of judgment, and hence of potential disagreement and uncertainty.[23]

Cavell's treatment of modern philosophical skepticism lies at the heart of his work, and it is essential for any appreciation of its political purchase. If this sounds odd, it is in part because political theory and epistemology are often presented as having little to do with one another. Eminent political theorists and philosophers such as Wolin, Hannah Arendt, Charles Taylor, Richard Bernstein, or Hans-Georg Gadamer hearken more directly than Cavell back to Aristotle's defense of *phronesis* and his claim that "the educated person seeks exactness in each area to the extent that the nature of the subject allows; for apparently it is just as mistaken to demand demonstrations from a rhetorician as to accept [merely] persuasive arguments from a mathematician."[24] Here the exacting demands of Cartesian epistemology appear irrelevant to politics and political theory, even scientistic and distorting, to the extent that they encourage expectations of exactitude and proof that cannot be met, thereby leading us to denigrate distinctively political judgment and deliberation. The attempt associated with Dilthey to establish the human sciences as separate but equal to the natural sciences is extended to politics and, for those who most prize the political, radicalized. Cavell, however, declines to compartmentalize human life and language use in this ultimately unsatisfying way, just as he refuses to abandon the real gains achieved in (and by) modernity. "I understand ordinary language philosophy not as an effort to reinstate vulgar beliefs, or common sense, to a pre-scientific position of eminence, but to reclaim the human self from its denial and neglect by modern philosophy" (*CR*, p. 154). "Modern philosophy"—that is, philosophy since Descartes established the primacy of epistemology and the centrality of the threat of skepticism—cannot be dismissed or evaded; and if there is a politics adequate to "the human self," that politics will be achieved only by those who pass through skeptical doubt.[25]

This insistence upon the importance of skepticism will also sound strange to those who appreciate the depth of Cavell's debt to Wittgenstein, who is taken by many more readers than Hacker as having consistently held the view advanced in his early *Tractatus Logico-Philosophicus* that "skepticism is *not* irrefutable, but palpably senseless, if it would leave doubt where a question cannot be asked. For doubt can exist only where there is a question; a question can be asked only where there is an answer, and this only where something *can* be *said.*"[26] In *The Claim of Reason* Cavell addresses a version of this argument advanced by prominent Wittgensteinians Norman Malcolm and Rogers Albritton in the context of an evaluation of Wittgenstein's use of the notion of a criterion. On the latter's account, criteria provide a basis for a sort of certainty. In a linguistic version of a Kantian transcendental argument, they suggest that attending to the necessary conditions of language demonstrates the incoherence and hence impossibility of philosophical skepticism.[27] One of those conditions is that we agree upon the criteria of the existence of things and the correct use of concepts to identify these things. In the case of another's pain, for instance, I can be certain that she does have pain if various criteria are fulfilled (she groans, holds her cheek, rocks back and forth, and so on). No doubt, these actions might be done in jest, as part of a psychological test, a piece of performance art, or a Candid Camera TV show. But, Malcolm argues, this fact does not open the door to skepticism, to doubt in every given case:

The abnormal reaction *must* be the exception and not the rule. For if someone *always* had endless doubts about the genuineness of expressions of pain, it would mean that he was not using *any criterion* of another's being in pain. It would mean that he did not accept anything as an expression of pain. So what could it mean to say that he even had the *concept* of another's being in pain. It is senseless to suppose that he has this concept and yet always doubts.[28]

Cavell points out that this argument does not do much to dispel any actual doubts, as the concepts of pain and pain behavior are used in the case of both actual and feigned pain. "Criteria are 'criteria for something's being so,' not in the sense that they tell us of a thing's existence, but of something like its identity, not of its *being* so, but of its being *so.* Criteria do not determine the certainty of statements, but the application of the concepts employed in the statements" (*CR*, p. 45). The possibility of skepticism therefore remains. While it may not be raised in ordinary practical circumstances, it is a response to questions that no rules of language or reason prohibit. More, it is "a response to, or expression of, a real experience which takes hold of human beings," an experience "of being sealed off from the world," in which "the world drops out" (*CR*, pp. 140, 144, 145)—an experience, that is, of profound alienation.[29]

This experience is a very particular one. Indeed, it is an *uncanny* one. If Malcolm is wrong that the rules of our language or concept use prohibit skeptical doubt, it remains true that skeptical doubt is a peculiar projection of the ordinary (manner of raising and expressing) doubt out of which it allegedly grows, a projection so radical that—as the skeptic gladly acknowledges—the nature of doubt appears fundamentally altered. Ordinarily we doubt some*thing* in a context of assumption. But when Descartes is done with us we have moved to doubting *everything*, a shift that Malcolm is right to seize on as extraordinary. Descartes's doubt both does and does not resemble my doubt that, say, the white dot on the horizon really is a boat, if only because I also doubt the alternative possibilities (that it is a seagull, a wave, etc.). It resembles those ordinary cases enough that it is recognizable as a doubt, but it is a doubt that no set of circumstances alone could raise or justify. (If the experience "of being sealed off from the world" takes place within the world, it is not an experience of anything within that world.) As Cavell says, skepticism "is *not* fully natural, and . . . it is not *fully* unnatural," either (*CR*, p. 160). In his analysis of this, Cavell focuses not upon the rules for concept use, as does Malcolm, but upon the nature of a *claim*, which he argues is not so simple a thing as it might at first appear. "There must," Cavell argues, "in grammar, be reasons for what you say, or be point in your saying of something, if what you say is to be comprehensible. We can understand what the *words* mean apart from understanding why you say them; but apart from understanding the point of your saying them we cannot understand what *you* mean" (*CR*, p. 206).[30] And you, as a human being, always act in specific situations, responding to specific features of those situations. A claim is thus intelligible in a particular *context*. I can't simply announce a claim (say, a doubt) at any time, in any place, and be (myself, in my claim) intelligible. I will not yet have quite *said* or *claimed* anything. If I simply announce, out of the blue, "There are no physical objects," and you happen to be standing by me, you will at best take that to be a rather bizarre invitation to philosophical debate—and indeed, only that if you have reason to think that I am someone interested in such conversation, and not someone driven mad by life on the street, chronic drug abuse, or some other trauma. That is to say, your likely response will be, "Huh?" or, "Come again?"[31]

The skeptical epistemologist wants to say that knowledge *in general* is impossible. But in order to demonstrate this he needs to show that he is unable to know anything, that is, any particular thing. To do this, he needs an example of a specific object, like Descartes's ball of wax, that somehow transcends its specificity so as to exemplify *all* other possible objects of knowledge—something Cavell terms a *generic object*. "When those objects present themselves to the epistemologist, he is not taking one as opposed to another, interested in its features as peculiar to it and nothing else. He would rather, so to speak, have an unrecognizable *something* there if he could, an anything, a thatness. What comes to him is an island, a body surrounded by air, a tiny earth. What is at stake for him in the object is materiality as such, externality altogether" (*CR*, p. 53). But *externality altogether* is not a specific object about which a claim can be made. The skeptic is thus left in an impossible position: he needs to be making a claim about an object that he cannot know, but for his claim to have the reach he wants it to, he cannot be confronting such an object. Likewise, for his claim to be intelligible, he must be making it to someone, for some reason. But on his own account there is no other person there, either because they have no mind (as in other minds skepticism) or because they simply don't exist (as in general skepticism): "My noting of the epistemologist's context as non-claim focuses," Cavell writes, "on a feature dramatized in Descartes' description of his context (as one in which he is seated in his dressing gown before the fire . . .), namely that the epistemologist, in his meditation, is alone" (*CR*, p. 220). The skeptic is, as such, *alone*, making a claim that is no claim, in what Cavell terms a *non-claim context*.

If the epistemologist were not imagining a claim to have been made, his procedure would be as out of the ordinary as the ordinary language philosopher finds it to be. But, on the other hand, if he were investigating a claim of the sort the coherence of his procedures require (or going over in imagination a case in which a concrete claim has in fact been made) then his conclusion would not have the generality it seems to have. (*CR*, p. 218)

Cavell argues that the epistemologist's attempt to have it both ways is indicative of a broader tendency in modern philosophy: "In philosophizing we come to be dissatisfied with answers which depend upon *our* meaning something by an expression, as though what *we* meant by it were more or less arbitrary. . . . It is as though we try to get the world to provide answers in a way which is independent of our *claiming* something to be so" (*CR*, pp. 215–16). "I must empty out *my* contribution to words, so that language itself, as if beyond me, exclusively takes over the responsibility for meaning."[32] For Cavell it is this fantasy, which he describes as "the human drive to transcend itself, make itself inhuman" (DD, p. 57), that really gets skepticism going: the skeptic attempts to find something that will guarantee the intelligibility of his practices and, ultimately, himself. It is his failure in this enterprise (his conclusion that there is no indubitable basis for certainty) that most philosophers identify as his skepticism. But for Cavell skepticism names the initial turn to epistemology in the evasion of one's own responsibility for one's responses.[33] (Here again the etymology is felicitous.) The attempt to defeat or banish skepticism is on this account merely another expression of it and of the fantasy of self-effacement that underlies it (CR, pp. 351–52).

What this analysis achieves is to take epistemology seriously while at the same time decentering it and, relatedly, to situate sociality and interpersonal responsibility at the heart of subjectivity. Skepticism is not, say, what Rorty claims, a peculiar hang-up picked up by over-eager undergraduates who have read too much Descartes and Hume and not enough Dewey; it is a particularly pure example of a more general attempt to claim something without accepting responsibility for the conditions that make claims intelligible, an attempt to speak without speaking to someone, to speak without being someone who needs or wants to speak. The claim to knowledge is thus, as a claim, an interpersonal matter; and it can never be fully grounded in a way that will provide the certainty that the epistemologist seeks. As each claim requires a claim context, no claim can be so abstract as to speak to and in all such contexts, or serve as an ultimate foundation for them. Cavell concludes from this that the truth or moral of skepticism is that "the human creature's basis in the world as a whole, its relation to the world as such, is not that of knowing, anyway what we think of as knowing" (CR, p. 241). Instead it is a matter of *acknowledgment.*[34] This is a turning within the epistemological, not a (hermeneutic) replacement of it: "I do not propose the idea of acknowledgement as an alternative to knowing but rather as an interpretation of it, as I take the word 'acknowledge,' containing 'knowledge,' itself to suggest (or perhaps it suggests that knowing is an interpretation of acknowledging)."[35] Knowledge is not undermined; if it seems it is, that is because "a condition presents itself as a limitation" (CW, p. 164). Our knowledge of things in the world is possible, not on the basis of an indubitable foundation of certainty, but in the context of the acknowledgment of other people and commitments.

One can think of this argument as an extension of Kant's identification of subjectivity with the activity of judgment, rather than with passive observation, as in the empiricist tradition. But where Kant's subject is notoriously difficult to situate, and whereas it remains difficult to relate Kant's synthesizing transcendental ego, legislating moral will, and empirical subject, for Cavell the subject of responsibility in language is always *us*, here and now—the human beings whom modern philosophy has, he argues, obscured and occluded.[36] These beings are plural, in conversation. What Arendt finds to be the sine qua non of politics is on Cavell's account the sine qua non of speech. If we return to the above comments on Hobbes and Bush, we can see that Cavell is if anything in a stronger position than Arendt to critique them. What Arendt will name a betrayal of "the political" for philosophy, Cavell will name a descent into uncanny unintelligibility.[37] One clear advantage for Cavell here is that he leaves open the possibility that the substance of politics might be of philosophical import and interest. (If it were not, why would we care about it, or care about it as deeply as we sometimes do?) Moreover, Cavell's defense of sociality, as he puts it,[38] directly addresses two of Hobbes's most basic assumptions: that human beings find themselves (initially) unburdened with responsibilities to one another, and that it is the business of political or moral philosophy to identify, explain, and justify what responsibilities they ought to assume. This project has been notoriously problematic, generating as it has more disagreement than consensus. One implication of the above is that it is not necessary in the form it has assumed up to now.[39]

If Cavell's analysis of skepticism rules out the "atomism" of Hobbesian contract theory, that has not led Cavell to reject all forms of contract theory. Cavell's own approach to the question of the distinctively *political* community begins with speaking beings in a context within which their speech with one another is intelligible, and asks how they will elaborate or evade that basic community. Hence he follows Rousseau, who in *The Social Contract* steers away from the Hobbesian notion of the pre-social state of nature and emphasizes instead that of a contract immanent to the present community that might transform it from within.[40] Properly understood, the contract concerns not just what responsibilities I will *assume*, but who

I *am*—if only because my deepest commitments are ones that express who I am.[41] "Moral philosophers in our liberal tradition," Cavell suggests, have come to "look upon our shared commitments and responses . . . as more like particular agreements than they are" (*CR*, p. 179). Rousseau corrects this, and proposes the contract as a means of self-examination. The politics of the legislative activity of a general will requires that all citizens, at some time, be capable of asking themselves whether the defining activity of that society expresses their will. We cannot all be forced to be free all the time. Such inquiry is, in a crucial sense, a matter of *self-interpretation*:

When a law is proposed in the people's assembly, what is asked of them is not precisely whether they approve of the proposition or reject it, but whether it is conformity with the general will which is theirs, and each by giving his vote gives his opinion on this question, and the counting of votes yields a declaration of the general will. When, therefore, the opinion [*l'avis*] contrary to my own prevails, that proves only that I have made a mistake [*je m'étais trompé*], and that what I believed to be the general will was not so.[42]

No one has unmediated access to their (common) self, and their opinions as to that self and its will are worked out in concert. In *The Social Contract* Rousseau himself has little to say about this moment of reflective self-interpretation, and turns to the state as the proper vehicle and site for this political hermeneutic.[43] Cavell, in contrast, keeps the focus squarely on the subject as citizen. For him, the point of the teaching of the theory of the social contract remains

its imparting of political education: it is philosophical because its method is an examination of myself by an attack upon my assumptions; it is political because the terms of this self-examination are the terms which reveal me as a member of the polis; it is education not because I learn new information but because I learn that the finding and forming of my knowledge of myself requires that finding and forming of my knowledge of that membership (the depth of my own and the extent of those joined with me). (*CR*, p. 25)

From this perspective, the thought of the contract throws into high relief the potentially political implications of our use of the first person plural, our ability to speak for one another by giving voice to the will that is common to us.[44] "To speak for oneself politically is to speak for the others with whom you consent to association" (*CR*, p. 27), because if you aren't in any such association you aren't yet political. But my attempt to speak for others is, as noted above, never more (or less) than a *claim*. "The authority one has, or assumes, in expressing statements of initiation, in saying 'We,' is related to the authority one has in expressing or declaring one's promises or intentions. Such declarations cannot be countered by evidence because they are not supported by evidence" (*CR*, p. 179). Far from identifying a source of impersonal authority, the claim to community is itself always open to repudiation. I can only say that this is what *we* say. Moreover, the context required for the intelligibility of the claim as claim is that of an absence of consensus. As Richard Eldridge puts it, such claims are

attempts to speak as a member of a community would speak, attempts which are called forth by the facts that not everyone does speak that way, that community habits of speech have been lost or forgotten or that the community of which one is or hopes to be a member has not yet learned how to project its habits of speech onto new situations and so is under threat of dissolution, in so far as different people may come to conceptualize important new situations differently, thus distancing themselves from one another.[45]

Examples of such new projections in contemporary political life might involve the rules or definition of war when the alleged enemy is no longer a nation-state, or, the nature of democracy when the democratic polity has assumed the privileges and burdens of empire. If you reject my claim— say, that *we* now find a place for invading countries that have not attacked us, or that *we* are not the sort of people who will compromise democratic principles of transparency in government this much—I am evidently wrong: since that's not what you say, it can't be what *we* say. But your countering claim is left hanging in precisely the same way (since I evidently don't second it), and therefore it is unable to disprove my claim. Cavell concludes that in such a situation, "it is not a matter of saying something false. Nor is it an inability or refusal to say something or to hear something. . . . At such crossroads we have to conclude that on this point we are simply different; that is, we cannot here speak for one another." And of a speaker who ends in this bind he writes, "He hasn't said something false about 'us'; he has learned that there is no us (yet, maybe never) to say anything about" (*CR*, pp. 19–20).

　　This conception of the relationship between publicity, identity, representation, and speech opens up a wide political-theoretic terrain for

Cavell. The obvious commonalties between the political use of the first person plural and the ordinary language philosopher's appeal to *what we would say* has allowed him to tease out subtle and important philosophical features of political life and political features of philosophical life. More generally, the focus on the nature of the subject assumed and denied in each of these sheds light upon political identity and representation and on the preconditions of commitment in the absence of certain grounds. In both liberal Anglo-American and "Continental" political theory there is still a widespread assumption that reasons, to operate as reasons, must be grounded in certainty. Prime examples of this would be the existentialist celebration of politics as something beyond rational deliberation (as in the endlessly repeated suggestion that a free choice is a decision made in "a moment of madness") and this existentialism's mirror image, the fetishizing of economic, instrumental rationality and "utility maximization" (the choice of the so-called Rational Choice theorists). Cavell's work offers enormously thoughtful and sensitive therapy for both, showing as it does how little we have understood what it is to appeal to reason or community, and how crude our conceptions are of the nature of (political) speech, judgment, and the distinctions between the public and private.[46] If Cavell's contributions to political philosophy have not been widely recognized, this is in part a function of the fact that he expresses almost no interest in political institutions such as the state or in the violence to which it claims a monopoly. Even in his few explicit engagements with political theory, he is quick to say that he writes for a society in which "good enough" justice prevails. But he is hardly alone in being more interested in political subject formation than rules of governance, as the examples of Michel Foucault, Judith Butler, and Alasdair MacIntyre remind us. As in their cases, the claim is that no set of rules or institutions or acts of violence could truly be legitimated in the absence of an understanding of the subjects who will confer this legitimacy, and experience its result.

If Cavell's work thus has enormous political implications and range, his own focus has been on the ways Thoreau and especially Emerson deepen and draw out lessons Austin and Wittgenstein began, their appeal to "the common, the familiar, the everyday, the low, the near" referring, as does ordinary language philosophy, to "an intimacy, an intimacy lost, that matched skepticism's despair of the world."[47] Cavell acknowledges that "to most of my colleagues the underwriting of ordinary language philosophy by transcendentalism would be about as promising as enlivening the passé by the extinct."[48] Even those less dismissive than these colleagues have felt that, Cavell's protests notwithstanding, this turn has more to do with ethics and culture than it does with politics. In his most recent book, the 2004 *Cities of Words: Pedagogical Letters on a Register of the Moral Life,* Cavell goes out of his way to confront and discourage such doubts. The book's title is an obvious reference to Plato's *Republic,* the main body of which ends, at the close of Book Nine, by turning away from the *polis* to the individual. In words Cavell cites as one of his epigraphs, the "city in words . . . is a model laid up in heaven, for him who wishes to look upon, and as he looks, set up the government of his soul. It makes no difference whether it exists anywhere or will exist. [The man of sense] would take part in the public affairs of that city only, not of any other." Set politics aside, and tend your own garden—advice that many, even after Cavell's *Senses of Walden,* think of as Thoreau's as well as Candide's lesson.

But Cavell cites these lines only to immediately emphasize that moral perfectionism as he understands it stymies any such easy division of the moral and the political, as well as the compromises and resignations such divisions make possible, suggesting that the perfectionist's "imagination of justice is essential to the aspiration of a democratic society" (*CW,* p. 14). Perfectionism, Cavell proposes, names a register of moral life in which the self is experienced as divided against itself, as in Kant, where the noumenal self stands above the phenomenal and sensual self, or, more pertinently, in Plato's image of the cave, which counters the self capable of inhabiting the intelligible world of the just with that bound in and to its degraded shadow.

Each of these variations provides a position from which the present state of human existence can be judged. . . . The very conception of divided self and a doubled world, providing a perspective of judgment upon the world as it is, measured against the world as it may be, tends to express disappointment with the world as it is, as the scene of human activity and prospects, and perhaps to lodge the demand or desire for a reform or transfiguration of the world. (*CW,* p. 2)

This sense of disappointment is of course registered in the lines cited from the *Republic.* But Cavell's response is not to turn away from the world of shadows and the self that dwells there, to abandon politics for ethics. On his account, Emersonian perfectionism requires that we "transfigure Kant's metaphysical division of worlds into a rather empirical (or political) division of the world" (*CW*, p. 2):

> If the world is disappointing and the world is malleable and hence we feel ourselves called upon for change, where does change begin, with the individual (with myself) or with the collection of those who make up my (social, political) world? This question seems to make good sense if we contrast Emerson and Freud with, say, Locke or Marx . . . , but its sense is questioned as we consider what perfectionist encounters look and sound like. I would say, indeed, that it is a principal object of Emerson's thinking to urge a reconsideration of the relation ("the" relation?) of soul and society, especially as regards the priority of one over the other. (*CW*, p. 3)

The question of the relation of soul and society is hardly a pre-political matter but arguably the central question of politics, as the example of *The Republic* reminds us. Cavell stakes himself as a political thinker upon his sense that its answer(s) requires both politics and philosophy, and neither in isolation from the other. If this makes politics more "idealistic" than many contemporary political theorists would have it, it hardly pushes it in a utopian or moralistic direction. The perception of a higher world and self, of oneself as fallen, demands not the simple replacement of one world by another—as if we could simply enter the city in speech, or the kingdom of ends—but a reinterpretation of the very sense of being split, divided against oneself. This is alluded to in the picture of a claim to community as requiring an interpretation of myself and of those with whom I am joined. A life made up of moments of such interpretation is not an abandonment of either pole any more than it is an escape from the testing of one's claims in conversation with others. Alienation is not overcome (in a happy conformity), but refigured, reinterpreted, in ways that allow one moments of peace in which the demands of both worlds—of the "ideal" and "real"—come to terms with one another. Cavell does not oppose the fallen real of what he calls our actual ordinary to an *ideal*, but to *an eventual ordinary*. This is, I take it, why he can make the apparently paradoxical proposal that "the condition of democratic morality" is living "as an example of human partiality, . . . which means, being one who lives in promise, as a sign, or representative human."[49] To simply deny partiality in favor of a representative humanity somehow opposed to it would be a denial of our condition of a piece with "the human drive to transcend itself, make itself inhuman" that Cavell finds in skepticism. Representing humanity requires making some sort of peace with that partiality, not abandoning it, just as representing my community is not to speak in a voice other than my own, but to speak in that voice for us—speech that invites your correction, and hence your assistance, and hence speech that hails you as being one with me, but in a position to amend what that has meant to me up to now.

CHAPTER TWO

Wittgenstein and Cavell: Anthropology, Skepticism, and Politics

Sandra Laugier

Many commentators have seen an anthropological dimension in the thought of Wittgenstein, notably in his notion of form of life and in his reflections on rules and on the communal nature of language. But this alone is not sufficient for there to be political ideas in Wittgenstein: only since Stanley Cavell's radical reading of Wittgenstein, in *The Claim of Reason*, are we able to see a genuine political dimension (beyond the usual banalities about Wittgenstein's conservatism, of the recourse to a form of life). Cavell, well beyond anthropological and social readings of Wittgenstein, offers an original reflection (inspired by both Wittgenstein and his own master, J. L. Austin) on the subject of language, and the authority of this subject, over others and over oneself, thus on the authority that society has over one: In short, this is the question of us. This question, as Stanley Cavell has presented it in *The Claim of Reason* and his later work (*This New Yet Unapproachable America* and *Conditions Handsome and Unhandsome*), is also the question of skepticism. It is a question that poses itself when we deal with ordinary language, which is Cavell's starting point.

1. Ordinary Language and Society

The appeal to ordinary language poses in effect a new problem. Cavell says in the introduction to his first book, *Must We Mean What We Say?*, that the idea "that what we ordinarily say and mean may have a direct and deep control over what we can philosophically say and mean"[1] has a significance that goes beyond the philosophy of language: the idea is often rejected by philosophers (Continental as well as analytic) who find it simplistic and blind to the nature of philosophical questions. It poses the problem of the pertinence of this ordinary saying. The philosophical problem of appealing to "what we say" appears when we ask ourselves not only what saying is, but what we are. How do I know what we say in this or that situation? How is the language that I speak, inherited as it is from others, *my* language? These are the questions that we encounter in the opening sections of Wittgenstein's *Philosophical Investigations*, which curiously begins with a quotation from Augustine about the learning of language: since one always begins with the words of another, one comes into agreement with one's "elders."

What is at issue in Cavell is our criteria, that is, our shared agreement on, or rather *in,* language, and more particularly the *we* in "what we would say when." What basis is there for the appeal to ordinary language? All we have to go on is what we say and what we agree on in language. Our agreement is not a matter of inherent meanings, but of uses. We determine "what a word means" by its uses. The investigation of our agreement (asking "what would you say if . . . ") is founded on everything but meanings or the determination (even problematized) of "shared senses" among speakers. The agreement that Austin and Wittgenstein speak of is not an intersubjective agreement; it is not founded on a "convention" or on any actual agreements made between speakers in society. It is an agreement that is as objective as anything (Austin speaks in this connection of "experimental data"). But what is this agreement? Where does it come from, and why should we give it such weight? This is the problem Cavell sets out to address. In all of his work, he poses the question: What allows Austin and Wittgenstein *to say what they say about what we say?* From what do they derive their right? And the answer is fertile in paradoxes. For Cavell, the radical absence of any foundation for the claim to "say what we say"—his first discovery—is not a mark of any absence of logical rigor or rational certitude in the procedure that arises from this claim—his second discovery. This is the meaning of what Wittgenstein says about our "agreement in judgments" and in language: it is not founded on anything but itself, on *us*. Clearly, there is in this the makings of skepticism, and this is thus quite properly the central topic of *The Claim of Reason*. But to understand the nature of our language and our agreements is also to understand that it "does not abolish logic" (*Philosophical Investigations*, §242) and that rather the lack of any external foundation for our agreement in language represents something fundamental to our rationality—this is what Cavell defines as, in the strict sense, *the truth* in skepticism. *The Claim of Reason* is, as a whole, a development of a remark in one of his first essays, "The Availability of Wittgenstein's Later Philosophy": "We learn and teach words in certain contexts, and then we are expected and expect others to project them into further contexts. Nothing insures that this projection will take place (in particular, not the grasping of universals nor the grasping of books of rules) . . . It is a vision as simple as it is difficult, and as difficult as it is (and because it is) terrifying."[2]

One can see here the movement that is accomplished in Cavell from the question of shared language to the question of the sharing of forms of life, a sharing that is not merely a matter of being part of social structures, but of everything that makes up human activities and existences. This is why sociological interpretations and uses of Wittgenstein always miss the true force of his anthropology: it never suffices for Wittgenstein to say "this is what we do." The problem is to know how to connect the I to the us and vice versa. In this way, skepticism is inherent in every human practice, linguistic or otherwise: all certitude or confidence in what we do (follow a rule, count, etc.) is modeled on the confidence that we have in our shared uses of language. The "acceptance of forms of life," immanence, does not afford us a pat response to philosophical problems. From this point of view, one of the merits of Cavell's reading is its radically putting in question such a conception of "form of life," a conception that might be called "conformist." Putting the conformity question inevitably raises skeptical doubt. Cavell shows at once the fragility and the depth of our agreements, and he seeks out the very nature of the necessity that emerges, for Wittgenstein, from our forms of life. A rule is neither a foundation nor an interpretation: it is *there*—but this in no way diminishes its rigor, for it is natural. A unique aspect of Cavell's position is his redefinition of the necessity of ordinary usage in terms of *nature*.

There is not, then, an "answer" to the skepticism that emerges from the fragility of our agreements. That our ordinary language is founded on nothing but itself is not only a source of anxiety as to the validity of what we do and say: it is the revelation of a truth about ourselves that we do not want to recognize—that "I" am the sole possible source of their validity. To refuse this, to attempt to surpass skepticism, ends up reinforcing skepticism.

The accepting of this fact, then, does not come as a relief, a deliverance, but is the recognition of finitude and of the everyday. It is on this condition that we can regain our lost contact with reality, the nearness of the world and of words, which is broken in skepticism. So a response to the question of "realism," so much discussed today in the philosophy of language, is not to be found except in ordinary language, in what Austin and Wittgenstein show to be the entanglement, the reciprocal involvement of language and life. The adequacy of language to reality—the truth of language—is not to be constructed or to be proven: it is to be shown in language and its uses.

The philosophical problem that ordinary language philosophy raises has therefore two parts: First, with what right does it found itself on what we ordinarily say? Second, on what, or on whom, does it found itself in determining what we ordinarily say? These questions are in reality the same: they are the question of my (my words') connection to the real (to our world), that is to say, for Cavell as for Wittgenstein, of our criteria. To see this, let us return to the question of our agreements in language. We share the criteria by means of which we regulate our application of concepts, through which we establish the conditions of conversation. What Wittgenstein investigates and determines, in the *Investigations*, is our criteria, which govern what we say. But *who is he* to claim to know these things? It is this absence of foundation for the claim to know what we say that supports the idea of criteria, and that defines the claim to ordinary language. "The philosophical appeal to what we say, and the search for our criteria on the basis of which we say what we say, are claims to community. And the claim to community is always a search for the basis on which it can or has been established. I have nothing more to go on than my conviction, my sense that I make sense."[3] The central enigma of community is thus the possibility that I can speak in the name of others. It is precisely here that we find the problem of "Other Minds": "But how does he [Wittgenstein] know such things? . . . how can he so much as have the idea that these fleets of his own consciousness, which is obviously all he's got to go on, are accurate wakes of our own?"[4] This accounts for the very unusual tone of the *Investigations*, that they have something of autobiography. It is this tone of confidence that brings Wittgenstein close to Rousseau and Thoreau, and leads Cavell to find in Wittgenstein's reflection on agreement in language an interrogation of the nature of subjectivity.

There is not then in Wittgenstein a refutation of skepticism by the ordinary. For Wittgenstein as for Austin, there is nothing obvious or immediate about the ordinary: it is to be discovered, and that is the task that Austin's minute analyses and Wittgenstein's innumerable examples set themselves. What I mean is that the appeal to ordinary language does not hold out an easy solution to the philosophical problems, and that it certainly cannot be reduced to any falling back on shared meaning. This is what most strongly distinguishes Wittgenstein from a philosopher like Moore, who would seem to know, right off the bat, what our shared meaning is, what we ordinarily say or think. But in reality there is nothing that is more difficult to know: Wittgenstein has need of the whole of the *Investigations* to know, for example, if we *think* that we have access to the mind of another person or that the world exists. These are questions that do not have a straight off answer, and they show the impossibility, or the danger, of responding to skepticism with arguments that appeal to our ordinary beliefs. This returns us again to the question of the foundation of our agreement: that of the nature of *me*, of my capacity to speak, and so to conform in the use of shared criteria. It is not enough to invoke community; we still have to know what authorizes me (what gives me the right) to invoke it.

When I remarked that the philosophical search for our criteria is a search for community, I was in effect answering the second question I uncovered in the face of the claim to speak for "the group"—the question namely about how I could have been party to the establishing of criteria if I do not recognize that I have and do not know what they are . . . the claim is not that one can tell a priori who is implicated by me, because one point of the particular kind of investigation Wittgenstein calls grammatical is exactly to discover who. (*CR*, p. 22)

The strength of Cavell's analysis of convention is that it makes us revisit the problematic character of every appeal to convention. That it is problematic is shown by this passage of the *Philosophical Investigations*:

It is what human beings *say* that is true or false, and they *agree* in the language that they use [*in der Sprache stimmen die Menschen überein*]. That is not agreement in opinions but in form of life. If language is to be a means of communication there must be agreement [*Übereinstimmung*] not only in definitions but also (queer as this may sound) in judgments. This may seem to abolish logic, but does not do so.[5]

It is of the first importance for Cavell that Wittgenstein says that we agree *in* and not *on* language. That means that we are not makers of the agreement, that language precedes agreement just as much as agreement makes language possible, and that this circularity amounts to an irreducible element of skepticism. Most conventionalist interpreters of Wittgenstein (e.g., one may say, in a sense, Kripke) take a false path: they suppose that convention can help us to define agreement in language. The idea of convention does indeed mean something: it acknowledges the strength of our agreement, and the extraordinary character of our capacity to speak together. But it cannot be the basis of an account of the real practice of language, and furthermore it can encourage us to avoid seeing that language is natural. As Cavell puts is, "we *cannot* have agreed beforehand to all that would be necessary."[6]

That we agree in language means that language—our form of life—produces our understanding of one another just as much as language is a product of agreement, that it is natural to us in this sense, and that the idea of convention is there to at once ape and disguise this necessity. "Beneath the tyranny of convention, there is the tyranny of nature," Cavell writes. At this point, the criticism mounted by Cavell of usual interpretations of "form of life" becomes relevant. Cavell opposes these interpretations by his use of the formulation "form of *life*," by contrast with "*form* of life." What is given is our forms of life. What leads us to want to violate our agreements, our criteria, is the refusal of this given, of this form of life in not only its social but also its biological dimension. It is on this second (vertical) aspect of form of life that Cavell is insisting, while at the same time recognizing the importance of the first (horizontal) dimension, that is, social agreement. What discussions of the first sense (that of conventionalism) have obscured is the strength in Wittgenstein of the natural and biological sense of form of life, which Wittgenstein picks out in evoking "natural reactions" and "the natural history of humanity." What is given in forms of life is not only social structures and various cultural habits, but everything that can be seen in "the specific strength and dimensions of the human body, the senses, the human voice" and everything that makes it the case that, just as doves, in Kant's phrase, need air to fly, so we, in Wittgenstein's phrase, need friction to walk (*Investigations*, §107). In thinking of convention we resist the naturalness of language, which is just as or even more essential than convention to language's being public:

It is a wonderful step toward understanding the abutment of language and the world when we see it to be a matter of convention. But this idea, like every other, endangers as it releases the imagination. For some will then suppose that a private meaning is not more arbitrary than one arrived at publicly, and that since language inevitably changes, there is no reason not to change it arbitrarily. Here we need to remind ourselves that ordinary language is natural language, and that its changing is natural.[7]

Cavell, in concluding the first part of *The Claim of Reason*, asks in this way about what he calls "the natural ground of our conventions":

What is the natural ground of our conventions, to what are they in service? It is inconvenient to question a convention; that makes it unserviceable, it no longer allows me to proceed as a matter of course; the paths of action, the paths of words, are blocked. "To imagine a language is to imagine a form of life" (cf. [*Philosophical Investigations*] §19). In philosophizing, I have to bring my own language and life into imagination.[8]

This leads Cavell to redefine the task of philosophy as *education for grown-ups*. But "for grownups this is not natural growth but change" (*CR*, p. 125).

2. Community, Language, and Politics

It is at this point that the question of language becomes political. One part of the American political debate at the end of the last century, notably the opposition between "liberals" and "communitarians," concerns the relationship of the individual to the community, and therefore of the "I" to the "we." What is criticized by communitarians is the liberals' insistence on the individual; what is rejected by liberals is the affirmation of community values and virtues as against the claims of the individual. Rather than rehearsing this tired debate, let us consider this specific point, namely that of the relation between the two claims fundamentally at issue here: that of the "I" and that of (or to) the community.

One often dates the emergence of the communitarian critique of liberalism to the publication, in 1981, of Alasdair MacIntyre's book *After Virtue*. MacIntyre attacks the liberalism that originated with the Enlightenment, attributing to it the evils of modern civilization, and in particular the present disarray of moral philosophy, crisscrossed as it is with insoluble debates and incapable of resolving even the least concrete moral problem. MacIntyre's point of departure, then, is a critique of contemporary moral (and therefore political) philosophy, and *After Virtue* is useful in the first instance for its putting in question certain consensus views in analytic moral theory, especially the heritage of emotivism. Modern moral thought is in a state of chaos and emptiness, a chaos and emptiness so profound that we ourselves are at a loss to account for it. Once we get past the purely reactionary surface of MacIntyre's kind of pessimistic picture of contemporary reality, we can see the depth and importance of MacIntyre's description. The words of moral discourse are devoid of sense; they do not speak to us *at all.* "The most striking feature of contemporary moral utterance is that so much of it is used to express disagreements; and the most striking feature of the debates in which these disagreements are expressed is their interminable character."[9]

After Virtue is most pertinent not in its opposition to contemporary civilization, but in its opposition to the scholasticism of analytic moral philosophy as it had developed up to the 1970s. This recognition of the emptiness of the moral discourse that had developed in our time brings *After Virtue* into connection with the quasi-contemporary work of Cavell in *The Claim of Reason*. The absence of meaning in our words, parallel to the absence of meaning in our lives, is a theme that Cavell and MacIntyre have in common. We can find a common source of their ideas in Emersonian perfectionism and in Emerson's denunciation of conformity in "Self-Reliance": "This conformity makes them not false in a few particulars, authors of a few lies, but false in all particulars. Their every truth is not quite true. Their two is not the real two, their four not the real four; so that every word they say chagrins us, and we know not where to begin to set them right."[10] In raising the question of the "content" of our moral discourse, which is also asking after the everyday, ordinary value of our moral theorizing, MacIntyre, like Cavell, reintroduces ordinary moral questioning into the heart of a hypertheorized moral philosophy.

But at this point Cavell and MacIntyre diverge, and the remedies they offer for our condition differ. The passage from Emerson that I quoted, with its characteristic expression of the "self-reliance" that allows me to make language my own and to give meaning to our shared words, is distant from the point of view of MacIntyre. The pessimistic description in *After Virtue* is aimed as well at a second target, and this second target is at the root of the debate over communitarianism. If our language has become hollow and empty and if even we ourselves are unable to account for this, it is because modernity—to use the standard terminology—even while depriving us of our moral foundations and points of reference, has given us the illusion of being able to speak about them. Our political and moral language is a language of objectivity, of rationality: but this language does not refer to anything, it does not give us any criteria. What gives us the illusion of speaking about morality is the Enlightenment project that has dominated our culture and our philosophy for three centuries, putting forward a conception of rationality independent of social and political context and of every specific conception of man. For MacIntyre, not only has this project failed, but its recent prolongation—in the form of contemporary liberalism—maintains us in the illusion of a pertinence long since lost. It is here that the second target of MacIntyre's thought becomes clear: individualism, characterized by demand for the rights of the isolated individual, founded on his reason alone, detached from every higher authority, and independent of any prior conception of good. Contemporary liberal theories have denied all content to moral reflection, and in giving political and legal primacy to the individual, in isolating him from his social and historical context, they have deprived him of every connection to the good (to the *virtues*, to take up MacIntyre's moralizing terminology).

It is on this point that some of the discussion about the moral self is focused. According to MacIntyre (and others such as Sandel and Taylor) the moral self cannot have access to an understanding of itself if it is considered simply as such, unconditioned in any way and outside of its social and historical conditions. If I do not take up the question here in these terms, this is not because the debate is not important, but because precisely what is most often taken for granted in this debate is what is here in question: the connection of myself, of the individual, to the community, or rather the difference between considering a person as isolated and disengaged, and considering a person as part of a community (or a history, a tradition, etc.). This, one might say, is exactly the problem posed by MacIntyre and others: the inscription of man in a historical and social context (a great discovery, or, if one prefers, an emergency exit from the great mess of analytic philosophy at the end of the century). It seems to me, however, that the question of the relation between the individual and the community can be posed in an entirely different way.

In opposing liberal individualism, MacIntyre upholds not so much community as *tradition*, defined in terms of *practices*. A practice is "any coherent and complex form of socially established cooperative human activity through which goods internal to that form of activity are realized in the course of trying to achieve those standards of excellence which are appropriate to, and partially definitive of, that form of activity" (*AV*, 175). Every activity or practice, like playing chess, presupposes an internal norm of excellence that is not determined by those who participate in it, but, so to speak, by the practice itself. According to MacIntyre, it is on this model that one should understand morality in general and the virtues in particular: acting well is not a matter of making choices as an individual, but of recognizing the virtues internal to the practice in which one is engaged.

This sort of view can indeed find support in a certain reading of Wittgenstein, or of Wittgenstein as rehabilitated by the English Thomist Catholicism that was current at the time of MacIntyre's British education. Certain formulations in Wittgenstein can be interpreted in a conservative or traditionalist sense, and one can find the influence of this sort of interpretation in MacIntyre. We can recall in this connection an article by J. C. Nyíri, "Wittgenstein's New Traditionalism," according to which "Wittgenstein's attitude toward the liberal idea of progress is that of a conservative" and there is in Wittgenstein's later philosophy "a conservative-traditionalist view of history . . . and a logical foundation for such a view."[11] In

Nyíri's conception here we can find a certain resemblance to that of MacIntyre and other contemporary communitarians. Some of Nyíri's arguments appeal to facts about Wittgenstein's life; others look to his discussions on ethics with Schlick:

Schlick says that in theological ethics there used to be two conceptions of the good: according to the shallower interpretation the good is good because it is what God wants; according to the profounder interpretation, God wants the good because it is good. I think that the first interpretation is the profounder one: what God commands, that is good. For it cuts off the way to any explanation "why" it is good, while the second interpretation is the shallow rationalist one, which proceeds "as if" you could give reasons for what is good.[12]

One can see how a remark like this of Wittgenstein's can be used for reactionary purposes. But when Wittgenstein says that "what God commands, that is good," he does not mean that the good is to be *defined* as what God commands, or that all there is to good is simply what God commands. Wittgenstein's point here is antifoundationalist, and if, for him, the "first interpretation" is more profound than the second, this is precisely because it cuts off any definition of the good. Any interpretation of Wittgenstein's remark as giving a foundation for the good is therefore cut off as well. To read this remark as an affirmation of the force of divine authority, or of tradition, is to take it in a sense exactly opposed to what Wittgenstein meant. Certainly Wittgenstein constantly maintains that there is no explaining or justifying our customs and what we do. But that a tradition (or *form of life*, that is to say, for Wittgenstein, "what must be accepted, the given") is not to be justified does not mean that it is *good*, or that it can in any way provide a foundation for a substantial conception of the good. Yet it is precisely this sort of inference that the neo-traditionalists aim to draw: they refuse to see that the criticism Wittgenstein mounts against "shallow" rationalism holds just as much or even more against a traditionalism that wants or takes itself to discover substantial values or foundations in tradition taken as given.

To make Wittgenstein's position clearer (we now see how difficult it is to see it clearly) we should examine more closely the "accepting" of the given that it seems to advocate. This is the work that I mean to begin, or at least sketch, in what follows.

3. Agreement and Society

A community, a society, is founded on agreement: this is the shared point of departure for both liberal and communitarian theories. What is the nature of this agreement? This question, rarely posed in these terms in moral and political philosophy, is precisely the question of the relation between the individual and (her) community. When we think about being a member of a community, we always think of it—the liberals as well as the communitarians—as a renunciation or a substitute for rationality. Thus the recourse to tradition, in MacIntyre, allows us to escape the illusions that come with rational decision making, and the veil of ignorance, in Rawls, allows us to escape the prejudices that go along with being an individual in a community. But why should we understand community in this way? What exactly is my connection with my community or my tradition? The answer to this question is hardly as clear as is generally imagined by the parties engaged in this debate.

If we turn again to Wittgenstein's view, we see that it raises the problem of agreement in the form of a dilemma: contractual agreement or communitarian agreement. Are we dealing here with the same sense of agreement? In the (liberal) contract, I am the source, the point of departure for the agreement; but I am not alone, and so we, the others and I, come to an agreement with one another. On the communitarian view, it is not for me to enter into an agreement: I already am in an agreement, as a member of the community. In *The Claim of Reason*, Cavell shows how Wittgenstein in fact unseats these two conceptions of agreement, neither one of which represents the reality of our agreement in society. The liberal contractualist thinks of agreement as if it were something that we entered into at some particular moment, and does not see what, in this agreement, is already "given." The communitarian, on the other hand, is excessively focused on the given, and thinks of my membership in the community as something immediately acquired. Thus we can see that the liberal/communitarian debate fundamentally rests on an internal division in the notion of agreement, between agreement as contract (object of rational decision) and agreement as harmony (belonging to a shared tradition). What is significant in Wittgenstein's position is that it dissolves this division in order to define agreement as something at once both given and decided, and to define the philosophical problem of agreement as precisely the problem of this duality. On this point we can look back at a passage I already cited in which Wittgenstein defines agreement as agreement "in" a form of life: "It is what human beings *say* that is true or false, and they *agree* in the language that they use. That is not agreement in opinions but in form of life."

Wittgenstein's model for agreement in society, is, as we have seen, agreement in language: we agree *in* the language that we speak. This parallel between ordinary language and politics is fundamental to understanding the nature of political and social agreement. The predominant interpretations of this passage of the *Investigations* take it for either a formulation of a naïve hypothesis about agreements that we have made about how we are to use language (the French translation has: they agree *on* the language that they use), or for a recognition of what, in language, is already there, given, and to which we cannot but submit. Those who uphold a Wittgensteinian traditionalism have certainly seen something important: that language (like the whole of our form of life) is given, that is to say inherited, that we have not chosen it any more than we have chosen our parents.

There is a pervasive and systematic background of agreements among us, which we had not realized, or had not known we realize. Wittgenstein sometimes calls them conventions, sometimes rules . . . The agreement we act upon he calls "agreement in judgments" (§242), and he speaks of our ability to use language as depending upon agreement in "forms of life" (§241). But forms of life, he says, are exactly what have to be "accepted"; they are "given" (p. 226).[13]

What they fail to see who wish to interpret Wittgenstein as speaking of an obligation to accept what is socially given is that my agreement or my membership in *this* form of life is not itself given, and that not everything is to be "accepted." That forms of life are given does not mean only that what we are given are *forms* of life, but also that *our* form of life is a given. What the notion of form of life involves, then, is not conservatism, but, as Cavell puts it, "the mutual implication of the natural and the social."

In being asked to accept this, or suffer it, as given for ourselves, we are not asked to accept, let us say, private property, but separateness; not a particular fact of power, but the fact that I am a man, therefore of *this* (range or scale of) capacity for work, for pleasure, for endurance, for appeal, for command, for understanding, for wish, for will, for teaching, for suffering.[14]

Here the sense of the comparison between the agreement in a community and the agreement in a language becomes clear. That language is given to me does not imply that I know how I am going to go on, to agree *in* language with my fellow-speakers.

I should emphasize that, while I regard it as empty to call this idea of mutual attunement "merely metaphorical," I also do not take it to prove or explain anything. On the contrary, it is meant to question whether a philosophical explanation is needed, or wanted, in the fact of agreement in the language human beings use together, an explanation, say, in terms of meanings or conventions or basic terms or propositions which are to provide the foundation of our agreements. For nothing is deeper than the fact, or the extent, of agreement itself.[15]

I alone can determine the extent of "our" agreement. What constitutes the community is my claim to speak for it, for others. The I, far from being given a priori, *is* the staking of this claim. And here is the fundamental problem most often avoided in contemporary political discussions of community, that of:

The claim to speak for "the group"—the question, namely, about how I could have been party to the establishing of criteria if I do not recognize that I have and do not know what they are . . . the claim is not that one can tell a priori who is implicated by me, because one point of the kind of investigation Wittgenstein calls grammatical is exactly to discover who.[16]

This, then, is precisely the question. How is my society, my community *mine*, and how can it speak in my name, and I in its? How, with what right, can I speak in the name of the group of which I am a member? How can I have acquired such an extraordinary privilege? This is the sense of the claim (the demand for recognition) in Cavell: my claiming to speak for "us," which makes language a social matter, that is to say a political matter. Agreement in language can be broken, it can happen that my criteria are not shared. "Disagreement about our criteria, or the possibility of such disagreement, is as fundamental a topic in Wittgenstein as the eliciting of criteria itself is."[17] Recourse to the notion of community is in no way a solution, in Wittgenstein, to the political problem. Even if I look to my community, there is still the problem of whether I belong. "The only source of confirmation here is ourselves. And each one of us is fully authoritative in this struggle."[18] This can lead to the suggestion that the opposition on which the liberal/communitarian debate is founded, between the voice of the individual and the voice of society, is artificial, and is based on a misunderstanding of the nature of my belonging to the community. On this point we can look to the analysis of Rousseau's theory of community that Cavell proposes at the beginning of *The Claim of Reason.*

What [Rousseau] claims to know is his relation to society, and to take as a philosophical datum the fact that men (that he) can speak for society and that society can speak for him, that they reveal one another's most private thoughts . . . The problem is for me to discover my position with respect to these facts—how I know with whom I am in community, and to whom and to what I am in fact obedient.[19]

I don't have, so to speak, a choice between myself and others, the individual and the community. The present debate, in which communitarians and liberals have been led to modify their claims by each adopting certain theses of their opponents, has perhaps revealed this fundamental impasse, but without doing anything to resolve it. The community both gives me a political voice, and can take that voice back from me, or deceive me, and betray me so far that I do not wish to speak for it, or to let it speak for me, *in my name.*

My participation is what is constantly in question, in discussion— in *conversation,* to take up an essential and shared theme in Rawls and Cavell—in my connection to the community. Belonging to a community is as obscure and threatened as is my own personal identity: I do not know to what tradition I belong. Cavell remarks that my belonging to a shared form of life is always threatened, by me or by others: "To speak for yourself then means risking the rebuff—on some occasion, perhaps once for all— of those who claimed to be speaking for you" (*CR,* p. 27). But—and here is what is paradoxical about community structure understood in this way— in refusing my agreement, I do not withdraw from the community: the refusal is itself part of my belonging. *Uncritical* membership in a community is the founding myth of communitarianism, which opposes a central element in English and American liberal thought: the possibility of my withdrawing at once *from* and *in* society, of taking back from it my consent:

Since the granting of consent entails acknowledgment of others, the withdrawal of consent entails the same acknowledgment: I have to say *both* "It is not mine any longer" (I am no longer responsible for it, it no longer speaks for me) *and* "It is no longer ours" (not what we bargained for, we no longer recognize the principle of consent in it, the original "we" is no longer bound together by consent but only by force, so it no longer exists). (*CR*, p. 27)

At the foundation of communitarian approaches to moral philosophy is the idea that our inability to arrive at substantial agreement on moral questions is a reflection of our fundamental irrationality. Cavell holds just the reverse: the difficulty of arriving at agreement is rather, on his view, constitutive of what he calls *the claim to rationality*. Reason is never something merely given; it has to be claimed. Reason is as much the object as the subject of *The Claim of Reason*. The individual's demand to speak in the name of others, even if it has no further foundation, is *rational*, and is definitive of something essential to human rationality. When Wittgenstein says that human beings "agree in the language that they use," agree in a form of life, he thus makes an appeal to an agreement that is not founded on anything other than the validity of a voice. In *Must We Mean What We Say?*, Cavell, following Kant, defines the rationality of the appeal to ordinary language, on the model of aesthetic judgment, as the claim to speak in a "universal voice": this claim is founded on *my* saying what *we* say. What is affirmed, then, in Kant, is the demand for universal assent, "and in fact everyone presupposes this assent (*Einstimmung*), without the subjects who judge opposing one another about the possibility of such a demand." This demand is what defines our agreement, and community is then, by definition, something to be demanded, not something that furnishes a foundation. It is *I*—my voice—that determines the community, and not the other way around. Finding my voice means, not finding it in harmony with the rest, but achieving recognition of my competence.

A moral assertion, for Cavell, is thus a claim that is concerned as much with itself as with its object. This is what raises the problem of morality as a question of skepticism. One can say that in Cavell and in Wittgenstein the community cannot exist except in its being constituted by the claims of individuals and by the recognition of the claim of the other. The community cannot, then, be *presupposed*, and it is nonsense to speak of resolving moral disagreement or political conflict by appealing to it. Community is only possible in our recognition that we live in a shared moral world, and of it, again, I am, *me*, the only possible foundation. The impossibility of arriving at agreement would then be a proof of the existence of a community—and not an indication that we have lost it. We are not talking here about a solution to the problem of morality, but rather a transferring of the problem and of the foundation of agreement in community, onto the recognition and the claiming of oneself. In the case of moral agreement as in the case of political claims, I am turned back upon myself, to discover my own position and my own voice. The question then comes to: how can I avoid skepticism if I can have no foundation but myself? This is just the question of what it is to "follow a rule."

4. Rules, Skepticism, and Conformity

Wittgenstein announces in *Investigations* §224 the connection between the terms "rule" and "agreement" (they are family relations, in fact "cousins"). The anxiety of learning is the anxiety of a rule: nothing assures us that we are on the right "rails" if our forms of life do not. Skepticism is thus inherent in every human practice: all confidence in what we do (follow out a series, count, etc.) is modeled on the confidence that we have in our shared uses of language. John McDowell makes the following comment on the passage I quoted above from Cavell about the "terrifying" character of the ordinary fact that we do not have any other foundation but our form of life: "The terror of which Cavell writes at the end of this marvelous passage is a sort of vertigo, induced by the thought that there is nothing that keeps our practices in line except the reactions and responses we learn in learning them."[20] But the treatment for this "vertigo"—the anxiety inherent in the use of language—is not to be found in a recourse to community, for this anxiety is induced precisely by the problem of connecting the individual to the community. This shows the limits of a certain sociological conception of rules, that would find in the agreement of the community the "background" of all justification of our actions. Wittgenstein aims to show at once the fragility and the depth of our agreement, and the very nature of the necessities that emerge in our forms of life. There is no "answer" to this skepticism, which is not only a doubt about the validity of what we do and say, but also reveals the point at which *I* am the sole possible source of that necessity.

The reading of Wittgenstein that I am opposing, then, is that of *the ordinary*. One makes as if the recourse to the ordinary, to our forms of life (as something given), is a solution to skepticism: as if forms of life were, for instance, social institutions. There are here two opposed pictures, one that of the background (notably in Searle,[21] who holds that institutions constitute the background that permits us to interpret language and to follow social rules); and the other that of the naturalness of our form of life. The term "background" appears in the *Investigations* as a name for a picture that we make for ourselves, not as an explanation of *anything*. The background cannot then have any causal role, for it is the language itself—our *ordinary* uses, the whirl of which Cavell speaks,[22] and that Wittgenstein describes in these important passages from *Remarks on the Philosophy of Psychology*: "We judge an action according to its background within human life . . . The background is the bustle of life. And our concept points to something within *this* bustle." And: "How could human behavior be described? Surely only by showing the actions of a variety of humans, as they are all mixed up together (*durcheinanderwimmeln*). Not what one man is doing now, but the whole hurly-burly (*Gewimmel*), is the background against which we see an action."[23] Here we see the inadequacy of the idea of a background, for what we in fact see is action, set in the whirl of our form of life. To say that the application of a rule is *determined* by a background is not the same thing as to say that the application of a rule is to be described against the background of human actions and connections. Following a rule is part of our life in language, and is inseparable from our other practices. What is at issue here is not a contrast between an isolated individual and a community, but between a rule and the multiplicity of rules within which it is set and entangled. To the overly perceptual and static imagery of the background, we can prefer then that of the texture or whirl of life.

Our practices are thus not exhausted by the idea of a rule. On the contrary, one thing that Wittgenstein is aiming to show—if we follow Cavell's reading—is that one hasn't said particularly much about a practice (such as, for instance, language) when one has simply said that it is governed by rules. In reality, discussion of rules is distorted by the (philosophical) idea of an explanatory or justificatory power in the concept of a rule—an idea that leads directly to conformity. We must have done then with conformist interpretations of what a rule is and with the idea—

shared by many contemporary political doctrines, like Rawls's—that certain claims are impossible, or out of place, that they do not have a meaning in our society, because they take place outside of its rules and deny the basic agreement that founds it. But precisely what agreement? This is, precisely, Cavell's question. What have I agreed to? What is the measure of consent? *Conditions Handsome and Unhandsome* follows the idea, first expressed in *Pursuits of Happiness*, that consent is neither measured nor immeasurable. I cannot have consented to everything that happens in my society, or *in my name*, just because I am a member of this society or part of this practice. Cavell's early discussion, in chapter 3 of *The Claim of Reason*, of Rawls's seminal paper "Two Concepts of Rules" (1955), assumes a greater significance here: agreement to a practice, and to a set of rules thus defined by a practice, is never given, but is always under discussion: it is the conversation of justice.

There is, adjoined to the idea of community, the idea that one must somehow learn to make claims as people generally do, that one must consent to certain *rules* in order to be able to make a claim to anything. But, as Cavell reminds us, there is no rule that tells us how to stake a claim. Thinking about community and about politics from the side of the ordinary then means learning to recognize a skeptical dimension even in the *rule* itself.

CHAPTER THREE

Bringing Truth Home:
Mill, Wittgenstein, Cavell,
and Moral Perfectionism

Piergiorgio Donatelli

There are many paths one can wish to take in approaching Stanley Cavell's idea of perfectionism. He has written that "there is no closed list of features that constitute perfectionism" and that we should better conceive of it as "an outlook or dimension of thought embodied and developed in a set of texts spanning the range of Western culture."[1] In this paper I try to suggest one possible entry into Cavell's idea of perfectionism. In order to do so I shall help myself with two authors Cavell mentions in his list, John Stuart Mill and Ludwig Wittgenstein.

I

In trying to detect the reasons for the state of homelessness in which perfectionism finds itself in modern philosophy, Cavell mentions two points he connects to the thought of Emerson and Nietzsche. He cites a "hatred of moralism—of what Emerson calls 'conformity'—so passionate and ceaseless as to seem sometimes to amount to a hatred of morality altogether," and a "disgust with or a disdain for the present state of things so complete as to require not merely reform, but a call for transformation of things, and before all a transformation of the self."[2] Cavell wants to make appropriate room both for the idea of a dissatisfaction of the self with itself and also for the intuition, as he says, that "a higher or further self is one to be arrived at in person, in the person of the one who gives his heart to it."[3] So Cavell offers here two suggestions. In the first place, perfectionism is connected to judging what we do and say and feel from the point of view of a further and unattained self.[4] In the second place, however, what is essential to Cavell's thought, as I read it, is that this further self is not given to us from the outside, as it were, but constitutes the development of our present self to its state of fullness and clarity with itself. This emerges most explicitly when Cavell works at making clear his thought (and Emerson's) in connection with Kant. He writes at one point:

While the idea of the noumenal plays a role in what I understand as Emersonian Perfection (as when in "Experience" Emerson breaks into his thoughts by saying "I know that the world I converse with in the city and in the farms, is not the world I *think*"), and is related to an idea expressed as being true (or false) to oneself, I assume no role for the idea of a true (or false) self. Such an idea seems rather something imposed from outside oneself, as from another who has a use for oneself on condition that one is beyond desire, beyond change . . . . [5]

This is also connected to the thought that if one's ideal of perfection—of what truth is for us—is given from the outside, if it isn't one's own, the love and search for this ideal—for truth—is a form of idolatry, that is, an extreme case of the self falsifying itself.[6] One of the points of this essay is also to envisage a notion of truth in a perfectionist perspective, of truth conceived as a dimension of the self. Therefore, we need to take into consideration both invitations of Cavell's perfectionism: to think of truth as the expression of a perfect self, that is, as the result of a radical transformation in our way of seeing and taking things, and to think of this perfect self as our further and yet unattained self which has reached clarity with itself. Truth—the object of our assessment of things which we find so problematic and which demands this sort of response—is the expression of our further self, of one's elevated state of mind. Cavell draws our attention to the fact that a certain dissatisfaction with things[7] needs to be responded to by being seen as internal to a state of the self which lies in confusion and asks for clarity.[8] A truth, therefore, is never something external to the individual, as is shown by perfectionism's hatred of moralism and idolatry, but stands as the natural expression of her yet unattained self.

This way of conceiving the perfectionist response to this dissatisfaction brings Cavell to state what I take to be a central paradox of perfectionism. He expresses it by way of commenting on Emerson's and Thoreau's understanding of the relation of their books with their readers:

If the thoughts of a text such as Emerson's (say the brief text on rejected thoughts) are yours, then you do not need them. If its thoughts are *not* yours, they will not do you good. The problem is that the text's thoughts are neither exactly mine nor not mine. In their sublimity as my rejected—say repressed—thoughts, they represent my further, next, unattained but attainable, self. To think otherwise, to attribute the origin of my thoughts simply to the other, thoughts which are then, as it were, implanted in me—some would say caused—by let us say some Emerson, is idolatry.[9]

If truth is not yours already it will not do you good; but if it is yours already you will not need it. The paradox signals the special problem that perfectionism has in establishing the relation between my present point of view and that of truth. Whatever I am aiming at, the solution to my present dissatisfaction will bear this sort of connection with my own self. I need the truth I am aiming at to be the natural expression of my own self, yet as my present self is not such as to express such truth but is in a state of confusion, it appears as distant from me. But in being distant and independent from me it cannot count as a truth for me, as a solution to my dissatisfaction. There is an emphasis on transformation and cultivation of the self here. Cavell mentions this as one central trait of perfectionism: "Perfectionism's emphasis on culture or cultivation is, to my mind, to be understood in connection with this search for intelligibility, or say this search for direction in what seems a scene of moral chaos, the scene of the dark place in which one has lost one's way."[10] The search for truth requires a transformation of the self. It is a search for direction, therefore we need a guide, which Cavell epitomizes in the figure of the friend; yet we need to be helped out of our scene of chaos in such a manner that we will find our own way: "With respect to the issue whether virtue is knowledge, whether virtue can be taught, whether to know the way is to take the way, perfectionism's obsession with education expresses its focus on finding one's way rather than on getting oneself or another to take the way."[11] There is a difficulty, which is central to the project of perfectionism, in accounting for what it is to show someone the way out of her scene of chaos. I am concerned here with this difficulty. I will try now to offer a reading of it. In order to do so I will go first to the thought of Mill as an important example of perfectionism; then I will briefly treat Wittgenstein; finally I will go back to Mill and Cavell.

II

John Stuart Mill's *On Liberty* is mentioned by Cavell in his list of texts which embody and develop the idea of perfectionism.[12] I will examine some thoughts from Mill in order to suggest a reading of the idea of a perfectionist path. *On Liberty* (1859) is certainly, among other things, a perfectionist text. Mill expresses there the result of a long journey around the themes of perfectionism that he had started at the beginning of the 1830s while exploring for the first time new directions of his thought and especially romanticism and Saint-Simonism. Larger areas of his vast intellectual work could be described as a reading of romantic themes into a more traditional empiricist associationist philosophy.[13]

One early text is relevant here, "On Genius" (1832). In this essay Mill explores themes to which he returns later in *On Liberty*. Mill is interested in showing what genius is and he finds it in the capacity of the active mind to find truths by itself. "Knowledge comes only from within; all that comes from without is but *questioning*, or else it is mere *authority*."[14] The person of genius is one who discovers truths for herself. "There may be no hidden truths left for him to find," writes Mill, but in a different sense many of the truths that were discovered at one time may be "hidden to *him* as those which are still unknown."[15] If knowledge comes from within, from an active mind capable of entering into the spirit of a truth, to make it her own, there can be no knowledge apart from that which is the expression of a higher state of mind. All knowledge decays into a state of apparent truth, in a mere formula, in what Mill calls cram, "latin cram, mathematical cram, literary cram, political cram, theological cram, moral cram," if it isn't directed at the elevation of the mind.[16] Mill's central example here, as it will be in *On Liberty*, is Christianity. Mill draws a speculative history of epochs and while he finds a true capacity for knowledge in the great moments of the Greek mind he registers a decay which takes place afterwards. As he writes: "The attempt to think for oneself fell into disuse." It was in this spirit, says Mill, that the teachings of Christ were taken, and "the effect was fatal."

The words of him whose speech was in figures and parables were iron-bound and petrified into inanimate and inflexible *formulae*. Jesus was likened to a logician, framing a rule to meet all cases, and provide against all possible evasions, instead of a poet, orator, and *vates*, whose object was to purify and spiritualize the mind, so that, under the guidance of its purity, its own lights might suffice to find the law of which he only supplied the spirit, and suggested the general scope.[17]

The teaching of a truth is connected to a purification and spiritualization of the mind so that that truth will be the result of the mind's own understanding. We see here at work the perfectionist idea that a truth is what the mind can know for itself as the natural result of its elevation. Mill is tackling here the perfectionist problem that Cavell has signaled. And it is no surprise therefore to find Mill presenting a line of reasoning very similar to what I have called the perfectionist paradox in a letter from February 9, 1830, to his Saint-Simonian friend Gustave d'Eichthal.

. . . you imagine that you can accomplish the perfection of mankind by teaching them St Simonism, whereas it appears to me that their adoption of St Simonism, if that doctrine be true, will be the natural result and effect of a high state of moral and intellectual culture previously received: that it should not be presented to the minds of any who have not already attained a high degree of improvement, since if presented to any others it will either be rejected by them, or received only as Christianity is at present received by the majority, that is, in such a manner as to be perfectly inefficacious.[18]

There is no truth in a doctrine apart from its being the natural result of a high state of mind. Thus there is no use in teaching a doctrine if the mind has not been elevated because it will not be able to receive it; but if it is already elevated it will not need that doctrine because its being able to hold it is the effect of the high state achieved.

What interests me is Mill's understanding of the two states of the mind, the difference between "the man who knows from the man who takes upon trust—the man who can feel and understand truth, from the man who merely assents to it, the active from the passive mind."[19] Mill distinguishes between an apparent understanding of a truth from a real understanding of it; there is a difference between truths which remain traditional, truths "which we have *only* been taught and learnt, but have *not* been *known*" and truths which one has made truly one's own.[20] Mill develops this distinction in the second chapter of *On Liberty*. Mill is engaged there in defending the principle of liberty on the grounds that it is necessary in order to preserve truth. He has three main arguments. In the first he supposes that conflicting opinions that one would be willing to suppress are, reasonably, true; in the second he supposes that they are, reasonably, false; and in the third he imagines that they reasonably contain a portion of both truth and falsity. The second argument is interesting here. Mill argues in favor of free discussion of opinions even when we have every reason to suppose that the opinions we discuss are false, because, in the absence of discussion, truths are held in the mind in the manner of mere habits of thought or prejudices, and thus they are not truths anymore. Free discussion and debate require that we are able to offer grounds for our beliefs, that we connect those beliefs with reasons, sentiments, and personal experience, realizing them in consciousness, as Mill says, making them connect with "the inner life of the human being."[21] Mill draws here from his arguments in "On Genius," and explains in more detail what was there suggested, that is, that the mind can be in a state of apparent knowledge, a state in which "a dull and torpid assent" is given to a truth but no real entry is earned by that truth in our imagination, feelings, and understanding.[22] Now Mill explains the nature of these two states of the mind as a difference between the appearance of meaning, the illusion of understanding, and the real phenomenon of understanding and meaning. What happens is that we retain a few words, says Mill, but the meaning is lost: "the shell and husk of the meaning is retained, the finer essence being lost."[23] Mill applies this analysis generally to all kinds of beliefs, but his argument is especially concerned with ethical and religious creeds.[24] He presents again the case of Christianity, which was transformed from a teaching of living beliefs capable of irradiating and penetrating into the individual to a habitual respect for the sound of certain formulas, with "no feeling which spreads from the words to the things signified and forces the mind to take *them* in and make them conform to the formula."[25] But he also writes about what happens with general observations on life such as proverbs, "of which the full meaning *cannot* be realized until personal experience has brought it home."[26]

Mill furnishes here an analysis of what I take to be a perfectionist path from a state of confusion, of apparent belief, to a state of clarity, where a truth is fully realized, taken in oneself. The improvement of the human being is conceived as the capacity to know truth, that is, to be able to reach truth not as something external to us but as the point of view of the yet unattained clarity of the self with itself. Mill is treating mainly instances of what Cavell would count as conditions in which one has lost one's way, in which our wanting to make ourselves intelligible to ourselves and to others fails. This is Mill's general analysis of his time—an analysis which he goes into at length in the third chapter of *On Liberty*—a time in which people think, feel, and choose in crowds, a time in which the truths one holds are entertained merely as the shell and husk of meaning, whereas the essence is lost. Therefore he offers an analysis of the notion of truth which asks us to regain a true knowledge of the truths, to regain confidence in what we say and feel. But Mill also gives this as a general analysis of the notion of truth. The purpose of this part of the argument in chapter two is to show that truth is always to be entertained as if it were to be regained after having been lost. This way Mill arrives at a tension, which is also a tension internal to his own philosophical view, between the fact that progress is measured by the "number and the gravity of the truths which have reached the point of being uncontested"[27] and the other fact, that the consolidation of an opinion contributes to its loss of internal life, and marks the first step toward a passive acceptance of it. Mill is interested in defending the idea of progress of knowledge, but he also wants to say that there is no progress which doesn't also manifest itself as progress of the individual mind.[28] So all truths are to be known as if they were being saved from decay and corruption, known as if for the first time, as the opening of new possibilities to us. (There might be a connection here, in *this* strand of Mill's thought, with Cavell's notion of skepticism as a possibility which is always open to us, as a constitutive fact about humanity.[29] Mill thinks that our capacity to make ourselves intelligible to ourselves and to others through the words we say is always open to this threat of corruption, of becoming a mere shell and husk of meaning, "incrusting and petrifying" the mind.[30] Therefore we should always conceive of our knowledge of truth from the point of view of this skeptical threat, that is, from the point of view of what truth is for people who have lost their intimacy and confidence with it.)

Mill gives us a model of how to think about the sort of truth which is faithful to a progress of the individual mind. We are asked to think about truth as the natural result and effect of a high state of mind, that is, a condition in which the mind has achieved a solution to the sort of dissatisfaction to which that truth is a response. In this sense, Mill's notion of truth offers an example of perfectionism, because he regards truth as the expression of one's further self, a self which has reached a point where our search for truth has found a response. Mill says that we should understand the self's perfectionist journey as one in which there is a transition from the appearance of meaning to the real phenomenon of meaning. The condition of truth is one where meaning is regained from what was a mere shell and husk of meaning. Therefore we are asked to conceive of the fact of knowing truth as a regaining of the fullness of meaning from the poverty of a mere appearance of meaning. The condition of the further self—the high state of mind—is one where clarity has conquered confusion and illusion of meaning. I take this to be a central fact about Mill's understanding of truth in this part of *On Liberty*. Mill is working on a contrast between the way in which words are connected to our life in the present unsatisfactory state and from the point of view of a high state of mind. He wants us to see what a truth looks like when its meaning is regained from the state of a mere illusion of meaning. We are asked to realize what it means to understand a truth in contrast with what it meant to retain only the shell and husk of the meaning of *that* truth. So with proverbs he says that "most people first truly learn [their] meaning when experience, generally of a painful kind, has made it a reality to them"; "the full meaning *cannot* be realized until personal experience has brought it home."[31] There is a contrast here between the self that has learnt from experience what those words mean and the mere shell of meaning that impressed the mind with no experience. The way in which proverbs can be striking is disclosed by their capacity to show us a sense in which we can take their words, a sense which destroys the previous illusion of having meant anything at all, and which is connected to, and is the expression of, our experience.

Mill furnishes an analysis of truth which makes use of a distinction between truth and the appearance of truth. But Mill says that we need to understand truth as the natural expression of a mind that has reached clarity with itself, that has overcome its state of confusion. So the truth of a proverb strikes us in its special way in that we see it as the expression of a self that has learnt from experience what those words really mean. What strikes us as special and important lies in those words' being filled with our experience, in contrast with their being signs for an empty space. There is a matching of those words with our experience that we find striking in contrast with our previous acceptance of what we took those words to mean. I am interested in pointing out the fact that the sort of truth Mill is interested in is striking to us in such a special way because it is seen as the emergence of meaning from a state of confusion. Mill is interested in showing how we can recover meaning from *those* shells and husks, how meaning can be expressed by those dead signs once again. And he thinks of knowing truth, in the sense that is proper to an individual conceived as a progressive being,[32] always as if it involved such a discovery, as a recovery of meaning from a state of confusion and illusion.

III

Mill has helped us make some progress in understanding the nature of the perfectionist journey from one's present self to the as yet unattained further self. Now I want to suggest a reading of what Mill is doing with the notion of truth in *On Liberty* which draws from Wittgenstein—and especially from a Wittgenstein made available by Cavell's reading. There are many ways we can try to approach Wittgenstein as a perfectionist author. I will not be concerned here with the difficult task of exploring these different ways, but only with finding in Wittgenstein suggestions as to how to make perspicuous Mill's idea of a progress of the self toward truth. In order to do so, I will suggest one perfectionist lesson which we should be able to learn from Wittgenstein. I will try to express this briefly and in doing so I will often refer to "Wittgenstein," with no further qualification. There are great differences between different moments of Wittgenstein's work, but what I want to say with regard to perfectionism represents a line of thought which should be seen as a common inspiration to all his work—the *Tractatus* and the later work.

Cavell has written about the interest perfectionism holds for philosophy as for "a (an untaken) way of life."[33] I think we can use this as a general characterization of Wittgenstein's concern for philosophy. Wittgenstein thought that philosophy was not a question of putting forward doctrines or theses of any kind. He took philosophy to be involved with a form of liberation of the self from fantasies and confusions. There is no truth which philosophy can deliver. A philosophical work is composed of illustrations through which the author enters imaginatively into the reader's or the interlocutor's confusions and tries to move her perception and understanding to a direction where what appeared to be a problem is not a problem anymore. Philosophy, as Wittgenstein wrote around 1933, is "a work on oneself. On one's own conception. On the way one sees things. (And what one demands of them)."[34] "What has to be overcome is not a difficulty of the intellect, but of the will,"[35] says Wittgenstein, because what needs to be overcome is an attachment to certain forms of words, a wanting them to mean something in spite of their failing to do so. Philosophy therefore delivers no truths, no theses, apart from their being the expression of a state of the self which has overcome its problems. The solution to these problems lies in their disappearing, that is, in the self's attainment of a perspective from which there are no problems anymore. Cavell has taught us, since his very early essay "Aesthetic Problems of Modern Philosophy," to see an inspiration here which is common to the *Tractatus*—where Wittgenstein writes that "the solution of the problem of life is seen in the vanishing of this problem"[36]—and the *Investigations*—where we find him saying that "philosophical problems should *completely* disappear":[37] "the problems of life and the problems of philosophy have related grammars, because solutions to them both have the same form: their problems are solved only when they disappear, and answers are arrived at only when there are no longer questions—when, as it were, our accounts have cancelled them."[38] Philosophy, therefore, is not something which can be expressed in truths that have a standing and validity independent from the self, but is a way of life which can bring us to a condition in which the need for those truths is overcome. Philosophy aims at a transformation not in the doctrines, in something which has a life independently from us, but of the self—that is, in what we find problematic or unsatisfactory in things—of the demands we make of things. There are no truths of philosophy, therefore, apart from their being the expression of the fact that the self has reached a position in which it has transformed itself, transformed its demands on things which were creating that dissatisfaction.

There is a specific teaching of Wittgenstein from which I wish to draw now. I shall refer to the *Tractatus*, but similar things can be said if we turn to the *Investigations* as the inspiring work. Wittgenstein's analysis of the perfectionist path in the *Tractatus*, the journey of the reader who follows the author's indications ("He who understands me . . . ," says Wittgenstein in *Tractatus* 6:54) through the book in order to arrive at a solution to one's problems, is a movement from confusion to clarity, which Wittgenstein frames as the overcoming (*überwinden*) of the impression that we find sense where we realize eventually that there was no sense to be found. As a conclusion to the *Tractatus*, Wittgenstein writes that one "who understands me finally recognizes them [the propositions of the *Tractatus*] as senseless" (6:54), that is, she will have overcome certain kinds of demands, whereby she took certain combinations of words, concerning the nature of the world and logic and the foundations of ethics, as expressing a *problem* for her, as being something which called for a solution. So Wittgenstein's understanding in the *Tractatus*—and I would take this, with Cavell, as a line common to the later work—of the perfectionist path from confusion to clarity is expressed as a movement from nonsense to sense, that is, a movement from a state of illusion where we take nonsensical combinations of words as meaningful sentences to a condition where such illusion is overcome and we realize that we were doing nothing at all when we thought we were meaning such and such a thing.[39] As Wittgenstein writes in *Tractatus* 4:003, "Most propositions and questions, that have been written about philosophical matters, are not false, but senseless. We cannot, therefore, answer questions of this kind at all, but only state their senselessness." But stating their senselessness turns out to be a difficult task to which the whole of the *Tractatus* is dedicated. The passage in fact from nonsense to sense is not one from one region of language and thought to another; it isn't a contrast that can be drawn that way. This is a contrast which is only available to be drawn by entering imaginatively into one's nonsensical perspective, that is, by entering into the imagination of a speaker's wanting to mean something and failing to do so while thinking she is meaning *that*. This is Wittgenstein's lesson for perfectionism: truths aren't anything independent from the self because a truth, the response to our demand for knowledge, is the condition of the mind when we realize that we have said nothing, that we cannot read any meaning in our demand for knowledge, in what seemed to us a problem that needed to be solved. As Wittgenstein will say later in "Philosophy," in one sense philosophy doesn't require any renunciation, it doesn't order us to do something that we wouldn't naturally do: "I do not abstain from saying something, but rather abandon a certain combination of words as senseless." Yet in another sense, "philosophy requires a resignation, but one of feeling and not of intellect."[40] That is, when we abandon a combination of words as senseless we are not renouncing something, we do not abstain from saying something that we would want, feel inclined, to say, but we do feel that abandoning, that leaving behind what doesn't show a meaningful face to us anymore, as a sort of resignation, as a letting go of an intention of meaning, a form of attraction which had powerfully cast its spell on us.

IV

I am interested now in drawing together Wittgenstein's illustration of the journey of the self from confusion to clarity and Mill's (and Cavell's) perfectionist understanding of the notion of truth. Mill writes about the necessity of establishing an intimate connection with a truth (a connection with the inner life of the human being), of truths being taken into oneself—in one's imagination, feelings and understanding—, of personal experience as bringing truths home. Cavell is also interested in this fact of the human mind. He is interested in how we come to be able to take in facts, to establish a personal connection with them. In *The Claim of Reason* he draws a contrast between this capacity to take in facts, a "capacity for making connections, seeing or realizing possibilities," which he relates to imagination, and a different approach to things that might be vivid without being imaginative. As a comment on this he mentions Dickens: "Dickens, who was superlative in both capacities, both in imagination and in imaginativeness, came to recognize this problem: he could get the Pecksniffs and Murdles of the world to cry over the pictures he presented of poverty and the deaths of children, but this did not get them to see their connection with these pictures." This capacity "to take the facts in, realize the significance of what is going on, make the behavior real for oneself, make a connection,"[41] is central to the perfectionist project of accounting for an intimate relation of the self with the self's concerns and preoccupations.

In this connection Cavell goes into Wittgenstein's treatment of the phenomenon of seeing-as. There are interesting considerations which parallel what I shall try to suggest here. But I shall not pursue this very line. I want to propose a different connection between Mill's, and Cavell's, interest in the way truths are realized in oneself and Wittgenstein. We can try to gloss these interesting cases using Wittgenstein's suggestion of thinking of a truth in the light of its being recovered to the self. The phenomena that Mill and Cavell mention are all instances in which we are struck by the power and significance of a truth, we are struck by the capacity a proverb has of bringing light to one's experience, to render it perspicuous to oneself, struck by the capacity of a description of pride by Dostoevsky, say, in the *Brothers Karamazov*, to touch and illuminate our own sense of pride. These are instances where a description of something, or a suggestion or a rule of prudence or ethics, is taken in not as a description of something or a prescription on how to act; it isn't simply that, a description or a prescription among others, but it strikes us as special and illuminating.[42] We don't just see people's suffering or being tyrannized by their pride, but we realize it as a true possibility, something that concerns us intimately, not humanity in some abstract sense but our very selves.[43]

I have suggested before that the *Tractatus* offers a possible understanding of this in terms of truths recovered to the self from a state of illusion. Mill speaks of recovering the meaning of a truth from the shell and husk that we retained. We may wish to gloss this picture of the shell and husk of meaning—with Wittgenstein—as the process through which we overcome our condition of nonsense and achieve clarity. Mill is interested in our capacity to acknowledge that shell and husk as the mere phrases ("phrases retained by rote," incrustations outside the mind)[44] which personal experience fills up with meaning. But, drawing from the teaching of the *Tractatus*, this capacity should be seen as internal to the imaginative journey of the mind that compares a sense she has achieved with her previous supposition that she was perceiving a sense where she now realizes there was none. We can see and realize a truth among other truths in its ordinary conceptual dimension, but we can also do something different. We can enter into the imagination of seeing such a truth from the point of view of the illusion of sense whereby we thought we understood a truth whereas we were only clinging to a certain combination of words that meant nothing. Thus a truth appears special and impressive in contrast with what is the mere shell and husk of its meaning. But it is important that we see that this contrast is available to be drawn only from within the imagination of nonsense, the imagination that led us to take a certain combination of words as meaningful.

There are two directions of interest for an analysis inspired by Wittgenstein that need to be distinguished here. Mill talks about a fact that concerns certain doctrines and beliefs, especially the belief in Christianity, or the belief in certain maxims and proverbs. He gives an interesting analysis according to which many of these beliefs are only apparent. There are strings of words to which we give our consent without there being enough of what we do in life and in language to show that there is really a belief there. I am suggesting that Mill here can be glossed, with Wittgenstein, as working his way to the analysis of a phenomenon which we could describe otherwise as one in which we seem to entertain concepts when we do not really have concepts in our minds at all: no meaning but only incrustations of meaning. This is one phenomenon that can be treated by showing how what we seem to understand and hold in our minds is only the illusion of our holding a concept: in Fregean terms, words exercise only a psychological influence on our minds but play no conceptual role. This situation was famously illustrated by Elizabeth Anscombe for the notion of moral "ought" in her article "Modern Moral Philosophy."[45] But then we might be interested in showing what it means to move from a state of confusion, from a failure to mean something by using certain words, to the overcoming of this confusion, to the state in which we can give those words a sense. This is also part of the general interest—exemplified by Anscombe's treatment—in the history of concepts, as we might want to say (I take this expression to mean the history of how concepts are born and how it happens that they disappear),[46] but it also shows an interest in how words—mere signs which happen to exercise a mesmeric force on us—can acquire a meaning. In that article Anscombe seemed more interested in diagnosing instances in which we fail to give words their sense even though it seems we can, instances where philosophical persuasion should encourage us to see ourselves as entertaining illusions of sense and therefore enable us to abandon such illusions, abandon the impression that we have concepts,

like the moral ought, to which we are (or we consider we should be) responding. But here I am interested in looking at those instances where
we are able to give words a meaning once again, to find a place for them
in our life.

I take Cavell's notion of perfectionism to be concerned with a variety
of forms of liberation and improvement, with ways in which it can be said
that "problems are solved only when they disappear."[47] The sense in which
at the end of the *Tractatus* (6:54) we are asked to recognize its propositions
as senseless is connected to Anscombe's treatment of the notion of moral
ought. They are both cases in which at the end of the perfectionist process
we are able to recognize that what we took to be meaningful appears now
only as an illusion of sense. We free ourselves of the impression we had
that there was anything meaningful in our attraction to those signs. The
truth of philosophy here, the truth of the words of philosophy, lies in this
explosion of the illusion of sense, in the liberation it affords from what we
considered we had to engage with, from what *had* to be attended.[48] And
we can account for this truth only from the imaginative point of view of
our previous state of confusion. It is only in our capacity to enter into the
impression that there was something that we were able to mean by those
combinations of words that we can appreciate our present incapacity to do
so as a liberation and an achievement.

I am however interested here in a different progress of the mind.[49] In
the case of the *Tractatus* we end up exploding the illusion of having meant
anything by certain words; that is, we abandon certain combinations of
words. But our exploding the illusion of sense might work differently, en-
abling us to give a meaning to those words. That is, our realization that
we had meant nothing by them might turn in our capacity to read meaning into them. Cora Diamond has discussed a similar yet different case
in her essay "Riddles and Anselm's Riddle." In the case of riddles there
is a search for a solution to the riddle that ends up being a solution only
in that it fixes at the same time the meaning of the riddle itself. I am discussing a case, as in Mill's notion of truth, in which we do not start from
any such self-consciousness about our being in search of a sense, from any
such manifest puzzlement about the meaning of the form of words in the
riddle. But there is also an analogy in this: we recognize those words as
meaning something, as expressing some thought, only insofar as we re-

alize that we had meant nothing until then. With riddles the solution is internally connected to our being able to fix a meaning for those words; in Mill's case, understanding the real sense of a proverb is internally connected to our being able to fix a meaning, realizing that we had previously meant nothing. This realization is part of the game of searching for a solution to a riddle, whereas it is a discovery in Mill's case: the discovery of being freed from a state of confusion. (This is also the discovery the reader makes in the *Tractatus*.)

I am interested in giving an entry, in my reading of Cavell's perfectionism, and of its connection with Mill, to the idea of the finding of a truth for ourselves as a case in which we experience words becoming a living entity once again for us, in which personal experience brings the meaning of a proverb home, in which human reality is taken in ourselves as something real. I am glossing this sort of case—the case, say, where experience, in Mill's example, brings the full meaning of a truth home—as one where personal experience shows how to give meaning to words, what kind of bearing they can have on our life. But this can be appreciated from inside the perfectionist progress of the mind as the filling of words with meaning, that is, as seeing the connection between words and experience, seeing experience under the description of the sort of truth expressed by a proverb. This realization, this bringing truth home, this taking in of facts, cannot be captured in conceptual terms; it cannot be a realization of an experience which we had already conceptualized, of a certain truth which was already grasped by us. Experience here teaches something not in the ordinary inductive way, as Mill would say, teaching about the tendencies of things. The relevant notion of experience here can only be grasped from within the perfectionist path of the mind. We learn from personal experience through a process in which we work toward giving a meaning to words retained in a state of illusion of meaning. We can imaginatively appreciate this, as I said, from the point of view of the progress of the mind from confusion to clarity. We can see how the truth in a proverb illuminates our experience, as if we could have the experience without holding the concept for that experience, and conversely how experience illuminates the words, as if we already had those words to be illuminated as a concept previously grasped.

I think there is a connection here, which I shall not be able to explore, between the way in which a truth becomes a living principle in us and the special nature of this kind of experience. After commenting on the relationship of a reader with a text (Emerson's text in particular), which I proposed to call the perfectionist's paradox, Cavell writes that "In becoming conscious of what in the text is (in Emerson's word) unconscious, the familiar is invaded by another familiar—the structure Freud calls the uncanny, and the reason he calls the psychoanalytic process itself uncanny. Emerson's process of transfiguring is such a structure, a necessity of his placing his work in the position of our rejected and further self, our 'beyond.'"[50] Recovering a truth is bringing that truth home, being able to give a sense to it, that is, bringing it back to our ordinary ways of making sense of things; yet this invasion of the familiar by another familiar appears to us in an uncanny light. In another text, "The Fantastic of Philosophy," Cavell describes the experience of the uncanny (and the fantastic) as a "hesitation between the empirical and the supernatural."[51] This invasion of the familiar by another familiar has this uncanny nature because what is recovered as familiar appears, from the point of view of what we thought was to be recovered (from the nonsensical imagination of it), as unfamiliar, as uncanny. What is recovered, the meaning which fills the words of the proverb, is in a sense something familiar, our being able to give those words of the proverb a sense; yet it is also seen as a *meaning* that fills those words with a sense as from outside, a meaning detached from the ordinary meaningful connections—the empirical world in Cavell's words above—and seen supernaturally, as it were, as something which makes those words a living entity once again. We experience those words as mere signs (sounds) which are being filled by meaning. (We have this feeling of signs becoming symbols, to use Tractarian phraseology.) Our experience with truth (that sort of experience which perfectionism explores) shows this hesitation and ambivalence in our wanting to grasp truths as familiar facts about our success in expressing ourselves meaningfully, and in our experiencing truths in the light of their being a response to our state of confusion, as truths recovered from confusion, brought home to us.

We can now try to appreciate the perfectionist paradox in this light. The paradox expressed the thought that if truth is not yours already it will not do you good; but if it is yours already you won't need it. We can see this now as a difficulty internal to the fact that what counts as a truth for the self lies in the disappearance of what was felt as a problem, in clearing away the illusion of sense and thus in being able to give those words a meaning. There is a progress of the self which can be accounted for as a search for something to be achieved; yet this goal—truth to be regained—is a goal which is internal to the self, it needs to be yours already because it is a response internal to the illusion of the self, to the failure of the self to mean something: it is a response to that. It is a truth only in its being the overcoming of the illusion. The difficulty expressed by the perfectionist paradox can be appreciated, in the light of the reading that I have suggested, as constitutive of the kind of learning and progress Cavell's perfectionism is interested in exploring.

V

I have not explicitly connected this reading of Cavell's idea of perfectionism with political philosophy.[52] I now want to suggest one possible connection, even though I will not be able to explore it. Cavell has described moral perfectionism as "the condition of democratic morality,"[53] placing the idea of perfectionism at the center of the question of consent to a political community. There are many interesting issues that should be discussed here. The connection between the kind of consent that the self gives to others (community) and the extent to which the self can be representative of others—which Cavell connects to a line of thought central in Rousseau's philosophy—is also central to Mill's thought and especially to his discussion and reaction to Tocqueville's analysis of democracy in America.[54]

I want to raise a different (though related) issue here. A perfectionist understanding of the relation of the self to a political community can also be broached from the point of view of finding political claims, for example, in the field of justice, as not expressible though in ordinary conceptual ways, but as claims which make sense from the perspective of a further and yet unattained self. There is a difficult issue involved here, which would need a larger and separate treatment. This issue concerns the difficulty of expressing claims regarding justice when the language one uses necessarily fails one's linguistic intention. An example is when language seems to take sides with a certain position so as to pre-empt the dissenter's attempts to refute such position. Hate speech is an instance of this, but it is a much wider phenomenon.[55] I want to suggest that there are cases where this failure might be illuminated by a perfectionist understanding of what counts as claiming that an injustice has been done. These are cases where the issue of justice lies in a transformed vision of things, in a further and yet unattained vision of things and social reality that affords us the possibility to give voice to our sense of injustice. So the kind of claim we want to make inhabits that dimension which stands between our present condition, in which we find ourselves helpless in our incapacity to draw from our conceptual resources in order to say what we intend to say, and a further condition where this difficulty is overcome. I would think Cavell has an eye to this (among other things) when he notes Nora's changed attitude to Torvald in Ibsen's *A Doll's House* and writes

I am taking Nora's enactments of change and departure to exemplify that over the field on which moral justifications come to an end, and justice, as it stands, has done what it can, specific wrong may not be claimable; yet the misery is such that, on the other side, right is not assertible; instead something must be shown. This is the field of Moral Perfectionism, with its peculiar economy of power and impotence.[56]

The field of moral perfectionism extends beyond or below the reach of assertible claims, it moves in a region of thought which imagines a further and possible world where a cry of injustice, say, can find its proper voice, but as a world which is yet unattained, imagined as a transformation of our present capacities of expression. In this sense, as Cavell's writes, "Nora's imagination of her future, in leaving, turns on her need for education whose power of transformation presents itself to her as the chance to become human";[57] it is an imagination of a transformed condition of the self, an imagination of new rules and duties that can make sense of her newly acquired vision of things.

Perfectionism in this light warns us of the difficulties and the distances which may shape political claims in a society. Perfectionism should make us aware that the space where this difficulty resides is that of the self, it is the difficulty which lies in participating in a community and yet wanting to transcend that community. This difficulty can be accounted for as internal to a progress of the self that draws from the conceptual resources of the community but works its way to transforming them. A cry of injustice may require the imagination of a further self capable of rendering *that cry* intelligible to oneself and to others. Finding a solution, giving expression, to one's sense of injustice may require, that is, the perspective of that imagined further self. But this also shows the kind of distance that claims of justice can make, a distance that is not internal to the same conceptual space but needs to be bridged differently by a change in our conceptual world. In drawing together Cavell's idea of perfectionism with Mill and Wittgenstein I have wanted also to suggest a reading of these difficulties and distances.[58]

Telling the Dancer from the Dance: On the Relevance of the Ordinary for Political Thought

Joseph Lima and Tracy B. Strong

MIRANDA:

O, wonder!
How many goodly creatures are there here!
How beauteous mankind is! O brave new world,
That has such people in't!

PROSPERO:

T'is new to thee.

—SHAKESPEARE, *The Tempest*

I. A Short Historical Parable

By the middle 1960s two separate but related intellectual forces were taking root in American social sciences and humanities. Both were a response to the positivism that had dominated the professions in the period immediately following the Second World War. The appeal of that positivism was widespread—in social science, in philosophy, in the New literary Criticism—and was itself in great part a reaction to what appeared to have been an extremely dangerous subjectivism and irrationalism in the 1930s. Both of these reactions had the effect of breaking the intellectual hold—or were at least taken to have broken the hold—of the positivist understandings of the social world and of how one should go about trying to understand that world.

Central to positivism had been three claims. The first was that there was a clear-cut conceptual separation between facts and values and that, in consequence, values were subjective, not of the world, and could be kept apart from one's analysis of social reality. This was not a denial that values were "important," but it was a denial that values were objects of knowledge.[1]

The second claim was parent to the first. It was a claim that propositions about the world could and should be made to speak for themselves—thus that propositions about the world should have a validity independent of whoever advanced them. One could and should clearly separate the speaker from the spoken, for if one did one's work right, not just empirical claims about the world but concepts themselves would stand independently of the speaker. In its simplest form, the claim was that a statement like "mass equals force times acceleration" was true independently of who said it and of when and where it was said.

The third claim derived from the first two. It held that certain forms of discourse (claims to knowledge) were responsible and responsive to the real world in ways that other forms (one might think of them as emotive, or expressive) were not.[2] In the first form honesty toward the world required something of the thinker; in the second anything (apparently) went.

Into this vision of the world came a critique that came to carry the shorthand name of "Kuhn." Thomas Kuhn's book, *The Structure of Scientific Revolutions*, argued that claims about the world carried with them participation in a broader understanding—to some degree social and historical in nature—without which those claims would not be possible. Kuhn called these broader understandings "paradigms." Kuhn, in other words, appeared to question the distinction between the two forms of speech or knowledge, between the expressed and the un- or inexpressible.

Soon, everyone was citing Kuhn.[3] Crudely, what most people took him to have done—whether or not they approved of it—was to have brought "values" or cultural commitments back in scientific discourse. It is important to realize that in this reading of Kuhn, however, "values" were still understood precisely in the terms that positivism had cast them in. They were, in other words, the unexpressed, the non-cognitive, and so forth. That facts, as one learned to say, were "theory [or value] laden," and "embedded" in "webs of meaning" did not seem to join culture, value, or meaning any more tightly to the world nor make knowledge of these things any more shareable. The emphasis was rather in the other direction—loosening the grip of facts on the world, introducing a scrim of "values" before everywhere we might look for the former.

This terrain was fertile enough to foster a second development. Pretty soon those who read Kuhn in this manner—whether favorably or not—were reading Wittgenstein and allowing themselves free passage between paradigms, pictures, forms of life, and language games. Central here was the claim taken from Wittgenstein that language, or certain linguistic conventions, so shapes our understanding of the world that we do not see around their corners. Wittgenstein's apothegm that "a picture held us captive" came to stand for a peculiar kind of blindness forced on one through language itself.[4] For those who were favorable to this so-called "linguistic turn,"[5] however, Wittgenstein's proposition about imprisonment became a slogan of liberation. For if what seemed to constrain our thought was merely a picture, then it would certainly seem one could get out of it, or at least change pictures—or so it appeared. The irony here is that Wittgenstein's passage expresses a *disappointment* with knowledge. Wittgenstein continues: "And we could not get outside it, for it lay in our language and language seemed to repeat it to us inexorably." The irony is compounded in that *two* disappointments are captured here simultaneously: the initial one, a disappointment with the failure of knowledge to satisfy its own inveterate demands (in the *Investigations* this appears as the demand for a crystalline pure ideal of language), and the succeeding one, a disappointment with this initial disappointment—a finding of the latter to be in effect empty, a disappointment with success. It is this second disappointment that drives Wittgenstein to his famous turning around of the axis of his investigation (*PI*, §108). We shall have more to say about such turnings below.

In the social sciences, however, it was not long before some were proclaiming that "what you see depends on where you sit."[6] Kuhn's paradigms—already carried from scientific practice into society itself—were now radicalized by being located in the plurality of "language games" that were suddenly found to mark the differences among everything from academic disciplines to political projects. Ironically, since Wittgenstein's earlier work, the *Tractatus Logico-Philosophicus,* had been a central document in the rise of positivism (whether properly understood or not), his later work, the *Philosophical Investigations*, acquired its prestige in part as a recantation of an earlier "positivism."

We shall not be concerned here directly with the status and importance of Kuhn's work for the social sciences. However, leaving aside the question of whether or not those who read Kuhn got him right—and the answer to that would have to be for the most part "no"—it is important to realize that Kuhn's work drew heavily on certain developments in philosophy which were associated with the designation "ordinary language philosophy," a practice of philosophy variously associated with the work of J. L. Austin and Ludwig Wittgenstein. Its most prominent contemporary American practitioner is Stanley Cavell, who has extended Austin and Wittgenstein beyond any point that might have seemed obvious. We shall focus here on the importance and implications of this practice of philosophy for political theory and political science.

II. Sources and Resources

We believe many of the above developments associated with the enthusiasm for paradigms and language games to have been harmful to political theory and social science.[7] However, we do not think them harmful because they falsely blurred lines between the speakable and the unspeakable, between facts and values, between theory and commitment. We think them harmful because they blurred those lines incorrectly. We don't, that is, take them as an unfortunate departure from the comparative clarities of an earlier positivism. (We more nearly take them as a continuation, if in ironic guise, of positivism's never-avowed obscurities.) But, in any case, we find ourselves unsatisfied with *this* inheritance of the practice of ordinary language philosophy for political thought—which for us is to say that we find the ordinary as yet uninherited for political thought, hence for political science; and this precisely in those precincts of political theory most receptive, on their own account, to all things linguistic. To examine what an alternative inheritance of ordinary language philosophy might mean for political theory, we will look at the work of J. L. Austin, of Wittgenstein, and of Cavell. Cavell serves us doubly here: he is a guide to the understanding of the other two thinkers; he has also developed their thought in ways that are new and hard or impossible to anticipate from even a deep reading of the first two.[8] We hope that our reading here will be fruitful, fruitful in the sense that if one were to take it seriously it would affect the way in which one does political theory and potentially political science.

Wittgenstein has been, for the philosophical community, a difficult person to place. Three broad approaches to domestication seem to have developed. First, to some he appears as a Humean (or "mitigated") skeptic. In this reading, the central part of Wittgenstein's achievement is to have shown that philosophically we can always raise questions, but that these questions will, however, have little to do with our ordinary life. This view places great weight on passages such as "Justification comes to an end" (*PI*, §194) and "My life consists in being able to accept many things" (*PI*, §44). In this reading, the task of philosophy is to keep itself in its own, proper, corner and not to pretend to be part of life as we live it. This view is held in different ways by Richard Rorty and Saul Kripke.[9]

A second reading holds that Wittgenstein is a kind of empiricist justificationist. The *Investigations* are taken to be a justification of cultural common sense. Hence: "Our mistake is to look for an explanation . . . where we ought to have said 'This language game is played'" (*PI*, §654). This view derives ultimately from G. E. Moore for whom philosophical problems can and should be eliminated by reinforcing what all people know unproblematically. A contemporary exponent of this understanding of Wittgenstein would be the late Peter Winch.

A third view is a kind of Kantian justificationism. Kant, as is commonly known, tried to determine those categories of the understanding which delineated the realm in which reason was possible. David Pears, for instance, refers to Wittgenstein as a "linguistic Kantian." In readings such as this, Wittgenstein wants to show the limits of human reason by reestablishing the boundaries between the phenomenal and the noumenal realms. Thus: "Grammar tells us what kind of object anything is" (*PI*, §373). Grammar, in this reading, becomes the equivalent of the synthetic a priori; however, it is understood as conventionally based.[10]

It is important to realize that all three of these readings see Wittgenstein as concerned centrally with the *justification* of knowledge. Thus to the degree that any one of these views would be correct, Wittgenstein's thought will not be of much use in political theory. There is also a danger when addressing these questions—more present in Wittgenstein and Cavell than with Austin—of falling into one of three interpretive modes. The first is that of the valorization of ineffability—these authors are taken to point at the power of what cannot be said, at a realm of mystery lying beyond language and to which language is inadequate. A second mode is to hold that these authors are not talking about philosophy at all but rather about that which is pre- or non-philosophical, a kind of anthropology. Here the expectation is that these readers desire to keep philosophy in its proper place. The last mode is to think that these men are attempting to turn philosophy into literature—a kind of edifying discourse that since it makes no real claims to the truth need not bother about being "right." Here they are read into a particular version of continental thought, with its emphasis on reading as opposed to (in Anglo-American analytic thought) argument. Gerald Bruns may be thought to hold this position.

III. Life and Form

The first two dangers come from a particular conception of the often invoked but rarely examined Wittgensteinian concept of the *Lebensform*—the "form of life."[11] Accordingly, we begin our investigation by looking at this term.

"Form of life" is often taken to imply that there is some sort of (anthropological) bedrock beyond or behind or beneath which one cannot go, that it has simply to be accepted. The standard citation is from *Investigations,* §241. There the voice that answers has been questioned by a somewhat Russellian interlocutor: "'So you are saying that human agreement decides what is true and what is false?'" The response is: "It is what human beings *say* that is true and false; and they agree in the *language* they use. That is not agreement in opinions but in form of life." In turn this exchange is most often taken to imply that human understanding is shaped by some thick, pre-existing set of affairs about which one can do nothing because that is simply what or who one is. There are parallels in this to contemporary "communitarian" thought, with its opposition of the thick social self to the "thin" liberal one.[12]

In this reading, Wittgenstein would be calling to our attention that about which we can do nothing. It would constitute, as Cavell remarks, a kind of "rebuke [of] philosophy for concentrating too much on isolated individuals."[13] The implication here is that we can do nothing about what are essentially conventions, constitutive conventions to be sure, but conventions none the less. This reading makes Wittgenstein conservative—a person who neither can nor wishes to do anything about the way the world is.[14] Bertrand Russell, once Wittgenstein's teacher and champion, had such a reaction to the *Investigations*. Such accusations, one might note, were also made about J. L. Austin by Ernest Gellner, the anthropologist and philosopher, among others.[15]

The accusation of conservatism revolves around an understanding of forms of life that generally presumes it to be ethnological, that is, the sort of thing that sociologists and anthropologists talk about. But this, standard, interpretation of "forms of life" with its emphasis on the ethnological, slights the weight that "life" carries in Wittgenstein's formula—that is, it flattens out one of the most striking and original features of the *Investigations*, which is its seeming alteration between finding that language makes the reach of convention effectively unlimited for humans—"To obey a rule, to make a report, to give an order, to play a game of chess, are customs (uses, institutions)" (*PI*, §199)—and that those same conventions have the quality of being or becoming a part of our nature—"commanding, questioning, storytelling, chatting, are as much a part of our natural history as walking, eating, drinking, playing"(*PI*, §25).[16] While Wittgenstein surely teaches the pervasiveness of convention, he is equally a teacher of the detailed extent to which the conventional is natural to the human. At best, what the exclusively ethnological weighting of Wittgenstein's conventionalism gives us is a plea to stop thinking, to let things be.[17] Behind it is the idea that philosophizing—what one might call language on idle—creates only false problems, and that one should attend instead to real problems, which are presumably problems of and in life, itself understood as something else than the entanglements of (philosophical) language. For such a reading, when Wittgenstein speaks of giving philosophy peace, he is taking about the finality of euthanasia.[18]

The perception of Wittgenstein's philosophical practice as having the necessary consequence of political conservatism is, as Cavell remarks, rooted in this reading of Wittgenstein as a (one-sided) conventionalist[19] (DD, p. 43). Such a reading takes Wittgenstein's notion of form of life in what

Cavell calls an exclusively ethnological or "horizontal" sense—as meaning *forms* of life.[20] Cavell proposes to contest this interpretation by attending to the "vertical" or "biological" sense of the formula—form of *life* (DD, p. 41). Cavell means the contrast between the horizontal and the vertical to call up the difference between conventions that are exclusive to (and thus serve to set off) one human group among others, and those that set the human off from other forms of life altogether—classically, both those "lower" and "higher" than the human—animals and gods.[21] It is a matter, it seems, of the human scale ("the specific strength and scale of the human body and of the human senses and of the human voice") (DD, p. 42).[22] That is the sense, or spirit, in which Cavell reads Wittgenstein's remark, "What has to be accepted, the given, is—so one could say—forms of life" (*PI*, p. 226). To this, one may adduce, as does Cavell, those passages in Wittgenstein which speak of "our real need" (*PI*, 108), and suggests that we must be "turned around" in order to be able to see this need. The idea is that acceptance of the human (that is, the taking) form of life (as opposed to this or that cultural mode of it) involves (or requires) the possibility of radical transformation of that life as it stands. Wittgenstein's language ("turned around") in passages such as these (Cavell remarks on its characteristic "fervor") calls to mind writers such as Plato and Rousseau who diagnosed the human form of life as one imprisoned by false necessities and in need of the liberation that comes from being turned around to face truer necessities. (Cavell mentions also Thoreau and Luther, and directly analogizes Wittgenstein's idea of rotating the axis of philosophy's investigation to that of a conversion.) We might also think in this connection of Nietzsche, with his notion of the need, at a certain stage of history, for the "breeding" or "cultivation" of a new form of life. He refers to it either as an *Erziehung*—an education—or as *Züchtung*—as breeding. In this context Nietzsche will speak of the need to "attempt to produce (*gewinnen*) a *Lebensform*, which has not yet been produced."[23] In short, the shift from the one-sided conventionalist reading of Wittgenstein to this reading in which the conventional and natural are endlessly interwoven in the human seems to open up for Cavell new vistas of radical transformation in the idea of the appeal to the ordinary.

So far, however, this does not seem to get us any where except into deeper waters. The notion of a "real need" appears to imply some kind of notion of false consciousness, the stance that one might be mistaken about what one's "real" needs in fact are. To this we can only say here that we have no choice in fact, if we follow Wittgenstein and Cavell on this, but to swim in these waters. What about false consciousness? The notion of a real need can be taken in one of two manners. First, it can imply that there is some-one who knows better than I how it is with me *and that* this person does so because s/he has greater insight, knowledge or skill, insight or knowl-edge or skill that is not available to me. This idea of false consciousness is endemic to Leninism where the idea of the party and the professional rev-olutionary (who, remarks Lenin, is trained to see through ordinary judg-ment on these matters and is thus not, as he remarks in *What is to be done?*, a "wretched amateur").

The problem is that this picture of false consciousness gives one no picture of what it would mean to *change* from seeing the world as one sees it to seeing it as it "really" is. The presumption is that the world will it-self take care of that change (perhaps this is akin to the presumption of Marx—before the 18th Brumaire of Louis Napoleon—that the senses of the proletariat would become their theoreticians). It is also the case that those who see the world as it "really is" are simply enforcers of the world, are not acting on their own. (If the senses were to have been theoreticians, and they fail, what then?) Therefore if they insist that one must see the world in such and such a way, the responsibility is not theirs. In this Lenin shares a march with the positivism identified in the first part of this essay. The pic-ture of change here is too influenced by the drama of Jastrow's well-known duck-rabbit, where the effect of (suddenly) seeing the duck when you have only seen the rabbit overwhelms the transition process and makes the pro-cess of change seem magical, almost instantaneous.[24] Rather we must ask what it means to undergo this kind of change.

In any case it would appear that the question of false consciousness is not well-posed when addressed in the Leninist/Gestalt fashion. For the change to be a change, it will have to be my change, not simply the ac-ceptance of a picture which has been presented to me, even if that picture be true. (The parallel with psychoanalytic practice is strong here: The ana-lyst cannot simply tell the patient what is wrong with her and what would be right—the patient has to tell herself, as it were.[25]) In other words the change will have to be one in which you, as the author of my change, disappear by virtue of my making the change.[26] Key here will be a concept of the "human" or the "ordinary" which occurs when beings like ourselves begin to talk to each other.

But we get ahead of ourselves here and risk making Wittgenstein and Cavell sound like Habermas.[27] We were saying that Cavell is trying to correct the conservative reading of Wittgenstein—hence of the appeal to the ordinary—as dependent on, or as amounting to, a kind of contingent foundationalism. Such a view would see the upshot of Wittgenstein's teaching in something like the following claim: There really is something that grounds or guarantees all (true) philosophical claims, only this something turns out to be nothing more than our practices, our customary ways of doing things; and this is enough for all but the hopelessly metaphysical—it silences doubt, at least for all practical purposes. On such a view, as noted, Wittgenstein looks like Hume, the philosopher who accommodates and mitigates the threat of skepticism by offering a skeptical solution. (This is Kripke's reading of Wittgenstein.)

Against such a reading,[28] Cavell offers a Wittgenstein who would have us accept, not "private property, but separateness, not a particular fact of power" but that of our having a certain "range or scale" of human capacities (DD, p. 44). With this acceptance, says Cavell, comes the possibility of transfiguration, of radical change to a different order of natural reactions (DD, p. 44). Note that this implies that the human is something that beings like ourselves do not always have, that it is something that we have lost and need to re-cover or re-member ourselves with and by.

Now, one might well ask at this point: Just how does shifting from the ethnological to the biological sense of forms of life get Wittgenstein (or Cavell) off the hook of a necessary political conservatism? A plausible reaction to such a move might be: Doesn't this, if anything, make matters worse? Doesn't it get Wittgenstein out of the conventionalist pan only to drop him into the essentialist fryer? How does the move from urging acceptance of *forms* of life, to urging acceptance of forms of *life*, get us to possibilities that deserve the names of transfiguration or radical change? It would seem, on the face of it, if anything, to move us even further away from such possibilities. It seems, that is to say, as though we are only being asked to accept even more—or to accept even more completely, at a deeper level so to speak—exactly what one might conceivably want to change. It sounds as though we are being denied or debarred from wanting change: Now our desire for it would violate not just convention (important as that might be), but nature as well. What is going on here?

It seems to us that there is only one answer possible here that makes sense of Cavell's claims: To say that the acceptance of forms of life (of the human form of life) counts as radically transfigurative is to say that the possibility of radical change is presently blocked by (in addition to what-ever else may be blocking it) our refusal of this very acceptance. In place of the traditional picture, in which change is to be wrested from a recal-citrant future, and in which, in our pursuit of it, we are held back by the dead hand of the past (what Milan Kundera once called the "kitsch of the Left"); this gives a picture in which change is seen to be already impinging on the present, but kept from breaking in on it by something we are re-peatedly doing. Radical change goes on not happening because we are not letting it happen. Here one glimpses the profound negativity of Wittgen-stein's philosophical practice as Cavell understands it. The move to the ac-ceptance of form of life is radically transfigurative precisely because it is the one move that is being refused, say endlessly deferred. Refused by whom? (Who is this "we" that refuses?) And in what sense refused? How does the opposition of power to what harms its interests, for example, relate to this refusal? What can this claim mean politically?

The idea is that the refusal to accept forms of life—or the refusal to accept that they must be accepted—is what creates, or has created, or sus-tains, false need in opposition to true need—artificial necessities in op-position to genuine ones (DD, pp. 43–44). The implied diagnosis is that the prevailing picture of change (but also—presumably—the prevailing pictures of stability or security) is already based on the denial of the hu-man form of life (DD, pp. 45–46). This denial, we take it, is not some-thing we are being warned against doing—a desire for something real that we are being urged to forgo—but, rather, something we are being told we must stop doing, for our doing it—our activity—is blocking real, gratify-ing change, by blocking the manifestation of "true need" (Cavell will also say "desire")(DD, p. 45).

It is on this idea that Cavell stakes his radical interpretation of Witt-genstein's remark that philosophy "leaves everything as it is" (*PI*, §124). Like the remark about accepting forms of life, this description of (Wittgenstein's) philosophical practice appears to deny the possibility of actually changing what is—the world as it stands, let us say. Hence it seems, by an old definition of what politics consists in, to be at best apolitical in its implications, if not anti-political. But such a reading of the remark depends on the unexamined assumption that present alternatives in philosophy (and why shouldn't political theory be added in here?) are already leaving everything as it is (an assumption that goes back at least to Marx's eleventh thesis on Feuerbach). On Cavell's reading, however, Wittgenstein's diagnosis of the situation is something like the reverse of this: The assumption that everything is already being left as it is—the assumption that theory, let us say, is perpetually in a condition of needing to be carried more effectively into practice—in fact drives the current and endlessly repeated intellectualization of all the problems on which philosophy touches—including those of ethics and politics.[29] And, crucially, this is not, we take it, a claim exclusively about, e.g., professional thinkers. Rather, the claim is directed to what Cavell later calls "philosophy unconscious of itself" (DD, p. 64), to philosophy adrift in the everyday. This is why Cavell has Wittgenstein finding "the (actual) everyday to be as pervasive a scene of illusion and trance and artificiality (of need) as Plato or Rousseau or Marx or Thoreau had found" (DD, p. 46). So while it is true, according to Cavell, that Wittgenstein's struggle is of philosophy with itself, this struggle is said to take place on the field of the everyday. And since this is a field already pervaded by philosophy—but, as it were, by philosophy which denies the fact of its own presence there—Wittgenstein is in the line of Rousseau and Marx and Nietzsche in being an unmasker simultaneously of philosophical illusion and of the artificiality, or say the false naturalness, of current practices. He sets a philosophical practice against philosophy as it stands precisely in the hope of releasing an (eventual) everyday from its imprisonment in the (actual) everyday, "as if the actual is the womb, contains the terms, of the eventual" (DD, p. 46). To refuse the (false) ascent, or transcendence, constantly offered up by philosophy, in its drift through the actual everyday, is then to refuse a kind of violence—an intellectualization that is, and results in, the forms of violence by which we hold ourselves captive to a false picture of what the everyday must be for us (a cave?).[30]

If Cavell is right about his Wittgenstein, is Wittgenstein serious? Are we to accept that philosophy—of a violent kind—so pervades the everyday that it prevents real, gratifying change, in our every effort at such change? (Then it also prevents gratifying preservation; then we are as disabled, in this sense, in our conservative impulses as in our revolutionary ones—something Arendt pointed out in "What Is Authority."[31]) Without the accuracy of this diagnosis, at any rate, it would be hard to see how Wittgenstein's philosophical practice could claim the status of cultural criticism that Cavell wants to give it (or the status of a work of ethics that Wittgenstein himself wished for it); and it would be hard, likewise, to see this practice as having more than a narrowly technical or methodological relevance for political theory. On the other hand, if Cavell's reading is right, the appeal to the ordinary has truly profound implications for political thought—and for politics itself. In particular, it has profound implications for the whole question of theory and practice, which makes itself felt inescapably in virtually every problem taken up by, or in, or as political theory.

What does it mean to try and change or dislodge a given picture of the relation between thought, or language, and life in the manner that Wittgenstein was at pains to? (See *PI*, §§19, 23, 241; §§174, 226). Twenty-five years ago, Hanna F. Pitkin argued that Wittgenstein's deeper significance for social and political thought lay not in a methodology that helps avoid theory, let alone "refute" philosophical "mistakes," but in a way of exposing the role of theoretical presuppositions in our lives as we live and use them, including therefore the lives of those who study political and social phenomena. Her point then was that we could no longer presuppose, as had earlier generations of social scientists, influenced by their reading of what Max Weber was presumed to have said in "Science as a Vocation,"[32] that open avowal of presuppositions was sufficient to provide perspectives on ourselves. The problem was rather "becoming aware of what our presuppositions are."[33] It is not the case that one has only to say what they are to overcome them. Rather one has to become aware of what one's commitments to them actually are.

For Pitkin, writing near the beginning of the new emphasis on language in the study of political life, Wittgenstein promised exactly this kind of awareness or, as he and Cavell call it, "acknowledgment."[34] With it, they and she had some hope for relief from the "reification" that seemed to many, in those years, to stand in the way of genuine political change.[35]

Thanks in part of the intervening influence of the linguistic turn, in all its various forms, the presuppositions that color contemporary social and political thought are no longer as thoroughly determined as they were, when Pitkin wrote, by the legacy of positivism. Yet having simply taken the linguistic turn is not to have freed political theory from that earlier range of presuppositions. There is more then one way to be held captive by a picture.[36]

What is missing from the ethnological readings of "form of life" and what continues to be missing in most versions of Wittgenstein and Austin that have gotten themselves formalized in contemporary political thought is an understanding of the full implications of seeing language itself (and not just these or those words) as an activity, a mode of action. If "words are also deeds" (*PI*, §546), that is no guarantee that this understanding has sunk in, nor indeed of what it means to say this.[37] Think for a minute that most contemporary discussions of language tend to see words exclusively as signs and not also, as Wittgenstein and Austin would have it, as signals, or better still, as tools with widely varying purposes and uses.

IV. Some Attempts at Use

The most interesting recent work being done with attention to those procedures, or at least to some of their results, has emphasized Austin's work on performatives—verbs the uttering of which, in the first-person singular present indicative, constitutes the performing of the action named in the utterance.[38] Performatives were shown by Austin, who is responsible for the term, to be a mode of discourse that did not fit easily into either "factual" or "normative" statements. Nor did they "correspond" to a supposed "fact" in the world as a kind of descriptive tag. Rather, they did something: language was action.

Taken in relative isolation from Austin's, not to say from Wittgenstein's, other work, however, the treatment of performatives can itself occlude the larger implications of seeing language as action, as a (as the human) form of life. Very roughly, a focus on performativity that is drawn from too narrow a range of examples, or language games, lends itself to another iteration of the ethnological understanding of language as a (culturally specific) form of life—this time with the addition of an element of ironic subversion: If a language is such a form of life, sustained by the repetition of its performatives—Nietzsche thought we remained tied to God by our faith in grammar—one might hope to subvert its effects by performing them (ethnologically) *incorrectly*. While this may look vaguely liberating when set against the ethnological view of language as form of life, it is but a different (skewed) angle on the same picture, and ultimately carries the same conservative implications. This is, if we understand, more or less what Cavell has recently objected to in Derrida's appropriation/critique of Austin.[39] Pitkin had already issued a similar warning in *Wittgenstein and Justice*:

The existence of these [performative] verbs is relatively uninteresting compared to the far greater discovery implicit in Austin but made explicit by Wittgenstein: that much or perhaps all of language is performative in a looser sense, is what we might call quasi-performative. Though speaking may not always be performing the action named in the speech, it is always performing an action, for whose consequences the speaker is responsible.[40]

Is it quibbling to cite this passage as saying something that has yet to be fully appreciated about the social and political implications of ordinary language procedures? Those now making use of Austin in ways inspired by Derrida have surely seen the need to expand the application of the idea of performative utterance (rather than confining the interest of the approach to a subset of verbs, for example), and that expansion has obviously involved seeing language as performative, hence as something enacted. What more could one want from Austin, or from the view of language as action?

What needs to be shown here is that the way in which Austin's work on performatives as extended by Cavell has so far been applied to problems in political theory fails to release the full, liberatory—and, we will say, democratic—potential of seeing language as a mode of action. The current reception of Austin, hence of the ordinary, fails, in particular, to draw the right implication from the fact of the existence of performative utterances, and it fails to do so because its view of them is colored, still, by the old ("positivist") picture of the relation of words and the world. In short, performatives mainly work for contemporary political theory as a handy way of inverting the positivist picture—and this despite a real desire, on the part of those drawn to the view of language as action, to escape from mere antithesis. (This is increasingly evident in Judith Butler's work, especially. It is, however, evidently very hard not to end up merely inverting such a picture.)

In the work of Judith Butler, Bonnie Honig, and others, Derrida's appropriation and critique of Austin's work on performatives has been received and deployed as the basis for recasting the terms of a debate, or anyway of a theoretical puzzlement, brought on by the contemporary (or late?) politics of identity, one involving something called "essentialism" and something else, thought to be the opposite of that, called "constructivism."[41] The puzzlement in question can be rendered as a dilemma: To see identity (or political subjectivity) as something essential is to render it a political cudgel in whoever's hands seize it; to see it as something purely constructed is to risk failing to understand, or resist, or harness, its power.

Cavell, meanwhile, has raised serious questions about Derrida's Austin, asking in effect whether the former has not both praised and blamed the latter for the wrong things.[42] Specifically, Derrida attributes to Austin the view (with which he concurs) that the analysis of performative utterance is properly made in terms not of truth (adequation to reality) but of force (perlocutionary and illocutionary, as everyone now knows), and the view (with which he strongly disagrees) that such analysis shows meaning to be controlled, or determined, or guaranteed by the presence of a speaker's intention. Against this reading, Cavell aims to show two things. First, he argues that Austin's work on performatives was meant to contest precisely the view (as embodied in positivism) that only statements of fact could be adequate to reality, hence meaningful, and that other sorts of utterances, notably moral and aesthetic judgments, were "emotive" or "noncognitive." Thus, having "discovered" the category, Austin wanted exactly to defend performative utterance as (logically) capable of, indeed governed by, adequation to reality in a no less serious sense than is "constative" utterance. Second, Cavell shows that intentionality is not, for Austin, a presence that guarantees meaning in language—or even what Austin called the "felicity" of performative utterances—and that Austin does not, therefore, deny what Derrida imagines him to be denying, namely, the ubiquitous failures of human intention to carry through to outcome. (Cavell here gently chides Derrida for being unfamiliar with Austin's work on excuses and pretending,[43] for which there would clearly be no place if the latter had philosophically repressed the failures of intention as Derrida supposes he had.) Rather than being a metaphysical guarantee of successful performative utterance, intention is for Austin a constituent of sense, and, as such, is itself controlled by the kind of necessities, or conventions (both terms apply if either does) that, in Wittgenstein's lingo, are called "grammar." Thus, Cavell takes Derrida to task for two related misreadings: on the one hand, for praising Austin for having opened up a gap where none in fact exists (viz., between performative utterance and reality) and, on the other, for criticizing Austin for having repressed a gap where he in fact acknowledged one (viz., between intention and outcome).

If Cavell's criticisms are credited, then the version of Austin, or anyway of "performativity," circulating in some of the most interesting contemporary political theory may be significantly misleading with respect to Austin's and, by extension, ordinary language philosophy's possible contribution to political thought—even this late, so to speak, in the history of the linguistic turn. Whether and in what way all this might matter, to political theory and practice, are of course what interests one here, or what, at least, should.

Derrida and, after him, Butler want a "performativity" which is open-ended, "futural," to use Butler's term. Both suppose that the idea of the ordinary, with its conventional contexts, describes a use of performative utterance that is significantly constrained, conservative. If the (politically relevant) possibility of the projection of performative utterances, of "speech-acts," into different contexts is not to be found in "ordinary language," then where? The answer is clearly: from an idea of "iterability," or "citationality"—a possibility grounded differently for Derrida (in the arbitrariness of the sign) than for Butler (in the body's rhetorically exceeding the "speech-act" it performs)—but in either case considered internal to the use of language. On such a reading of Austin, he leaves us with a kind of either/or choice: Either account for the so-called "force" of "speech-acts" by accepting that they are determined, in effect, by prior social conventions, hence fixed; or else accept their indeterminacy, their (Derrida more-or-less says necessary; Butler settles for possible) "failures" in repetition, and receive, in return for such acceptance, what Butler calls "the political promise of the performative."[44] Having begun from the premise that performatives are not responsive to reality—that, in Derrida's phrase, they call for the replacement of "truth" by "force"—Derrida and Butler find (different kinds of) hope (philosophical for him; political for her) in the idea that performatives are also not entirely successful in responding to their sup-posedly-originary (and, as they both insist, "ordinary") contexts. The first gap—between words, or mind, and the world—is thus to be "redeemed" by a second gap—this one between words and their (conventional, social) contexts of use.

Here we want to consider what difference it makes that the Austin-ian, or say "ordinary language," contexts, from which escape is thus sought through iteration, are taken, by both Derrida and Butler, in a sense that (in reference to Wittgenstein's parallel, or at least related, notion of "forms of life") Cavell would call "ethnological" or "horizontal"—and clearly *not* in the competing sense he calls "biological" or "vertical." Given this com-peting sense, would Austin—hence would the ordinary—come out differ-ently with respect to "the political promise of the performative"?

With this in mind let us reexamine a bit Austin's understanding of the "performative,"[45] that is, the realm of describing or naming something in such a manner that that is what it is. (To say "I promise" is actually to promise, not to refer to something.) We recognize this most easily as a po-litical question when such a contest over such namings arises.[46] Take the following case.[47] In 1789 Louis XVI of France found himself urged by his minister Neckar to call the Estates General into session. The Estates Gen-eral were composed of the nobility, the clergy, and the Third Estate, which stood for the non-privileged classes. The Estates had not been summoned since 1614, when the meeting dissolved without agreement after the Third Estate refused to consent to the abolition of the sale of offices unless the nobility gave up some of their privileges. The convocation of the Estates was thus essentially a medieval practice, hardly an institution, but it was nonetheless a practice the availability of which led to their being called in 1789. On June 17, 1789, the Third Estate declared itself to *be* the National Assembly of France. The question immediately raised is to the authority by which, in terms of which, this claim has legitimacy and more importantly to what it means to declare oneself something that had not previously ex-isted as itself. The assembled delegates (they are not even really delegates in that they are not for the most part elected) cannot be calling upon an existing authority—they are trying to call one into existence—to create a past—so as to give themselves a reality in the present. The King, it should be noted, had the Assembly building surrounded by troops and ordered the delegates to disperse, stating that their naming of themselves the National Assembly meant nothing and was therefore null and void.

The political question here is then which performative is to be efficacious, what one might call the ethnological, social conventional (that of the King), or the biological, that is the claim to life advanced by the would-be Assembly.[48] Is it too much to see the contrast that way? The would-be Assembly is clearly doing something other than wrongly performing a conventional performative. We might say that it is introducing a new performative. (It is not as though they are claiming to speak as a *different* Estate.) What had been a part now claims to speak as and for the whole. The deeper question then has to do with the status of this authority—the authority of the political voice. What is it that serves as the entitlement to speak in this voice? The Third Estate is claiming the right to think of itself as a National Assembly—how may this right and, more important, this would-be actuality be established? This is the question of foundation, of constituting oneself as a person, a body, a people—perhaps the fundamental modern political question. It is, as we shall see, the question of sovereignty.

What has to be the case for a performative to be accepted as performing, for something new to come into existence—in the above case, for the National Assembly to in fact exist, where existence comes both in the acknowledgment from others and that it is what it says that it is? Most of the discussion of performatives explicitly assumes a particular form of life (one might call it an institutional structure) such that when one says "I do" in a particular set of circumstances and in response to a question posed at a particular time and place, then one is *in actuality* a married person and in no ways an unmarried one. In the above case, however, we are one step below or beyond that, in a realm of what we might call a hyper- (or vertical) performative, when the saying of particular sentences calls up the possibility of conditions that make a new authority actual. Such a change is in fact a transformation or a transfiguration of the world. If we have been naught, how shall we be all?

The case above gives us a spatial debate between the King and the (would-be) Assembly; the spatially situated debate, however, is a debate about time, over the hold of the past. From our reading of Cavell, we want and need to understand the discussion as a temporal debate, that is, one between the transformation of the present and the past. In speaking as the National Assembly, what the delegates of the Third Estate had going for them was something the King had inadvertently provided in bringing them all together—call this their chance to be in one another's present, that is, to share a present (as opposed to, or in addition to, a social framework defined by past performatives). The conditions had been created for one of those political moments in which there occurs what Slavoj Zizek has called "the elementary gesture of politicization."[49] The case raises, we mean, the possibility that the time of the political is always now, for the reason that it is only by sharing a present that those who have not been heard can speak as a "we." (Political skepticism, and we do no more than assert this in passing, might be thought of equally as a fear of such moments, or a hope that they will come to pass without our participation.) Another way to say this is that what comes to the fore at such times is the fact of politics as a recurrent possibility of the human (talking) form of life. This might be nothing but a restatement of the old Aristotelian conception of the political as being as natural to the human as speech (or language) itself is. But, if it is, it is a restatement in full awareness that the polis does not now exist for us. (Something like that awareness might have driven Rousseau to speak of the English being free for a day only.[50]) If it is true that we can look back and see the polis's (re-)emergence at moments across our history, then we equally see that it is constantly escaping us—or that we are constantly fleeing, or say turning, from it (as if in disappointment). This should prompt the question of why it is we are so constantly disappointed by the political present? Does our disappointment stem from too *few* occasions for our participation—too few occasions in which we might find ourselves sharing a political present with others? We don't exactly require, anymore, the invitation of a King.

It might indeed be the case, as Sheldon Wolin has argued, that the polis is always at hand, but always slipping through our grasp, whenever we try to force it into forms designed to endure without our wholehearted participation.[51] It might be, in other words, that polis exists, if at all, only in its articulation. This is not dissimilar to what Rousseau said about sovereignty in the *Social Contract*. Recall that for Rousseau sovereignty does not exist and cannot exist over time. It is pure presence. Each moment of sovereignty—what Rousseau calls "law"—is "absolute, independent or the preceding, and never does the sovereign act because he willed (past tense) but only because he wills (present tense)."[52] This thought, given formulation in several places in Rousseau's drafts as he worked on the *Social Contract*, appears in final form in the extraordinary claim that "yesterday's law carries no obligations today."[53] And Rousseau makes no concession to the pragmatism of politics by his immediate recognition that "consent is presumed from silence." Rather he is saying that our very act of saying nothing about a law is a recognition of our complicity in it. Sovereignty and the very being of political society are held to exist solely in the present tense, in and as their performance. Not only can the future not be tied down, it cannot be rightly named without sin. There is not "any kind of obligatory fundamental law for the body of the people, not even the social contract." Note that this means that whether or not obligation is an important component of a political society, politics and society cannot be properly conceived of as *resting* on obligation, for I cannot be obliged without some form of representation, and representation cannot be a ground of rest.[54] In politics (at least), the dancers can only be told from the dance.[55] How does obligation reveal political society and how to we know political society apart from obligation?

If so, then this calls attention to ways in which philosophy's predicament, as diagnosed by Cavell in his reading of Wittgenstein, and that of contemporary politics match one another. This is to say that politics and philosophy seem to be in the same position with respect to their respective present possibilities—or, to put it otherwise, they share a problematic of authority. The authoritative utterance must be rooted in a present, and for constituting such a present, every moment is as good as every other. For Cavell's Emerson, "the conditions of a philosophical practice are set before *us*," meaning in the first instance nineteenth-century Americans.[56] (Hence to pick up Emerson's and Cavell's challenge we must grasp the "us"—this is the "ordinary" in ordinary language philosophy—before which practices are set.) For Wittgenstein, as Cavell teaches us to read him, the ordinary or the everyday (to which words are to be led back, as if from metaphysical exile) is no refuge from skepticism, as Cavell names philosophy's preeminent temptation and threat, but rather the only place where the latter can truly be confronted, or say engaged. This is because the ordinary is the place away from which we are always turning, in reaction to skepticism's threat, which arises precisely there, among "our" "ordinary" words (where else?). So, as Cavell is constantly reminding us, the ordinary partakes of the uncanny, an extraordinary of the ordinary that consists in our non-presentness to it—which comes across as its non-presentness to us, as when Wittgenstein's procedures cause us to be struck by the richness of a term that had grown. stale with philosophical use, or when Emerson's or Thoreau's (as Cavell makes them available to us) allied procedures cause us to be struck by the philosophical weight of words that seemed too ordinary to bear such significance. For Cavell, what the temptation to skepticism shows us (once we stop trying to defeat it by philosophical main force or strategic retreat) is that and how we come to grief in our ordinary life with words by treating them as if they could (that is, as if knowledge could make them) go on meaning, but without us.[57]

Is there a similar dialectic of estrangement and attraction at work in the political everyday? One in which skepticism (about the possibility of the political) is similarly our path away from, but also our royal road back to, the political present? Over thirty years ago, Sheldon Wolin introduced the notion of "epic political theory" in an explicit analogy with Kuhn's paradigm shift. The great political theorists, Wolin argued, were those who faced the death of their civic gods, the political anomalies of their times, and thereby became paradigm creators—whose decidedly extraordinary work, in other words, was to envision transfigurations of the political world.[58] If, however, skepticism shows that the task of finding or founding a philosophical present falls to the ordinary, the everyday (because that is where every opportunity for doing so is lost, if it is not found there); and if politics partakes of this same uncanniness of the ordinary (because it too goes forward now, if at all, under the threat and temptation of skepticism, according to which it is here that the political present is lost or found); if all this is so, then the condition of epic theory is the everyday condition of politics, and the situation of the epic theorist is the ordinary situation of all who now give thought to action in the political present.

CHAPTER FIVE

Political Revisions: Stanley Cavell and Political Philosophy

Andrew Norris

> But play, you must,
> A tune beyond us, yet ourselves,
> A tune upon the blue guitar
> Of things exactly as they are.
>
> —WALLACE STEVENS[1]

When political theorists read the work of Stanley Cavell, they are initially likely to be drawn to his discussion of contract theory.[2] In a substantial body of work devoted to topics such as skepticism, Romanticism, tragedy, film, and the problem of other minds, Cavell's discussion of the social contract emerges as one of his few extended considerations of an explicitly political topic. And it serves to unify Cavell's briefer discussions of disparate other political themes, such as chattel slavery and civil disobedience. Not surprisingly, then, it is also the subject which has drawn him into his most prominent critical engagement with a political theorist, in this case John Rawls. If this makes Cavell's discussion of the contract an obvious place to begin studying his work, his unusual line of approach provides great rewards for those who do so. Cavell's extensive engagement with ordinary language philosophy and his work on the universal voice of Kantian aesthetics allow him to produce a rich account of the Rousseauian social contract that casts considerable light upon our ability as citizens to speak politically for one another in the first person plural. Cavell thus has much to teach us about how an individual can represent her community, thereby making her community present in this world.[3]

It is important, however, to see the limitations of a reception of Cavell's work that focuses too intently on his discussion of the contract. The examples of Rousseau and, to a somewhat lesser extent, of Rawls encourage us to focus on a model of politics as legislation. In Rousseau the general will is a specifically legislating will; likewise, in Rawls we speak for one another first and foremost in the Original Position, where the only task we engage in is that of choosing the principles of justice for the basic structure of society. But Cavell is not just concerned with our ability to speak *for* one another but also our ability to speak *with* one another. Hence conversation takes the place of legislation as the primary mode of political speech. Or, perhaps better, if legislation is to occur, it will occur, for the most part, in conversation. Most citizens are not founding fathers. But that only means that the voice of the democratic citizen who speaks in our name is not first and foremost the voice of such a patriarch. This is something to which Rousseau in particular is simply not open. As much as Cavell can use his work as a model of how an individual can speak for a community, Rousseau's own theory of the contract is one in which the citizenry use speech only to acclaim or not acclaim the mode of government and the identity of the governors. He can picture a healthy polity in this way because the issue for him is one of the correct answer to the questions posed to the citizenry. In this way he is a classic instance of a modern philosopher who takes the difficulties we have acknowledging one another in our differences to be an abstract problem of knowledge—an evasive transposition of the political and existential into the epistemological that Cavell names "skepticism."[4]

Noting this complicates Rousseau's own categorical distinction between the general and the private wills, and hence between the voice of the people and the voice of the alienated, corrupt individuals portrayed in the second *Discourse*. Appreciating this in turn alerts us to the limitations of another initially tempting way to read Cavell. If the liberal polity needs a richer understanding of voice and agency if it is to continue justifying itself with the thought of the contract, it also needs to clarify how its public institutions can be truly public, and not simply the smokescreens and tools of privileged classes and factions. This has been a major concern of political theorists like Hannah Arendt who have drawn upon Aristotle's categorical distinction between the public and the private. In this context Cavell's explication and defense of the first person plural sound like a familiar rebuke to individualistic forms of liberalism in which the private as it were swallows up the public, leaving only a night-watchman state regulating clashes between individuals who can speak only for themselves and their own interests. And this is certainly how Cavell is read in the first major work of political theory to draw upon his work, Hanna Pitkin's 1972 study *Wittgenstein and Justice*.[5] But though such a rebuke is to be found in Cavell, it is neither as straightforward nor as categorical as Pitkin suggests. If the public is not, as in Arendt, the name of a realm, but rather that of a voice we use in conversing with one another, the line between the public and the private is not one that can cleanly separate an *agora* from a household.[6] If Cavell demonstrates that the personal is political, he also shows us how the political is personal. This sometimes makes his work difficult to untangle; but given the problems to which Arendt's own spatial language and insistence upon categorical distinctions have given rise, that may be all to the better.[7]

Rather than being seen as a latter-day Aristotelian, Cavell is better understood as a Socratic figure: Like Socrates, Cavell traverses the public and the private distinction without simply denying it. And, like Socrates, he does so in an attempt to criticize his political culture from within, showing it to be lacking in its own terms, terms it uses without understanding. Consider in this regard Socrates' surely intentionally provocative claim that he is "one of the very few among the Athenians, not to say the only one, engaged in the true political art."[8] To say this in the city that prided itself as being the most political in the world is to deny that its citizens know what politics is or where it can be found. Socrates' claim is precisely that the Athenians are not yet in a position to give that endorsement of his claims about them, although these claims are correct, and are correctly made by a loyal Athenian, a man who is not able to divorce himself from the city he condemns. More: that that city is not yet truly a city, inhabited as it is by people who fail to practice the true political art, and that

Socrates cleaves to it, and treats it as a city to which he owes his loyalty, because he recognizes it to be something it has not yet become. Socrates as citizen must precede the eventual city in which he will be at home. Much the same logic that is at work in the *Republic*'s account of the noble lie(s), the telling of which, as a lie, is the condition for the story it tells to become true, insofar as it allows the citizens to become the people they truly are, members of a *polis*.[9] Quite aside from Cavell's fondness for (Emerson's and Nietzsche's reiterations of) Pindar's injunction, Become what you are!, one is reminded here, first, of Cavell's observation that Wittgenstein's definition of a philosophical problem as one in which *ich kenne mich nicht aus* identifies me as not knowing my way *and*, in such ignorance, as not knowing myself; and, second, of Cavell's linking of this conception of philosophy with Kierkegaard's claim that "most men live in relation to their own self as if they were constantly out . . . in a foreign land."[10]

What should already be clear is that for Cavell, as for Socrates, the activity of philosophizing is where private deeds take on a public significance. It is too easily forgotten that Cavell's work on the use of the first person plural did not begin in a set of reflections upon politics, but rather upon *philosophy*. Cavell sought to explain how ordinary language philosophers might justify their regular and characteristic appeals to what "we would say." It is obvious that such appeals are not based upon statistical surveys or anticipations of the same. Cavell sees them as expressions of commitment: "The authority one has, or assumes, in expressing statements of initiation, in saying 'We,' is related to the authority one has in expressing or declaring one's promises or intentions. Such declarations cannot be countered by evidence because they are not supported by evidence."[11] What concerns us here are not the details of this argument, but simply the fact that Cavell's insights in the social contract are won by assuming a commonality between the political and the philosophical of precisely the sort that comparisons with Aristotle (particularly an Arendtian version thereof) would discourage us from seeing.

The connection between the philosophical and the political is in each case a therapeutic one. Here Cavell draws his direct inspiration not from Socrates but from Wittgenstein, whose work lies behind Cavell's discussions of publicity and privacy.[12] Contrary to a popular misconception, Wittgenstein does not simply deny the possibility of a private language.

Instead, he asks why we would be inclined to think that such language might be possible, why we would even want to consider such a thought. And Wittgenstein's approach is to consider such things by presenting a dialogue in which it is far from obvious when he speaks in his own voice, and when he takes up views he considers false or misguided. His therapy, like Plato's dialogues, does not allow easy summation or citation. As may already be clear, the same is true of Cavell's. This is further complicated by the form that philosophical and political therapy takes in Cavell's work. While Wittgenstein presents conversations with imaginary interlocutors, Cavell works through readings of the canon. In *The Claim of Reason* he writes, "I have wished to understand philosophy not as a set of problems but as a set of texts."[13] A corollary of that is that his own work is a set of readings which defy easy summation in programmatic statements of a philosophical "position" that can be evaluated with straightforward arguments. Instead, these readings must themselves be "read"—something that will surely strike some as a requirement that one kneel in order to believe. Stanley Rosen, for instance, has attempted to dismiss Cavell simply by quoting him, as if his resistance to unqualified assertion were embarrassment enough.[14] We would do better, I think, to accept that Cavell is not in the business of offering proofs, but rather that of providing new perspectives on texts and difficulties that we have seen already. And here the measure of his success is what he allows us to see.[15]

If Cavell's intertextuality distinguishes his work from Wittgenstein's, it does not disentangle the two. It is Wittgenstein who initially teaches Cavell that philosophy is a conversation that reflects upon its own preconditions as a conversation—and this is at the heart of Cavell's significance for political theory. In the foreword to *The Claim of Reason*, Cavell writes that in his doctoral dissertation he sought to draw out "the implications of Austin's procedures for moral philosophy—implications, let us say, of the sense that the human voice is being returned to moral assessments of itself."[16] A page later, Cavell tells us that he came only with time to experience Wittgenstein's *Investigations* as "a discovery for philosophy of the problem of the other." While the chronology is not entirely clear here, the five years or so between his first working with Austin and his perception of this about the *Investigations* leads one to ask whether Cavell's own approach to the voice in moral philosophy was initially to a voice experienced as speaking alone, as not yet properly in conversation with an other. If this were so, it would fit well with the centrality that questions of narcissism and isolation assume in his work in the next forty years.[17] It is in any event clear that the "feat of writing" that Cavell associates with the *Investigations* and what it contributed to Cavell's understanding of "the connection of writing and the problem of the other" have everything to do with Wittgenstein's depiction, in writing, of "the recurrence of skeptical voices, and answering voices"—that is, with its enactment of conversation.[18]

Disfigured Politics

I have suggested that Cavell is not so Aristotelian as Pitkin proposes, yet it is undeniable that he encourages the comparison.[19] Consider in this regard this identification of conversation with the political, which is taken from a discussion of narcissism and cannibalism in "*Coriolanus* and Interpretations of Politics":

This is not a play about politics, if this means about political authority or conflict, say about questions of legitimate succession or divided loyalties. It is about the formation of the political, the founding of the city, about what makes a rational animal fit for conversation, for civility. This play seems to think of this creation of the political, call it the public, as the overcoming of narcissism, incestuousness, and cannibalism; as if it perceives an identity among these relations.[20]

This passage seems calculated to remind one of the Aristotelian claim that man is a political animal because he is a speaking and rational one, and that a polis is different from all other forms of association in that it is only in a polis that we can truly speak:

Nature, according to our theory, makes nothing in vain; and man alone of the animals is endowed with the faculty of language. The mere making of sounds serves to indicate pleasure and pain, and is thus a faculty that belongs to animals in general. . . . But language serves to declare what is advantageous and what is the reverse, and it therefore serves to indicate what is just and unjust.[21]

To give and receive orders as in the Persian empire is not truly to realize the *telos* or end of speech; that is achieved only when deliberating and arguing as a citizen about justice and injustice. "Justice belongs to the *polis*; for justice, which is the determination [*krisis*] of what is just, is an ordering of the political association" (1253a). This identification of justice with its own determination fits well with Cavell's sense that the speech that we engage in unendingly is devoted to determining who we are and what the order of our association is.[22] And the parallel here is reinforced by the fact that it does not occur in isolation. Other commonalties include: *phronesis*, homonymy, vagueness, exactitude, friendship, walking, the primacy of the practical, and the ordinary life as opposed to the philosophical life.

How then are we to explain the fact that Cavell almost never refers to Aristotle? Perhaps the best way to begin to answer this would be to look at a place where one might initially be most surprised by Cavell's reticence in this regard. Cavell has repeatedly returned to Emerson's description of "the *divided* or social state" as one in which the One Man is cut into parts that attempt to live monstrous lives of false independence: "The state of society is one in which the members have suffered amputation from the trunk, and strut about so many walking monsters,—a good finger, a neck, a stomach, an elbow, but never a man."[23] Cavell proposes that this passage from Emerson is transcribed in the passage from the chapter "Of Redemption" of Nietzsche's *Zarathustra* that reads, "I walk among the fragments and limbs of men. This is what is terrible for my eyes, that I find men in ruins and scattered as over a battlefield or butcher-field."[24] Without contesting that claim, I take it to be clear that both passages are also transcribing other texts, among them Aristotle's *Politics*:

the city is prior in the order of nature to the family and the individual. The reason for this is that the whole is necessarily prior to the part. If the whole body is destroyed, there will not be a foot or a hand, except in that ambiguous sense in which one uses the same word to indicate a different thing, as when one speaks of a "hand" made of stone. (P. 1253a)

As the hand of Aristotle's destroyed body is not a real hand, so Emerson and Nietzsche's partial men are not men at all. More significant, though, than the metaphor of the body politic is the democratic nuance Aristotle adds to the image when he comes somewhat reluctantly to defend the suggestion that the people at large should be sovereign:

when they all come together it is possible that they may surpass—collectively and as a body, although not individually—the quality of the few best, in much the same way that feasts to which many contribute may excel those provided at one person's expense. For when there are many, each has his own share of goodness and practical wisdom; and, when all meet together, the people may thus become something like a single person, who as he has many feet, many hands, may also have many qualities of character and intelligence.[25] (P. 1281a)

Lest this seem to be too much a celebration of the power of numbers, Aristotle goes on to say explicitly that it will not be true of every group, or it would apply to beasts as well. The citizens must be perfected to some extent (Aristotle says they must not be "too debased in character") before they can be brought together into a whole that is greater than its parts (pp. 1282a and 1281b). Reading this as transcribed in Emerson's and Nietzsche's words—and thus in Cavell's citing of them—we can see that their longing for the One Man is already a longing for a democracy within which unity is not bought at the expense of difference. Aristotle calls this form of association a polis, allowing it to bear the name of its genus; the longing for it, then, can be seen as a longing for the political as such.

Cavell is drawn to uses of this imagery that picture "the social state" as disfigured, not yet a(n Aristotelian) political state.[26] In the passage cited above from the essay on *Coriolanus* he speaks of "the *formation* of the political, the *founding* of the city, about what makes a rational animal fit for conversation, for civility"—in short, about the "*creation* of the political, call it the public." And he goes on in that essay to characterize the narcissism and cannibalism that resist such foundings and formations as, for Coriolanus at least, an alarm "at simply being part, one member among others of the same organism." This repulsion is one that alienates him from his own language: Cavell understands Coriolanus to equate the exchange of language with cannibalistic consumption, and he proposes that Shakespeare's play "asks us . . . to try to imagine a beneficial, mutual consumption, arguing in effect that this is what an audience is."[27] We are to imagine, then, a way of speaking, and in so imagining to open ourselves up to language—here, the language of this political play. Similarly, Cavell writes of the possibility that "some of the things [Wittgenstein] says have lost, or have yet to find, the human circle in which they can usefully be said."[28] Aristotle, in sharp contrast, pictures our speech as already full and present to us, the polis as achieved—as the initial passage I cited from Book I speaks of the political, deliberative nature of man as something that is already produced or achieved. The deliberation between citizens that Aristotle presents as taking place within the polis is on Cavell's account one that takes place, as it were, at the city's gates: we are asking how we can found a city in a way that only those who are already somehow citizens can. We are asking, that is, how we can become who we are, and why we might be resistant to doing so. The reasons we will recount will, as Cavell indicates in the opening pages of the *Coriolanus* essay, be as much psychological or intimate as they will be political. Indeed, it is because they will be both at once that their recounting can be political at all—that is, that it can consider the construction of the public that is the true concern of the political. It is precisely this incorporation of the intimate that will distinguish Cavell's evocations of Aristotle from, say, those of Gadamer and Arendt.[29]

Acknowledgment Versus Recognition: Becoming Political and Becoming Human

Cavell's philosophical work revolves around his sense of the existential relevance of modern skepticism. And it is surely of crucial significance—though surprisingly overlooked—that *The Claim of Reason*'s first discussion of political philosophical topics is introduced with the claim that "the philosophical appeal to what we say, and the search for our criteria on the basis of which we say what we say, are claims to community. . . . The wish and search for community are the wish and search for reason."[30] These lines and their reference to our claims to community provide a reading of the title of the magnum opus in which they occur, as they indicate the reason for the distance Cavell keeps from the Aristotelianism he comes so close to embracing. Aristotle writes in supreme confidence of the rationality of his world, a confidence with which Cavell is constitutionally out of temper.[31] But as the Aristotelian image of the body politic can be appropriated for Cavell's very different purposes, so can we read Aristotle's identification of the *telos* of the polis in a Cavellian light: "Justice," Aristotle writes, "belongs to the *polis*; for justice, which is the determination [*krisis*] of what is just, is an ordering of the political association." From Cavell's perspective this *krisis* can present itself as a recurrent critical condition that requires a decision as much as a determination. As such, it requires that we cut ourselves off from our polity, or understand ourselves as already so cut off, so as to choose again to bind ourselves to it.[32] Hence in *The Senses of Walden* Cavell describes *Walden* as "a tract of political education, education for membership in the polis [which shows] that education for citizenship is education for isolation."[33]

A politics of acknowledgment that grows out of such a sense of crisis, of our being at once within and without our political community, will be sharply contrasted with the superficially similar politics of recognition. While each understands the political as being a question of our authentic identity,[34] the identity in question, as well as *how* it is questioned, in each is quite different. Consider Charles Taylor's brief genesis of the authentic self that he perceives behind the new political demands for recognition (in addition to formal rights):

The most important philosophical writer who helped to bring about this change was Jean-Jacques Rousseau. . . . Rousseau frequently presents the issue of morality as that of our following a voice of nature within us. . . . Our moral salvation comes from recovering authentic moral contact with ourselves. Rousseau even gives a name to the intimate contact with oneself, more fundamental than any moral view, that is the sense of joy and contentment: "*le sentiment de l'existence.*"[35]

This sentiment is introduced in the Fifth Walk of Rousseau's *Reveries of a Solitary Walker*, a book that revolves around Rousseau's miserable sense that he is the victim of a society that has conspired against him and in so doing conspired against itself. All of this is crystallized in his defensive celebration of "the simple feeling of existence," which can make even "an unfortunate man [like Rousseau] who has been excluded from human society" "self-sufficient like God."[36] (Significantly, in both his book and his article Taylor begins his citation from the fifth walk immediately *after* this passage, and ends it immediately one line *before* Rousseau explains that this sentiment is a "compensation" for one who has been "excluded from society.") Resemblances to God are not usually what one thinks of when confronted with a claim to an authentic individual or political identity. Does it make more sense to credit such a confusion to Rousseau than it does to take these reveries of a solitary walker as being aware of the Peripatetic Philosopher's claim that "the man who is isolated, who is unable to share in the benefits of political association, or has no need to share because he is already self-sufficient, is no part of the city, and must therefore be either a beast or a god" (*Politics*, p. 1253a)? The very sentiment that Taylor isolates as the sense of self that, previously (apolitically) existing, can be asserted (or not asserted) in the political realm is itself political from the start.[37] Rousseau's point is precisely the opposite of what Taylor takes it to be: he cannot be himself—a human being—because he cannot be a member of a community, and at the same time it is in being aware of this that he becomes aware of (senses) his existence. Likewise, he is cast out of society by men who have forfeited his affection, who could only forfeit his affection, "by ceasing to be human."[38] This is politics that does not move from me to you, but hovers over the borders between us, between in and out.

Some may object at this point that if Rousseau is alluding to Aristotle here he is surely also alluding to Aristotle's description of the life of the philosopher as a god-like life that is "superior to the human level."[39] Rousseau is asserting, that is, not simply his loss of the human, but also its transcendence. Here, however, it is important to recall that Aristotle in the *Ethics* gives us two quite contradictory definitions of self-sufficiency: in the first book, which celebrates the political life, he writes that "what we count as self-sufficient is not what suffices for a solitary person by himself, living an isolated life, but what suffices also for parents, children, wife and in general for friends and fellow-citizens, since a human being is a naturally political [animal]" (p. 1097b). In the tenth book, however, he gives a different definition that celebrates in sharp contrast the philosopher's god-like independence from others:

Admittedly the wise person, the just person and other virtuous people all need the good things necessary for life. Still, when these are adequately supplied, the just person needs other people as partners and recipients of his just actions. . . . But the wise person is able, and more able the wiser he is, to study even by himself; and though he presumably does it better with colleagues, even so he is more self-sufficient than any other. (P. 1177a)

What is decisive here is that Aristotle does not reconcile these two ideals with one another.[40] In both, the human life—the ordinary life?—is the *political* life that allows for and demands the practice of justice. Book Ten and its redefinition of *autarkes* only ask whether that human life is truly good—for humans. If the philosophical is a standing possibility to be something other than human, that possibility is always a human possibility.[41] Reading Rousseau with the Aristotle he invokes allows us to see that this transcendence can be a kind of political exile, or an exile from politics, and vice versa. Rousseau celebrates his divine philosophical status with the same gesture that indicates his abandonment from the political community of his fellow men. This surely sets out the conditions within which Wittgenstein's struggle to end philosophy takes a philosophical form. What is in question is the limit or horizon of the human—in *The Claim of Reason* Cavell refers to it as "the frame of the world."[42] Such limits, once recognized and crossed, remain there to be seen and crossed again. It is, I think, in response to this that Cavell will identify the struggle with skepticism as an argument that can never be won, and that should never be won, insisting that that would only close down one or another side of the human. The conversation is a conversation of philosophy against itself, carried on in the gates of an eventual *polis* that will, it seems, never be fully entered. This is, of course, quite a different claim than the historical claim that identifies the *polis* with the city walls that separate the inside from the outside—quite the opposite claim, in fact.

Cavell writes of Thoreau and his native Concord:

Concord is stranger to him, and he to it, than the ends of the earth. But why does this watchman of the private sea insist especially on his readers' outward condition or circumstances in the world? Because the outward position or circumstance in this world is precisely the position of outwardness, outwardness to the world, distance from it, the position of the stranger. The first step in attending to our education is to observe the strangeness of our lives, our estrangement from ourselves, the lack of necessity in what we perceive to be necessary. The second step is to grasp the true necessity of human strangeness as such, the opportunity of outwardness.[43]

If the critique of ideology entails "making problematic . . . what has hitherto seemed to be natural and necessary," Cavell is clearly enough championing it.[44] Indeed, one might see him as proposing an existential politics of anti-hegemony, one that questions every attempt to foreclose discussion through appeals to common sense and its sense of the possible. Cavell writes of "how at odds I find myself with those who understand Wittgenstein to begin with, or to assert thesis-wise, the publicness of language, never seriously doubting it, and in that way to favor common sense. I might say that publicness is his goal. It would be like having sanity as one's goal. Then what state would one take oneself to be in?"[45] We might answer: the state that Rousseau describes in his *Reveries*.

Conversation, Conversion, and Revision

A philosophical politics calls for a political philosophy. As the conversation of the political moves from the center to the border of the polis, which as it were turns itself inside out, so does the philosophy that counters philosophy assume a new and different guise. In discussing Wittgenstein as a "philosopher of culture" Cavell argues that the common perception that Wittgenstein's leaving things as they are amounts to a form of "political or social" conservatism is not so much inaccurate as it is incomplete. To emphasize this about the *Investigations* in the manner of Ernest Gellner's *Words and Things* "neglects the equally palpable call in the book for transfiguration, which one may think of in terms of revolution or of conversion."[46] This call for transfiguration takes the form of contesting (rather than blindly conserving) the culture's understanding of its true needs.[47] Such a call, and such a contestation, Cavell hears and sees enacted in more famously and explicitly political texts "such as the *Republic* and *The Social Contract* and *Walden*." It is striking that the first two of these are perhaps the classic texts of philosophical legislation, texts in which philosophers or novices to philosophy lay down the laws or design blueprints for a just polity, one that as much as possible meets the demands of philosophy. This is all the more striking as Cavell goes on in the same page to place the author of the *Investigations* in an apparently much different genealogy, that of "a line of apparently contradictory sensibilities, ones that may appear as radically innovative (in action or feeling) or radically conservative: Luther was such a sensibility; so were Rousseau and Thoreau. . . . Sensibilities in this line seem better called revisors than reformers or revolutionaries."[48] *Revisors*, presumably, because they see and show things again and differently, in writing like Wittgenstein's that presents conversations that draw us in, and are themselves therefore open to our interpretation, our rewriting. Rousseau's presence in both of these lists is I think easily understood, given his explicit and deep ambivalence about the possibilities of politics.[49] More significant is the decision Cavell quietly makes here concerning the sort of transfiguration called for in the *Investigations*: while one "may think of this transfiguration in terms of revolution or of conversion," insofar as the *Investigations* is the work of a revisor, its call for transfiguration will be a call for conversion, and not revolution, at least not in the sense that that could be called for by, say, a Marxist revolutionary.[50]

In reference to this claim that the particular intensity of the *Investigations* amounts to a call for conversion that goes beyond ethical prescriptions and proscriptions, Cavell invokes §108: "One might say: the axis of reference of our examination [*Die Betrachtung*] must be rotated, but about the fixed point of our need [*um unser eigentliches Bedürfnis als Angelpunkt*]."[51] I assume that in taking this as a call for conversion Cavell is well aware that it might be taken instead as an echo of the book's preface, specifically of Wittgenstein's characterization of the *Investigations* as a book of sketches of landscapes in which "the same or almost the same points were always being approached afresh from different directions, and new sketches made." Taken in this light, §108 might be seen as a call for a rotation rather than (or in addition to) a conversion, in much the sense of Aristotle's celebration of the polity as a mode of association that capitalizes on our differences from one another, or of the "perspectivism" Nietzsche arguably derives from it: "There is *only* a perspective seeing, *only* a perspective 'knowing'; and the *more* affects we allow to speak about one thing, the *more* eyes, different eyes, we can use to observe one thing, the more complete will our 'concept' of this thing, our 'objectivity' be."[52] Having more eyes could well be understood as involving a conversion or exchange of views (in conversation). Taken as a figure of conversion within the individual, §108 is somewhat more complicated. Conversion is typically a figure for a turning in which we aim toward rather than away from our real need (the sun, the Good, God) so that we can see (*betrachten*) the truth. I assume *Angelpunkt* has a figural meaning here as well; how after all does it add anything to the idea of "our real need" to say that it is the crucial point? But insofar as it does have such a meaning it figures our real need as the point *about which* we turn. I think of this as taking two possible forms, the first in which our real need is, as it were, attached to the beam of our life like a hinge; the other in which the beam of our life is more or less centered and balanced on our real need. What is striking is that in each case the *Angelpunkt* of our real need is behind us whichever way we turn.[53] If we begin by not seeing it, then nothing changes but the context of our aversion. In looking out we do not see it so much as see what the world looks like from its perspective; as if to say, with this experience behind us, we can see the world for what it is—as something that reveals itself in the acknowledgment of a need that it itself does not contain. Perhaps not a surprising figure for a philosopher who spends as much time grappling with solipsism as Wittgenstein, and more or less what we might expect from a lesson on the necessity and fruitfulness of alienation such as Cavell's.[54]

Cavell's sense of the need for such conversion is one in which our world is as a whole inadequate, in need not of discrete reforms or institutional changes, but of a complete transfiguration that will give our every word a meaning that it presently lacks, at the same time leaving everything as it is. An uncanny change, one that will respond to the extraordinary in the heart of the ordinary, and allow us to speak not new phrases but in a new way. As Emerson puts it in a "totalizing remark" that Cavell is particularly fond of citing, "Every word they say chagrins us."[55] So every word needs to be changed, though not for another language of the same sort (e.g., German, or Hindi). Cavell's own response to this chagrin has been to try and see "whether I could speak philosophically and mean every word I said."[56] In its emphasis upon the total at the expense of any particular fault or reform this is reminiscent of Augustine's variation on the Platonic figure of the conversion. As he argues in *The City of God*, as God could not have made anything evil, and as God made all things, evil cannot be a thing or derived from a thing. We cannot therefore point to the thing that offends God; it must instead be a matter of our own movement within things, our turning from the truth: "How can a good thing be the efficient cause of an evil will? How can good be the cause of evil? When the will abandons what is above itself and turns to what is lower, it becomes evil. This is true, not because what it turns toward is evil, but because *the turning itself is a deformity*."[57]

In Cavell too there is a focus upon our posture toward things rather than the things themselves, and a repeated use of the language of redemption and deliverance, though always in an avowedly secular sense. While one finds in Cavell a focus upon the totality at the expense of the particular, this is not, as it is in Augustine, in the service of the humbling of the particular—quite the opposite. The chagrin in the face of "every word" can only be addressed by the individual who finds her own particular voice—a claim that is at the heart of Cavell's response to Rawls. In his discussion of *A Doll's House* in "The Conversation of Justice," Cavell focuses entirely upon Nora's inability to participate in this conversation and to argue for her "position" as being a function of her not yet having a voice of her own.[58] "Nora," he says, "has no reasons that are acceptable."[59] This entails disregarding the reasons that she does offer—most pertinently, her complaint that the law is unjust because it is inequitable, a complaint that is ironically motivated by Torvald's attempt to remind her that she has moral sense[60]—as well as the web of connections and parallels Ibsen establishes between Nora and the play's other characters. But while a full reading of the play would need to take account of all of this, Cavell's emphasis is not misplaced, nor does it render the play apolitical. As Cavell's comparison of Nora with Marx's vision of the [German] proletariat as a universal class reminds us, this is a play of emancipation: It begins with the sound of a door opening, and its first word is "hide";[61] it concludes by bringing everything out into the light, bringing Nora back out of the doll house, to a new outside, one that will be made possible by what transpires on her circuit through the house. Nora says that she and Torvald must be liberated from one another before they can begin to construct a world in which they can find themselves. But that liberation is not that world, that free life. To imagine otherwise is to imagine a series of plays that end with slamming doors, as this one does, and imagine that they are a happy cycle of plays.

Revolt like this has a secondary quality as regards its source as well as its effects. The first and most basic movement is the one that drives Nora from Torvald's house, not that of crossing the threshold. If we think of this as spiritual and not political, it may be helpful to recall that the image of the individual soul's conversion is political in its origin: When Socrates describes the aristocratic or monarchical alternative to politics as it is known (timocracy, oligarchy, democracy, and tyranny) he must provide an account (he says, "an image") of "our nature in its education and want of education" (*Republic*, p. 514a) so as to explain the possibility of forming (they have already been "bred") the characters of the men and women who shall in turn give the city its character and form. Significantly this education will differ as much from the conversation pursued by Socrates and Plato's brothers as the philosophers it produces will differ from the skeptical Socrates.[62] As Plato repeatedly emphasizes, the potential philosopher must be "compelled" to leave the cave and forced to face the light that has cast the shadows that formerly beguiled him. Conversation is quite insufficient: "If they were able to discuss things with one another, don't you think they would hold that they are naming these things going by before them that they see?" (p. 515b). So the image Socrates presents is not yet the education it depicts—not yet, we might say, a revision. It is, nonetheless, a conversion:

> Education is not what the professions of certain men assert it to be. They presumably assert that they put into the soul knowledge that isn't in it, as though they were putting sight into blind eyes. . . . But the present argument, on the other hand, indicates that the power is in the soul of each, and that the instrument with which each learns—just as an eye is not able to turn toward the light from the dark without the whole body—must be turned around. (P. 518c)

In his own account of the *Republic*—one openly selectively concerned with "the features it contributes to the concept of perfectionism"—Cavell glosses over the distinction here between the Socratic conversation and the education in compulsion the future philosopher-kings will suffer and undertake. He begins his account by singling out the conversational aspect of the *Republic* and infers from that the conversion, as if the conversion were not the topic but the effect of the conversation.[63] If such a reading is possible (reasonable, responsible), one might conclude that the *Republic* is giving us two models of conversion, which presumably are meant to comment upon one another. Is it?

   The fact that Socrates proposes this as an image encourages us to apply the image's own terms to it. It is seen, and hence can be seen again or revised, from another perspective. In what perspective ought we to see it? From where ought we to look at it—from within the city in words, within the story Socrates is depicted narrating, or from somewhere else (nowhere else) altogether? The image is one of the philosopher's training, of the experience of philosophy as a nonpolitical event that prepares one for political rule. This disparity is underscored by the fact that the philosopher who will be the product of the conversion will not be at home in the city, at least not as others are. Others will find their personal fulfillment in the city, they will be made whole by it: if I cannot rule my lower desires with my spirit as guided by my reason, I will find such guidance in the city, and in so doing will be able to see the city as an organic whole of which I am a part. Its reason will be my reason.[64] But the philosopher Socrates depicts is not in this situation. He has already (in the conversion) attained the proper balance others find only in the city.[65] Hence Socrates must address the problem of how one will persuade and "compel" such characters to join the city, to be its reason *rather than* their own (p. 520a). Where others will find fulfillment and harmony, the philosopher will find an alienation from his true self and an assumption of a false self. For how can it be my self if it is not necessarily mine?[66]

Raising the question of what my self is brings us back to where we started, reflecting upon the place of intimacy in the political. Raising that of the necessary gives us a hint of how Cavell might go on from here. In "The Philosopher in American Life" Cavell proposes that *Walden* is linked with "works of our culture specifically devoted to an attack on false necessities"—among which Cavell counts "Plato's vision of us as staring at a wall in a cave."[67] But the alternative of turning toward the sun is itself a false necessity. It only appears that if we aren't in a cave we must be outside of one. But if there is no cave there is not (necessarily) any outside either: "We have abolished the real world: what world is left? the apparent world perhaps? . . . But no! *with the real world we have also abolished the apparent world!*"[68] Seeing this involves a way of reading, a way of (approaching) writing, that Cavell characterizes as the work of revision. That this work is philosophical is clear enough; we need think only of Cavell's characterization of Wittgenstein's work as "breaking up one's sense of necessity, to discover truer necessities."[69] But it is political as well. We can see this in Cavell's description of Thoreau's political education as beginning in the recognition of "the lack of necessity in what we take to be necessary." And we can see it in Cavell's use of precisely the same language when he opposes "political tyranny" to "the freedom to convene":

What [tyranny's suppression of this freedom] prevents is not merely, as Mill urges, the free exchange of truths with partial truth and with falsehoods, from the fire of which truth rises. That *might* happen in an isolated study. It prevents the arising of the issue for which convening is necessary, viz., to see what we do, to learn our position in what we take to be necessaries, to see in what service they are necessary.[70]

If there is no cave, we do not leave it as Nora leaves the doll house. The work of seeing that we are not in a cave, though we may be staring at a wall, is thus not only a philosophical preparation for politics: it is politics. If this doesn't look like what politics has been thus far for us, that, presumably, is the point.[71]

Perfectionism Without Perfection: Cavell, Montaigne, and the Conditions of Morals and Politics

Richard Flathman

He also found a certain energy with a tendency toward abstraction, a disposition to seek a shape for life from within himself and not in what he could wrest from others.

—DON CALOGERO, CONCERNING DON FABRIZIO. IN GIUSEPPE DI LAMPEDUSA, *The Leopard*, TRANS. ARCHIBALD COLQUHOUN (NEW YORK: SIGNET BOOKS, NEW AMERICAN LIBRARY, 1960), p. 143

Six months before they [the Sicilian peasantry] used to hear a rough despotic voice saying, "Do what I say or you'll catch it." Now [the male peasantry having been accorded the suffrage] there was an impression already of such a threat being replaced by the soapy tones of a money-lender: "But you signed it yourself, didn't you? Can't you see? It's quite clear. You must do as we say, for here are the I.O.U.s; your will is identical with mine."

— *The Leopard*, p. 118

Finding a good deal to agree with in Stanley Cavell's conception of moral and political perfectionism (MPP), my objectives in this modest essay are twofold: in Part One I identify some of the main elements of MPP and the differences between it and other prominent moral and political theories. My aim is to raise a question concerning its implications for the good and the better life. In the second part, I attempt to augment somewhat Cavell's articulations of MPP by giving attention to the thinker Michel de Montaigne, who makes appearances in Cavell's work but is not a primary focus of his attention. I argue that Montaigne offers ways of further enriching MPP by giving a somewhat different inflection or tonality (anticipated by the first of the epigraphs) to Cavell's treatments of Self/Other relationships.

Pursuing the first objective requires engaging with Cavell's numerous identifications of the elements of MPP and how they differ from other theories with which Cavell compares and contrasts them. Here my focus will be on his conception of "conversation" and its role in thinking and acting on the register and under the conditions of moral and political life. In Part Two I ask whether there are comparable elements (whether affirmatively or negatively valorized) in Montaigne, and, if so, whether attention to them enhances MPP or something like it. The point is not that Cavell should have given (more) attention to Montaigne. Given the extraordinary compass of his reflections this would be small-minded if not churlish. The objective, rather, is to follow his example by taking our thinking into (both with and against) further formulations that address problematics similar to his and bring to them a sensibility akin to his. My hope is that doing so will contribute to giving a somewhat different accent—but not more than that—to the relationships mentioned above.[1]

Part One. Some Elements of Cavellian Perfectionism

Cavell identifies MPP both by contrast with other influential moral and political theories and by elaborating upon its own leading commitments and characteristics. Beginning with the former, he distinguishes it from other versions of perfectionism, in particular those that claim to have identified the *telos* toward which all human thought and action should be directed and by the standards of which all thinking and acting should be assessed. He attributes versions of this view, which I will call perfectionist perfectionism (PP) to Plato, to Raz and Murdoch,[2] to Shaw, to aspects of Aristotle's thinking, and he notes (but rejects) Rawls's attribution of such a view to Nietzsche. He also distinguishes MPP from what he takes to be the two types of theory, Kantianism (mainly Kant and Rawls) and Utilitarianism (mainly John Stuart Mill), that he claims have for some time been dominant in moral and political philosophy. He develops his objections to PP and his conception of MPP by drawing on Emerson, Thoreau, Whitman, and various other thinkers with whom he has worked over the years, and articulates his views by commenting on various films, plays, and other works of art.

Although objecting to PP, Cavell credits such theories with being on the same "register" of moral and political thinking as MPP. Their concern is less with the rightness and wrongness of this or that action or policy than with the quality of the lives or, as he sometimes puts it, of the "souls" of human beings (*CW*, pp. 11, 49). This focus is present in all perfectionist theories and is part of their concern with the "standing" of persons as participants in the conversations of moral and political life. It is a "precondition" of moral and political thinking (p. 222).

A further similarity between MPP, or Emersonian Perfectionism (EP), as he often calls it, and PP theories is that both work with one or another version of a distinction between the way the world now is, its inhabitants now are, and how the world and its inhabitants might become different and better.

Each of these variations provides a position from which the present state of human existence can be judged and a future state achieved, or else the present position judged to be better than the cost of changing it. The very conception of a divided self and a doubled world, providing a perspective of judgment upon the world as it is, measured against world as it may be, tends to express disappointment with the world as it is, as the scene of human activity and prospects, and perhaps to lodge the demand or desire for a reform or transfiguration of the world. (p. 2)

The chief difference between Cavell's MPP and PP theories resides in their respective treatments or figurations of the future self and world. The former deploys the distinction as between the attained and the not yet attained self, but refuses to offer a universal or even a general substantive specification of the shape and character of the as yet unattained self or even (or hence) a single path from the one to the other. The unattained self emerges out of or through "conversations" that take place among attained selves. To the limited extent that it is appropriate to identify affirmatively the "aim" or "purpose" of these conversations, it is to achieve greater self-

and mutual clarity and understanding ("to lead the soul, imprisoned and distorted by confusion and darkness, into the freedom of the day" [p. 4]); it is not to arrive at universalizable or even widely generalizable conclusions concerning the shape and character of the selves and the relations among them. The latter (PP) distinguishes between the attained and the attainable self and world and specifies in general and in some cases universal terms the shape and character that the attainable self should have and—in some versions—the path that leads from the first to the second. Thus in the former "perfectionism" means seeking improved clarity and understandings with the substantive content of the understandings left open[3]; in the latter, it means achieving a substantively specified quality of life and character deserving of being called the best or the right.

Perfectionism, whether of the MPP or the PP variety, "has not been much esteemed among (academic) philosophers in my part of the philosophical forest" (p. 15). In some cases, most notably Rawls's rejection of what he (mistakenly) takes to be Nietzsche's version of it, this is due to misunderstandings of its best formulations. More generally, however, the animus toward it is due to the concern of the latter with and for the quality of lives rather than the merits of particular actions and policies. The philosophers Cavell has in mind (with important exceptions in regard to Mill) have either relegated perfectionist questions to "those who work . . . between philosophy and literature" (p. 13), or have assumed that good lives supervene upon good, right, or just decisions concerning actions. Questions about the quality of lives are either not philosophical questions or they are answered by determining what is good, right, or just in this, that, and the next decision/action situation. Intimately associated with this view is the idea that decisions about what to do are made by assembling evidence and argumentation that leads to (is the path to) right answers to what proponents of these theories regard as clearly formulated questions.

One of Cavell's remarks concerning what he calls "moral standing" and "conversation" draws the contrast very clearly: "It is my impression that in established academic moral philosophy the question of moral standing, if it comes up at all, is grounded in one's conviction that one knows what is good or right for the other to do, so that the philosophical issue is essentially how to provide convincing, rational reasons for one's convictions. . . . The point accordingly assigned to moral conversation is that of rationally persuading the other to agree, or to do, something that you are, independently of the conversation, persuaded that she ought to do" (p. 235; see also *CHH*, p. 31).

The notion of conversation—what "stirs" it, what can and cannot be hoped for from it, what part it plays in morals and politics—is at the center of MPP. It should first be underlined, however, that the remarks just quoted do not support the conclusion that Cavell accords no value to the "register" on which moral and political philosophy most commonly operates or to the kinds of argumentation that it champions. As noted, he thinks MPP is a precondition of such philosophizing; but rather than being its "competitor" (*CHH*, p. 2) or an alternative (p. 11) to Kantianism and Utilitarianism, it can be viewed as what might be called a supplement to or an augmentation of them. It concerns itself with the intelligibility (and lack thereof) of the self to itself and the self to others. But as is emphasized by the rejection of PP, "Everything else is still open." The reach of rational argumentation always exceeds its grasp, but it can and sometimes does help to answer questions concerning obligations, justice, and rights. MPP supplements argumentation by addressing questions such as "whether there are limits to the obligation to be intelligible, whether everyone isn't entitled to a certain obscurity or sense of confusion," "what one is to do about persisting disagreement," and the like, questions that often remain open when argumentation has done what it can do (p. 25). It moves moral and political life to a different but not an incompatible register.

Mention should be made of some other aspects of the relationship between MPP and Kantianism and Utilitarianism. Cavell finds elements of perfectionism in both, particularly in Mill's version of the latter (p. 11). As noted, both distinguish between the attained and the attainable life. Cavell thinks that Kant spoils (debases?) his perfectionism in several ways, most importantly by positing the perfect but unattainable condition of moral purity, a demand that leads to moralism and snobbery on the part of those who think they are pure and to complacency and cynicism among those who despair of achieving the ideal (chap. 7, esp. pp. 138, 143–44).

Insofar as Utilitarianism promotes the maximization of good, if adopted as a complete theory it has—albeit for different reasons—comparable tendencies. But Cavell (rightly) finds a good deal to admire in Mill's version of the theory. His admiration radiates out from a question that

Mill poses. In his discussion of the conformism pervasive in his society, Mill ends by asking: "Now is this, or is it not, the desirable condition of human nature" (*On Liberty*, quoted by Cavell in *CHH*, p. 97). The pertinence of the question lies in its impertinence, in the fact that few if any of his fellow citizens so much as ask it and few if any would fail to be annoyed by having it posed to them. And, especially in comparison with Kant, it resides in the terms in which it is posed, namely as a question about what is *desired*. Of course Mill's use of these terms reminds us of a familiar objection to him. "Then what can it mean—why is it not a contradiction—for Mill, taking as the only proof that something is desirable the fact that people do desire it, to say that liberty is desirable, when he has just asserted that hardly anybody does in fact desire it?" (*CHH*, p. 96).

Cavell's answer, which is part of his rehabilitation, against Kant, of desire, is as follows: "The irony [in Mill's use of these terms] goes beyond any doubts philosophers have felt toward Mill's reasoning. Having established to his satisfaction . . . that with respect to self-regarding actions we are free to dispose of ourselves, Mill now finds that it is we who are . . . the threat to our own liberty. As if liberty consists only in the rightful claiming and taking of it, as if it is otherwise an item in pawn waiting for redemption" (p. 97). He continues:

The condition of human nature in which we . . . do not ask whether our condition is desirable is one in which our nature does not exist for us. . . . Mill's writing, his philosophical mission . . . , is to *awaken* us to the question he poses: Is this, is our experience of the currency of our world, desired by me? It is a question meant to show us that we have a right to our own desires, to have them recognized as touchstones for social criticism and reform. A right, one could say, to invoke the principle of utility "in the broadest sense." (p. 97)

Of these thoughts of Mill, especially as developed in *The Subjection of Women* and hence in Cavell's discussion of marriage ("a special case of the want of liberty," p. 98), he says no less than that "If a bible of perfectionism were to be put together, the paragraph of Mill's containing this perception, together with whatever is necessary to understand it, would demand prominence in it" (p. 98).[4] No competition, no alternative, here; and the augmentation that is supplied draws importantly on resources that Mill himself makes available.

Taking conversation as including the converse of myself with myself as well as with others (this assumption will have to be examined below), Cavell says that he is more interested in what "stirs" it than in "the various ways in which" it "may or may not be seen as coming to rest" (p. 315).[5] To the (again) limited extent that there is a general answer to this question, Cavell's proposals bring together many of the thematics developed throughout his works. The impulse to conversation arises from a sense of disappointment or dissatisfaction with oneself, one's language, and one's relationships with others; perhaps a feeling of aversion toward myself and/or others, toward what I say about myself and what others say to, about and for me; perhaps the sense of not having anything (more) to say, or of not being able "to find my feet" with others; perhaps the sense of my life being in a crisis such that I cannot continue to choose it. Having a strong feeling of dissatisfaction, even a sense of crisis in their lives and relationships (and finding no argumentative means of escape or satisfaction), the characters in the films, plays, and stories that Cavell discusses are either stirred to conversation with themselves and their partners or impelled to break their relationships in the hope of finding new conversational partners.[6]

Given that confusion, unintelligibility, isolation, disagreement, disappointment, and the like are ineliminable features of moral and political life (of the ordinary), and also given the limitations on what argumentation can do to relieve or diminish them, the choice between engaging in or refusing conversation seems to be no choice at all, certainly not a choice worth making.[7] But many people make this choice. Emerson's and Mill's and Thoreau's conformists make it, Othello and Lear make it. The result is that they live lives of "silent melancholy," of "quiet [or not so quiet] desperation," lives in which their nature does not exist for them. Can we understand this seemingly destructive choice?[8]

It may help us to do so if, following Cavell, we recognize that to enter into (perfectionist) conversation is to put oneself at risk, to make a wager at high stakes and with uncertain odds. What we can hope to win is (generically) clear from what on Cavell's account prompts or provokes us to initiate conversation or to be responsive to the initiatives of others. We are confused, isolated, weighed down by disappointments, and feeling estranged from others who matter to us and alienated from our political society. Argumentation has failed us. There are no rules or generalizable maxims to guide us. In such circumstances entering into conversation opens the possibility of making ourselves intelligible to ourselves and to others, of establishing or reestablishing meaningful relations with others and overcoming our alienation from our society. In ways reminiscent of the state of nature conceptions of the social contract theorists, but also and more directly of many of the depictions of the human condition presented by Emerson and Thoreau, Mill, Kierkegaard, and Nietzsche, Cavell frequently characterizes human beings and their relationships as dismal and disheartening.[9] But he is a hopeful, not a despairing, thinker, and the hope, perhaps our last best hope, is in (perfectionist) conversation.

What if we have made the leap of faith, risked conversation and then--and then—conversation goes badly, fails us. Confusion and misunderstanding increase, disappointment becomes aversion, the participants despair of themselves and one another, the relationship may be broken. If high-stakes wagers hold out the promise of large winnings they necessarily risk huge losses. Cavell is certainly aware of the risks. He speaks of "the inevitable feature of classical remarriage comedy in which the pair becomes incomprehensible to (most of) the rest of the world," and says that "this may be taken as the essential risk perfectionism runs, since at the same time it fully recognizes the moral demand for making itself intelligible— but first, in the case of our couples, to each other" (p. 153).[10] In succeeding for the couple, conversation has made their relationships with (most of) the world more difficult (see also p. 299).[11]

Cavell's identification of the difficulties that conversation addresses strongly suggests that failures will be frequent. We are heavily invested, or rather deeply embedded, in the ordinary ordinary, in ordinary language. The confusions, incomprehensibilities, disappointments, and estrangements that we experience develop within and because of the ordinary, owing to our disappointments with ordinary language and its criteria. Yet the ordinary and its languages are all we have to work with; our reliance is, finally, on them. Hence we can readily understand why the languages of resurrections, transformations, and metempsychoses, the languages of the providential and the miraculous, come to Cavell's mind when he finds instances of "transcendental" successes, successes that diminish opacity and make possible moments of happiness (see *CW*, esp. pp. 436–37).

Certainly instances of failure are recognized in the course of his discussions. Through much of Ibsen's *A Doll's House* Torvald Helmer exemplifies the losses incurred by refusing conversation (with Nora). Challenged by Nora to talk seriously with her, he treats her as a child and says things like, "You must have *some* moral sense." Cavell treats this as refusing conversation, as refusing to consider her position and instead presenting her with an argument based on a conviction he has formed prior to her challenge. This is certainly a plausible reading. But what if we read it as his attempting to awaken in her a conviction he has reason to think that she has shared with him in the past? On this reading the problem is not that Helmer refuses conversation, it is that he says the wrong things, thereby rupturing a relationship that has been of great importance in both of their lives. (Of course we are led to believe, or at least to hope, that the break opens a new and better life for Nora.)

In *Adam's Rib*, both Amanda's saying "Let's all be manly" to Adam and Adam's later saying to Amanda that he is not sure he wants to be married to "the so-called New Woman" deepen the growing rift between them. Perhaps, as with Helmer, these too are refusals of conversation rather than examples of conversation gone bad because the wrong things have been said. Perhaps conversation is resumed only later in the film and when it does it brings the couple back into marriage (but it also closes "a curtain upon the rest of the world") (*CW*, pp. 72–73).

The merits of these alternative readings are less important than a general question that they raise, namely the question of the criteria by which we distinguish between conversation and, for example, argumentation, conversation, and academic didacticism or pious preaching.

In considering this question it will be helpful to follow Cavell's lead and consider the same question with regard to consent to the government and laws of a political society. Cavell says: "Perhaps we do not require an answer to the question of what positively shows express consent so long as we have an answer to the question of what negatively shows that this consent is no longer in effect, that it has devolved into our individual hands, that a time has come in which [quoting Locke] 'People . . . may provide for themselves'" (p. 65). For most people most of the time, it is part of their ordinary lives that they are members of a politically organized society (they are born into it, choose to immigrate to it). (Can we also say that genuine conversation is a part of our ordinary lives? If so, would there be much work for MPP to do?) They show their consent to it by their day-to-day activities, by (usually) obeying its laws and paying their taxes, by participating from time to time in (conversing with one another about?) its political processes, and the like.[12] The important question, then, the question that, Cavell argues, interests Locke (and Emerson and Thoreau and Milton and numerous of the partners in the remarriage comedies in respect to divorce and separation from marriage) is less what counts as consent than what brings about, justifies, and counts as its withdrawal or revocation.

Consider in this connection the second of my two epigraphs from di Lampedusa. The male peasantry has been accorded the suffrage and many of them have cast their ballots. We are familiar with the argument that to vote in an election is to consent to the political system in which the election is held, precisely the claim that the ruling aristocracy made in saying, "But you signed it yourself, didn't you? Can't you see? It's quite clear. You must do as we say, for here are the I.O.U.s; your will is identical with mine." But because the votes of a large part of the peasantry were deliberately, fraudulently, miscounted, in saying this the aristocrats were speaking to, not for, the peasantry. On this and virtually all other matters, there was no "conversation of justice" between them and the peasantry. (Given that they didn't expressly register their outrage—or did so only in grumbling together—is the political society "theirs"?)

The notion of speaking for, as well as to, others is central to Cavell's idea not only of consent but of conversation generally. "Conversation . . . means . . . my speaking for others and my being spoken for by others, not alone in speaking to and being spoken to by others. So we shall not be surprised by the urgency of the question: How do you know you are speaking for anyone and being spoken for by someone?" (p. 51). Doing so requires "mutual responsiveness" (p. 54), it requires "that you have sufficiently appreciated the situation from the other's point of view, and . . . have articulated [in 'your own {not a "hollow"} voice'] the ground of your conviction" (p. 235). It requires acknowledgment of the "awful . . . awesome truth that the acknowledgment of others, of ineluctable separation, is the condition of human happiness. Indifference is the denial of this condition" (p. 381). In a further comment that will be important below, he says that the "idea of conversation expresses my sense that one cannot achieve [the needed] perspective alone, but only in the mirroring or confrontation of what Aristotle calls the friend . . . " (p. 174).

The conversation of MPP, then, carries the familiar meaning of "living or having one's being *in or among*," and "interchange of thought and words," but it means and requires more than "familiar discourse or talk" (*OED*, pp. 1 and 7). Cavellian conversation is an achievement, an overcoming (but never a final, now for all time overcoming) of the opacity of self and other, a willingness to live with skepticism concerning other minds and doubts about one's own intelligibility to oneself. No book of etiquette will tell you how to converse when you and/or your conversational partner find yourselves in estrangement or other crisis.[13] If the sensitivities and other aptitudes essential to such conversation were regularly and amply displayed by attained selves, lives of secret melancholy and quiet despair, political societies marked by alienation and sour submission, would be less prevalent than we know them to be.

Before moving on I underline a couple of related questions explicit or implicit thus far. Cavell recognizes that his perfectionism is susceptible to debasement (pp. 11–12). It is protected from familiar forms of debasement by its refusal of PP, its rejection of sentimental slogans such as "Love thyself" and "Be all that you can be" (*CHH*, p. 16; *CW*, p. 11), of misunderstandings such as the elitist views that Rawls attributes to Nietzsche (*CW*, pp. 13–14, 90–91), of the self-centered, self-congratulatory snobbery of Rawls's notion of a "life above reproach" (*CW*, pp. 174–79) and Kant's related notion of purity. Also, there is a strong commitment to equality evident throughout his texts. As he emphasizes in rejecting Aristotle's belief that friendship in the highest sense can only be among men, friendship can be among (almost) any two or more people (*CW*, pp. 363–68).[14] (This might be called, not an equality of opportunity, but an equality of potentiality or possibility, the possibility of attaining a better life than I have attained thus far.)

These things insisted upon, questions may nevertheless be raised concerning MPP's focus on conversation and argumentation as the two primary means of engaging with oneself and others. These are of course to be preferred to the obvious alternatives—self-satisfaction or self-hatred, conformity, indifference toward or disdainful dismissal of others, pious preaching, punching out scoundrels and villains and other uses of force, violence, intimidation, bribery, and the like. Certainly Cavell is aware of the frequency with which these are chosen. (Later I ask whether the notions of conversation and argumentation place too much emphasis on seeking self- and mutual intelligibility through interaction with others, as being tasks "not accomplished alone" [p. 218], whether it underestimates the respects in which I can, perhaps must, "wrest" my intelligibility "from myself.")

Human beings perceive and respond to themselves and one another in a multitude of registers and through a great variety of signs and signals. Cognitively and conatively, through mood, demeanor, stance and posture, tone and inflection. All of these are part of conversation, all of them play a vital role in "familiar discourse and talk," in being "conversable." We might say that they help to sustain the selves we have thus far attained, that they diminish the likelihood of the loss of self- and mutual intelligibility, that they forestall crises. There is of course much quoting, mimicking, idle chatter, and conforming in such exchanges. They can deaden and stultify. But they are also sources of reassurance, of comfort.

Certainly it is a merit of MPP that it calls us to something better than this, inspires us to look around, above and below us, for heretofore unrecognized possibilities. Perhaps it is true that we are fully, genuinely, receptive to better possibilities only—or at least primarily—when we experience ourselves and those who matter to us as desperate, as in crisis. It may be that it is only then that we can envision "a further possibility of ourselves, which it is the task of the genuine educator to encourage us to find" (p. 218). But Nietzsche, to whom Cavell is responding here, knew that the concepts "peaks" and "abysses" require the concept of smoother, habitable terrain. If I am mired in the swamp or numbed by the repetitive buzz of "familiar discourse and talk," what are the prospects of raising my gaze to the pinnacles and opening my ears and voice to genuine conversation? In what I take to be a contrast with Rawls's insistently rationalist or reasonable justice, Cavell talks of "good enough justice" (p. 163). Would it be wrong to say that one of the risks MPP runs is making the better life the enemy of the good life, of the life that is desired by some?

Part Two. Complementing Cavellian Perfectionism: Montaigne and Cavell

There are numerous commonalities or affinities between Montaigne's thinking and Cavell's. Cavell regards Montaigne's skepticism as pre-Cartesian and not inspired by or responding to the same concerns as those he (Cavell) repeatedly addresses. Granting for present purposes that this is the case, as regards skepticism the two thinkers come together in that—rather than taking their task to be to defeat skepticism, to refute it by proving that we can and do have reliable knowledge of the material world and of other minds—they attempt to understand why it arises in or for us and try to find ways to live with it. Following Pyrrhonian skepticism generally, Montaigne is deeply skeptical about both our senses and our reason.[15] He also thinks that overestimation of and excessive reliance on reason is dangerous, in part because reasoning often excites the very passions that it seeks to control but more importantly because the "penetrating clarity [claimed for it] has too much subtlety and curiosity in it. . . . Therefore common and less high-strung minds [those who live in, with, the ordinary?] are found to be more fit and more successful in conducting affairs. And the lofty and exquisite ideas are found to be inept in practice" ("We Taste Nothing Pure," II, 20, p. 51).

We might say that Montaigne, while never simply rejecting the senses or reason, welcomes skepticism because it helps him to achieve moments of "tranquillity," moments at which his feelings of frustration, distress, and disappointment, his sense of being at odds with or against himself and alienated from others, are diminished or partly relieved.

In the "Apology for Raymond Sebond," Montaigne appears to argue that we must look, all but exclusively, to God's grace to make good the deficits left by the "uncertain and deceivable" senses and "puny," "lame and blind" reason. I agree with the view that, read together with his hundred and some essays, "Sebond" is exceptional in the dogmatic character of its skepticism and in its fideism ("exceptional" is not the same as anomalous; both skepticism and fideism are present throughout his writings). Some interpreters argue that he is best characterized as a Stoic, as counseling withdrawal from and cultivated indifference to other people, to the world generally, and especially to public affairs.[16] This view, which finds substantial support from the essays in Book One and those parts of Books Two and Three that were first written, is largely responsible for Montaigne's partly deserved reputation as a conservative thinker, one who advises himself and others to conform to, to go with the flow of, whatever customs, conventions, and laws happen to be established, for whatever reason or for none, in one's community, culture, or polity.

In his later writings Montaigne does not abandon Stoicism, but he strongly criticizes features that he finds excessively prominent in it. He continues to find "many useful things" in Seneca but objects to the Stoical disposition to give the law to other people (he calls this vanity). He has come to "dislike inculcation" and especially "the practice of [Seneca's] Stoical school of repeating, in connection with every subject, in full length and breadth, the principles and premises for general use, and restating ever anew their common and universal arguments and reasons" ("Of Vanity," III, 9, pp. 734–35). In "Of Physiognomy" (III, 12) he complains of the "scholastic probity" "that I see held in greater price than it is worth, . . . almost the only one practiced among us, a slave to precepts, held down between fear and hope" (p. 811). In "Of Experience" (which was important to Emerson) he says "Since the ethical laws, which concern the individual duty of each man in himself, are so hard to frame [so hard to state the maxim of], as we see they are, it is no wonder if those [laws] that govern so many individuals are more so" (III, 13, p. 819); indeed, "there is no way of life so stupid as that which is conducted by rules and discipline" (p. 830).

The affinities, the resonances, between these passages and EP are impossible to miss. But how are we to square them with Montaigne's conservatism, with his advice to himself and others to conform to the going beliefs and practices of his time and place, with the great value he accords to "Queen Habit"?[17] Do these views debase his perfectionism?

Montaigne wrote essays (he invented the genre), not treatises. His essays express the thoughts prominent in his mind at the time he wrote them, and he was little troubled by the dissonances and real or apparent contradictions among them. The question is not whether he harmonized his various views but whether we can find in them, perhaps appropriate from them, ideas—sensibilities might be what we should look for—that enhance our own thinking and judging. Read in this spirit, the answer to this question is yes.

Returning to the question of his conservatism or conformism will help us to see why this is the case. As to custom and convention generally, while we should accept them as general guides to action, we should not do so "blindly" or "slavishly." In "Of Ancient Customs" (I, 49), he says: "I should be prone to excuse our people for having no other pattern and rule of perfection than their own manners and customs; for it is a common vice, not of the vulgar only but of almost all men, to fix their aim and limit by the ways to which they were born. . . . But I do complain of their particular lack of judgment in letting themselves be so thoroughly fooled and blinded by the authority of present usage" that, like chameleons, they change their colors with every passing social fancy and are entirely incapable of appreciating the ways and mores of other peoples (pp. 215–16). In "Of Experience" (III, 13), we find him asserting that "We should conform to the best rules, but not enslave ourselves to them. . . . " Customs and conventions should be brought before the bar of reason or conscience. Along with the benefits that conforming to them provides (most importantly that doing so contributes to our tranquility) a "principal effect of the power of custom is to seize and ensnare us in such a way that it is hardly within our power to get ourselves back out of its grip" (p. 83).

We must remember what reason is not and cannot be, but we should also bear in mind that "it has pleased God to give us some capacity for reason, so that we should not be, like the animals, slavishly subjected to the common laws, but should apply ourselves to them by judgment and voluntary liberty" (II, 8, p. 279). This advice also applies to those "common laws" that we—often mistakenly—take to be laid down by Nature itself. While "we must indeed yield a little to the simple authority of Nature," we ought not "let ourselves be carried away tyrannically by her: reason alone must guide our inclinations."

There are obvious tensions, dissonances and perhaps contradictions among these several views. To repeat, there is reason to think that Montaigne realized this but was not troubled by it. He does, however, make distinctions—in particular a distinction between "externals" and "internals"—that ease somewhat the tensions, muffle the dissonances that we have encountered in following his discussions. Underlining these distinctions will help us to foreground what is most estimable in Montaigne's thinking concerning perfectionism

He has argued in "Of Custom" that the absurd and even monstrous character of many laws and customs ought not deter the "man of understanding" from conforming to them. This is in part because such a man, for example Socrates, will understand the higher-order reasoning according to which obedience is "the rule of rules," the "law of laws." This reasoning, however, concerns what Montaigne calls "externals"; it concerns "our actions, our work, our fortunes, and our very life (that is the possibility of staying alive)," all of which we must "lend and abandon" to society. Encompassing and consuming as these notions (nostrums?) appear to be, there is much in human experience that is not only outside of but properly independent of their domain. In particular, "society in general can do without our thoughts" and in respect to them "the wise man will withdraw his soul within, out of the crowd and keep it in freedom and power to judge things freely" (p. 86). Those of understanding can conform to law and custom and yet sustain and perhaps enhance that which is distinctive to them as individual persons. He agrees with Cavell that there are often tensions and conflicts between the internal and the external, between the personal and the social, public dimensions of life, but those who understand both can achieve and sustain a *modus vivendi* between them. (In contrast to Rawls, neither Montaigne nor Cavell regards the notion of a *modus vivendi* as a pejorative or diminishing term.)

Appearing as it does in an early essay, we might take this distinction between "externals" and the inner life of the soul to be an expression of the Stoical notion of the retreat to the Inner Citadel. But strongly analogous distinctions recur in later essays and acquire a far greater prominence and articulation. And while they do not entirely escape the difficulties with the Stoic notion of retreat, they present a conception of the self and its relationships to various "externals" that is far more fruitful and engaging than the latter.

One of the most pathetic of the human tendencies he notes in "Of Democritus and Heraclitus" (I, 50) is precisely to pretend indifference toward distinctions such as between body and soul, internal and external, personal and public. Although hardly one either to diminish the role of Fortuna in human affairs or to exaggerate the possibility of human control over the flow of events and outcomes, Montaigne insists that there are dimensions or domains of life that can be made by us to depend more on us than on the circumstances into which Fortuna flings us. Notwithstanding his numerous diminishing assessments of our powers of judgment, he insists that "it is a tool to use on all subjects, and comes in everywhere" (p. 219). For various practical purposes we may agree that, viewed externally, things "in themselves may have their own weights and measures and qualities" (p. 220), but even in the lowliest of its moral, political, and other practical functions, the soul "treats a matter not according to itself, but according to herself," allotting to each its "qualities as she sees fit" (p. 220). And because souls differ enormously from person to person "Death is frightful to Cicero, desirable to Cato, a matter of indifference to Socrates. Health, conscience, authority, knowledge, riches, beauty, and their opposites—all are stripped on entry and receive from the soul new clothing, and the coloring that she chooses— . . . and which each individual soul chooses; for they have not agreed together on their styles, rules, and forms; each one is queen in her realm" (p. 220).

To deny the role of personal judgment in these matters is at least self-deceiving and in most cases hypocritical. "Wherefore let us no longer make the external qualities of things our excuse; it is up to us to reckon them as we will. Our good and our ill depend on ourselves alone" (p. 220). (Take responsibility for yourself as Cavell *sometimes* says?)

This radical perspectivalism coexists with rather than contradicts or takes back Montaigne's repeated insistence on the ways in which our judgments and our dispositions are shaped and directed by custom, convention, and the opinions of those around us. To this extent he agrees with Cavell that we cannot do it alone. He nevertheless insists not only on the possibility but the reality of an ineliminable plurality of judgments and hence of dispositions, sensibilities, tendencies and orientations toward thinking and acting. This aspect of his argumentation can be construed as an expression of his skeptical rejection of the dogmatic view that "the external qualities of things" are given, dispositively and indisputably, by impersonal or intersubjective Nature or Reason. But it is clear that Montaigne also has a heavy normative investment in the distinctions now under discussion and in particular in the conception of a self (or the possibility of selves) that not only cannot be reduced to a resultant of the forces that play upon it but that celebrates, revels in, and seeks to make the most of its particular, distinguishing, perhaps unique characteristics.

Employing a later terminology, we might say that it is Montaigne's view that those who deny or attempt to explain away this self are guilty of a kind of *mauvaise foi*. We now must explore the respects in which those who recognize this self, but seek to suppress, shrivel or even apologize for it, fall short of and perhaps betray their humanity. Yet more important, we must appreciate Montaigne's intense appreciation for those, high and low according to conventional assessments, who, each in their own way, embrace, celebrate, and seek to enhance a self that is for as well as against itself, a self that recognizes and combats its weaknesses and deficiencies but does so first and foremost in the name of and for the sake of enhancing itself.

I begin by gathering a number of the passages in which Montaigne presents variants on the theme of external submission accompanied by internal independence. Most of the pertinent passages concern relationships between self and other, and particularly more or less institutionalized relations (of which he regards marriage as one) between self and others.

Montaigne never seriously entertained the notion of a way of life or of being untouched by or unindebted to tradition, culture, society, neighbors, fellow citizens, etc. In an extended series of figures, however, he attempted to convey his understanding of the ways in which one should maintain what Nietzsche was to call a "pathos of distance" from others. The essay "Of Husbanding [*Mesnager*] the Will" (III, 10) is pivotal in this regard: "Few things touch me, or to put it better, hold me; for it is right that things should touch us, provided they do not possess us" (p. 766). He cultivates this "privilege of insensibility" and "in consequence grow[s] passionate about few things" and does not "engage" himself "easily." He particularly opposes those passions "that distract me from myself and attach me elsewhere." His conviction is "that we must lend ourselves to others" but "give ourselves only to ourselves." When "pushed . . . into the management of other men's affairs," he has been willing "to take them in hand, [but] not in lungs and liver, to take them on my shoulders, not incorporate them into me; to be concerned over them, yes; to be impassioned over them, never." "We must husband the freedom of our soul and mortgage it only on the right occasions; which are in very small number, if we judge sanely" (p. 767).

Although clearly expressed in respect to relationships and attachments such as marriage, the family, and involvements with neighbors,[18] this sensibility was especially marked as regards affairs that are public in the sense of involving formally delineated institutions and obligations, including marriage and the family but in particular citizenship, government and politics. Influenced by his two unsought and happily relinquished terms

as mayor of Bordeaux, he believed that life that is "public" in this sense
is inherently depraved, requiring "offices which are not only abject but
also vicious." The morally iniquitous actions that they often demand may
sometimes "be excusable . . . inasmuch as we need them and the common
necessity effaces their true quality," but this is a corrupting way of thinking
and even when it is justified he prefers to leave it and the actions it con-
dones to others (III, 1, p. 600).

With more than a little irony, he remarks that he would leave this
part in the human drama to "be played by the more vigorous and less fearful citizens, who sacrifice their honor and their conscience, as those an-
cients sacrificed their life, for the good of their country. We who are weak-
er, let us take parts that are both easier and less hazardous. The public
welfare requires that a man betray and lie and massacre; let us resign this
commission to more obedient and suppler people" (p. 600). Montaigne
also allows that a passion that often animates rulers and other actors on
the public stage, namely the craving for glory, can be "salutary" and sometimes must be cultivated even by the dissemination of fables and myths
that, if believed, inspire heroism and sacrifice ("Of Glory," II, 16, pp. 477–
78). With the possible exception of its close cousins vanity and arrogance,
however, Montaigne regards the quest for glory as the worst of the human
attributes or dispositions. He favorably cites Chrysippus and Diogenes as
"the first and firmest exponents of the disdain for glory" ("Of Glory," II,
16, p. 468). "All the glory in the world," they argued, "did not deserve that
a man of understanding should so much as stretch out his finger to acquire
it: 'What's in the greatest glory, if it be but glory?'—Juvenal" (p. 469).

Worse, the quest for glory and honor demeans and diminishes the
self because "of all of the pleasures there was none more dangerous or more
to be avoided than what comes to us from the approbation of others" (p.
468).

These last thoughts, particularly the thought that even apparently
high-minded forms of other-regardingness are deflecting, diminishing,
and finally corrupting, lead Montaigne to give favorable consideration to
an extreme version of the view that the self should be solely for itself—
should direct its attentions and concerns exclusively to living tranquilly—
"tranquilly not according to Metrodorus or Arcesilaus or Aristippus, but
according to me. Since philosophy has not been able to find a way to tran-

quillity that is suitable to all, let everyone seek it individually" (p. 471). He goes so far as to entertain "one of the principal doctrines of Epicurus," namely "conceal your life," a precept that "forbids men to encumber themselves with public charges and negotiations" and thereby "necessarily presupposes . . . contempt for glory, which is an approbation that the world offers of the actions that we place in evidence."

Accordingly, Epicurus counsels himself and his followers "not to regulate [their] . . . actions at all by common opinion or reputation" except out of the consideration of small prudence "to avoid the . . . accidental disadvantages that men's contempt might bring him" (p. 469). Montaigne pronounces these precepts of Epicurus to be not only clearly superior to those of Aristotle and Cicero but "infinitely true . . . and reasonable" (p. 469). What is more, the apparent consequent, namely that every "person of understanding" among us, should accept them and endeavor to live by them, is powerfully reinforced as the essay continues. "I do not care so much what I am to others as I care what I am to myself. I want to be rich by myself, not by borrowing." "All these judgments . . . founded on external appearances are marvelously uncertain and doubtful; and there is no witness so sure as each man to himself." "I hold that I exist only in myself; and as for that other life of mine that lies in the knowledge of my friends . . . , I know very well that I feel no fruit or enjoyment from it except by the vanity of a fanciful opinion" (pp. 474–75).

These remarks, particularly the dismissive stance he takes toward friendship, seem to put Montaigne in sharp disagreement with Cavell (but also, as will emerge, in conflict with himself). Cavell frequently emphasizes that the movement from the attained to a better self cannot be "accomplished alone"; with rare exceptions the conversations he foregrounds are between two persons and lead to mutual understanding and the creation or—most often—the renewal of a partnership marked by enhanced mutual understanding. Early in *Cities of Words* he writes: "the other to whom I can use the words I discover in which to express myself is the Friend—a figure that may occur as the goal of the journey but also as its instigation and accompaniment. Any moral outlook—systematically assessing the value of human existence—will accord weight to the value of friendship. But only perfectionism, as I understand it, places so absolute a value on this relationship" (p. 27).[19] The concerns of EP "are characteristically for friends, hence based on attraction not obligation" (p. 133). He objects that "the featured four examples Kant presents after introducing the first formulation of the categorical imperative seem to me fantasies of essentially isolated, friendless people" (pp. 133–34).

The differences between Cavell and Montaigne are real and important. They are not, however, as sharp as it has thus far appeared and they coexist with significant points of agreement.

Montaigne's dismissive reference to that "other life of mine that lies in the knowledge of my friends" clearly concerns friendship in the casual, perhaps distinctively American, sense of amicable but shallow relationships with neighbors, colleagues, and casual acquaintances. But he has another and entirely different understanding of friendship that is developed in the essay of that title (I, 28). In it he describes and celebrates the deep, mutually ennobling, relationship that he had with La Boetie. He speaks of "true" friendships and says that in them "our souls mingle and blend with each other so completely that they efface the seam that joined them, and cannot find it again" (p. 139); there is a "complete fusion of the wills" and the relationship becomes "that of one soul in two bodies" (p. 141), thereby seeming to obviate the self-other distinction on which the passages quoted earlier depend.

Cavell's most extensive discussion of friendship (in *CW*) is through an engagement with Aristotle's thoughts on the subject. In remarks that closely parallel statements in Montaigne's "Of Friendship," Cavell quotes Aristotle as saying, "The blessed person decides to observe virtuous actions that are his own; and the actions of a virtuous friend are of this sort. Hence he will need virtuous friends"; "The excellent person is related to his friend in the same way he is related to himself, since a friend is another himself"; "Someone's own being is choiceworthy because he perceives that he is good, and this sort of perception is pleasant in itself. He must, then [in order to perceive his own being], perceive his friend's being, together [with his own], and he will do this when they live together and share conversations and thoughts" (quoted by Cavell from *Nichomachean Ethics*, pp. 1170a and 1170b, in *CW*, p. 366; the material in brackets is Cavell's). "The friend becomes," Cavell adds, "as it were, my next self" (p. 367).[20]

These are respects in which these two sets of passages are not only fully compatible but strongly complementary. There are, however, significant differences between the two conceptions of friendship. In order to explore them let us recall that Cavell rejects Aristotle's view that friendship can only be between men and holds that any two people can be friends. As a general proposition that may influence the sense of the possibilities open to myself or to others, this is surely right. This contrasts sharply with Montaigne's dogmatic rejection of the possibility that women are capable of true friendship (and that fathers and children and brothers and business partners (and so on through a long list) cannot be (true) friends with one another. There is no more to be said for these presumptuous remarks than for Aristotle's judgment about women. In the cultures that Aristotle, Montaigne, and Cavell have in mind, it may indeed be difficult for women to develop friendships with men, fathers with their children, et cetera, but this is more because the general proposition that they are incapable of doing so is widely believed and asserted than because of any congenital or otherwise incapacity to do so. In this respect the difference between Cavell and Montaigne is clearly in Cavell's favor.

This may or may not be true concerning Aristotle's and Montaigne's distinction between true friendship and those of its less valuable forms that are based on, or have an admixture of, utility and pleasure. Cavell endorses, or rather extends, Aristotle's view which allows that "almost any relationship of cooperation or mutuality—any we might say that further sociability—may be seen to manifest some register of friendship, as between host and guest, or seller and buyer, or a ruler and his swineherd. But while Aristotle can say [as I read the sentence, 'say' should be in italics or scare quotes to emphasize 'merely' say] that character friendship includes the two lesser grades of friendship he distinguishes, the relationships drawn in remarriage comedy seems to demonstrate its possibility" (*CW*, p. 363).

By contrast, while Montaigne sees the value of these "lesser" forms of relationship, he refuses them the name of friendship. All "associations that are forged and nourished by pleasure or profit, by public or private needs, are the less beautiful and noble, and the less friendship, in so far as they mix into friendship another cause and object and reward than friendship itself" ("Of Friendship," p. 136). (Those familiar with Eric Rohmer's film *A Tale of Winter* may find an analogous hierarchy in Felicie's distinctions among the kinds of love she feels for, respectively, Charles, Lolic, and Maxence. See *CW*, chap. 23.) He regards true friendship as extremely rare and holds that no person can have more than one true friend.

In the same paragraph, Montaigne refers approvingly to Aristotle's view "that good legislators have had more care for friendship than for justice" and says that "the ultimate point of the perfection of society is this."[21] We might say that for Montaigne friendship is not the only thing that you can't "accomplish alone" (Cavell), but that it is the most important thing that you can't accomplish in that way.[22] We can and must say that for Montaigne true friendship is exclusive, that in Cavell's words it "closes the world on others." This is not merely a *risk* that Montaignian friendship must run; it is not merely one possible or even usual outcome of true friendship; it is a condition of achieving true friendship, one sought by those who seek such a friendship.

In this respect Montaignian friendship is exclusive: it excludes other persons from the relationship. In other respects, however, it is open to, perhaps conducive to, a wide range of possibilities. That Larry and I are true friends in no way prevents Mary and Tom or anyone else from becoming true friends. Our example, the joy that others see us take from it, may awaken others to the possibility of such a relationship and encourage them to seek their own. (I believe that I have had this experience and I do not think it is uncommon.) Nor does it exclude the "lesser" forms of relationship. Montaigne appreciates the value of relations based on pleasure and utility; he simply refuses to accord them the same esteem. These other, lesser, relationships include those he thinks appropriate to citizenship. "There was never a better citizen or one more devoted to the tranquillity of his country [than La Boetie]" (p. 144). We might say that, assuming that Montaigne was justified in his belief that he was a good citizen, he had learned to be one by having La Boetie as his friend. This thought may inform his endorsement of Aristotle's view that friendship is the first concern of the good legislator. If justice is "good enough," and if many of its citizens form true friendships with one another, the *bonum civile* of the polis, the *respublica* (the democracy?), will be as fully accomplished as its circumstances permit.

Cavell is prepared to run the risk that friendship as he understands it may "close the door" to "most of the rest of the world," the risk that by becoming friends Larry and I become incomprehensible to others. It is a strength of his view that, by comparison with Montaigne and Aristotle, he wants to equalize (democratize?) the possibilities for friendship. It is also a strength of his view, but one that I think is also a strength of Montaigne's, that closing the door to the world does not mean that our friendship cannot contribute to changing the world for the better.

I am inclined to say the following: Montaigne risks making friendship so pure that few can attain it and, perhaps—though I doubt it, because it would be vain and presumptuous—engendering in those few who attain it a snobbery toward those who do not. For him friendship is a soaring ideal, a vision of the highest, the most joyous and ennobling, relationships possible for human beings. It is also an ideal for Cavell, perhaps even the highest ideal of his perfectionism, and it is also an ideal that can be realized in many different ways. (As well as their being perfectionists, in their thinking both Montaigne and Cavell are deeply pluralistic.) If he finds it realized in, exemplified by, relationships in which—I believe—Montaigne would not recognize it, this can be regarded, on the one hand, as making more room for it or, on the other, as a thinning out, a watering down of the ideal. It makes it more widely available, but at the cost of diminishing its grandeur and perhaps its inspiring quality.

If these are our choices, how should we choose? There is no right or best answer to this question. What place or role do we want ideals to have or to play in our lives? If one thinks, as I think Nietzsche thought, that the role of ideals should be more than to offer us the possibility of partial relief from our melancholy lives, if we value them because they inspire us to scale the heights and dance on the edge of abysses, then Montaigne's conception of friendship may draw us to it. As both Montaigne and Nietzsche would be among the first to say, the greatest part of our lives will be lived on lower ground, trying through what Montaigne calls "small prudence" to make ordinary relations with family, neighbors, colleagues, and fellow citizens mutually acceptable. But as Cavell himself and virtually all of the writers and texts that draw and hold his attentions teach us, lives lived exclusively on this lower ground will from time to time lose their savor, may become so dreary as to seem no longer worthy of our choice. To the extent that Montaigne found this to be the case, the soaring ideal of friendship gave him the resolve, the courage, to continue. Others, finding it unattainable, may take it to be an affront to them. No matter how high perfectionism pitches its ideals (of self- and mutual intelligibility, of justice, of individuality, of happiness, as well as of friendship), this is a risk it must run.

We now must ask whether Montaigne's idealization of friendship is compatible with his esteem for what we can call his self-made individuality. If the most joyous moments of his life were due to, if he could not conceive of their possibility apart from, his relationship with another person, has he not betrayed his ideal of being "rich by myself, not by borrowing," of existing "only in myself"? To consider this, I return to his praise of the counsels of Epicurus.

As with other doctrines that are, abstractly, "infinitely true . . . and reasonable," as a practical matter the Epicurean principles are easier to formulate and articulate than steadfastly to apply. The notion of a concealed, entirely private solitary life, while worthy and indeed inspiring as an ideal, will of itself provide few if any of us with a sufficient guide to the day-to-day conduct of ourselves and others.

How then can/should the self supplement its concern for itself? With what considerations can the latter be combined consistent with and complementary to its proper self-preoccupation? Elements of the answers to these questions are already before us and are quite straightforward. So long as we do not do so vainly and presumptuously as do the Protestants, we should hearken to God's will for us as it is made available to us in and through the teachings of the church that is established in our society. As long as we do not do so blindly we can and should let secular custom, convention, and law direct much of our conduct. If or to the extent that we can accomplish the difficult feat of sustaining the freedom of our internal judgment concerning the merits of the rules to which we conform, the guidance with which they provide us could well answer many of the quotidian questions of conduct with which we are confronted.[23]

In respect to these sources of guidance in "external" matters Montaigne supplements and qualifies positions discussed above primarily by invoking a view of "nature" and of following the "natural" (the ordinary?) as distinct from and often as opposed to the artful and the artificial, the abstract and the theoretical, the contrived and the needlessly convoluted. Speaking "in good earnest," he says: "Isn't man a miserable animal? Hardly is it in his power, by his natural condition, to taste a single pleasure pure and entire, and still he is at pains to curtail that pleasure by his reason: he is not wretched enough unless by art and study he augments his misery."

"Human wisdom very stupidly exercises its ingenuity to reduce the number and sweetness of the sensual pleasures that belong to us. . . . " (p. 148; compare Cavell on Mill on desire). Moderation, yes; monkish abstinence and self-abnegation, no. The sensual pleasures are ours by nature and we should let ourselves enjoy them.

Montaigne returns to this theme many times, at greatest length in the frequently bawdy "Of Some Verses of Virgil" (III, 5). Anticipating Cavell's views of academic and professional philosophy, he complains that those who are learned or philosophically disposed treat "of things too subtly, in a mode too artificial and different from the common and natural one." More specifically as regards sexual intercourse, "Nature pushes us on to it, having attached to this desire the most noble, useful and pleasant of all her operations." But she leaves us free to assess it as we see fit, and, stupidly, we "shun it as shameless and indecent, blush at it, and recommend abstinence. Are we not brutes to call brutish the operation that makes us? . . . What a monstrous animal to be a horror to himself, to be burdened by his pleasures, to regard himself as a misfortune" (pp. 669–70).

He rejects any very sharp distinction between the corporeal and the mental or spiritual (see III, 13, p. 849, as well as the discussion about to be cited), but insofar as he treated the "soul" as the seat of judgment he argued that, rather than being cool toward bodily pleasures, it should "hatch them and foment them, to offer and invite herself to them." "For it is indeed reasonable, as they say, that the body should not follow its appetites to the disadvantage of the mind; but why is it not also reasonable that the mind should not pursue its appetites to the disadvantage of the body?" (p. 68).

This association between mind or soul and body shows up again but in broadened form in other places where he expresses his preference for the natural over the artificial. In "Of Experience" he says: "I, who operate close to the ground, hate that inhuman wisdom that would make us disdainful enemies of the cultivation of the body. I consider it equal injustice to set our heart against natural pleasures and to set our heart too much on them" (M, III, 13, p. 849). How, then, in addition to being respectful and responsive to our bodies, does one go about "operating close to the ground"? What, in addition to our bodies, constitutes the "ground" to which we should remain "close"?

Following Socrates, who like himself is of the common sort in every respect except that he knows it (II, 17, p. 481), he asserts that "we need hardly any learning to live at ease. And Socrates teaches us that it is in us, and the way to find it and help ourselves with it. All this ability of ours that is beyond the natural [beyond the ordinary, questing for the metaphysical?] is as good as vain and superfluous" (III, 12, p. 794). He is convinced that "most of the instructions that learning uses to encourage us are more showy than powerful and more ornamental than effective. We have abandoned Nature and we want to teach her her lesson, she who used to guide us so happily and so surely." We must seek the "evidence of her that is not subject to favor, corruption, or diversity of opinion" (p. 803; compare III, 13, p. 844; and Cavell, *CW*, 368). "I let myself go as I have come. I combat nothing. My two ruling parts, of their own volition, live in peace and good accord" (M, III, 12, p. 811).

The passages just considered seem to be distinctive in that in them Montaigne appears to be generalizing quite freely concerning the human condition and to be quite prepared, on the basis of those generalizations, to advance principles and precepts that should be followed by all of humankind. Whereas he claims that his essays are written solely for himself and a few friends, we now see him claiming to be "guided by the general law of the world" (M, III, 13, p. 821) and prepared to guide the world by giving general laws to it.

What is the range and who are the addressees of these generalizing remarks? As to their range, the characterizations of the human condition are general and hence consistent with great variations from society to society and person to person. "Men are diverse in inclination and strength; they must be led to their own good according to their nature and by diverse routes" (M, III, 12, p. 805). As to their addressees, my view is that they are addressed primarily by Montaigne to Montaigne himself and perhaps to those akin to him. Having experienced the temptations of learning, philosophizing, and dogmatizing, hence no longer able to rest his head on that "sweet and soft and healthy pillow" that is "ignorance and incuriosity" (III, 13, p. 822), Montaigne must teach himself to attend to himself, to make the study of himself both his "metaphysics" and his "physics" (p. 821). "There is nothing so beautiful and legitimate as to play the man well and properly; no knowledge so hard to acquire as the knowledge of how to live this life well and naturally; and the most barbarous of our maladies is to despise our being" (p. 852). "It is an absolute perfection and virtually divine to know how to enjoy our being rightfully. We seek other conditions because we do not understand the use of our own, and go outside of ourselves because we do not know what it is like inside. Yet there is no use our mounting on stilts, for on stilts we must still walk on our legs. And on the loftiest throne in the world we are still sitting on our rump."

It is not an easy thing to let one's self go as it comes, to let the self be first and foremost for itself. This is because the idea of doing so, as with the idea of true friendship, is not merely an idea but a soaring ideal, a vision of what fully human, fully humane, lives—in all of their diversities—would be like. The first of these is the ideal that Montaigne urged upon himself. As I read him, the ideal of friendship is subordinate to, a means of achieving, the first of these ideals. A life relieved of, freed from, self-diminishing forms of "combat" requires struggle with and against elements and forces that, given the unavoidably situated character of our selves, are almost certain to have installed themselves deeply within us. The possibility of sustaining that second form of combat can be greatly enhanced by true friendships. But it depends above all on sustaining—no easy thing to do—the conviction that "You are as much a god as you will own/That you are nothing but a man alone" (Amyot's Plutarch, III, 13, p. 857). This is the ideal that Don Calogero glimpsed in the life of Don Fabrizio.

I have raised two main questions about Cavell's perfectionism. The first is whether it tends to undervalue the ways in which "familiar discourse and talk" may provide reassurance, comfort, and perhaps a sense of understanding oneself and one's important others well enough to make life worthy of choice—we might say worthy enough to take the risks involved in trying to make it better. My second, seemingly disparate, but I think closely related, question concerns the perfectionist ideal of conversation with others, the ideal of attaining self- and mutual understanding primarily through relations of a certain intense and otherwise elevated quality with others.

As to the first, Cavell, Emerson, Thoreau, and Mill are certainly right that many lives are weighed down by feelings of disappointment and desperation and right to press us to confront those feelings and to take the risks involved in trying to attain to better lives. They are correct that there are lives in which familiar discourse and talk make matters worse, lives that have come to such a crisis that only conversation of a qualitatively different kind can redeem them. A part of my question is whether those who experience such a crisis have to bring something, bring enough, of or from their attained selves to it to be able to confront the crisis, to take the risk that conversation might fail them. We might say enough that they can regard their lives as worth redeeming.

I have turned to Montaigne because he recognizes the seriousness of these questions and responds to them in ways that complement the answers given by MPP. He has experienced first-hand the dull, repetitive, stupefying banality of much familiar discourse and talk. But he has also experienced its quieting, supportive, reassuring qualities, the ways in which it diminishes the incidence of destructive hatred and conflicts and allows of moments of tranquillity. His advice to himself and others is to accommodate to it externally, to conform conduct to established customs, conventions, and laws. This advice is not given out of admiration for their content but in the hope that by following it he and his acquaintances and fellow citizens can be comfortable with one another, can enter into true friendships with one another, and, with the help of such friendships, can give a shape to their lives that they find pleasing to themselves.

Addendum

I have alluded parenthetically to important issues, concerning democracy and democratization, that I cannot adequately address here. These questions form something of a *leitmotiv* in those of Cavell's works primarily discussed here. Emersonian perfectionism as Cavell understands and promotes it is "understood not only to be compatible with democracy, but its prize" (*CHH*, p. 28). "If there is a perfectionism not only compatible with democracy, but necessary to it, it lies not in excusing democracy for its inevitable failures, or looking to rise above them, but in teaching how to respond to those failures, and to one's compromise by them, otherwise than by excuse or withdrawal" (p. 18). "If I say that the aim of Emersonianism . . . is to suggest the richest conception of perfectionism compatible with, and indeed essential to, a democratic disposition, then the question arises as to whether, or in what sense, the democratic city is an image of its citizens, or whether it is precisely of that city that it can be said the face of its citizens remains open to their imagination" (*CW*, p. 321).

Montaigne is certainly no democrat. To my knowledge, the terms democracy and democratization never appear in his work and if he had used them he certainly would not have said that his perfectionism is essential to democracy or that it is perfectionism's prize. Of course these differences between him and Cavell are readily understandable in terms of the differences between his times and Cavell's. No one was thinking about democracy in Montaigne's century; now it is on just about everyone's lips.

It should nevertheless be noticed that there are some commonalities between his political thinking and Cavell's. Some of his favorable references to Aristotle suggest that he might have agreed that the city, that is, the politically organized society, is an image of its citizens and that it must be open to the imagination of its citizens. He might also have said that his perfectionism teaches its citizens how to respond to the failures of the city. He "excused" those in authority in that he said that their often atrocious actions are sometimes necessary, but he did not hesitate to criticize them and frequently took and promoted positions that they condemned.[24] Having no taste for regular, active participation in public affairs, for the most part he left their conduct to others. His preferred means of contributing to the life of the city was to make his personal life and relationships exemplary to others while registering his dissent from decisions and policies that he found unacceptable.

This is of course a kind of withdrawalism and could be called parasitic, squeamish, perhaps even selfishly self-regarding. Is it so very different from Cavell's couples closing the door (the curtain, the blanket) on most of the rest of the world? More important, is there a single ideal of democracy, a single best model or figuration of the democratic disposition? I take it that Montaigne agrees with Cavell and Emerson in rejecting this Perfectionist Perfectionism view. I think that they are right to do so.

Perfectionism, Parrhesia, and the Care of the Self: Foucault and Cavell on Ethics and Politics

David Owen

But, then, what is philosophy today—philosophical activity, I mean—if it is not the critical work that thought brings to bear on itself? . . . The "essay"—which should be understood as the assay or test by which, in the game of truth, one undergoes changes, and not as the simplistic appropriation of others for the purpose of communication—is the living substance of philosophy, at least if we assume that philosophy is still what it was in times past, i.e., an "ascecis," *askesis,* an exercise of oneself in the activity of thought.

—MICHEL FOUCAULT

Work on philosophy is—as work in architecture frequently is—actually more of a // a kind of // work on oneself. On one's own conception. On the way one sees things. (And what one demands of them.)

—LUDWIG WITTGENSTEIN

This essay explores an intuition initially expressed by Arnold Davidson that Cavell's reflections on the topic of moral perfectionism involve "working toward a conceptualization of ethics that shares with Foucault and Hadot the idea that what is at issue is not only a code of good conduct but a way of being that involves every aspect of one's soul"[1] and most recently supported by Cavell's own characterization of moral perfectionism "as emphasizing that aspect of moral choice having to do, as it is sometimes put, with being true to oneself, or as Michel Foucault has put the view, caring for the self."[2] My purpose in exploring this thematic affinity in the works of Cavell and Foucault is to attempt to show how they can help to elucidate aspects of each other's philosophical projects, although my primary emphasis will be on using Foucault's reflections on ethics to aid our understanding of Cavell's concern with moral perfectionism. Since Foucault's work may be less familiar to readers of a volume dedicated to Cavell, I'll begin by sketching out the nature of, and reasons for, Foucault's turn to consider ethics in his late work before using this as a basis on which to engage in the main quest of this essay.

I

In his late works, Michel Foucault turns from attending to the forms of government to which we are subjected to a focus on the forms of government to which we subject ourselves, that is, on *ethics* conceived as a mode of the self's relationship to itself. More precisely, Foucault is concerned with the ways in which one seeks to govern the formation of one's ethical subjectivity in relation to a given morality or, as Nietzsche would have it, give style to one's character.[3] He proposes a general analytical apparatus in terms of which different forms of ethical *rapport à soi* can be addressed under four aspects: the ethical substance (the aspect or part of oneself or one's behavior which is concerned with moral conduct), the mode of subjectivation (the ways in which one establishes one's relation to moral obligations, rules, etc.), the form of ethical work (the ascetic practices through which one acts on oneself) and the ethical *telos* (the kind of ethical being that we aspire to be when we act morally). There are four guiding reasons for this shift in focus and the consequent development of this analytical apparatus.

The first reason expresses Foucault's concern that the one-sided character of his genealogical studies of, for example, punishment and sexuality, the fact that they focus on the forms of government to which we are subjected, may (and, indeed, did) generate the misleading impression that he takes contemporary society to be a scene of domination in which our forms of subjectivity are shaped without remainder by powers that we have no effective capacity to resist. In this respect, Foucault's focus on ethics is designed to insist on the point that "power is not a relation which molds passive receptacles into obedient subjects, but one which presupposes free subjects." "Our mode of existence *in* any field of power and knowledge is clearly as practitioners of self-awareness and self-formation, in which we think and act and have our ethical mode of being, and conduct ourselves in relation to power."[4] Ethics is, thus, to be understood as "the considered form that freedom takes when it is informed by reflection."[5]

The second reason is that just as Foucault takes modern political theory to have failed in large measure to cut off the King's head (i.e., move beyond a juridical, sovereignty-based picture of politics), so too he takes philosophical reflection on morality to be governed by a picture of morality as a (quasi-) juridical code of laws and prescriptions in which moral action is conceived in terms of conduct in accordance with moral rules. This is, if you like, a picture of morality in which the question "What ought I do?" is privileged in a way that obstructs our acknowledgment of the importance of ethical *rapport à soi* in two respects.

First, it obstructs our recognition that action in accordance with a given set of moral rules may involve very diverse ethics. Taking the example, "a code of sexual prescriptions enjoining two marital partners to practice a strict and symmetrical conjugal fidelity, always with a view to procreation," Foucault points out that "there will be many ways, even within such a rigid frame, to practice that austerity, many ways to 'be faithful.'"[6] In respect of the *ethical substance*, the practice of fidelity can relate to "the strict observance of interdictions and obligations in the very acts one accomplishes" or the mastery of desires through constant struggle such that "the contradictory movements of the soul—much more than the carrying out of the acts themselves—will be the prime material of moral practice."[7] In respect of the *mode of subjectivation*, Foucault notes that one can practice conjugal fidelity "because one acknowledges oneself to be a member of a group that accepts it, declares adherence to it out loud and silently preserves it as a custom" or "because one regards oneself as an heir to a spiritual tradition that one has the responsibility of maintaining or reviving" or "in response to an appeal, by offering oneself as an example, or by seeking to give one's personal life a form that answers to criteria of brilliance, beauty, nobility, or perfection."[8] In respect of the form of *ethical work*, Foucault points out that "sexual austerity can be practiced through a long effort of learning, memorization, and assimilation of a systematic ensemble of precepts, and through a regular checking of conduct aimed at measuring the exactness with which one is applying these rules" or "in the form of a relentless combat" or "through a decipherment as painstaking, continuous and detailed as possible, of the movement of desire in all its hidden forms."[9] Finally, with respect to the *telos* of the ethical subject, conjugal fidelity can be part of forms of moral conduct that aspire "to an ever more complete mastery of the self" or manifest "a sudden and radical detachment vis-à-vis the world" or "strain toward a perfect tranquillity of soul .. or toward a purification that will ensure salvation after death and blissful immortality."[10] Thus, Foucault's point contra the juridical picture of morality is this: "There is no specific moral action that does not refer to a unified moral conduct; no moral conduct that does not call for a forming of oneself as an ethical subject; and no forming of the ethical subject without 'modes of subjectivation' and an 'ascetics' or 'practices of the self' that support them."[11]

Second, this quasi-juridical picture of morality obstructs our recognition that insofar as our ethical lives involve both reference to moral rules, on the one hand, and ethical *rapport à soi*, on the other hand, and it is the case that these elements "may develop in relative independence from one another,"[12] different forms of ethical life may exhibit different relations to these two features. Thus, and here Foucault has in mind post-Reformation Europe, "in certain moralities the main emphasis is placed on the code, on its systematicity, its richness, its capacity to adjust to every possible case and to embrace every type of behavior" such that "the subjectivation occurs basically in a quasi-juridical form, where the ethical subject refers his conduct to a law, or set of laws, to which he must submit at the risk of committing offenses that make him liable to punishment."[13] By contrast, and here Foucault is thinking of Greek, Roman, and early Christian examples, other moralities place the main emphasis on "the forms of relations with the self, on the methods and techniques by which he works them out, on the exercises by which he makes himself an object to be known, and on the practices that enable him to transform his own mode of being" and, in these cases, "the system of codes and rules of behaviour may be rather rudimentary."[14] It is, however, moralities of this second kind that the quasi-juridical picture of morality fails to enable us to grasp, and it does so in virtue of its failure to acknowledge its own status as an artifact of the prevalence of the first type of morality in post-Reformation Europe.

The third reason for Foucault's turn relates to the forms, inherited and adapted from the Christian tradition, characteristic of modern ethics, on the one hand, and the resources offered by the Greek and Roman focus on "an aesthetics of existence,"[15] on the other hand. The nature of this reason can be elucidated, albeit somewhat schematically, by reference to Foucault's concern that modern society is characterized by a paradox of the relations of capacity and power, in that the ways in which we develop and enhance our capabilities for thinking and acting are linked to the intensification of power relations,[16] that is, the practices of normalization to which we are subject and which Foucault refers to as "bio-power."[17] The salient point has been neatly expressed by Dreyfus and Rabinow:

Bio-power spread under the banner of making people healthy and protecting them. Where there was resistance, or failure to achieve its stated aims, this was construed as further proof of the need to reinforce and extend the power of experts. A technical matrix was established. By definition there ought to be a way of solving any technical problem. Once this matrix was established, the spread of bio-power was assured, for there was nothing else to appeal to: any other standards could be shown to be abnormal or to present merely technical problems. We are promised normalization and happiness through science and law. When they fail, this only justifies the need for more of the same.[18]

Foucault's argument is that the maintenance and reproduction of this matrix are, to a significant degree, facilitated by the fact that forms of resistance to particular manifestations of it are themselves conducted in terms of ethics that exhibit this appeal to science and law—or, more precisely, that combine a quasi-juridical mode of subjectivation and ethical *telos* with a notion of ethical substance defined by the modern psychosciences and a form of ethical work focused on techniques of interpretation and avowal of the truth about the self developed by these sciences.[19] Foucault puts the point this way: "Recent liberation movements suffer from the fact that they cannot find any principle on which to base the elaboration of a new ethics. They need an ethics but they cannot find any other ethics than an ethics founded on so-called scientific knowledge of what the self is, what desire is, what the unconscious is, and so on."[20] Examples are provided by the ongoing political debates concerning nature and culture and philosophical debates concerning essentialism and anti-essentialism within the feminist[21] and gay liberation[22] movements. The salience of Foucault's investigations of ancient ethics for this concern is twofold.

First, it allows Foucault to show that the historical emergence of this problematic form of ethical *rapport à soi* is tied to the shift from Greek and Roman conceptions of ethics as a mode of care of self that affirms the self to early Christian conceptions of ethics as a mode of care of the self directed to renouncing the self. On the one hand, Christian ethics involved a quasi-juridical mode of subjectivation: "In Christianity what is very interesting is that the sexual rules for behavior were, of course, justified through religion. The institutions by which they were imposed were religious institutions. But the form of the obligation was a legal form. There was a kind of . . . internal juridification of religious law inside Christianity."[23] On the other hand, Christian ethics involved a hermeneutics of suspicion:

This new Christian self had to be constantly examined because in this self were lodged concupiscence and desires of the flesh. From that moment on, the self was no longer something to be made but something to be renounced and deciphered. Consequently, between paganism and Christianity, the opposition is not between tolerance and austerity, but between a form of austerity that is linked to an aesthetics of existence and other forms of austerity which are linked to the necessity of renouncing the self and deciphering its truth.[24]

This combination of features, Foucault argues, persists even as the religious framework of self-renunciation drops away after the eighteenth century in the competition between, and combination of, scientific and juridical elements in contemporary ethics.[25]

Second, it provides Foucault with an alternative "model" to propose, namely, the ethics of care of the self as an aesthetics of existence. The distinctive character of this kind of ethical *rapport à soi* is that, in contrast to Christian ethics, it does not aim to eliminate the conflicting forces within the self (e.g., desires) but to govern them such that they serve "the objective of living or manifesting in one's life an ethos of freedom,"[26] where "the ethos of freedom in question is an agonal ethos, an ethos that celebrates freedom not, or not exclusively, as unobstructed or unopposed thinking and doing but as a triumph over conflicting and antagonistic forces within the self."[27] Hence this ethos of freedom takes the form of "an 'aesthetics,' a 'stylisation' of the self by itself."[28] As Foucault comments, "in this form of morality, the individual did not make himself into an ethical subject by universalizing the principles that informed his action; on the contrary, he did so by means of an attitude and a quest that individualized his action, modulated it, and perhaps even gave him a special brilliance by virtue of the rational and deliberate structure his actions manifested."[29] It is important to be clear about two points with respect to this passage. The first is that this activity of self-stylization takes place, for the Greeks, within an ethical space that is structured by the "few great common laws . . . but it was as if they traced a very wide circle in the distance, inside of which practical thought had to define what could rightfully be done" and "for there was no need of a text that would have the force of law, but rather of a *techne* or 'practice' a *savoir-faire* that by taking general principles into account would guide action in its time, according to its context, and in view of its ends."[30] The second point is that this form of care of the self is not simply self-directed: "To the extent, always important, that I am what I am because of my relations with others and my participation (or my resistance to participation in) shared practices, institutions, and activities, I cannot know who or what I am, hence cannot care for myself, without close attention and responsiveness to others and to arrangements that I share with them."[31] Governing oneself appropriately is integrally connected with conducting one's relations to others in ethically appropriate ways—and Foucault points out that the view that this form of care of the self is connected to the domination of others is a later view that arises from the Christian suspicion of love of the self as a form of earthly attachment.[32] This is not to deny that what the Greeks took as ethically appropriate ways to conduct their relations to women and slaves would not strike us as such but to note that this does not impugn the point that the care of self is necessary to achieve the self-government required to conduct oneself in ethically appropriate ways. The central point stressed by Foucault in relation to this alternative model is that it disconnects ethics from the idea of a true or final self and thus dissolves the paradox of power and capacities that he takes to characterize contemporary ethical life.[33]

The fourth, and final, reason for Foucault's turn to a focus on ethics concerns the relationship between ethics and the emergence of, what Foucault calls, "the critical attitude" by way of the connection, established by Socrates, between care of the self and *parrhesia* (a form of truth-telling in which the truth-teller runs a risk by telling the truth). Focusing on Plato's *Laches*, Foucault shows how Socrates establishes this link by inquiring into the relationship of *bios* and *logos* in the accounts offered by his interlocutors: "Socrates is inquiring into the way that *logos* gives form to a person's style of life; for he is interested in discovering whether there is a harmonic relation between the two. . . . Socrates' role, then, is to ask for a rational accounting of a person's life."[34] Here Socrates serves a "touchstone"[35] who determines "the true nature of the relation between *logos* and *bios* of those who come into contact with him."[36] The distinctive feature of this form of *parrhesia* is that its aim is "to convince someone that he must take care of himself and of others; and this means that he must *change his life*."[37] As Foucault goes on to note:

This theme of changing one's life, of conversion, becomes very important from the Fourth Century B.C. to the beginnings of Christianity. It is essential to philosophical parrhesiatic practices. Of course conversion is not completely different from the change of mind that an orator, using his *parrhesia*, wished to bring about when he asked his fellow citizens to wake up, to refuse what they previously accepted, or to accept what they previously refused. But in philosophical practice the notion of changing one's mind takes on a more general and expanded meaning since it is no longer just a matter of altering one's belief or opinion, but of changing one's style of life, one's relation to others, and one's relation to oneself.[38]

This kind of *parrhesiastic* practice is, thus, concerned not simply with self-knowledge but, more generally, with becoming intelligible to oneself through a form of critical testing of oneself by way of engagement with someone—typically a friend[39]—who acts a *parrhesiastes*.

The significance of this turn to ethics for Foucault is not least that it enables him to understand his own activity better by allowing him to situate his genealogical investigations as exemplifications of the critical ethics of modernity; an ethics that can be described as "a *limit-attitude*" that seeks to interrogate the contemporary limits of the necessary by asking this question: "In what is given to us as universal, necessary, obligatory, what place is occupied by whatever is singular, contingent and the product of arbitrary constraints?"[40] Such a critical attitude is given expression through a *parrhesiastic* practice (genealogy) "in which the critique of what we are is at one and the same time the historical analysis of the limits imposed on us and an experiment with the possibility of going beyond them."[41] As such it manifests a form of care of the self in which we engage in the free activity of testing what are given to us as bounds of reason—it is "a patient labor giving form to our impatience for liberty."[42]

Having laid out Foucault's reasons for turning to attend to ethics and, in doing so, clarified his commitment to the ethics of care of the self as a practice of freedom characterized by an aesthetics of existence, we can note four initial affinities between Foucault's stance and Cavell's reflections on moral perfectionism.

The first is that the province of moral perfectionism in Cavell's sense is directed to that dimension of moral life that Foucault refers to as ethics. Commenting on the cinematic comedies of remarriage he addresses as illustrations of moral perfectionism, Cavell notes: "The issues the principal pair in these films confront each other with are formulated less well by questions concerning what they ought to do, what it would be best or right for them to do, than by the question of how they shall live their lives, what kind of persons they aspire to be."[43] More particularly, Cavell explicates this dimension of moral life in terms of "the aesthetic dimension of (moral) judgment," relating moral perfectionism to the (artistic) activity of self-formation that Foucault glosses with the thought that we "should relate the kind of relation one has to oneself to a creative activity" and which he, like Cavell, relates to Nietzsche's notion of giving style to one's character, that is, becoming what one is.

The second affinity is that moral perfectionism is not presented by Cavell as "a competing theory of the moral life," but rather, as Cavell puts its, "something like a dimension or tradition of the moral life that spans the course of Western thought and concerns what used to be called the state of one's soul, a dimension that places tremendous burdens on personal relationships and on the possibility or necessity of the transforming of oneself and of one's society."[44] We can explicate the precision of Cavell's apparent equivocation in the statement "something like a dimension or tradition of the moral life" by reference to Foucault's reflections on ethics. It is like a dimension in that, as Foucault points out, "There is no specific moral action that does not refer to a unified moral conduct; no moral conduct that does not call for a forming of oneself as an ethical subject; and no forming of the ethical subject without 'modes of subjectivation' and an 'ascetics' or 'practices of the self' that support them."[45] It is like a tradition because, as Foucault notes, it has come to the fore relative to the moral code dimension of morality at various points in the course of the Western history of morality.

A third affinity arises from the fact that moral perfectionism, like the ethics of care of the self, addresses "what used to be called the state of one's soul" in that it is specifically concerned with one's intelligibility to oneself as a (moral) agent.[46] In other words, it focuses on what Foucault commenting on Socratic *parrhesia* refers to as the relation of *bios* and *logos*. This is manifest in the significance of the theme of conversion and the figure of the friend in Cavell's discussion of moral perfectionism (I'll return to this elsewhere in the essay).[47] Another way of describing this affinity is to say that Foucault's conception of the ethics of care of the self as a practice of freedom oriented to freedom (i.e., self-government) can be aligned with Cavell's statement that "Emersonian perfectionism is not primarily a claim as to the right to goods . . . but primarily as to the claim, or good, of freedom. . . ."[48]

The final affinity to which I draw attention at this stage concerns the point that Cavell conceives of the *modern* mode of moral perfectionism as necessarily processual rather than teleological in character, that is, the activity of "becoming what one is" does not have an endpoint in some perfect state of self-realization but, rather, is an ongoing process of struggle[49]—as Foucault has it "we are always in the position of beginning again."[50] Hence while Cavell acknowledges certain Christian texts as examples of engagement with moral perfectionism,[51] he opposes Emersonian Perfectionism to the teleological variant of moral perfectionism advanced within the Christian tradition. I'll address this issue further in the following section, but it is perhaps worth noting that Cavell's acknowledgment of a Christian mode of moral perfectionism and his rejection of that mode as incompatible with the commitment to autonomy that is a constitutive feature of our modernity exhibits the same structural relationship to Christianity found in Foucault's acknowledgment of a Christian mode of the ethics of the care of the self and his rejection of that mode from the perspective of the *ethos* of modernity as articulating, in its religious and secular variants, a threat to the principle of autonomy. In this respect, both Foucault and Cavell align themselves with the Greek and Roman view of the ethics of care of the self as an aesthetics of existence (that re-emerges in Romanticism and in Nietzsche) against the Christian view of the ethics of care of the self as the renunciation and transcendence of the self.

Taking these points of affinity seriously as signposts for our discussion, I note that one initial product of a dialogue between these thinkers is to provide a way of rereading, in the light of Foucault's turn to ethics, his notorious claim in *Discipline and Punish* that "[the] judges of normality are present everywhere"[52] and his elaboration of this claim in the following passage: "We are in the society of the teacher-judge, the doctor-judge, the educator-judge, the 'social-worker'-judge; it is on them that the universal reign on the normative is based; and each individual, wherever he may find himself, subjects to it his body, his gestures, his behaviour, his aptitudes, his achievements."[53] One standard response to this passage has been to take Foucault as endorsing something like Adorno's conception of the administered society, where this is taken to imply a totalizing view of modernity as a panoptic scene of domination.[54] However, a more productive approach is suggested by recourse to Cavell's reflections on a passage that, as Cavell reminds us,[55] is not written by Foucault but by John Stuart Mill:

In our times, from the highest class of society down to the lowest, everyone lives under the eye of a hostile and dreaded censorship. Not only in what concerns others, but in what concerns themselves, the individual or the family do not ask themselves, what do I prefer? Or, what would suit my character and disposition? Or, what would allow the best and highest in me to have fair play and enable it to grow and thrive? They ask themselves, what is suitable to my position? what is usually done by person of my station and peculiar circumstances? or (worse still) what is usually done by persons of a station and circumstance superior to mine? I do not mean that they choose what is customary in preference to what suits their own inclination. It does not occur to them to have any inclination except for what is customary. Thus the mind itself is bowed to the yoke: even in what people do for pleasure, conformity is the first thing thought of; they like in crowds; they exercise choice only among things commonly done; peculiarity of taste, eccentricity of conduct are shunned equally with crime, until by dint of not following their own nature they have no nature to follow: their human capacities are withered and starved; they become incapable of any strong wishes or native pleasures, and are generally without either opinions or feelings of home growth, or properly their own. Now is this, or is it not, the desirable condition of human nature?[56]

On the surface, Mill's remarks are open to precisely the same criticism that has been vigorously directed at Foucault's comments, namely, that if this depiction of the state of affairs of contemporary society were true, the author would not be in a position to offer such a description. Yet this objection misses, on Cavell's view, the point of Mill's prose:

> The condition of human nature in which we . . . do not ask whether we find our condition desirable is one in which our nature does not exist for us, a perpetuation of the threat I formulated . . . as of our haunting society, unable to sense our participation in it. Mill's writing, his philosophical mission as I put it, is to *awaken* us to the question he poses: Is this, is our experience of the currency of our world, desired by me. It is a question meant to show us that we have a right to our own desires, to have them recognized as touchstones for social criticism and reform.[57]

Mill's prose is directed to identifying and addressing what Foucault would describe as "the main danger" and so acting as a provocation to an audience that fails, as yet, to acknowledge the ethical issue raised by this danger. On this model of (re-) reading, Foucault's remarks are to be taken—as his later stress on ethics suggests—as attempting to awaken us to a threat that, on his view, our captivation by a juridical picture of freedom obstructs us from recognizing. Indeed, it is notable that Mill's argument in *On Liberty* is able to bring this issue into focus only by freeing itself from a view of our (degree of) freedom as specified by the universe of general and particular legal constraints to which we are subject. To be sure, Foucault moves from Mill's notion of custom to a focus on practices of normalization and the normalization of law (i.e., the spread of biopower) but the essential point is akin to Mill's in that it expresses the worry that "it is we who are, in the current dispensation of advanced society with progressive aspirations, the threat to our own liberty."[58] (Without developing this thought here, I note that Mill's defense of developing, and exhortation to develop, one's own individuality may be read as proposing a form of aesthetics of existence.) Notice that this reading has implications for how we are to understand Foucault's practice of genealogy by casting it as an inquiry designed to make visible the issue of, and threats to, our freedom and so prompt a change in our practical relations to ourselves and our society.

II

It may be sensible to begin the task of showing how Foucault's reflections on ethics can elucidate features of Cavell's project by exploring the fact that both are fundamentally concerned with the character and prospects of human freedom, where freedom is not to be identified with an individual's possession of a causal power to initiate action by an act of will in some way independent of antecedent causal conditions but with a certain kind of self-relation. Since Foucault and Cavell both broadly endorse Nietzsche's (Emersonian) account of freedom in terms of becoming what you are or, as he also puts it in *Twilight of the Idols,* "having the will to be responsible to oneself,"[59] it may be useful to start by sketching this account.

We can get a grip on the nature of this self-relation by considering Nietzsche's commitment to the following three claims: first, fully effective agency requires acknowledging and internalizing the norms and necessities of the practices through which agency is exercised; second, the artist exemplifies such agency; third, fully effective agency, so conceived, is freedom.[60] In advancing the first of these claims, Nietzsche is drawing attention to the fact that agency is not opposed to necessities as if capricious constraints but, rather, involves acknowledging such necessities: "A person who insisted, for example, that 'submitting abjectly' to the 'capricious' rules of grammar and punctuation inhibited or limited his powers of linguistic expression would show that he had no idea what linguistic expression *was.*"[61] In advancing the second claim, Nietzsche is adapting Kant's claim concerning genius to the notion that second nature gives the rule to art via genius and hence "that since exemplary artistic activity is neither arbitrary nor chaotic, but rather appears law-like . . . and yet since the procedures for such activity cannot be codified, the 'rule' that is given to art cannot, in Kant's words, have 'a *concept* for its determining ground': it cannot be taught, but must instead 'be gathered from the performance, i.e., from the product, which others may use to put their own talent to the test, so as to let it serve as a model, not for *imitation,* but for *following.*'"[62] Nietzsche regards such agency as exemplary because the necessities "that are in operation here are, because unformulable, also inconceivable *except as* internal to what Kant calls the 'performance,' that is, to the exemplary exercise of artistic agency itself; therefore those [necessities] cannot be held up as a standard *external* to the exercise of that agency, and so cannot be chafed against, from the perspective of that agency, as any kind of limitation upon it."[63] Because necessity is integral to all forms of agency, artistic agency as a form of agency that acknowledges necessity as a condition of itself is exemplary of agency as such. In advancing the third claim, namely, that fully effective agency conceived in terms of the exemplary character of artistic agency is freedom, Nietzsche is simply drawing the implication of the point that the "necessities through which artistic agency is exercised are . . . *internal* to the exercise of that agency, and so cannot be adduced as independently specifiable standards against which any given instance of that exercise can be assessed" by reformulating it thus: "in the exemplary exercise of agency, success is marked by the fact that the agent's will—his intention—becomes 'determinate' *in* its realisation, and only there."[64] In acting thus, I discover myself precisely *in* so acting and hence my agency is free because it is *mine*, and, as mine, I acknowledge and affirm my responsibility for it. To give style to one's character is to acknowledge and affirm one's character as one's own and thus to exhibit the will to be responsible for oneself. In the terms adopted by Emerson, freedom is the process of seeking to express (and hence realize) one's own genius.[65]

The initial issue concerning this concept of freedom that I wish to raise in relation to Cavell and Foucault hangs on noting that freedom is conceived here as an agonistic self-relation and hence as a perpetual process—there is no final *telos* to be realized. Cavell expresses the processual character of this self-relation in Emersonian terms, as the (ongoing) movement from the attained to the attainable self,[66] whereas Foucault's stance can be glossed as the (permanent) critical stance of becoming otherwise than one (currently) is.[67] To put it another way, the closely related ideas of being true to oneself (stressed by Cavell) and caring for oneself (emphasized by Foucault) do not appeal to—indeed, reject—both the idea of a true self that is to be discovered and the idea of a transcendence of selfhood.[68] I have noted that this involves a rejection of Christian forms of perfectionism, but there are two related issues with respect to Cavell's project that should be addressed here.

The first is that Foucault sees modern culture as characterized by practices that are predicated on the idea of a true (or false) self, and, in particular, he relates this dimension of modern culture to what he takes to be the secular inheritance of Christian forms of care of the self in psychoanalysis and related forms of knowledge. As Bernauer and Mahon note:

The greatest support for the psychoanalytic project as a normative discipline is the notion that sexuality is the index of one's subjectivity, of one's true self. The capacity of sexual desire to become the most revealing sign of our truest, deepest selves depends on a long historical formation through which we were constituted as subjects in a special relation to truth and sex. Traditional Christian confessional practices were reconstituted in scientific terms. . . . This modern medical management of sexuality resides "at the heart of the society of normalization."[69]

I raise this point to suggest a possible tension within Cavell's project between his rejection of the idea of a true self and his recourse to Freudian psychoanalysis. Foucault's suggestion that, to put it polemically, psychoanalysts are to be seen as secular forms of ascetic priest does, I think, place some pressure on Cavell's broad endorsement of this form of knowledge (pressure that may be seen as adding to that arising from feminist critics of Freudianism).[70]

The second point relates to a line of criticism directed at Cavell by Mulhall with respect to Cavell's attitude to Christianity. Referring to Cavell's remark that one ought to "find the *words* of the Christian to be the right words. It is the way he means them that is empty or enfeebling,"[71] Mulhall comments:

If, however, we acknowledge the truth of this remark—if we see Cavell as wishing, and so presumably needing, to employ Christian words in essentially unchristian ways—and if we put it together with his perception of the cultural impertinence of Christianity to America, then it becomes clear that Cavell's own practice runs the risk of being culturally impertinent to his fellow Americans. For if his position is characterized by its need to employ words whose original grammar articulates a perspective that is both distant from and hostile to the modern, liberal democratic conception of individual autonomy, how can he know that he avoids that estrangement?[72]

To respond to this in terms of Cavell's recourse to Emerson merely threatens to suggest that it is Emerson who is culturally impertinent and that Cavell inherits this condition. Here I think that it is pertinent to note that Foucault's investigations of Greek and Roman practices of care of the self and the transition to Christian practices of care of the self suggest that the words that Cavell (or Emerson) needs to articulate the standpoint of moral perfectionism are not words whose original grammar is tied to Christian practices (hence distant and hostile) but words whose original grammar is tied to Greek and Roman practices that Cavell (or Emerson) can be seen as reclaiming from Christianity. I note, for example, that Cavell's need of the word *conversion* may be seen as reclaiming this word from the Christian tradition that appropriated it from its central place in Greco-Roman culture.

Given that Cavell and Foucault share a commitment to this concept of freedom and to the question of its relation to modern culture, we can develop this engagement further by attending to the ways in which Foucault can help to elucidate features of Cavell's reflections on this question in its personal and political dimensions. This is the task of the following two sections.

III

In *Pursuits of Happiness* and, most recently, *Cities of Words*, Cavell explores the issue of moral perfectionism through reflection on the Hollywood comedy of remarriage—a genre of film which addresses the concern of getting a (separated) couple past some internal obstacle between them and hence back together again.[73] In taking up (and specifying) this genre, Cavell is concerned to show how, in projecting the requirement of the creation of a new woman or the new creation of a woman, films such as *The Philadelphia Story* explore the theme of the education of a woman, her becoming what she is, through exchanging words with a man to whom she was previously married such that her achievement of conversation with this man will find expression in remarriage. To begin the task of bringing Foucault to bear on this locus of Cavell's reflections on moral perfectionism, I note two points. The first is that, on Cavell's account, "marriage is an allegory in these films of what philosophers since Aristotle have thought about under the title of friendship, what it is that gives value to personal relationships, and this is a signature topic of perfectionism."[74] Friendship is a "signature topic" of moral perfectionism because Cavell sees the process of coming to stand to oneself in the self-relation that comprises freedom as one that is accomplished or brought about through the agency of a friend (the attraction of an exemplar). The second is the centrality of conversation and the idea (drawn from Milton) of "a meet and happy conversation"[75] as a mode of association, a form of life that expresses the ideal of marriage (and friendship), to these films. My suggestion, on the basis of these two points, is that the dialogic interactions that, in significant measure, bear the weight of development within these films can be elucidated by reference to Foucault's reflections on that form of *parrhesiastic* encounter concerned with the care of the self—recalling that, for Foucault, this mode of mutual engagement is distinguished by the following features: that the friend who acts as *parrhesiates* is one who runs a risk in telling the truth, that this friend is distinguished by sufficient integrity and steadiness of mind to serve as a touchstone, that the purpose of the encounter is to test the relationship of *bios* and *logos* in the person subject to this truth-telling in order that she may change (convert) her relationship to herself, become intelligible to herself.

Consider in this regard Cavell's analysis of *The Philadelphia Story*. Cavell argues that the encounter within this film manifests an engagement with perfectionism because it addresses the issue of Tracy Lord's intelligibility to herself, the relationship between *bios* and *logos*, in terms of the question of whether she desires what she protests she desires (to marry George). Thus the topic raised here is one that Foucault finds central to Hellenistic culture, namely, self-delusion (that we are unable to know exactly what we are), which Plutarch suggests arises from a form of self-love (*philautia*) that serves as the ground of a persistent (and flattering) illusion about what we are.[76] Moreover, the film follows Plutarch in proposing that coming to an honest response to this question of what she desires, overcoming this state of self-delusion concerning what one is, requires the agency and perceptions of a true friend (C. K. Dexter Haven) and underscores the point that coming to see Dexter as a true friend leads Tracy to acknowledge the truth of the rebukes that he has directed to her (e.g., that she was a scold rather than a helpmeet with respect to his drinking when they were married) and to change her relationship to herself, to overcome the confusion within her relationship to her desires, such that she becomes intelligible to herself.[77] Now I note that in Cavell's reading, in *Pursuits of Happiness*, he describes Dexter as therapist and philosopher.[78] With these descriptions, Cavell wishes to draw attention to two features of Dexter's role. By referring to Dexter as "a true therapist of some kind," Cavell is highlighting Dexter's (pedagogic) practice:

Dexter's refusal to interfere with events, anyway with people's interpretations of events (as if always aware that a liberating interpretation must be arrived at for oneself) is expressed in his typical response to those who offer interpretations of *him*, either to toss their words back to them (George: "I suppose you pretend not to believe it?" Dexter: "Yes I pretend not to"); or to use his characteristic two- or three-syllable invitation to his accusers to think again, asking "Do I?" (have a lot of cheek); "Wasn't I?" (at the party); or "Am I, Red?" (namely, loving the invasion of her privacy).[79]

(I note that in this passage, if not elsewhere, Cavell somewhat elides the other dimension of Dexter's pedagogic practice, namely, his frank rebukes of Tracy for her failure to acknowledge her own human frailty.) By referring to Dexter as (making a claim to the status of) philosopher, Cavell is emphasizing his "demand to determine for himself what is truly important and what is not,"[80] where this refers to the fact that Dexter's mind (in contrast to that of George) is not subject to public opinion concerning what is important. Moreover, this feature of Dexter is linked to the fact that his concern for truth and self-knowledge has now found expression in the act of self-mastery by which he has cured himself of his substitute addiction, namely drinking (which he had conceived as a way of opening your eyes to yourself)—and that he has done so by reading.[81] The main point that I want to make concerning this analysis is that the features that Cavell highlights are precisely those that are drawn together in the figure of the *parrhesiastes*, whose integrity and steadiness of mind distinguish him from the flatterer and whose activity takes the form of a critical pedagogy designed to bring the one subject to it to change her relationship to herself by bringing her to see for herself the need for such conversion. Dexter's pedagogy involve two modes of speech that can be found in the tradition of *parrhesia*: first, a free-speaking frankness (the original sense of *parrhesia*) and, second, a mode of, or variant on, Socratic irony. I take it that the shift from Cavell's dual descriptions of Dexter in *Pursuits of Happiness* to the unitary description of Dexter as "a kind of sage"[82] in *Cities of Words* can be aligned with this point; however, we should note that Foucault distinguishes the *parrhesiastes* from the *sage*[83] not least in that he takes the former as both focused on the present and as one who runs a risk in telling the truth. If this identification of Dexter as *parrhesiastes* has the precision that I want to claim for it, then it must also be the case that Dexter in acting as a truth-teller is running a risk in so doing.

Cavell does highlight a risk run by Dexter when he points to Dexter's, at the conclusion of the film, saying to Tracy, "I'll risk it. Will you?" This risk is acutely specified by Cavell as Dexter "saying that he'll both risk their failing again to find happiness together, and also finally risk his concept of that happiness, to find out whether he has anything in mind."[84] But this is not the kind of risk salient to the identification of Dexter as *parrhesiastes,* and perhaps because the risk involved is all too obvious Cavell does not, so far as I can see, attend to it; if this is the case then this may be a way in which Foucault's reflections on *parrhesia* and care of the self may not only help to elucidate the moral perfectionist reading of these films but add to that reading. The risk that I have in mind is prior to, and a condition of, the risk highlighted by Cavell; it is the danger that Dexter runs in speaking frankly to Tracy, confronting her with a truth-telling whose discomforting status as such she may wish to disavow, and so risking that his efforts may go awry, that she will not be responsive to his teaching—indeed that he may alienate her such that she remains alien to herself and the condition of their (risking) happiness is not realized but further frustrated by his efforts. To be sure, his assumption of this risk is bound to the circumstances of her impending—and, to his mind, unsuitable—marriage to George, but that he runs such a risk is both undeniable and indicative of his own self-knowledge, his knowing that to fail to run this risk would be to surrender the prospect of true love (I take Dexter's announcement to Tracy that he may sell *True Love,* the boat that he built for them, as both an attempt to engage her in reflection on what she desires and, hence, what she wishes to be *and* an acknowledgment of the risk that he runs in so engaging her). This point matters because it also re-emphasizes the centrality of Dexter's achievement of (a degree of) self-mastery to his playing the *parrhesiastic* role of true friend. In the opening scene of the film, we see Dexter almost come to strike Tracy before instead pushing her to the ground as he abandons their home and later we learn of his alcoholism—yet the Dexter who serves as *parrhesiastes* can only play this role precisely because he has overcome his tendencies to violence and dependence on drink, successfully confronted discomforting truths about himself; given what hangs on the success or failure of his enterprise for him (for what he most cares about), his parrhesiastic activity imposes a burden of self-restraint on him that requires the full exercise of the self-mastery that he has struggled to achieve in the intervening period.

In advancing this claim that Foucault's reflections on *parrhesia* and care of the self can help to elucidate features of Cavell's readings of comedies of remarriage in terms of moral perfectionism, I venture one further dimension in which I take Foucault's concerns to help elucidate Cavell's readings—here the issue is the relationship between these films and democratic politics. For Cavell, the comedies of remarriage can be seen "as inviting a conversation with the society of which it is a reflection and upon which it permits perspective."[85] Here I simply note that, for Foucault, the ethics of care of the self links the personal and political in the sense that these are related domains within which the quest for self-mastery is worked out and the *parrhesiastic* practices tied to care of the self involve seeking to cultivate persons who, precisely because they have acquired (a sufficient degree of) self-mastery, are able to conduct themselves appropriately to others in both domains. It is notable in this respect that Tracy Lord's education concerns not only her private conduct (say, in her acting as a scold rather than a helpmeet in her marriage to Dexter) but also her relationship to the public sphere; as Cavell notes, it is a feature of the film that initially "her despising of publicity is rather too strong for one of normal democratic tolerances"[86] and yet by its conclusion she has come to accept the place of such publicity (pictures of the remarriage are taken to be published in *SPY* magazine). A similar point can be made with regard to Dexter's overcoming of his tendency to violence and alcoholism as not only the condition of his responsiveness to Tracy but also to the staff and editor of *SPY* magazine (in an early scene, Dexter is identified as having broken the camera of the magazine's photographer when she tried to get photographs of his original honeymoon with Tracy). To my mind these points confirm the sense in which Cavell's engagements with comedies of remarriage can be viewed as analyses of instances of the mode of *parrhesia* connected to the care of the self. However, having hereby raised the issue of the relationship of moral perfectionism and democratic politics or the ethics of care of the self in its political dimension, let me turn to focus more directly on this topic.

III

Consider to begin the following comment by Jim Conant:

Many a theorist of democracy has discerned within "the democratic movement" a tendency to suppress democracy's capacity for criticism from within—a pressure to collapse into (what de Tocqueville called) "a tyranny of the majority." John Adams, Matthew Arnold, William James, Thomas Jefferson, Alexander Hamilton, John Stuart Mill, Alexis de Tocqueville (not to mention Emerson and Thoreau) all dread that debasement of democracy that both Mill and Emerson refer to as "the despotism of conformity." There is a perfectionist strain within the tradition of democratic thought that takes it as a matter of urgent concern that the antiperfectionist tendencies latent within the democratic movement be kept from eroding democracy's resources for criticism from within—where the pressure of such criticism is taken to be essential to democracy's capacity to remain faithful to its own aspirations. Each of the theorists listed above emphasizes that democracy can flourish only if its citizens cultivate—rather than disdain—those virtues which were formerly the sole prerogative of aristocracy (such as independence of mind, disregard for fashion, eccentricity of conduct).[87]

We can distinguish two related kinds of threat to which this passage alerts us. The first is the failure on the part of political thought to discern the problem to which the perfectionist draws attention. The second is the failure on the part of political culture to cultivate citizens who manifest the appropriate virtues. This section endeavors to deploy Foucault to elucidate and extend Cavell's concerns in relation to these two threats.

When Foucault remarks that at bottom "despite the differences in epochs and objectives, the representation of power has remained under the spell of monarchy. In political thought and analysis we *still have not cut off the head of the king,*" he is drawing attention to "the importance that the theory of power gives to the problem of right and violence, law and illegality, freedom and will, and especially the state and sovereignty."[88] This claim has two dimensions. The first, and most commonly noted, is that Foucault is suggesting that this way of picturing power fails to grasp (renders invisible) forms of power, modes of government, that do not take the form of, say, legal prohibition—that is, forms of power that operate through disciplinary and regulatory normalizing practices (which we may take, I think, as an analogue or extension of the despotism of conformity). The second is that citizenship is construed in exclusively juridical terms as an office or status. What I'd like to venture at this stage is the claim that Foucault provides here a framework within which to elucidate Cavell's reflections on Rawls and, more specifically, his use of Nora from Ibsen's *A Doll's House* as a way of articulating his concerns about Rawls's theory of justice.

Discussions of Cavell's reflections on Rawls have understandably focused on the point that Cavell argues that Rawls is committed to too contractualist a view of democratic citizenship. I'll sketch the main features of this argument before turning to the closer focus on Nora that I want to develop.[89] There are, Cavell notes, two instances of what may be called the conversation of justice in *A Theory of Justice*. The first conversation concerns the constitution of the original position and involves a process whereby principles and intuitions are matched against one another. This conversation of justice comes to an end in a state of reflective equilibrium. The second conversation concerns the degree of compliance with, or departure from, the principle of justice decided in the first conversation, where "the measure of departure from the ideal is left importantly to intuition."[90] For Rawls, it seems, this conversation also involves the matching of principles and intuitions, not least in the sense that "if an initial [i.e., intuitive] judgement that an injustice is being perpetuated cannot ultimately be backed up by reference to (or articulated in terms of) a principle of justice, then it must be rejected; and those of us to whom the accusation was voiced can think of ourselves and 'our conduct [a]s above reproach.'"[91] Cavell's suspicion is that "Rawls is taking encouragement from the proof concerning the resolution for the original position, to regard 'above reproach' as a rational response to the question of affirming a plan of life in our actual society."[92] But this could only be the case if we could expect that the proof of an optimal resolution in the first conversation also held for the second conversation—and Cavell argues that there is "no such proof to be expected that the conversation of justice has an optimal, or any, resolution, when it is directed to the constitution of our actual set of institutions."[93] Cavell's grounds for this claim are articulated by sketching how the appeal to intuition in the second conversation differs from the appeal to intuition in the first conversation:

In the latter case, our "judgements of the basic structure of society" which are to be matched with the principles of justice are, before that matching, made "intuitively, and we can note whether applying these principles would lead us to make the same judgements . . . in which we have the greatest confidence . . . ; or whether, in cases where our present judgements are in doubt and given with hesitation . . . , these principles offer a resolution which we can affirm on reflection." . . . But the matching of principles with considered judgements yielding reflective equilibrium does not describe the process of bringing a present perception . . . under what Kant describes . . . as reflective judgement. In the former case, intuition is left behind. In the latter case, intuition is left in place.[94]

Cavell acknowledges that there is "an idea or picture of matching in play" in both cases, but insists on the difference between them. In arriving at reflective equilibrium "the picture is that judgement finds its derivation in a principle, something more universal, rational, objective, say a standard, from which it achieves justification or grounding."[95] Whereas in reflective judgment, "the idea is of the expression of a conviction whose grounding remains subjective—say myself—but which expects or claims justification from the (universal) concurrence of other subjectivities, on reflection; call this the acknowledgment of matching."[96] The failure to mark the distinction between the modes of matching at play in the two conversations— that is, the treatment of the second conversation as involving the same picture of matching as the first—entails that Rawls's principle-based picture of consent is carried over from the first conversation to the second. This has two related consequences. First, it appears that our (rational) consent to society is proportional to the compliance of society to the principles of justice. Thus, for Rawls, the degree to which I am joined to society is simply a function of the degree to which it embodies the principles of justice. But this picture precludes the possibility of the experience, highlighted by Cavell's non-proportional account of consent, of being answerable for society as mine. It occludes the sense in which I can experience myself as implicated in, and compromised by, unjust actions or practices performed in my name; the sense that I cannot, in truth, avoid responsibility for such actions and that this is part and parcel of the damage that such unjust actions or practices do. Second, it appears that we are only open to, or obligated to engage with, charges of injustice expressed in terms of these principles. The implication of this claim is that the nature and form of our political identities are (exhaustively) specified and fixed by the principles of justice. Political activity does not concern the exploration, extension, revision, or transformation of our political identities but, rather, the affirmation and reaffirmation of these identities—the depth and extent of our political identities is determined in advance. It is this point to which Cavell is referring us when he comments: "It seems to me that Rawls is taking encouragement from the proof concerning the resolution for the original position, to regard 'above reproach' as a rational response to the question of affirming a plan of life in our actual society. Whereas this bottom line is not a response to but a refusal of further conversation."[97] It is this failure to acknowledge this refusal as a refusal that Cavell stresses, and the implications of this are drawn out thus: what calls for response in my expression of a conviction of injustice is not that the conviction of injustice to which I give voice can be articulated in terms of a principle of justice, but, rather, that in giving voice to this conviction I speak for you as well as myself, I (claim to) speak for *us*; to refuse to acknowledge the conviction I express as an offer of conversation (if it is not—if it cannot be—expressed by reference to the principles of justice) is to deny me a political voice, it is to render me politically voiceless, mute. It is this experience of voicelessness which Cavell finds expressed by Nora in Ibsen's *A Doll's House*. In this play, Nora struggles to express, to bring to expression, her inchoate sense of injustice: "'I could tear myself to pieces'"[98] and "'I must find out which is right—the world or I.'"[99] The dilemma in which Nora finds herself is that to speak in the language of the moral consensus, represented by her husband, Torvald, who has managed "for the eight years of their marriage, to control her voice, dictate what it may utter and the manner in which it may utter it,"[100] is not be able to give expression to her conviction of injustice; while to find other, new, words and ways of speaking capable of expressing this conviction is to be held not to speak in terms which we are required to acknowledge, that is, not to speak (in the relevant sense) at all—as, for example, when Torvald responds to her need to know if she or the world is right "'You're ill, Nora—I almost believe you're out of your senses.'"[101] or, again, when he disqualifies her voice by claiming "'You're talking like a child.'"[102] What Cavell draws to our attention with the example of Nora (and Torvald) is the way in which the moral consensus of society denies Nora's (political) voice and, thus, leaves her out of the conversation of justice—her (political) identity remains obscure because the terms on which she could make intelligible (i.e., express) her sense of injustice are denied to her. Thus, as Cavell puts it, Nora has been deprived of a voice in her own (political) history.[103] The problem with Rawls's position on Cavell's reading is, thus, that Rawls's account of our political identities and the field of our political voices as (contractually) specified and fixed by the principles of justice entails that his theory of justice is blind to the possibility of the problem that "the whole framework of principles in terms of which [we] must conduct the second conversation of justice is experienced as so pervasively and systematically unresponsive to [our] suffering that it appears to stifle [us], to constitute a vocabulary in which nothing that can be said truly speaks [our] mind, gives expression to [our] experience."[104]

Now let us reflect on Nora as she is presented in Ibsen's play in the light of Foucault's attention to normalizing modes of power. We can note first that it is a feature of one type of such forms of power that they govern through practical identities by articulating norms that are authorized and underwritten by scientific knowledge of the subject of these identities (e.g., wife, mother, woman) and so discipline the formation of these forms of subjectivity in the name of truth. In this respect, Torvald's appeals to, and rebukes of, Nora can be read as invocations and expressions of the normative and normalizing determination of her identity against her inchoate appeal to a humanity that is not so fixed. If the language of Torvald's remonstrations suggests that Nora is being situated by him in relation to the (biopolitically privileged) figure of *the hysterical woman*, we can grasp Nora's struggle to articulate her sense of injustice as the necessary inchoateness of someone confronting a moral consensus that grounds its authority on the epistemic claim to know and determine the truth of her being. Here I link Cavell's sense of the plight of Nora as deprived of a voice in the conversation of justice to the following words of Foucault: "a system of constraint becomes truly intolerable when the individuals who are affected by it don't have the means of modifying it. This can happen when such a system becomes intangible as a result of its being considered a moral or religious imperative, or a necessary consequence of medical science."[105] And I introduce the following passage from Foucault as giving expression to the demand of responsiveness:

It is through revolt that subjectivity (not that of great men but that of whomever) introduces itself into history and gives it the breath of life. A delinquent puts his life into balance against absurd punishments; a madman can no longer accept confinement and the forfeiture of his rights; a people refuses the regime which oppresses it. This does not make the rebel in the first case innocent, nor does it cure in the second, and it does not assure the third rebel of the promised tomorrow. One does not have to be in solidarity with them. One does not have to maintain that these confused voices sound better than the others and express the ultimate truth. For there to be a sense in listening to them and in searching for what they have to say, it is sufficient that they exist and that they have against them so much which is set up to silence them. . . . All the disenchantments of history amount to nothing: it is due to such voices that the time of men does not have the form of an evolution, but precisely that of a history.[106]

In relation to Nora, we may say that the sense of Foucault's remarks is to claim that it is by virtue of the refusal of those who have been denied a voice in their own political history to accept this denial (to accept that the truth of their identities or the meaning of their words is fixed) that *we* inhabit historical time. The point, expressed here with deliberately polemical force, is that we are historical beings insofar as we are free beings, that is, beings who exercise their freedom in attempting to shape their own lives by, for example, resisting external determinations of who and what they are. In summary, then, my claim is that Foucault's reflections on biopower can helpfully elucidate Cavell's recourse to Nora by linking her plight to the two dimensions of the problem posed by the failure to cut off the King's head in political theory and that in doing so Foucault provides further illumination of the need for responsiveness to demands such as Nora's.

But if there is to be such responsiveness, if we are not to succumb to the Torvald in each of us, then our democratic culture must cultivate citizens who are responsive in this way, who cultivate the virtues of listening. In respect of Cavell, this returns us to the sense in which comedies of remarriage have a public or political dimension in that both gesture toward the possibility of a political ethics of conversation and indicate the fact that caring for oneself extends across both personal and political domains. Having argued that Cavell's analyses of comedies of remarriage may be read as engaging these films as portraying *parrhesiastic* encounters, I would like to suggest that Cavell's contribution to, and intervention in, democratic culture consists in both his efforts to provide us with examples of such responsiveness to others, to draw to our attention this overlooked dimension of modern culture, and to exemplify such responsiveness in his encounters with the works of modern culture (I note the democratic impulse in

Cavell's *choice*—perhaps as a necessity for him—to focus on Hollywood films rather than confine his attention to avant-garde art). Somewhat tentatively I would like to propose that Cavell's conversation with Rawls be viewed as such a *parrhesiastic* encounter in which Cavell addresses his colleague Rawls (and, given Rawls's exemplary status, so addresses contemporary liberal political theorists and, more generally, contemporary liberals) in order to try to bring him to acknowledge a blind spot in his understanding of liberal democratic society (and so in himself as a citizen of such a society). In this respect, the complexity of Cavell's prose in his Carus lectures, its hesitancy and evident anxieties, attests both to Cavell's concern as to his entitlement to act as *parrhesiastes* and to his commitment in virtue of his respect (that is, collegial friendship) for Rawls to so act. In this encounter, Cavell may be said to manifest the ethos that Foucault identifies with modernity, namely, a critical questioning of what is given to us as natural, necessary, and obligatory oriented to the undefined work of freedom.

Conclusion

In this essay I hope to have begun to sketch some ways in which a productive dialogue between the works of Foucault and Cavell might be initiated. Certainly I am aware that the sketches offered here constitute only a beginning, an entry point into such a process of reciprocal elucidation; not the least of the issues that I have passed over being the relation of Foucault's reflections on political criticism as an art of reflective indocility to Cavell's reading of the social contract. However, I do hope to have accomplished the main aim of this essay, namely, to have established a *prima facie* case for the value of constructing an encounter between these thinkers by showing how Foucault's work can help to elucidate features of Cavell's project (and, although this has not been my primary focus, vice versa) and I also hope that one product of the initial efforts presented here is to draw attention to the significance of Foucault's reflections on the ethics of care of the self and Cavell's work on moral perfectionism for political theory.

Acknowledgments

I am grateful to Bert van den Brink, Tom Dumm, Andrew Norris, Aaron Ridley, Jeff Stickney, and Jim Tully for rapid comments on the penultimate draft of this essay and to Andrew Norris for allowing me sufficient time to write it.

CHAPTER EIGHT

Stanley Cavell and the Limits of Appreciation

Ted Cohen

Introduction

Some of Stanley Cavell's earliest work was in aesthetics, and I am going to begin by saying something about a problem in aesthetics, making use of one of Cavell's most powerful and fruitful ideas, the concept of *acknowledgment*.[1] That idea was not offered by Cavell in one of his works in aesthetics, but I will adapt it nevertheless, and then I will try relating this aesthetical matter to a moral and political problem Cavell himself has discussed in terms of the human need to acknowledge one another.

I will say something about what it may mean to acknowledge one another when we do not feel the same way about certain works of art, and then I will ask how the burden of acknowledgment changes when our disagreements are not about how we feel, but about how we act.

Aesthetical Disagreement

I have argued elsewhere that sometimes when there are differences in the appreciation of art, neither side can claim to be right and the other wrong, but that this is not the end of the matter, or shouldn't be. In such a case if my feeling for the work is different from yours, I am entitled to my feeling, but I am not justified in thinking yours illegitimate, and, further, I must somehow incorporate your sensibility in my sense of things. I argued for this, taking as an example various degrees of appreciation of the music of Wagner. I will not repeat that argument, but simply offer its upshot.

I think there is something very nasty in Wagner's music, and I think I *hear* it in the music. In this I am like Thomas Mann, who said: "I find an element of Nazism, not only in Wagner's questionable literature; I find it also in his 'music.'"[2] And this has left the music so disturbingly offensive—as it sounds to me—that I do not care to hear it. Mann, on the other hand, continues his remark with this: " . . . albeit I have so loved that work that even today I am deeply stirred whenever a few bars of music from this world impinge on my ear."[3]

So: Mann finds Wagner's music disturbing, but he loves it nonetheless. Here is another assessment, this from someone who also cares for the music but hears it differently from Mann: ". . . Wagner expected his audience to admire his heroes and heroines when in fact he presents a succession of underbred neurotics, portrayed with consummate skill. As no one else can, he paints all that is irrational, morbid, cranky, self-destructive, 'Wagnerite' in human nature as it really is; that is to say, in all its formidable enchantment."[4]

That comes close to my own sense of this music, although I find the "underbred neurotics" less interesting than Auden does, and I find nothing "enchanting" about them. Nor do I find them curious and amusing, as perhaps Toscanini did when he said this, speaking of the second-act love scene in *Tristan*: "If they were Italians, they would already have seven children; but they're Germans, so they're still talking."[5]

I find the music disturbing and I do not love it at all; some listeners simply love the music and find nothing troubling. Mann loves the music despite feeling troubled by it. Auden cares deeply for the music, I think, but he hears it as an accurate portrayal of something disturbing and nasty. I cannot tell just how Toscanini heard the music, but he certainly found it worth playing.

My thesis, if I dare to dignify it with that word, is that Mann, Auden, Toscanini, and I are all secure in our relationships with Wagner's music. None of us is making a mistake, none of us is having an inept or inappropriate response.

A corollary to my thesis is that you cannot just dismiss these equally legitimate responses to Wagner's music and go on to say that however particular listeners may find themselves when hearing the music, there is still the question of whether the crap in Wagner's music does or should diminish the artistic quality of the music. You cannot do that because, in the end, the difficult fact is that the crap leaves the music unaffected for some, damages or distorts the music but not irretrievably for others, and ruins the music for yet others.

My claim is that the Wagnerite is perfectly legitimate in his enjoyment of this music, and in his capacity to overlook the anti-Semitism in the operas, but that he is no more legitimate than I in my disgust. My world is one in which the music of Wagner is distasteful. Your world is one in which the music of Wagner is endlessly engaging. I have to find room in my world for you and your Wagner along with me and my Wagner. If I don't, then I forfeit my claim to *human*, moral responsibility, for it comes with an obligation not to write you off, not to consign you to some other world I have nothing to do with. It has to *mean* something in my world that you are in it loving Wagner, for, after all, *the* world is no more mine than yours.

I hope you agree with this, but even if you don't, you likely will think it an innocuous idea. But when the idea is extended to differences in feeling about matters of moral and political gravity, the idea becomes more difficult and also more interesting.

Moral Disagreement

No philosopher I know has written better about what it is to be human than Stanley Cavell, and the question of what it is to be human arises with great force and drama in arguments over the permissibility of abortion. This, too, Cavell has written about with depth and sensitivity. In nearly a half-century's work, Stanley Cavell has contributed an astonishing variety of *ideas*, in the form of both new topics for philosophy and new ways of thinking about old topics. Less than theses or "methods," he has presented *ways* of thinking about things. One thing he has thought and written about is *conversation*, about what it means for people to speak with one another, which is a way—perhaps *the* way—in which people simply are *with* one another. One particular kind of conversation occurs in the arguments we have with one another over moral and political matters, and, in particular, when the matters have to do with what it is to be human.

My question is, what are we to make of it when we cannot carry these arguments to a conclusion? What we are to do to remain together when we cannot agree?

Cavell himself has discussed one striking example of such a conversation in his remarks about abortion and the abortion debate (*CR*, p. 373). Cavell's remarks are especially intricate because he is interested not only in the argument as an exchange between human beings, but also in the fact that what they may seem to be arguing about is whether some other thing is a human being. Thus the question of acknowledgment, or appreciation, as I am calling it, is reticulated. In my Wagner example I was concerned with my appreciation of someone whose appreciation of the music differs from mine. Here we are dealing with the question of how, and whether, to appreciate someone who himself fails to appreciate someone.[6]

There is no better statement of the topic than Cavell's. He says: "If it makes sense to speak of seeing human beings as human beings, then it makes sense to imagine that a human being may lack the capacity to see human beings as human beings" (*CR*, p. 378).

But Cavell goes on to conclude, in a brilliant piece of analysis and argument, that the abortion opponent cannot sincerely take a fetus to be *a* human. He notes, however, that one may indeed be struck by a feeling of abhorrence at the prospect of abortion, and then adds: "A person can understandably be blind to these perceptions. I claim not to be, and yet I claim to be a liberal on the issue of abortion—not merely tolerant of it but passionately in favor of its legalization, convinced that those who wish to oppose it legally are tyrannical and sentimental hypocrites" (*CR*, pp. 373–74).

I found this a startling, unexpected declaration. But perhaps Cavell is speaking of certain specific people when he calls them tyrannical and sentimental hypocrites, and, if so, he may well be right. In fact I'm sure Cavell was speaking of specific people, because it would be utterly uncharacteristic of him to speak crudely of all people, including ones of whom he knows nothing. If someone meant *all* those who wish to oppose abortion legally, then I would not follow him, for I think it simply isn't true that every abortion opponent is a hypocrite.

There is no doubt that some people are appalled by abortion, and even by its prospect, and there can be no question about the fact of their feeling. I suppose one might grant the feeling and still think these people wrong to push for legal sanctions, but why would that be *hypocritical?* I don't even see that it would be *wrong* for them to lobby for anti-abortion legislation.

But now we are talking morality and politics, and, you see, my defense of aesthetic toleration and mutual appreciation will have to play out differently, because now it is not merely a question of acknowledging the legitimacy of one another's feelings, because *something will have to be done.*

As I see it, it is a juvenile response to one's opponents simply to suppose them ignorant, stupid, or evil. That is a way of denying them a place in one's world, and although sometimes one's opponents are indeed benighted, they are not always so, and it is a grown-up sense of the world to recognize this.

But something has to be done, and what the pro-choicers want done is not what the pro-lifers want done. It is one thing for you to enjoy Wagner's music while I avoid it, and for both of us to credit one another with humanity and dignity, and quite another for us to engage in this mutual acceptance when something has been done that the other despises. And yet, surely, this is exactly what has to be done unless our conversation is to end and we are to be resigned, truly, to being in a war of all against all. This is not an easy thing to do (it is not really all that easy for the Wagner-lovers and the Wagner-haters to share a musical world), and I do not know that it is possible to do it. I do know that it has to be attempted, and that forsaking the attempt is no less than forsaking the idea that we might live together.

Living Together

I am not a political scientist, a political historian, or someone with any sophisticated understanding of politics, and so you will, I hope, forgive my attempt at a naïve formulation.

There are three ways in which we can imagine sharing the world with one another, if we think of them broadly and crudely. One would be for us to be the same as one another, with essentially the same feelings, attitudes, and preferences. One would be for us to be different from one another but to agree to live close by without interfering with one another. The third would be for us to be different from one another, but not only to live near one another but also to bend some effort at an *appreciation* of one another in all our differences.

This may well echo a classical distinction present in the works of Hobbes and Spinoza, and I leave it to others to articulate that source. I take the biblical story of the Tower of Babel to mean that the first option is closed, that God himself does not wish us to be the same, to speak the same language and have the same ambition. But then there are two remaining possibilities. One is tolerance of a minimal sort, in which we abide one another, rather as young children, not yet able to participate in group activities, are still playing near one another, aware of one another, and carrying on what is called "parallel play."

My preference, obviously, is for the other alternative, the one in which we not only abide one another, but try for something deeper, something more than a grudging concession that the world belongs to all of us. Whether we can manage that depth I do not know. I do know that it is to be hoped for.

Imagination

I may well already have departed from Cavell's idea of acknowledgment, but now I will move even farther away, although I think I am still in the spirit of that idea.

What does it mean to appreciate someone else, and, in particular, someone whose feelings are different? For a while I have been developing the thesis that the ability to imagine oneself to be another is an absolute prerequisite for the competent appreciation of much narrative art, and maybe other art as well.[7] It seems to me often required that one somehow put oneself in touch with the feelings, say, of characters in a novel or movie, and that one does this, if one can, by achieving a kind of imaginative identification with that character. It may also be required that one do this with an artist, say a poet, in order to gain a robust sense of how things seem to that person. It is only by doing this that one can pass beyond simply describing the relevant feelings and discover what it could be to *have* those feelings.

The same requirement seems to me to press on those of us engaged in moral conversations and arguments. We must somehow appreciate one another. Now of course this cannot mean that we must *agree* with one another, and so we cannot take agreement as the only sign that this appreciation has been achieved. It is for this reason that I have supposed that the critical "identification" is metaphorical, not literal, and I have tried to understand the phenomenology of that undertaking.

Of course, one can go too far with this thought. Suppose my opponent is someone who wishes to enact laws that would disenfranchise Jews, or maybe even kill them. What can it mean to share my world with this person? Am I required to appreciate him, and let it go at that?

One may go too far with this thought even in matters of aesthetics. When I had delivered a lecture in which my remarks about Wagner were a part, my friend Peter Kivy, an astute philosopher with a special interest in music, told me he'd found what I said compelling, but that he didn't think I could make the same points about Beethoven's music. I think he is right. I can find a place in my world for those who love Wagner, and I expect them to find a place in their worlds for me and my distaste for Wagner. But it is much harder for me to locate someone who finds Beethoven disagreeable. In fact I find it easier to keep company with someone who likes no music at all than with someone who loves some music but can't stand Beethoven. So I think Kivy is right, and yet I have no idea how to explain and justify the difference.

But then, how far is too far? There is no rule for this, but it isn't bad to deal with these monstrosities as they come up, sizing up their monstrousness and seeing whether one can live with them.

Playing Games

There may be a lesson to be learned from game-playing. What is it to be a good loser? It surely doesn't mean being happy that one has lost. But it also doesn't mean writing off one's loss as if it weren't real or somehow didn't count. This is the sort of thing one encounters with sporting opponents who, as my brother Stephen astutely puts it, never seem to feel that you've won. They feel that they've lost, and would have won if only they had played their best, or the sun hadn't been blinding, or the umpire had been accurate, or whatever. Thus they depreciate you and your victory.

Of course the analogy with game-playing is imperfect, but it is worth pressing. Unless the game is degenerate, your opponent wants to win, and you know he wants to win. You want to win, and he knows that. Your aim and his aim are incompatible, but neither is illegitimate, and you both know that. In order to win, you must risk losing. And when you lose, what then? In the moment you may be so disappointed and distressed that you have no equilibrium, but what do you think and feel when you've regained your balance?

One thing to think is that this is just how things are. It was always a possibility, when you took up game-playing, that this would happen. You may look forward to another game, hoping for a better result, but right now you will have to live with this.

Is political life a game? (Don't say "just" a game. There may be more to games than you've thought.) No, of course not: you never explicitly undertook to play with your political opponents. And yet there is a comparable need, the need to live *with* them even through winning and losing.

Let us have a final look at that apparently childish tale, the story of the Tower of Babel. God has placed us in one world, a world no more and no less yours than mine, and He has rendered us different from one another. The task, then, must be for us to make the best of it, and that, I suppose, at its best, is what political life is about. The dimensions of this task are enormous, and in charting them one does well to look to Stanley Cavell's appreciation of the idea of acknowledgment.

CHAPTER NINE

Cavell and Political Romanticism

Espen Hammer

On a first reading, Cavell's work may seem to have little to offer by way of political reflection. Although the force of his entries, say, on Rousseau and Rawls, or on chattel slavery and civil disobedience, is undeniable, it appears that his intellectual efforts have largely been spent on his attempt to lay claim to the inheritance of Wittgenstein's and Austin's visions of ordinary language philosophy (with Thoreau and Emerson as their American counterparts), as well as on the extension of his emphasis on the ordinary into a number of aesthetic domains, including film, drama, literature, music, and dance. Throughout his whole career, the problem of skepticism—its significance and location within the economy of human knowing and practice—has been the central and organizing concern of his work; hence his thinking seems intimately tied to epistemology, or rather to the dismantling of the traditional claims of epistemology by means of methods and procedures extracted from ordinary language philosophy.

This (I would say standard) picture of Cavell's work is not so much false as it is one-sided. The more one reads him, the clearer it becomes that most of his thinking, even when its distance from the political appears to be considerable, actually is inseparable from some form of socio-political articulation. This is true of his early writing on the first-person plural and continues to be true of his reflections on Shakespeare and Hollywood cinematic drama, and even of his approaches to seemingly autonomous subjects such as dance and opera. Although he never endeavors to provide final answers to the classical problems of political theory (such as "Why ought I to obey the state?" or "What is the correct relation between the individual and her society?"), his work as a whole seeks to articulate a vision of human intersubjectivity that can be neither divorced from the political nor identified with it. Rather, it represents a philosophical rethinking of the political that seeks to bring out and locate what Cavell calls a "grammar of society."[1]

Attempts to flesh out the political dimension of Cavell's thinking have often tended to focus on his interpretation and application of Rousseauian contract theory, and on how that position, providing an account of how citizens can speak politically both for and to one another, challenges Rawls's more static account of the contractual bond.[2] In conjunction with his reconstruction of the universal voice of Kantian aesthetics and his inheritance of Austin and Wittgenstein's methods of ordinary language philosophy, the deployment of Rousseau produces a powerful conception of the political as constituted by networks of communicative acts of self-expression that, in the absence of pre-given universals, seek to authorize themselves as representative. The "we" in Cavell is a contested, fragile space of individual human voices that are exercised without any communal or metaphysical assurances. While I certainly do not call into question the significance of this line of reception, there are at least two reasons why I believe it is limited. First, it is too easily restricted to becoming simply a minor corrective to liberal political theory, thus failing to record the existential and intellectual burden it places on those who seek to act rationally as social and political critics of their own society. Second, as Andrew Norris has argued, since Rousseau's own theory of the contract is directed toward uncovering a mode of speech whereby the citizenry can acclaim or not acclaim its government, that is, how legislation is possible, it does not fully do justice to Cavell's interest in conversation, where the task is not to found the republic or deliberate about its fundamental principles of justice but to provide ongoing challenges to the political content for which citizens (implicitly or explicitly) take responsibility.[3]

In this paper I want to think of Cavell's philosophical vision as a form of political romanticism, and I want to question it in terms of criticisms raised from a realist political perspective by Hegel and Carl Schmitt.

By exposing Cavell's political thinking to these, in my view, significant criticisms of political romanticism, I hope to bring out its strength as well as its potential weaknesses. While I believe there are readings of Cavell that escape the Hegelian and Schmittian charges, his political romanticism is inherently unstable and needs further elaboration in order to avoid an unacceptable aestheticization of the political. The way I set this up is to suggest that there is a vacillation in Cavell's work between a politics of beauty and a politics of the sublime. Only the latter is consistent with Cavell's philosophical modernism. I also argue that Cavell seeks to juxtapose and ultimately combine elements from at least three different traditions of political thought: liberalism, republicanism, and what I call a redemptive mode of political reckoning. In so doing, I will be interested in the relationship between politics and aesthetics, and in how the totalizing political critique that preoccupies Cavell involves acts of radical negation of accepted social authority.

Political Romanticism

The relationship between politics and romanticism has recently received considerable attention among philosophers interested in the intersections between literary studies and wider social and political issues. In the work of Jean-Luc Nancy and Philippe Lacoue-Labarthe, for example, romanticism, while often conspicuous in its apparent naiveté, is being viewed as having been an unacknowledged, deep source of motivation for many of the most radical political movements that have arisen since the French revolution. Politics, they write, must "[pass] through the literary."[4] Less radical, though equally intent on uniting the concerns of romanticism and politics, is the work of Richard Eldridge, which, like that of Nancy and Lacoue-Labarthe, inscribes romanticism within a philosophical modernism centered on self-authentication and self-authorization. Romantic writing becomes an arena for achieving autonomy or independence by articulating and making transparently endorsable the grounds on which human activity is able to count as reasoned.[5]

Hardly any contemporary philosopher has gone further than Cavell, however, in trying to envision what the political meaning and implication of romanticism amount to.[6] Starting with his 1972 study of Henry David

Thoreau, *The Senses of Walden*, and continuing in an extended collection of installments up to, and including, the important 1990 discussion of Emersonian perfectionism, *Conditions Handsome and Unhandsome*, Cavell has developed and elaborated a complex account of the praxeological dimension of romanticism, emphasizing not only self-authentication but also how the process of self-authorization involves reference to a community of mutually responsible individuals who consider each other as free and equal. Taking his lead from Rousseau's account of the idea (or explanatory myth) of the social contract, Cavell views each member of the polis, each consenting individual, as answerable not only to, but also for, the society and its normative arrangements. Thus, citizenship becomes extensionally equivalent with autonomy: it is in the field of the polis that the individual works out the normative content for which he or she is willing and capable of rationally taking responsibility, and in so doing uncovers the extent to which the individual's singular voice, aiming to speak for others while also accepting that others speak for it, is representative of others.

This—very roughly—is Cavell's idealized vision of pure politics. Its *modus operandi*, as it were, can be articulated in terms of what Ernesto Laclau calls an "empty signifier": that any particular act of political intervention determines itself as being of universal value or implication, thus aspiring to hegemony—hence the universal can never be fixed or endowed with a concrete content.[7] In some cases, though, a withdrawal from the community (exile inner or outer) may be required in order to rethink the conditions of consent. Following Rousseau, Cavell emphasizes that mere withdrawal from the community is different from withdrawal of consent from it: "Dissent is not the undoing of consent but a dispute about its content."[8] It is both possible and reasonable to reject society as it stands (because it is unfaithful to what I take us to have consented to) while consenting to the normative order which it should (because I take us to have consented to it) have conformed to. Indeed, the political romanticist will be someone who is prepared to speak in the name of a normative order which may fundamentally challenge present arrangements.

Being rational is thus to fully accept responsibility for one's own choices. The everyday conformist, on the contrary, rejects responsibility for the laws conferred on every citizen by the idea of the social contract. Rather than defining the extent to which he can conceive of himself as author of the social order, such an agent, by failing to estrange himself from prevailing opinion (as well as from himself), lets the community speak for him, yet without interrogating its right to do so. Conformity can thus be viewed as a form of unconsciousness; having repressed or forgotten their responsibility, conformists fail to define and express their (political) selves—as a result, they fall short, on Cavell's view, of obtaining a political existence.

Since it demands the reasoned agreement of all, the social contract can only be in full existence insofar as each individual is choosing to exercise freedom. In imperfect societies (that is, in societies as we know them) the bonds between citizens are secured by obedience to agreements that are partial and secret. In such societies, rather than acting openly on behalf of the polis, the citizens do not freely declare the basis of their consent; instead, they remain private, without a real voice, deprived of genuine citizenship. In Cavell's reading of Thoreau, which I will return to in a moment, the withdrawal from the community becomes a concomitant re-connection with it: the more isolated the writer is from his community, the more openly and freely can he call upon his neighbors. Acquiring citizenship becomes a question of finding one's own voice—of freely and individually assuming or declaring a position from which to speak.

Cavell's account of the polis, combining Rousseau's theory of the social contract with a Wittgensteinian version of everyday language, is thus radically different from that of many writers who, like him, have attempted to appropriate the philosophy of the late Wittgenstein for purposes of political reflection and analysis. In most cases, such attempts have generated some form or other of neo-Aristotelianism or communitarianism.[9] Hannah Pitkin, for example, relates the political dimension of Wittgenstein's *Philosophical Investigations* to his apparent wish to conceptualize the public nature of human speech—how intelligibility presupposes a publicly recognized and socially enforced system of rules that *a priori* excludes political aspirations toward the purely private and therefore partial.[10] Following Arendt, Pitkin regards the private as an entirely depoliticized sphere of necessity, whereas the public becomes the sphere of recognized judging and acting. In a kindred study, *Realism and Imagination in Ethics*, Sabina Lovibond tries to demonstrate that acceptable moral and political precepts are those that may find assent among communally authorized agents: thus judging correctly is to be in accord with the communal agreement under-lying our practices.[11]

While these are powerful extensions of Wittgenstein's work into the ethico-political realm, they advocate a strong division between private and public morality and, though Pitkin follows Arendt in conceiving politics as disruptive, future-oriented deliberation, and Lovibond makes a strong case for the role of ethical imagination, a potentially conservative vision of political life. The last point is reinforced by the fact that Wittgenstein's own views of politics were strongly shaped by organicist and communi-tarian metaphors, some of them stemming from Spengler, others from Tolstoy and similar proponents of virtue-based political moralities within closely knit communities. On typical readings of Wittgenstein's notion of life-form—in the work of commentators like Baker and Hacker—the rel-evant Wittgensteinian view is that the individual's resources of orientation are always a function of communal constraints, and that these constraints, spelled out in terms of grammar and the practices on which the gram-matical structure is based, rule out the possibility of private languages and hence serve to guarantee the seamless publicness of agents' utterances.[12]

Much of what goes on in Cavell, including his political reflections, hinges on his denial of such a view and his complimentary defense of a more nominalist vision of life-forms. Mutual understanding and intelligi-bility are not made possible by individuals' mastery of social conventions but by "our sharing routes of interest and feeling, modes of response, sens-es of humor and of significance and of fulfillment, of what is outrageous, of what is similar to what else, what a rebuke, what forgiveness, of when an utterance is an assertion, when an appeal, when an explanation."[13] By re-jecting the view that the individual's resources of orientation are a function of communal constraints, and that these constraints, spelled out in terms of grammar and the practices on which the grammatical structure is based, rule out the possibility of private languages and hence serve to guarantee the seamless publicness of speakers' utterances, Cavell is able to think of the *polis* not as constituted by a universal (whether traditional, communal, or metaphysical), but as a contested, fragile space of voices whose exercise is without external constraint.[14]

Cavell is in some respects rather close to a classical, Aristotelian view of politics. Citizens realize their true nature within the framework of a rational state; hence, freedom is nothing but the successful participation in such a community—or pure politics. What each single member of the polis can recognize as having assented to is not given *a priori* but constantly up for individual rethinking, discussion, and negotiation. However, Cavell significantly extends the polis—the sphere of mutual responsibility and citizenship—to include acts of negation and assertion that many theorists, both liberal and Aristotelian, would regard as of possible relevance only within the private sphere. As I will return to later, the most radical of such acts, as exemplified in the reading of Thoreau or in the melodramas of the unknown woman, may even leave the agent unrecognizable.

According to Richard Rorty, this is a good reason why these acts ought to be left to the private sphere.[15] If permitted to enter the public sphere, they would subvert the fundamental virtues of citizenship, namely, commitment to justice, equality, and social progress. While Rorty's distinction between private self-enlargement and public responsibility, by immunizing the public sphere from the effects of transformative intervention (they are all considered private pursuits), undermines the potential for radical social criticism, Cavell faces the opposite problem: On his account, the political seems without limits; indeed, the political, since it extends to the most intimate moments of literary self-authentication, stands in danger of losing the specificity it enjoys in the classical, Aristotelian view. Political participation risks becoming arbitrary, an aestheticized leap into a self-indulgent concern with individual purity, thus losing its responsiveness to the commitments that political activity (as opposed to aesthetic activity) exacts.

In the following I look at two classical criticisms of political romanticism that both focus on its failure to delimit the political from the poetic.

Hegel and Schmitt on Political Romanticism

Within the European tradition, the first significant critique of political romanticism appears in the chapter on spirit in Hegel's *Phenomenology of Spirit*.[16] Given the proliferation of non-political readings of this dialectic, it is important to stress that the romanticism Hegel attacks is of a *political* nature. Its aim, considered as a formation of spirit, is to articulate for itself a mode in which to actualize freedom most effectively and most coherently, and its context of appearance is intimately linked to the enthusiasm following the French revolution and the desire to understand its implications for contemporary liberal intellectuals.

In the chapter on spirit, which studies the ways in which the ideal of self-determination has been interpreted and implemented in various phases of European history, romanticism (which in real historical terms coincides with Jena romanticism and with authors such as Novalis, the Schlegel brothers, and Tieck) becomes the solution to the incompatibility that arises within Kantian ethics between the requirement that an action be motivated by duty alone if it is to possess moral worth and the conditions of the possibility of agency. By being exclusively preoccupied with the purity of moral judging, the Kantian agent alienates herself from all the ends that may matter and thus motivate; hence acting morally loses its point. As a response to this impasse, romanticism brings about a unity of pure practical reason and sensuous nature, thus overcoming the split between law and feeling, or transcendental and empirical subjectivity. Whereas, for the Kantian agent, the moral ideal hinges on obedience to a self-imposed law, for the romanticist it consists in authenticity—in being true to oneself *qua* sensuous *and* rational being: this is how moral beliefs are authenticated. The individual's essence becomes to act according to conviction; thus genuine freedom becomes extensionally equivalent with acting from a personal (or particular) point of view, as opposed to an impersonal (or universal) point of view.

Unsurprisingly, Hegel's critique of romanticism focuses on its arbitrariness. Since the conviction of the self can be attached to any random sensuous content (depending on the contingent social and historical position of the subject), what romanticism offers is freedom as *Willkür*, or simple volitional freedom (*arbitrium liberum*), rather than *Wille*, or free willing understood in terms of a notion of normative commitment. It should be unnecessary to rehearse the details of this well-known analysis. What is remarkable is how the romanticist's withdrawal from the world of political responsibility into a realm of subjective conviction and literary experimentation becomes, for Hegel, a form of evil. In a society of "beautiful souls," such a purity-seeker can gain recognition from like-minded beings without deciding to commit herself to anything in particular. Deprived of social engagement, however, inner life becomes empty; as with Kantian rigorism, the romantic brings about a disintegration of agency for which the only remedy, in Hegel's account, is to acknowledge her separation from arenas in which actions do come packed with consequences, and in which agents accept the implications of their linguistic and performative commitments. However, acknowledging such a separation entails confessing one's sins. According to Hegel, a confession of this sort asks for forgiveness from the community, and thereby reconciliation with the authority that is involved in communally authenticated norms. The forgiveness transports "the hard heart" to a higher level of Spirit.

Although in a somewhat different vein from that of the *Phenomenology of Spirit*, Hegel continues to elaborate his critique of romanticism in the *Aesthetics*.[17] Here, he relates romanticism, first, to a general subjectivization of the arts in painting, music, and literature and, second, to an aesthetization of Fichte's subjective idealism. This aesthetization is particularly manifest in the way in which, in authors such as Schlegel, Tieck, and Solger, Fichte's dialectic of pure activity and restriction, whereby the transcendental ego finds itself confronted with the "infinite task" of sorting necessary (self-authorized) norms from contingent (empirical) ones, and takes the form of a retreat to *Witz* and irony. In Hegel's view, the romantic ironist is a skeptic yearning for metaphysical plenitude who not only uses irony in order to signal that at a given point in the text the opposite of the ostensible meaning is intended but regards every production of meaning in terms of its inherently unstable structure of constitutive provisionality. The irony becomes an extreme version of the beautiful soul's wish to exempt herself from commitments that would position her as an individual within a social (and political) space. In the search for a higher and more adequate exercise of freedom than the world of the everyday allows for, she seeks to withdraw from the world into an inner sanctuary of pure, uninterrupted self-assurance. As Hegel puts it, "this virtuosity of an ironical artistic life apprehends itself as a divine creative genius for which anything and everything is only an unsubstantial creature, to which the creator, knowing himself to be disengaged and free from everything, is not bound, because he is just as able to destroy it as to create it."[18] As a result, he adds, "everything appears to it as null and vain, except its own subjectivity which therefore becomes hollow and empty and itself mere vanity."[19]

Although Hegel and Carl Schmitt have little in common as theorists of the political, they share many of the same judgments about political romanticism.[20] Unlike Hegel, for whom commitment to the political institutions of the Prussian state was a dominant concern, the dominant framework within which Schmitt, in the 1919 text *Political Romanticism*, launches his attack on romanticism is based on his assessment that the European bourgeoisie had embraced romanticism and thereby depoliticized the liberal social order by transforming political debate into an endless conversation in which an element of self-indulgence and a lack of seriousness rendered genuine political decisions impossible. Like Hegel, however, Schmitt accuses the romantics of wanting to "poeticize" all areas of political life: the very differentiation between art and politics that for Schmitt had become a hallmark of modernity thus stands in danger of collapsing: "Where political activity begins, political romanticism ends."[21]

Schmitt substantiates this view by arguing (as does Cavell) that romanticism is best thought of as a response to the process of secularization. Whereas the idea of a transcendent God offered a universal metaphysical principle by which to authorize the moral regulation of life, the romanticist, on her part, inherits the claim to authority while locating it in a source which is unable to sustain it, namely, the subjective imagination of the emancipated, private individual. In Schmitt's account, this displacement can be delineated with reference to Malebranche's occasionalism, which in the romantic movement is structurally retained though with God being replaced by the individual human being and his or her imagination. For Malebranche the skeptical problems arising from Descartes's metaphysical dualism can only be solved by invoking the notion of God as the final mediating instance between subject and object. According to Malebranche, the real agent of human action is not the individual human subject but God, and the world is reduced to providing contingent occasions for God's essential interventions. In the romantic secularization of Malebranche's occasionalism, the privatized romantic ego views the world as simply an arena for the free play of the individual imagination. The sense of what exists and what matters thus becomes a function of the interest that the individual aesthetic imagination happens to have: "Surrender to this romantic productivity involves the conscious renunciation of an adequate relationship to the visible, external world. Everything real is only an occasion. The object is without substance, essence, and function. It is a concrete point about which the romantic game of fantasy moves."[22] It is important to recognize that Schmitt rejects the commonly held view, especially on the Marxist left, that German romanticism was predominantly a reactionary movement. Indeed, throughout most of their public careers Schlegel, Fichte, Goethe, and Novalis adopted the republican values of the French revolution; thus politically, what they represented was the new and rising bourgeoisie and its demand for freedom and equality. In Schmitt's reading, there is an evident continuity between the reformation and the republicanism espoused by the romantics: by endorsing the principle of the free self, the basis of romanticism was a kind of restless spirit of infinite striving and self-overcoming. However, the romantics radicalized the claims of the French revolution by demanding not only political rights and liberties but also a new religion, a new gospel, a new creativity, and a new universal art. The problem, Schmitt claims, arising from this demand is that the romantics lacked a coherent vision of how such revolutionary reservoirs of sovereign, aesthetic meaning could be provided with an institutional form and basis. They remained fantasies entertained in private by individuals who strove to poeticize all other spheres of value but merely succeeded in disconnecting themselves from any real political influence and consequence.

Both Hegel and Schmitt recommend that the political should be protected from the unruly, essentially self-indulgent leap into arbitrariness that they see as the essence of romanticism. The political is an autonomous domain, marked by its own standards of rational behavior and engagement. Yet whereas Hegel ends up deriving these standards from the normative commitments entailed by, and developed in, his dialectical logic, thus ultimately subordinating politics to philosophy, Schmitt views the political as the realm of definition and decision. The reason, for Schmitt, why the romantic fails is that she refuses to engage with this realm.

Cavell's Reading of Thoreau

How does Cavell's approach to romanticism fare in the light of these criticisms? It depends, obviously, on the writings that are taken into account and how they are interpreted. On my reading, there is a strong presumption in favor of viewing *The Senses of Walden* (Cavell's 1972 interpretation of Thoreau's *Walden*) as his most sustained effort to articulate a political romanticism for our time.[23] In no other work by Cavell is the question of the "nation's promise" more strongly interweaved with considerations of a "literary withdrawal," and nowhere does he write with greater passion on the political dimension of reading and writing. A difficulty with this text, however, is that it deals with an extraordinary number of issues—with problems of language and selfhood, of political education, and of the relationship between reading and writing—and it is not always clear how they are to be connected.

Central to Cavell's account is his sense that Thoreau's withdrawal, commencing on Independence Day, or the Fourth of July, is a response to a political crisis whose implications must be measured in the light of "the idea of America." Referring to his reconstruction of Rousseau's version of the explanatory myth of the social contract, the suggestion becomes that America only exists in its discovery—that it can have no positive meaning but is, rather, an ongoing experiment for which its citizens are responsible. Unlike most other myths of statehood, the idea of America contains reference neither to origins (whether temporal, social or divine) nor to any fixed utopian future.[24] (The fact that Thoreau takes up the abode on the Fourth of July is in this respect an accident.) No specific dimension or feature of man's capacity for perfection is privileged. On the contrary, America entails a promise of unrestricted freedom, though not simply in the traditional definition of individual liberty to pursue happiness in the private spheres of family life, consumption, and enjoyment, but freedom understood as full mastery in what one does and says: America is what you and I, each on our own terms, are endlessly responsible for. It is where freedom, and hence full humanity, is to be achieved.

Walden is written, Cavell claims, in "a mood of absolute hope and yet of absolute defeat."[25] Thoreau addresses his fellow citizens, whom he views as conformists who have rejected the demand placed on them by the idea of America and are therefore mindlessly acquiescing in its partiality, and his ultimate aim in *Walden* is to educate people for citizenship by bringing them to a recognition that in spite of their conformism they *are* indeed self-determining beings: they are not fated to fate. Since every normative order of a political nature involves self-reflexivity, what seem like necessities are in fact possibilities—projects that we have and that we may either commit ourselves to fully or reject. Thus, the text of *Walden* must individualize its readers: it must help them to overcome false and dogmatic attachments to pre-given social arrangements and demonstrate "that education for citizenship is education for isolation."[26]

From what has been said so far, it seems evident that Hegel's attribution of *endlessness*, or infinite deferral, to political romanticism applies to Cavell's Thoreauian modification of it. Like the Fichte-Schlegel model of literature, which Hegel accuses of being incapable of satisfying its own definition, Thoreau's demand for auto-formation, auto-organization, and auto-dissolution is perpetually in excess in relation to itself.[27] There is a complete resistance to the determination of the Absolute as fixed and ultimate substance, and hence also an abandonment of the Hegelian labor of the Concept, however temporalized it may be. For Hegel, the result is a loss of determinacy and an arbitrariness that allows for any content, any claim, to appear as rationally binding.

Cavell's position in this regard is complex. As is clear from his readings of Derrida and Schlegel, he does not advocate the type of position that Hegel would think of in terms of "bad infinity" (*schlechte Unendlichkeit*). The mindful turn to the ordinary and the everyday that he finds in Thoreau does indeed allow thought to find "peace" and completeness in the perspicuous representation (or aphoristic formulation) of the diurnal and common. In Cavell's account, perspicuous representation (as in Wittgenstein's "The human body is the best picture of the human soul"[28]) is the achievement of transparency, of "completeness, pleasure, and the sense of breaking something off . . . words that epitomize, separate a thought, with finish and permanence, from the general range of experience."[29] The open-endedness of romantic writing consists merely in the rejection of dogmatism: namely, that thinking which transcends privacy inevitably enters the arena of public discourse, thus inviting challenge and possible rebuff. It is perfectly possible both to find peace and closure in a specific formulation *and* to find that one's judgment is not shared by the community. The risk in such cases, though, is that the speaker becomes unintelligible. However, what Thoreau does is to bring the reader into a relationship of being read or unpacked by the text: the text presents itself as representative of a position that the reader may be drawn to but has not yet attained; thus the text, while seeming to push the boundaries of the previously intelligible, is capable of educating the reader. The relationship between writer and reader must be thought of as a dialogue, involving mutual self-reflection, rather than the monological imposition of a view or claim.

Moreover, the notion of deferral, which regularly appears as an issue of contention in Hegel's account of how the romantics fall into the trap of bad infinity, would be a problem for Cavell only if it is falsely presupposed that, on his view, accounting for a word, authorizing its proper use, is an activity that can never be brought to an end. Bringing it to an end, however, does not involve claiming that nothing more can be said, but only that knowing a word is essentially a capacity to project it correctly into new contexts, a capacity that does not rest on proofs and hence is not open to the charge that something (a final account) is missing:

Simply because (or: precisely because) there is always more that *can* be said in accounting for a word, say tracing its meaning (because a *word* must always find itself elsewhere), it does not follow if I do not say more in a given exchange that I am *withholding* an account, or that it is *deferred*. If knowing a word is knowing how to go on with it, then showing how I go on is proving my knowledge.[30]

Yet the problem of endlessness or bad infinity is not the only one of which Hegel (and Schmitt) speaks. Just as important is his view that the political romanticist advocates a withdrawal to the private sphere—which subsequently is blown up to include the political—and that romanticism is never able to transcend privacy. On both Hegel's and Schmitt's accounts, for words to transcend privacy and *matter* it is required that they reach out beyond the contingencies of aesthetic play and into the ethical or political realm. How, if at all, does Cavell's Thoreau succeed in transforming his personal and most intimate moments into utterances that may have a bearing politically? For one thing, Cavell emphasizes that Thoreau is first and foremost a writer, and since his writing cannot in any way be recognized as political in the narrow sense, that is, as engaged or critical with respect to issues that a "political" writer would normally address, the political dimension of Thoreau's work is far from immediately self-evident. Readers of theorists such as Roland Barthes and Julia Kristeva will be familiar with the view that literary language itself, apart from its "content" or "surface meaning," may be subversive or in different ways resistant to current ideologies, et cetera. However, whatever Thoreau is doing, it is certainly not to uncover "a white writing" (Barthes) or "a semiotic level" (Kristeva) beyond the everyday structures of symbolic speech. For another thing, the writing that Thoreau is said to engage in requires total isolation, both physically and spiritually. What kind of isolation? Why would isolation allow Thoreau a space to exercise his political voice?

First, when Cavell, in *The Senses of Walden*, turns to Rousseau, he is less interested in bringing out the outlines of a theory of political legitimacy and freedom than he is in viewing Rousseau as a "grammarian of society." As I read him, what this means is that the remarks on contractualism should be taken as replying to certain specific questions-namely, how one can tell who is implicated by my own production of criteria, and how one could have been party to the establishing of them—that arise when someone asks what the philosophical search for our criteria implies. To be sure, the answer to these questions is not without political implications; it is rather that Cavell refuses to draw a clear-cut divide between philosophy and the fundamental questions of politics: both thematize the relationship between the individual and her community in terms of the notion of agreement; hence contractualism is an aspect of what Cavell more generally is interested in uncovering when he stipulates that the search for criteria involves making claims to community.

Second, the writing Thoreau is said to be engaged in "underwrites" the methods and procedures of ordinary language philosophy as represented by Austin and Wittgenstein: both Thoreau and the thinkers of ordinary language attempt to recount the specific conditions of language. Yet whereas Austin's and Wittgenstein's search for criteria is oriented toward "what we say when and the implications thereof," Thoreau's romantic transcendentalism offers, as it were, a more concrete way of recounting what ordinary language is *about*—that is, the world of the ordinary. The crisis—both personally and cosmologically—that Thoreau faces affects the very constitution of meaning and signification. Thoreau's fellow men speak, yet they have no voice; their language is devoid of affect and interest, there is no subject *meaning* what is said. What Thoreau teaches his readers is to accept the burden of language: that no impersonal structure can ever replace our responsibility for aligning word and world. Saying what there is—the redemptive dimension of Cavell's thinking—entails acknowledging an independent, separate world, one in which interest is taken, for only thus can we be responsive to the shared criteria that govern the world-directed use of words.

But this means that criteria, as Cavell analyzes them in *The Claim of Reason*, are not private possessions. Since language exists before the individual speaker, when Thoreau rethinks the conditions of his own speech he does so as a representative speaker. In explorations of the ordinary, claims made about one's own life simultaneously purport to be about yours: Thoreau takes himself to be representative of all human beings; he thus makes a claim to community. Since the claim is not based on an appeal to any kind of impersonal structure or presence but rather on one's readiness to make oneself intelligible to others with whom one is, as Cavell puts it, "mutually attuned" or "mutually voiced," there can be no guarantee, however, that when starting to elicit criteria we actually come to agree. Unlike the standard readings of the Wittgensteinian notion of life-form that I previously referred to, in which the individual's resources of orientation are a function of communal constraints, and where these constraints, spelled out in terms of grammar and the practices on which the grammatical structure is based, rule out the possibility of private languages and hence serve to assure the seamless publicness of agents' utterances, Cavell talks about arriving "at the completed and unshakable edifice of shared language from within . . . apparently fragile and intimate moments—private moments— as our separate counts and out-calls of phenomena, which are after all hardly more than our interpretations of what occurs, and with no assurance of conventions to back them up."[31] Indeed, "The drift of *Walden* is not that we should go off and be alone; the drift is that we *are* alone, *and* that we are never alone—not in the highest and not in the lowest sense."[32] Thoreau's fellow men—the conformists who fail to exercise their (political) voice—are, since they make no attempt to find their own voice, more isolated than the isolated Thoreau, who seeks to assume full responsibility for his own language by eliciting its criterial conditions. Only by withdrawing from his fellow men can Thoreau take up a position of "neighboring" in the sense of being both close to and distant from them. By being representative of what we might be, we recognize ourselves as presented in one another's possibilities.

Considered as a myth of the political, Cavell's Thoreauian account of the play of isolation and commonality draws heavily on the Platonic myth of the cave in the *Republic*.[33] The founder of the community does not so much find as re-find the voice which connects him with the universal. Re-finding one's voice becomes a joint effort of mutual education, an effort which defines the task of citizenship.

So does this mean that Hegel and Schmitt's privacy-objection has been met? Formally, at least, it seems that Cavell can have his cake and eat it too: by appealing to the logic of criteria, he can attribute Thoreau's literary exploration with a political significance, assuming that the most intimate acts of literary discovery are capable of posing as communally (and hence politically) binding. The question this raises, however, is whether Cavell, on a more material level, as it were, is entitled to extend the political to include the "serious speech" with which Thoreau is supposed to inspire his fellow citizens to become "reborn" as speakers. Apart from the criterial significance of Thoreau's writing, how can the writing of the literary romanticist avoid the trap of aestheticizing the political? Indeed, what kind of politics is this?

One problem with Cavell's construction is that political discourse normally unfolds within a framework containing divergent standards of rationality. It subdivides into pragmatic, legal, administrative, aesthetic, and moral discourses, each containing different norms and expectations; and, as Schmitt argues, if the aesthetic (or moral-aesthetic) discourse gets privileged above the others, it may easily have a destabilizing effect on politics and make it overly vulnerable to forms of what Max Weber would call charismatic, as opposed to traditional and formal-legal, authority. The difficulty is brought to the fore with Cavell's fascination, in *The Senses of Walden*, with the figure of the prophet. The interest in this figure is hardly balanced by a proper reflection on the prophet's inherent lack of accountability. Or rather, since the prophet is accountable only to a higher and ultimately inscrutable power, his incursion into politics is inevitably fraught with the well-known dangers of impartiality: injustice, mismanagement, discrimination, et cetera. Moreover, the tension between the right and the good—between, on the one hand, norms that are established as universally binding and can be appealed to as basis for a system of rights and, on the other hand, values that can serve as a rational basis for identity-formation and, by being articulated narratively, be the focal point of individual or collective aspiration toward the good life, which is crucial to contemporary neo-Kantian theory (Habermas and Rawls)—fails to be thematized in Cavell. The kinds of political deliberations and decisions that can establish legal norms that are in the interest of all those affected in a complex society would in general hardly be possible if the participants' main concern was self-transformation within a framework centered on questions concerning how to lead a good and perfected human life. In this respect, Schmitt (although he certainly was no Kantian) seems right in insisting that the political needs protection, rather than advice, from the romanticist. (Having said that, however, it is worth recalling how powerfully Cavell demonstrates how anyone comes to see the wrong of the institution of slavery for the first time. While the slave-owner "need not deny the supremacy of justice" yet sees the slaves as "not *purely* human," the overthrow of slavery is predicated on a changed *Weltanschauung*, an unwillingness to continue to make oneself unknowable by the slaves and private with respect to them. In this case, transformative experiences relating to one's identity effect radical changes in one's thinking about justice and equality.[34])

Nor does Cavell's Thoreau indicate any specific institution or normative order within which the activity of offering a "literary redemption of language" is to occur; hence he seems guilty of Schmitt's charge that political romanticism suffers from a socio-political naiveté. However, the absence of institutional anchoring may in some respect turn out to be an advantage: although his aim is to be in touch with the deeper commitments that his fellow men share and yet shun in their everyday lives, Thoreau writes from a perspective of complete denial. The only commitment he makes is toward the value of pure and unrestricted autonomy, a writing that seeks to become totally transparent and self-authorized, inviting others to reach the same standpoint. Thus, Thoreau's aesthetic politics does not rest its effectiveness on an appeal to objectively existing sources of moral and ethical authority: it is thoroughly modern in its rejection of such authority and its adoption of individual autonomy as the central focus of value.

As Adorno and Heidegger (among others) have argued, however, art's autonomy comes at a high price. While, in modernity, science takes the place of supreme and exclusive epistemic authority, the notion of art as offering instruction and insight gets replaced with that of art as illusion, a freely created source of pleasure and amusement. In short, the birth of the purely aesthetic coincides with the subjectivization of value and a general instrumentalization of nature. If writing today is *just art*, that is, at best an object of aesthetic admiration, and at worst one simply of entertainment, and if art has lost touch with its erstwhile ability to offer ethical and political instruction, then Cavell's artistically informed search for free expressiveness may seem strangely sterile or impotent. Isn't *Walden*, with all its celebration of simplicity, organicism, and natural beauty, in fact a good example of advanced writing that to a large extent has lost its capacity to provoke and instead—just think of the many cute little abridged versions you have seen!—become commercially exploitable kitsch?

On being brought to this juncture, however, the next natural step, I would argue, is to look at artistic movements, including Romanticism, in terms of how they may have responded to this loss of cognitive purchase. According to Adorno, for example, a hallmark of all serious modern art consists in its revolt against illusion (*Schein*).[35] In Adorno's dialectic, this revolt has essentially taken place on the level of form: resisting the aesthetic categories of beauty and harmony, advanced works of art have allowed external objects of nature and culture, and indeed contingency, to enter into their range of materials, thereby contaminating the purity of their principles of construction. Looked at more broadly, this may be considered as a form of resistance toward precisely the subject-centered reason that was responsible for the differentiation of art from the sphere(s) of cognitive validity; thus art aspires to sovereignty, the capacity to disrupt the successful functioning of nonaesthetic, cognitive discourse. It may also, however, be interpreted as a form of mourning: for the fact of art's continued imprisonment in Plato's cave, or for the social and cultural condition that generates and sustains this condition.[36] To be able to say this, however, requires a less Kantian account than the one we find in Cavell. Essentially, it demands a more Hegelian emphasis on how Romanticism represents a response to modernity, and not only a concentration on its potentials, however desirable they may appear on their own terms, for self-authentication.

It seems, moreover, as if Cavell's work cries out for a historical and social account that explains why the citizenry of modern states fails to exercise its freedom. While, on his view, the proneness to skeptical denial of the other, as well as denial, more generally, of responsibility to make oneself known and authenticate oneself before the other, certainly has strong motives (such as incapacity to come to terms with the human condition— its separateness, finitude, and fragility), it can often be difficult to see how they operate and make themselves felt under specifically modern conditions. The bad repetition that marks Thoreau's fellow men, their "lives of quiet desperation," in short their nihilism and indifference, gets accounted for by Adorno in terms of the dominance of identitarian reason and the principle of exchange, and by Heidegger in terms of techno-scientific forgetfulness of being. While I obviously would not suggest that Cavell should adopt any of these lines of thought, his philosophical modernism is abstract in the Hegelian sense of being unmediated by its social and political other.

There is another level at which Cavell's work may be accused of lacking historical specificity. I have already intimated how Adorno views the revolt against illusion taking place in high modernism as a response to the loss of cognitive purchase that stems from the differentiation of art into an autonomous sphere that, under modern conditions, encourages the degeneration of art into play and entertainment. In Adorno's thinking, it follows that advanced art needs to observe the Kantian distinction between an aesthetics of the beautiful and an aesthetics of the sublime. While the former seeks to obtain solace and pleasure in the contemplation of form only, where aesthetic form communicates with truth and moral rightness, the latter denies itself the solace of good forms in order to impart a sense of the unattainability of any ideas of the absolute that could unite the different value spheres (truth, moral and political rightness, beauty). Cavell vacillates, I would argue, between these two aesthetic orientations. As a theorist of the beautiful, he assigns to Thoreau the task of (re-)discovering criteria, thus placing him in a position to communicate, as a writer oriented toward the redemption of language, with moral and political registers. The risk here, as I have argued, is regression to a naïve, aestheticized politics that, despite its own aims, fails to obtain a binding character. However, as a theorist of the sublime, emphasizing Thoreau's potential unknowability and resistance toward cultural and political assimilation, he offers a much more powerful and relevant account of art's claim to be political.[37]

Consider Cavell's interpretation of Nora in Ibsen's *A Doll's House*.[38] Nora finds herself in a position of "[putting] the social order as such on notice"; she embarks, in other words, on a critique of what Adorno would call "totality" or "negative totality," a critique for which she has no reasons that can pose as acceptable.[39] It makes no sense to ask her to participate in the conversation of justice by showing, as Rawls requires, "why certain institutions are unjust or how others have injured them."[40] As a result she becomes a precursor of what Cavell, with reference to the Hollywood tradition of melodrama, calls "an unknown woman." All that her husband, Torvald, sees is a woman acting childishly, incapable of understanding the realities of the world she lives in. Cavell sums up his analysis by stating that he is "taking Nora's enactments of change and departure to exemplify that over the field on which moral justification comes to an end, and justice, as it stands, has done what it can, specific wrong may not be claimable; yet the misery is such that, on the other side, right is not assertible; instead something must be shown."[41] What must be shown, I would argue, is a sublime event whereby the claimant, in her unknownness and resistance toward discursive intelligibility, transgresses the social totality within which she has been involved and thus promises a radical, if not even utopian, political renewal.

Cavell's reading of Greta Garbo and her "hysterical conversion" toward absolute expressiveness points in the direction of such a sublime disclosure.[42] According to Cavell, Garbo's conditions of existence can be viewed as literally expressed in every single gesture she makes. As a result, Garbo remains unknown or beyond us—"visibly absent"—because a being capable of such an expressiveness is impossible to acknowledge. Indeed, the proof of Garbo's existence lies in her sublime transcendence of our powers of acknowledgment. She thus makes a claim as to how she would have to be acknowledged—if acknowledgment were possible. Cavell's point is not that the men she is surrounded by in the films fail to recognize her existence. Nor is it that she will remain forever beyond us. Rather, by exceeding our powers of acknowledgment, Garbo forces us to realize that our capacity for acknowledgment has limits, and that we ourselves, though at present incapable of change, are responsible for the maintenance of those limits. However, since Garbo's absence, in addition to the transcendence effected by the bodily expression of her psyche, is mechanically produced (it is an effect of the cinematic image's capacity to present a world from which the viewer is absent), it achieves a separateness that testifies to the radical finitude of the human condition. And as Cavell, following Freud, argues, the only progressive way of responding to finitude—to transience, separation, loss—is through mourning:

In Garbo's most famous postures in conjunction with a man, she looks away or beyond or through him, as if in an absence (a distance from him, from the present), hence as if to declare that this man, while the occasion of her passion, is surely not its cause. I find . . . that I see her *jouissance* as remembering something, but, let me say, remembering it from the future, within a private theater, not dissociating herself from the present moment, but knowing it forever, in its transience, as finite, from her finitude, or separateness, as from the perspective of her death: as if she were herself transformed into a mnemonic symbol, a monument of memory. . . . What the monument means to me is that a joyful passion for one's life contains the ability to mourn, the acceptance of transience, of the world as beyond one—say one's other.[43]

Garbo's *jouissance* becomes a declaration of independence so radical that, while subverting the logic of standard political discourse, it obtains a political significance of its own. In Garbo Cavell has uncovered a true modernist work of art—a sovereign act of remembrance endowed with utopian, redemptive qualities, capable of challenging the political, or rather the political individual being singled out, from a standpoint of unrestricted singularity.

Cavell's political romanticism deserves close scrutiny. What I hope to have suggested is that it stands up rather well to the classical objections raised by Hegel and Schmitt. While the privacy-objection can most certainly be met, I have argued that his romanticism is equivocal, however, as between an aesthetics of beauty and an aesthetics of the sublime. Only the latter, exemplified by the topos of the unknown woman, can provide art with a political dimension that evades what Hegel and Schmitt would see as an undue aesthetization of the political.

CHAPTER TEN

Stanley Cavell and the Pursuits of Happiness

Hans Sluga

I

Hollywood comedy and philosophy, remarriage and the nature of politics, dialogue in film and dialogue in philosophy—those are the unexpected conjunctions that give Stanley Cavell's 1983 book *Pursuits of Happiness* its unique, exhilarating, and, indeed, magic flavor. My modest goal in this essay is to determine the place of politics in this triad, for I want to show how Cavell's "comic" vision can help us to reconceptualize politics, and that at a moment when we are much in need of such a rethinking. Cavell's goal, I argue, is to get us away from reflecting on political principles and to attend, instead, to the political aspects of everyday practice. Such attention, he seems to think, will reveal what is needed at the large-scale level of national politics and, indeed, of global humanity. Politics, he appears to tell us, must be seen in dramatic terms. Film, more than any other medium, can show us the terms in which we must now interpret the human condition and even such a seemingly modest genre as Hollywood comedy can provide us with words essential for our political conversation. Before I turn to these perceptive and, indeed, profound observations, I find it useful to examine what Cavell writes in his book about philosophy and philosophical dialogue. From this I deduce that he really means to supplement the triad of comedy, politics, and philosophy with a fourth term—that of tragedy as the complement of the comic. But I ask myself whether Cavell's discussion of Hollywood comedy provides the means for fully accommodating the tragic in his new understanding of politics. *Pursuits of Happiness* may have to be read in conjunction with such earlier texts as Cavell's essay on *King Lear*, where the question of the pursuit and avoidance of love is treated in a different register. That project lies, however, beyond the limits of my discussion. I close, instead, with some words from Nietzsche, who proves to have been one of the inspirations of Cavell's book. No other thinker, I conclude, poses to us so sharply the precarious balance of tragedy and comedy in our lives.

The linkage of comedy and tragedy is made apparent in Cavell's book when he casually writes that thinking is "not required of beings exempt from tragedy and comedy" (p. 259).[1] The remark is surely provocative though not so much for connecting thought and tragedy as for finding an inherent link between thought and comedy, and it is the latter Cavell seeks to explore in *Pursuits of Happiness*. While there exists an acknowledged link between tragedy and philosophy, that between comedy and philosophy seems tenuous, if not obscure (at least to common perception). We know from Plato's Socratic dialogues that our whole philosophical tradition begins with a tragic conflict between the philosopher and the polis. In examining himself and investigating his fellow citizens, Socrates has performed a critical service to Athens. But the city fails to appreciate his work and condemns the philosopher to death and the inevitable consequence is a tragic alienation of philosophy from politics in which both are permanently left poorer.[2] The comic dimension of philosophical thought appears, by contrast, less well established. We are likely to remember at first only the unfortunate circumstance that Aristophanes' poking fun at Socrates may have contributed to his tragic death. Philosophy will, indeed, look ridiculous to the outsider, as Plato granted, but that seems to establish no inner link between comedy and philosophy. It is certainly easier to assume an asymmetric relation between philosophy, tragedy, and comedy. George Steiner suggests accordingly that human sensibility finds the tragic "more elevated, more fascinating" and, hence, "more conducive to . . . metaphysical suggestion." Tragedy, it appeared to Steiner, "not only seduces imagination and intellect, but *flatters* them," while comedy lacks the gravity to motivate philosophical thinking.[3] Cavell, however, identifies a substantial connection between the three. He maintains that philosophy is recognizably related to tragedy by beginning in wonder, but that it relates just as deeply to comedy by continuing in argument. His model in *Pursuits of Happiness* is the Platonic dialogue and specifically Plato's *Parmenides*, in whose vision of the ideas Cavell discovers a tragic beginning, while its arguments (over the idea of mud, and such) have for him a comical character. Philosophical thought is tragic in its beginnings, we may interpret these words, because it is thrust upon us and thus shares a sense of inevitability with all other tragedy. Philosophical wonder strikes us, we do not seek it out, and when it has struck we do not easily know how to escape. This sense of wonder isolates us from others and makes it impossible for us to live an ordinary human existence since, even in wonder, we are beings in need of others. Philosophical conversation, however, returns us to life and to the presence of others. But our dialogue with them is constantly plagued with confusions, pratfalls, misunderstandings. We are constantly saying too much or too little, constantly make fools of ourselves and thus reveal ourselves in a comic light.

Tragedy and comedy are, thus, on Cavell's terms equally part of the human condition. It is, however, the comic and not the tragic that preoccupies him in *Pursuits of Happiness*. And this holds not only with respect to philosophy but just as much for his reflections on politics. But we should not ignore the tragic element in the films that concern him in this book, and Cavell is by no means forgetful of this tragic angle. The lighthearted films he discusses all prove for him to have their darker dimension. For all that, he seems determined in *Pursuits of Happiness* to set their tragic aspect aside. It is left to the reader to find the balance between the comic and the tragic that must be, on Cavell's own admission, an essential ingredient in his new vision of politics.

2

Pursuits of Happiness presents itself innocuously enough as a reading of seven Hollywood comedies from the 1930s and 1940s—films that seem, to the unprepared eye, concerned with slight, unphilosophical, and unpolitical matters. Their heroines are, in every case, married women who have for some reason or other separated from their partners. The plot of each film is not to get the central pair together, as is so often the case in traditional comedy, "but to get them *back* together, together *again*" (p. 2). The fact of marriage is thus subjected to the fact or threat of divorce, and divorce, in turn, to the possibility of remarriage. None of this seems to bear in a major fashion on either philosophical or political matters.

Still, there is no doubt that *Pursuits of Happiness* seeks to rethink the nature of both philosophy and politics. Cavell assures us, in any case, that film in general—including, presumably, these comedies—exists "in a state of philosophy" (p. 13). This statement will admittedly sound outrageous to the traditional philosopher, but Cavell adds defiantly: "Philosophy, as I understand it, is indeed outrageous" (p. 8). And he deliberately courts such outrage by telling us that a face-off between film and philosophy "is positively called for" (p. 13). Only through such a confrontation will we see that film is "inherently self-reflective, takes itself as an inevitable part of its craving for speculation," and that the specific genre of the Hollywood comedy of remarriage "demands the portrayal of philosophical conversation, hence undertakes to portray one of the causes of philosophical dispute" (pp. 13f). By perceiving such affinities, Cavell assures us, we are likely to attain a deeper grasp of both film and philosophy. Film is particularly useful, to Cavell, in opening our eyes to thinkers like Emerson, Thoreau, Austin, Wittgenstein, and Heidegger, who all seek to bring philosophy back to the ordinary condition of everyday life. Precisely this condition is the concern of film and specifically of the comedies discussed in *Pursuits of Happiness.* Such films can therefore serve a distinctively philosophical purpose. In providing us with a richer view of the everyday, they illuminate at the same time the significance of the philosophers' interest in the ordinary.

This ordinary condition of everyday life proves, however, to be also a political one. Cavell alerts us to that through the title of his book. "Pursuits of Happiness" is evidently meant to recall the American Declaration of Independence, with its affirmation of the right of citizens to the pursuit of happiness. One must take note, however, that he changes the declaration's singular to the plural. He means to speak, in other words, not of a singular, officially ratified pursuit of happiness, but of multiple and individualized pursuits. We can see what he has in mind when we turn to his reading of *The Philadelphia Story* of 1940. The film is for Cavell not about the one kind of happiness that the American founding fathers, assembled at Philadelphia, guaranteed to citizens but about the diverse and quite specific kinds of happiness and unhappiness of its protagonists: Tracy Lord, C. K. Dexter Haven, Macaulay "Mike" Conner, George Kittredge, and Liz Imbrue. But in emphasizing this diversity, Cavell does not mean to depoliticize their pursuits. He intends, rather, to give the multiple pursuits depicted in *The Philadelphia Story* and in the other comedies discussed in the book a newly political meaning. This is possible, of course, only if we adopt at the same time a new and broader understanding of politics. Cavell seems to be telling us then that we will not begin to grasp the nature of politics unless we first grant the multiplicity of ways in which human happiness can be pursued and hence also the multiplicity of ways in which these pursuits can be achieved or can fail. Human happiness, we might rephrase him, has many shapes and embodiments. In politics, as it is traditionally conceived, we are, however, used to thinking (more problematically) only of a single form of civic happiness, and this thought draws, in turn, on our (problematic) philosophical preoccupation with the idea of unity. Where Plato identifies the idea of the good with the idea of the one, film tells us another story. Like myth and theater before it—but now with new and other techniques—film tells us that there is no single human drama, and hence no single human happiness. And these multiple stories are, in turn, political, in that they concern the ways in which people are forced to negotiate with each other the varying terms of their varying pursuits. That political character will not be apparent to those who think of politics only in terms of the unity of the state and hence of a great politics of government, of war and peace, of rulers and those who are ruled. One is reminded here of what Cavell writes of the particularity of the theme of Shakespeare's *King Lear*, that it is "about the interpenetration and confusion of politics with love."[4] *Pursuits of Happiness* is likewise about such interpenetration and confusion. Cavell discerns in that book a "split or doubling . . . between civilization and eros" (p. 64). It may be common, he writes, to call "a reasonable civilized existence" political and to think of the erotic as a stumbling block to political life, but the decisive fact is that "human happiness nevertheless goes on demanding satisfaction in both realms" (pp. 64f). And for this reason it may be necessary to reconceive politics, to think of it no longer as limited to the domain of reasonable civilized existence, but to find it also in all those areas of human life where we are engaged in the pursuits of apparently private forms of happiness. Following Thoreau, Cavell concludes that his films are determined to join "the thoughts of day and night, of the public and the private," that they seek to show that "what used to be a matter of cosmic public importance is now a private matter of what we call emotional difficulty" (p. 54). The old boundaries between the public and the private are thus redrawn and with them also the boundaries of the political. What had once seemed separated by sharp divisions has now come to be joined, and at this juncture appears a new understanding of the political.

Nowhere is Cavell's intention made clearer than in his chapter on *The Philadelphia Story*—a film replete with political references, from its title to the portrait of George Washington casually hung in the hallway of Tracy Lord's home. In writing on this film, Cavell proposes to weave a daydream, as he says, around the film's conversation (a conversation that must at once be seen as having a philosophical as well as a political character) "on the question of America, on whether America has achieved its new human being, its more perfect union and its domestic tranquility, its new birth of freedom, whether it has been successful in securing the pursuit of happiness, whether it is earning the conversation it demands" (pp. 152f). In his reading of *King Lear* Cavell had previously spoken of the need for an American "change of consciousness" in which "phenomenology becomes politics" (AL, p. 346). He had spoken then of tragedy intertwined with American history, its identity, and its insatiable need for love. "It is the need of love as proof of its existence which makes it so frighteningly destructive, enraged by ingratitude and by attention to its promises rather than to its promise, and which makes it incapable of seeing that it is destructive and frightening" (AL, p. 345). America "has never felt that union has been achieved. Hence its terror of dissent, which does not threaten its power but its integrity. So it is killing itself and killing another country"(AL, p. 345). Cavell was writing then, at the time of the Vietnam war, of America as King Lear, unable to accept love and the union that it allows. In *Pursuits of Happiness* some years later he writes of taking up these questions once again, but now in the light of comedy and with the hope for the possibility of conceiving a new and perfected union. Once again, Cavell's point is that the political cannot be so neatly separated from

what we have come to think of as nonpolitical. But now we can imagine
that question also in terms of the pursuit of happiness and not only in the
stormy light of tragedy. The political is seen to rest here at the level where
fates differ, where the public and the private intertwine, and where the
forms of human happiness (and unhappiness) multiply.

Cavell proves, thus, to be engaged in a rethinking of our classical
conception of politics—one that has come to us all the way from Plato and
Aristotle. According to this classical picture politics concerns the rule (*ar-ché*) or government of the polis or state. Only what happens at this upper
stratum of public life is to be considered genuinely political. The ordinary
and everyday may, no doubt, be subject to political regulation, but they
lack, on this traditional view, a political character of their own. If we are
to speak of a politics of everyday life, we can do so only in a derivative and
metaphorical fashion. There follows a sharp division between political and
civic life, whose ultimate outcome is the modern distinction between po-litical and individual liberty. We might, indeed, say provocatively that the
Platonic-Aristotelian conception of politics foreshadows Benjamin Con-stant. That is admittedly not so evident in Plato's *Republic*, which envis-ages, after all, an all-encompassing polis. But even there politics is thought
of specifically as the rule of the polis; civic life, by contrast, is conceived
to be intrinsically nonpolitical and subject only to political regulation. In
Aristotle's *Politics* the distinction between political and civic life becomes
even more sharply defined and manifests itself in the division of house-hold and polis. The former is the sphere in which man and wife, parents
and children, masters and servants interact, and it is as such a thoroughly
nonpolitical sphere. On this conception, politics occurs only in the public
arena, where independent males have the leisure to take turns in govern-ing their city.

Cavell, in contrast to this whole long tradition and under the influ-ences of philosophers of the ordinary from Emerson and Thoreau to Witt-genstein, Austin, and Heidegger, proposes a radical revisioning of poli-tics in which the ordinary, the private, the everyday, the small-scale, and
the insignificantly personal can all be conceived of as political in nature.
There exists for him then not only a politics of the state, but also a politics
of love, of marriage, of the family, of friendship, and of a manifold other
human conditions. This does not mean that he wants to ignore the large-

scale politics of government and the state. He seeks to broaden, rather, our conception of the political beyond the narrow confines of the Platonic-Aristotelian model. Not only that, but he expresses in addition an implicit commitment to the idea that the great politics of the public sphere is (historically, ontologically, and conceptually) based on the politics of the ordinary and can therefore be understood only in its terms and by means of its characteristic notions.

Cavell is thereby reviving, perhaps without realizing it, an understanding of politics first advanced by the sophist Protagoras—a conception explicitly denied in the Platonic-Aristotelian model. Protagoras, as it appears from Plato's dialogue named after him, had a threefold insight with respect to politics. The first was that human beings are forced to engage in politics because the gods do not take care of them and they are compelled, instead, to take care of themselves. His second thought was that human beings are political because they are not naturally equipped to take care of themselves. In order to survive and flourish, they must therefore create their own human world, invent language, produce clothes, build houses, and obtain food. Protagoras adds that human beings are also not naturally in possession of political institutions. There exists no natural political order and, indeed, no naturally established human hierarchy. Human beings are, rather, naturally unqualified for political life and awkward in their relations with each other. It follows, as a third point, that they need to foster both technical and political skills if they are to survive. While technical skills are specialized and may therefore turn out to be in each case the possession of only a few, political skills must be had by all, for "a man cannot be without some share of fairness, or he would not be human" (p. 323c).[5] Therefore, "when the subject is political competence . . . everyone must share in this kind of virtue; otherwise the polis could not exist" (pp. 322e–23a). Protagoras adds pointedly that the Athenians agree with him in this and defer to experts when faced with technical problems because they realize that technical competence is unevenly distributed, "but when the subject of their debate involves political wisdom . . . they listen to every man's opinion" (p. 323a).

But political competence for Protagoras begins with only a basic, raw, and undeveloped capacity. Its full realization is "not by nature or of spontaneous growth, but in whomsoever it is present the result of teaching and practice" (p. 323c). Only through care (*epimeleia*) can men develop respect for each other, a sense of fairness or justice; only through care can they learn to form bonds of friendship and thus, in short, become politically skilled. Politics in the broad sense is, in fact, embodied in all the acts of care that develop, nurture, and maintain these qualities. Politics is, in Protagoras' words, in effect, the *epimeleia koinonias*, and this care of the common is not merely the precondition of politics but constitutes its content and essence. Thus, even child rearing may be thought of as a political undertaking. And the same thing can be said of the inculcating of manners in school, of instruction in writing, the reading of good poets, and the learning of inspirational poems. Even instruction in music Protagoras declares to have a political function, since it teaches self-control and because knowledge of rhythms and harmonies makes a student more civil, more cultivated, "for to be more rhythmic and more harmonious is essential to speaking and acting" (p. 326b). The same holds for physical training, for it is essential "that a good mind may have a good body to serve it" (p. 326b). At yet a further and third stage in the formation of political competence the city compels boys to learn the laws and to use them as patterns for their own lives. "The city sets up laws devised by good lawgivers of the past, and compels citizens to rule and be ruled in accordance with them. Whoever strays outside the lines, it punishes" (p. 326e). While Protagoras' story stops at this point, it clearly calls for continuation, as we see when we turn to the storyteller himself, for Protagoras is also a teacher of political skills and must therefore have thought of himself as engaged in political action. All in all, we can call the Protagorean conception of politics then a pedagogic one. At the heart of politics lies, on this view, individual cultivation, not for selfish and personal ends but in order to make the individual a suitable member of the polis. Politics is, in other words, seen here not as rule or *arché* but as *paideia*, and it takes place not only in the public arena but also in the privacy of the home and the schoolhouse. In this conception of politics, the nursemaid, the parent, the teacher, and even the sophist can all see themselves as political agents. Once we have achieved maturity, we are indeed all of us political agents and in the political and democratic dialogue we are all and constantly teachers of each other.

It is to this Protagorean tradition in political thought that Cavell, in effect, refers us in *Pursuits of Happiness*. Like Protagoras he seeks to attain a broad understanding of the scope of politics. Like him, he allows for a politics of the everyday and the ordinary, not just a politics of government and the state. Like Protagoras, he conceives of politics, moreover, as a *paideia*, hence his emphasis on films of conversation and on the affinity of these conversations to philosophical dialogue. It is in the pedagogy of conversation that both the comedies of remarriage and philosophy acquire their political character. One must add here, however, that Cavell concerns himself with an aspect of such a political *paideia* that lies outside the Protagorean range of experience, and that is the political education of the woman. And this difference is surely decisive, for Cavell rediscovers the Protagorean conception of politics precisely by coming to understand that feminist concerns cannot be fully accommodated within the boundaries of the classical, Platonic-Aristotelian model of politics, for feminism concerns not just the attainment of new rights, but first and foremost the formation of a new woman and with that of the education or, rather, as it turns out, the self-education of woman. That such a process has a genuinely political character cannot, however, be comprehended in terms of our traditional model.

3

It is not the great economic and political issues of the time in which these films were made and in which their stories take place that matter to Cavell in these comedies. These films are preoccupied with private lives, not public situations; their stories are romantic in tone and full of the entanglements and uncertainties of love. They might for that reason be easily dismissed as escapist fare, as "fairytales for the Depression." Their stories are, moreover, typically isolated from the economic and political exigencies of their time by being set in affluent locations, often in a mythically wealthy "Connecticut" and sometimes in locations of great luxury such as the Lord estate in *The Philadelphia Story*. Only occasionally do we get glimpses of actual deprivation such as in *It Happened One Night*, in "the Depression vignette of a mother on the bus fainting from what her crying child informs us is hunger" (*PH*, p. 94). But Cavell points out that this passing over economic need and the settings of wealth are not unique to the comedies of remarriage. He writes: "If luxurious settings and fantastic sums of money were confined to the Hollywood films of this period, and if Hollywood films of luxury and expenditure were confined to works that form the genre of remarriage, then I would be more drawn to an economic interpretation of the films I have interested myself in" (pp. 2f). The remark dismisses the Great Depression, perhaps, too quickly as a merely economic matter and hence as not being of genuine political concern. But the decisive point for Cavell is that "the economic issues in these films, with all their ambivalence and irresolution, are invariably tropes of spiritual issues" (p. 5). Thus, the hunger, so prominent in *It Happened One Night*, should be seen as standing more generally for spiritual hunger. It is for this reason that public politics occupies so small a place in the world of these films. We may consider it emblematic when Cary Grant advises his newspaper editor in *My Girl Friday* to redo the front page, "to stick Hitler in the funny pages" and to leave the rooster story alone: "That's human interest" (p. 25). Cavell notes that newspapers generally represent the public in these films whereas the film itself "symbolizes the realm of privacy" (p. 64), and the two are formally distinct even though, as Cavell is keenly aware, they intersect in peculiar ways. We are not meant to conclude that the great political issues of the time do not concern these comedies. We are to understand, rather, first of all the political dimension of "human interest" and then the fact that the foundations of what we usually call politics lie in the affairs of the ordinary and everyday. Three specific issues, in fact, occupy Cavell's comedies and his reading of these films, which are of increasingly larger scope and lead thus from what we may think of as the more private to the more public-political. There is, first of all, a concern with "the creation of a new woman"; there arises from this, second, the question of a new understanding of the union of a man and a woman and with it the need for a rethinking of marriage; from this follows, in turn, as a third concern the question whether America has achieved its "more perfect union" and how we are to think still more broadly of the problem "of the perfected human community."

The first and most specific matter in these films is for Cavell a feminist one. The comedy of remarriage, Cavell writes, "is bound up with a phase in the history of the consciousness of women" (p. 16). But this phase is no longer that of the old feminist struggle which began in America with the Seneca Falls Convention of 1848 and culminated in the winning of the vote for women in 1920. The acknowledged leaders of that earlier women's movement—Eleanor Roosevelt, Frances Perkins, Margaret Sanger—are, indeed, entirely absent from these films. And so are all mother figures. Cavell writes: "Socially, it seems to me, the absence of the woman's mother in these films of the thirties betokens a guilt, or anyway, puzzlement, toward the generation of women preceding the generation of the central woman of our films—the generation that won the right to vote without at the same time winning the issues in terms of which voting mattered enough" (pp. 57f). The heroines of the comedies of remarriage are not public figures; they live for the most outside the political limelight; they are played, moreover, by actresses who, though they are recognizable in their own right, are not necessarily feminist leaders. Still, for all that, the comedies of remarriage represent to Cavell "a phase of feminism" (p. 19) since they concern "winning the issues in terms of which voting mattered enough." This new phase demands, as Cavell emphasizes, nothing less than "the creation of a new woman or the new creation of a woman" (pp. 16, 64, and 140). The repetitions of this formula make clear how central it is for Cavell's understanding of the comedies of remarriage. These films are, in other words, meant to be playing a peculiarly double role in this phase of feminism. They set out to create the new woman by means of the female roles in their stories, but they do so at the same time also through the leading actresses who perform these roles (Claudette Colbert, Irene Dunne, Katherine Hepburn, Rosalind Russell, and Barbara Stanwyck). While the cinematic narrative focuses on the heroine's identity, the cinematic medium highlights the physical and photographic presence of the actress herself playing the part. In using the new medium of the sound film and the capacity of film to allow an easy shifting of focus between the film's narrative and the physical reality of its actors and actresses, these comedies are engaged in both the creation of a new woman and a new kind of creative process, a new creation of woman. In their narrative content they can be said to be concerned with the one and in their reality as films with the other task.

Looked at either way, these films can be said to have an educational meaning. Certainly, "an essential goal of the narrative is the education of the woman" (p. 84). And in this we discover a direct connection between the Protagorean and the Cavellian understanding of politics, in that both see it as a pedagogic exercise. Even in these comedies, Cavell points out, men once again assign themselves the task of undertaking this education, hence their frequent, admonishing lectures. What is new, however, and could never have been contemplated by Protagoras is that women also "might attempt this direction" (p. 65) by taking an active hand in their own education. The effect is a new kind of intercourse between men and women. The concern with the creation of a new woman becomes thus at the same time a concern with the union of the two, that is, with marriage, and beyond that with the union between human beings in general. At stake is, in other words, "the problem and the concept of identity—either in the form of what becomes of an individual, or of what has become of two individuals" (p. 55). Cavell observes that in *The Philadelphia Story* the narrative's attention is paradigmatically directed toward this question of identity by asking "whether the heroine is a goddess made of stone or of bronze, or whether a woman of flesh and blood" (p. 140). And the symbolic death of the heroine as goddess and her rebirth as human are brought about through her engagement with the men who surround her. The transformation involves, in particular, the woman's acceptance of herself as an embodied, sexual being (as well as our acceptance of her as such).

The question of the new woman, of a new identity, thus forces us to examine what constitutes a union. "The overarching question of the comedies of remarriage is precisely the question what constitutes a union, what makes these two into one, what binds, you may say what sanctifies the marriage" (p. 53). It is taken for granted that the church has lost its power to authenticate the institution of marriage. Divorce is conceived as a legitimate way out of a failed relation. Since the couple is depicted as previously married, virginity (certainly not physical virginity) is no longer a condition for the new union, nor are children present in these films, for they, too, no longer authenticate marriage. The couple itself is rather seen to attain a new innocence in re-establishing their bond, and in doing so they often recover a childlike state in which the traditional social and legal definitions of marriage are no longer of concern. With such radical changes in the conception of marriage, the nature of its legitimacy is certainly now open to question, and so is, as Cavell sees it, "the question of the legitimacy of society" (p. 53). The old assumption that the man is or should be the active partner in the relationship and the woman the passive one is now overthrown. The new union assumes rather that the partners are equal in their ability to engage in a conversation in which their union is always at issue. Thus, "a willingness for marriage entails a certain willingness for bickering" (p. 86). While this may not be exactly a mark of absolute bliss, it expresses a sense of mutual caring and in consequence of the fact that in their search for a new union "the battle of men and women for recognition of one another" (p. 18) is both continued and renewed. Cavell points out that for all these reasons the comedy of remarriage can also be called "the comedy of equality" (p. 122), for "we are permanently in doubt who the hero is, that is, whether it is the male or the female, who is the active partner, which of them is in quest, who is following whom" (p. 122). The couple must rather work out a mutual understanding of what their union is to consist in. Cavell writes therefore: "The overarching question of comedies of remarriage is precisely the question of what constitutes a union" (p. 53). The validation of marriage is found under these conditions, as Cavell formulates in a deliberately paradoxical manner, in "the willingness for repetition, the willingness for remarriage" (p. 126f). And he makes sure that we do not forget this important point, first brought up in the discussion of *Bringing Up Baby*, by retelling it in his chapter on *The Philadelphia Story*, where he writes: "Our genre emphasizes the mystery of marriage by finding that neither law nor sexuality (nor, by implication, progeny) is sufficient to ensure marriage and suggesting that what provides legitimacy is the mutual willingness for remarriage, for a sort of continuous affirmation" (p. 142). In searching for such an understanding of their union, the couple will, no doubt, have to overcome obstacles. Even traditional comedy typically shows "a young pair overcoming individual and social obstacles to their happiness, figured as a concluding marriage that achieves individual and social reconciliations" (p. 1). What appears new in the comedies of remarriage is the fact that "the principal pair in this structure will normally draw the conclusion on their own, isolated within society, not backed by it" (p. 123). For all that, these films intend to depict no abyss between the couple and society at large. Every union in them is, rather, formed by recognizing continuities with society through "the inheritance of certain conditions, procedures, and subjects and goals" (pp. 28f).

These considerations lead Cavell immediately to his third and most far-ranging and explicitly political topic. The comedies of remarriage are, in Cavell's eyes, concerned not only with the creation of a new woman and the redefinition of her union with a man, they are equally occupied with the question of a perfected human community, and they, indeed, "propose marriage as our best emblem of this eventual community" (p. 152). Being concerned with the creation of a new woman these films deal, at the same time, with "a new creation of the human" (p. 16). They must thus be seen as parables for a new phase in "the development of consciousness" and a part of a "struggle for the reciprocity or equality of consciousness between a man and a woman" (p. 17). Marriage is, in this manner, to be seen as "an emblem of the knowledge of others not solely because of its implication of reciprocity but because it implies a devotion in repetition, to dailyness" (p. 241). In his treatment of *The Philadelphia Story*, the film's narrative concerning the marriage of Tracy Lord and C. K. Dexter Haven becomes for Cavell, accordingly, the occasion of a dream "about people convening for a covenant in or near Philadelphia and debating the nature and the relation of the classes from which they come" (p. 153). The question of their marriage is, thus, elevated to "national importance" (p. 147). The resulting debate is about "the rights of the sensuous or erotic side of human nature" against the claims of the necessary and the utilitarian (p. 155). The debate is also about "whether America will produce and recognize in human beings something to call natural aristocracy" (p. 155). It is a debate furthermore about the "balance between Western culture's two forces of authority [the Hellenic and the Hebraic] so that American mankind can refind its object, its dedication to a more perfect union, toward the perfected human community, its right to the pursuit of happiness" (p. 158). Essential in this is that all genuine union demands a constant re-union and that the true form of marriage is re-marriage. It follows that America cannot rest on the historical fact of having once established a union, but must seek constantly to "refind its object." And what holds for this particular political union holds, presumably, also for any other one.

But how useful, how compelling can these images be for us? What real help can Hollywood comedies provide us in rethinking our social and political condition? Our current global and "postmodern" situation is, of course, different from that of the period in which the Hollywood comedies of remarriage were made. It is different also from the conditions under which Cavell wrote his book on these comedies. Much has changed over the course of the last seventy years and just as much over the course of the last twenty years. Thus we realize today, in the early years of the twenty-first century, that we are facing more than the question of how to establish and maintain local, political unions. Our problem is rather that of a global society and we understand, for that reason, the need to establish a global community. But what could such a global union look like? We can, so it seems, extract some answers from Cavell's discussion, but they are admittedly tentative and incomplete. Thus, we can say, first of all, that we who contemplate such a global union will have to become in a sense new beings, that we must learn to acquire a new identity, learn to be and learn to see ourselves in new ways—yet in ways that do not obliterate who we have been before. Such a global union will have to be, furthermore, a re-union. In order to establish it, we will need, to use Cavell's words, "the reconciliation of a genuine forgiveness; a reconciliation so profound as to require the metamorphosis of death and revival; the achievement of a new perspective on existence" (p. 19). The many parties that make up global society must learn to see themselves as the same and yet also as different, as responsible for what has occurred before and yet ready to take a new turn. A global politics of the future cannot proceed without such reconciliation, forgiveness, and forgetting, without the alternation between taking responsibility for the past and opening up to a future renewal. We can see, perhaps, some of these processes already at work, but we can also see how much is needed to achieve a genuine union and re-union at a global level. Such a process would have to include Arabs and Jews, rich and poor, men and women, all races and classes, all the ruling nations and all the subjected tribes and communities and offer them part in a great reconciliation.

4

I ask myself, however, whether Cavell's comedies (and what he tells us about them) can offer us the means for dealing with such a challenge. It may turn out, first of all, that these films are overly concerned with American conditions. They may focus too much on a specifically American understanding of gender issues, and their women may be too much American and Hollywood creations. "Philadelphia" will certainly never mean as much to the world as it has meant and perhaps still means for Americans.

Katherine Hepburn is not likely to be the model for womanhood all over the world. The more general problem is that these comedies know only one model for the union and re-union of human beings and that is the union of man and woman as conceived at one moment in American history. The issues of American feminism in the 1930s or, for that matter, of American feminism in the 1980s may prove, however, too specific for understanding political union in general. Cavell and these comedies both see that there are many distinct kinds of pursuit of happiness but their pluralism carries only so far. At the time when the Hollywood comedies of re-marriage concerned themselves so exclusively with the union of men and women, other types of union were, in fact, already being imagined or invented around the globe: the new identities of as yet colonialized states, new or renewed forms of nationhood (such as that of the state of Israel), renewed religious communities (Islamic, Judaic, Christian), new commonalities of exile and refuge and transnational migration, new forms of labor relations, new understandings of sexual union, new forms of community based on new forms of communication. Enthralled by his comedies, Cavell is caught in thinking of marriage as being of unique importance for understanding the nature of social and political union and "not merely an analogy of the social bond, or a comment upon it" (p. 182). "The integrity of society," he summarizes, "is a function of the integrity of marriage, and vice versa" (p. 194).

But is this sufficient for dealing with the actually existing social diversity? To account for that one must, perhaps, turn all the way back to Aristotle and his recognition of the many-faceted nature of friendship (*philia*). Friendship is for Aristotle most broadly speaking that bond of mutual goodwill that makes human beings desire to live and act together and that makes them capable of doing so. As such it has for Aristotle numerous and distinctive forms. In one it is certainly the bond that unites men and women in marriage, but in other, distinctive forms it unites parents and children, lovers and their beloved, comrades in arms and fellow travelers, those who do business together, and also those who are politically united. There is, as Hannah Arendt has reminded us, even a form of *philia* that one can have to one's self—self-respect, in other words, a capacity to live with oneself, the ability to be at one with oneself. Understood as civic concord and trust, *philia* "would seem to hold cities together," as Aristotle writes famously in his *Nicomachean Ethics* (p. 1155a), and in his *Politics* he calls it once more "the greatest good for cities" (p. 1262b). But the specific bond of political friendship is for him different from the friendship that obtains in marriage and these two must once again be distinguished from other types of *philia*. Some forms of *philia* are, according to Aristotle, utilitarian in character, others are motivated by pleasure, yet others by our appreciation of the other person for his or her actual worth. Some forms of *philia* are relationships between equals, others between unequals. Some, like erotic love, are by their nature so close that those held together by them wish to become one; others are casual in nature like the friendships of young people or the one that unites travelers on a shared journey. Political friendship is one of the less intense forms of *philia* "for a city naturally consists of a certain multitude" and "not only of a number of people, but of people of different kinds" (*Politics*, 1261a). Civic unions are, in other words, of people already united in various forms of friendship. The relations of fellow citizens are, for that reason, of a distinctive sort. If they become too close, the city loses its uniquely political character and becomes like a household or even an individual. Aristotle concludes: "Even if someone could achieve this, it should not be done, since it will destroy the city-state" (p. 1261a). In order to maintain the diversity appropriate for city life, political friendship must then be less tight than the erotic kind, less tight than personal friendship, and less tight also than marriage.

Cavell is, of course, also a pluralist, but his variety of pluralism lies between the one espoused by Hannah Arendt, for whom the political domain is constituted as a plurality of human beings, and the one advanced by Aristotle, in which the political domain presupposes a plurality of *unions* of human beings. For Cavell, human diversity manifests itself in the fact that the union of human beings can succeed and fail in multiple ways, but there is for him in *Pursuits of Happiness* essentially only one model for a more perfected social and political union. He may, indeed, be right in thinking that the creation and maintenance of any kind of union shares characteristics with that of the creation and maintenance of a marriage. Cavell may also be right in applying the lessons he has learned from his comedies of remarriage to other types of union: namely, that all union is reunion, that all bonds require a constant reaffirmation, that forgiveness is a fundamental political virtue. But his concern with these similarities makes him forget the differences—and makes him forget, in particular, the difficulty with which, in different sorts of attempted unions, unity, reunion, reaffirmation, and forgiveness can be achieved, and this, in turn, makes him finally unable to accommodate in this context the full force of tragedy in human politics.

There are, no doubt, tragic marriages and tragic failures of marriage. But the fact remains that marriage is a chosen estate and if one marriage fails there is always the possibility of another successful one. If Tracy Lord in *The Philadelphia Story* fails to reunite with C. K. Dexter Haven, there is always the possibility of her marriage to Macauley Mike Conner, and if either of these chances falls through she can still go ahead and marry poor George Kittredge. She may even remain unmarried and still end up living happily ever after. But not all unions are voluntary, nor are all failures of unions under our control. Thus, we find ourselves thrown into a family with its history and its secret burdens or into a nation with its not so secret history, and these unchosen conditions have sometimes tragic consequences. Contrast Antigone to Tracy Lord. Antigone tells us that she would never have broken the city's law for a husband or child, since she could always have found a new husband or borne a new child, but she cannot replace her brother and, for that reason, owes him something that will bring her in conflict with the law. Her claim may sound harsh to modern ears but the message is clear. Tragedy comes from necessity and not from conditions we choose. Contrast Kreon to George Kittredge. The latter can give up his ambitions without much pain. Kreon has no other choices. He has no one to whom he could pass on the business of politics. His abdication means for him the abyss and also the abyss for the city he leaves behind. His tragedy is also the outcome of inevitability.

5

Cavell is not unaware that tragedy has its roots in necessity. In his essay "The Avoidance of Love" he grants, in fact, that "a radical necessity haunts every story of tragedy" (AL, p. 341). But in *Pursuits of Happiness* he hopes to transcend that necessity by means of a "gay and sociable wisdom" which he has taken from Thoreau and Kierkegaard (p. 238). This wisdom seems a far way off from Cavell's initial and unqualified recognition in

Pursuits of Happiness of the dual character of philosophy as both tragic and comic and the implication that the same duality must hold for both film and politics. That comedy is inherently linked to tragedy had, in any case, been already an insight in "The Avoidance of Love." Cavell had written there: "Comedy is fun because it can purge us of the unnatural and of the merely natural by laughing at us and singing to us and dancing for us, and by making us laugh and sing and dance. The tragedy is that comedy has its limits. This is part of the sadness within comedy; the emptiness after a long laugh" (AL, pp. 339f). This insight is, of course, not forgotten in *Pursuits of Happiness*. A tragic moment suggests itself for him in the films in that book that they may not actually help us navigate the rapids of our political existence. He discerns, indeed, a mythological and even Utopian element in his comedies, and the myths and Utopias they describe may forever remain just that. Acknowledging this "Utopian cast," Cavell writes of his films: "They harbor a vision which they know cannot fully be domesticated, inhabited in the world we know. They are romances. Showing us our fantasies, they express the inner agenda of a nation that conceives Utopian longings and commitments for itself" (p. 18). From the perspective of the early twenty-first century we may even conclude that these films have failed to provide us with the lessons that Cavell sought to extract from them. Against his hopes, they have not become the common possession of our culture. For many contemporary viewers they are, instead, now so dated that they have, in effect, become unwatchable. They have turned into curiosities in the local video library and their Utopias have been replaced in the public imagination by more violent, more disruptive, and altogether darker myths.

Cavell's films, by contrast, always envisage the possibility of a reconciliation of social solidarity and personal sweetness. They certainly know that there is tragedy. Like philosophy, they begin, in fact, in something like tragedy, though, perhaps, only mock tragedy. Jerry Warriner, the male protagonist in *The Awful Truth*, says therefore mockingly that his marriage "was one of those tragedies you read about in newspapers" (p. 235). And Cavell adds to this as his own commentary that "a tragedy is as likely as not to be what newspapers would make of it" (p. 244). But this is surely not all there is to it for him, for he also recognizes that "when sweetness and social solidarity conflict there may be tragedy, and in this world they will conflict" (p. 4). In discussing *His Girl Friday*, Cavell, indeed, draws our attention to the darkness and heartlessness of the world which the film inhabits. Looking back from this film to the other comedies of remarriage, he detects in each of them "a glimpse of the failure of civilization to, let me say, make human beings civil" (p. 184). Love, marriage, or more generally the union of a man and a woman will prove inevitably threatened under these conditions. Even so, Cavell is intent on downplaying the tragic consequences. He sees the comedies of remarriage, instead, as offering us "the possibility of reprieve, a real, if in each case temporary, relief from the pain of the world" (p. 183). And in this thought he draws on Michel de Montaigne's sentiment that "life is hard, but then let us not burden it further by choosing tragically to call it tragic, where we are free to choose otherwise." When experience is forced upon us and we are made to learn from it, there may be tragedy, but there is also hope for comedy as long as there is the possibility of experiencing and learning "in good time" (p. 183).

We may contrast Cavell's understanding of politics here with Max Weber's more single-mindedly tragic vision. For Weber it is clear that politics demands a "knowledge of tragedy with which all action, but especially political action, is truly interwoven" (PV, p. 115).[6] Politics is for him inherently tragic because it exposes us to radically conflicting demands, to the pull of fundamentally different kinds of obligation. One of these is an "ethic of ultimate ends," the other an "ethic of responsibility." Anyone guided by absolute moral ideals and by these alone will feel responsible only "for seeing to it that the flame of pure intentions is not squelched." In the worldly arena of politics, however, even the noblest ends are attainable only through dubious means (PV, p. 121), for politics inevitably relies on the use of power, force, and ultimately violence. The peculiar ethical problem of all politics and the one that provides it with its distinctively tragic character is thus the problem of "the specific means of legitimate violence" for "whosoever contracts with violent means for whatever ends—and every politician does—is exposed to its specific consequences" (PV, p. 124). Such violence will always and inevitably appear as problematic from the demanding viewpoint of an ethic of ultimate ends. It follows that the proponent of such an ethic "cannot stand up under the ethical irrationality of the world" (PV, p. 122). Anyone who feels called to politics must, therefore, accept the unavoidable ethical paradoxes in this field. He must let himself in for "the diabolic forces lurking in all violence," and he must know that he is responsible "for what may become of him under the impact of these paradoxes" (PV, pp. 125–26).

Cavell would have to respond that Weber has got hold at best of half a truth. While he is strongly (perhaps too strongly) attuned to the tragic potential of politics, he lacks an ear, so it seems, for its comic side. We must agree with Cavell that tragedy makes sense finally only as failed happiness. The right conclusion may be that tragedy and comedy are complementary characteristics of all politics. They originate from two ways of looking at ourselves that are both indispensable and yet also incompatible. Tragedy arises from looking behind ourselves and discovering that the suffering of the present is the inevitable consequence of past happenings, of long-forgotten errors, and of hidden crimes. "The mighty words of the proud are paid in full with mighty blows of fate, and at long last those blows will teach us wisdom," as Sophocles' *Antigone* concludes.[7] Comedy adds to this a very different insight, because it looks forward toward new possibilities; it perceives the present in terms of the promises it contains; it recognizes that happiness is never completely achieved but that the pursuit of happiness is always a possibility. Comedy tells us also that the miseries depicted by tragedy lose significance, if we cannot conceive of alternatives, if there is not even a glimmer of hope, if the pursuit of happiness is inconceivable. The tears of tragedy move us, in fact, only because there is always the possibility of laughter. Tragedy, thus, calls for completion through comedy and gains its meaning only in this connection. But the reverse may also be true, that the pursuit of happiness loses significance if it becomes a mere pursuit of enjoyment, that it gains its meaning only against the dark tapestry of the tragic. Cavell recognizes that sweetness and social solidarity will conflict in this world. He knows that for an angel, and only for an angel, "there is no distinction between comedy and tragedy" (p. 216). The Hollywood comedies of remarriage are, thus, for him, like Shakespeare's comedies, both "an opposite" and a "shadow of tragedy" (p. 223).

We can understand this best when we compare Cavell's discussion of *King Lear* with his reading of the comedies of remarriage. If we can take *Lear* as expressing archetypal features of all tragedy, we can say that both tragedy and comedy call for reversal and hence a return to the beginning. "We have, as tragic figures do, to go back to the beginnings, either to undo or to be undone," Cavell writes in "The Avoidance of Love." In the tragic situation we find ourselves repeating "the thing which has caused tragedy, as though at some point in the past history is stuck, and time marks time there waiting to be released" (AL, p. 349). In *Lear*, tragedy issues from the avoidance of love, but it appears from the comedies of remarriage that love can also be grasped, that history can become unstuck and time released. Cavell quotes approvingly Nevill Coghill's characterization of Shakespearean comedy as expressing "the idea that life is to be grasped," not avoided, and that such comedy is therefore "the opposite of Tragedy in that the catastrophe solves all confusions and misunderstandings by some happy turn of events" (p. 170). For Weber there can never be any such respite, not even a temporary one. Political tragedy arises for him from the inevitable conflict between power and ultimate ends. That picture certainly derives from Greek tragedy and perhaps specifically from Sophocles' *Antigone*. Or rather, it derives from a specifically Christian interpretation of Greek tragedy in which Antigone is said to be standing for an ethics of ultimate ends while her opponent Kreon is assumed to be driven by the needs of political power. But one may wonder whether this characterization is adequate for *Antigone* or any other Greek tragedy. Ethical paradoxes arise for the Greeks not, in fact, from a conflict between worldly responsibility and ultimate and unworldly ends, but from competing and conflicting claims on the tragic characters. These conflicts may derive from the opposing demands of the living and the dead, the chthonic and the Olympian gods, the family and the polis, civic order and Dionysian rapture, or the tension between individual intention and impersonal fate. Greek drama offers thus a multiplicity of accounts of the sources of tragedy and, hence, also the possibility of multiple forms of escape from the tragic consequences. Greek tragedy is therefore tied essentially to Greek comedy and the satyr play. This is the lesson Cavell also seems to be exploring in *Pursuits of Happiness*. The conflicts in which his couples are embroiled are never the product of a collision between an ethic of ultimate ends and one of worldly responsibility. His couples are, in fact, never concerned with ultimate ends but with the variable and contingent conditions of their own happiness. Cavell's comedies show us that conflict and hence tragedy have not only one possible source but that there are also manifold ways of seeking to overcome that conflict.

6

Cavell's political reflections in *Pursuits of Happiness* have the double goal of rethinking politics and rethinking political philosophy. Since its beginnings in the work of Plato and Aristotle our tradition has always seen political philosophy as concerned with providing binding formulas for human coexistence, solid foundations for the state, and a priori principles of political action and political judgment. In *Pursuits of Happiness* Cavell speaks differently, and this is to his credit. He understands his own philosophical purpose not as aiming at normative truths but as bringing "into question the issue of our common cultural inheritance" (p. 9) and as an effort to test "the limits or the density of what we may call our common cultural inheritance" (ibid.). Philosophy, he writes (and he must mean here philosophy properly, that is philosophically, understood), "seeks to disquiet the foundations of our lives and to offer us in recompense nothing better than itself" (pp. 8f). The philosopher is, in Cavell's picture, certainly not in a position to establish absolute, hard, and binding standards. He appears in Cavell's comedies and in his book, instead, as a father-figure endowed with a certain power of magic who knows at the same time that "renewal or reconciliation or restoration" exacts "the task of the laying aside of magic" (p. 50). The entire narrative of *It Happened One Night* can, in Cavell's account, be "summarized in the first of the newspaper headlines that punctuate it: Ellie Andrews Escapes Father" (p. 84). And it is not only the heroine that regularly escapes her father in this and the other comedies. Politics, more broadly speaking, escapes philosophy, because it is not the philosopher's job to make rules for those who seek political coexistence. Such rules will, rather, have to be elaborated by those engaged in defining, establishing, and maintaining their own social union. It follows from this among other things that politics cannot be simply a matter of justice (assuming that principles of justice *can* be laid down in a formula) but that it requires other qualities such as the willingness to accept guilt, the readiness to offer forgiveness, and the capacity for reconciliation, the acceptance of love.

In casting a disquieting eye on politics, Cavell comes up with insights that escape the common sort of political philosopher. I mean, in particular, his thought that politics can be seen as a form of *paideia* rather than rule, his discovery that the most ordinary business of everyday life can also be seen in political terms and that politics is therefore found not only at the level of government and the state but just as much in the daily do-ings of human life, and also the profound idea that all human union is a form of reunion and can be maintained only through a constant renewal. I mean here, above all, however, Cavell's insight into the comic aspect of politics. Philosophers see politics for the most part as a matter of rational calculation. That picture is certainly insufficient in that it overlooks the role of the emotions or passions in politics. Cavell adds to this the further observation that the release of these emotions in laughter is just as much part of our political life, that comedy, satire, wit, and joke are also essen-tial ingredients of our political existence. But in drawing such lessons from the Hollywood of remarriage we must not forget that tragedy, too, is "al-ways political." And it is so because it is always "about the incompatibil-ity between a particular love and a particular social arrangement of love" (AL, p. 347).

This brings me finally to Nietzsche and to Nietzsche's understanding of the human condition and to Cavell's relation to Nietzsche's thought. In Cavell's questioning of the role of philosophy in *Pursuits of Happiness* we can certainly discern an affinity to Nietzsche. Nietzsche is, indeed, central to Cavell's whole reading of the comedies of remarriage. Those films, he writes at the end of his book, recall for him "the two most impressive affir-mations known to me of the tasks of human experience, the acceptance of human relatedness, as the acceptance of repetition" (p. 241). One of these is Kierkegaard's study of the possibility of marriage in his book *Repetition*; the other is to be found in Nietzsche's thought of the Eternal Recurrence. Cavell summarizes the lessons he has learned from his two eminent prede-cessors in the thought that "redemption by happiness does not depend on something that has yet to happen," just as "redemption by suffering does not depend something that has already happened." Both, rather, "depend on faith in something that is always happening, day by day" (p. 241). Both Kierkegaard and Nietzsche call us, thus, to "a devotion in repetition, to dailyness" (p. 241). And this means for Cavell, in turn, "a massive break-through to the comic itself as the redemption of dailyness" (p. 242). At the end of his entire book, at the core of his whole philosophical argument, we encounter then Nietzsche's "new vision of time, or a new stance toward it, an acceptance of the Eternal Recurrence" (p. 262). This means, as Cavell writes, a coming together of "time and of childhood and of forgiveness and of overcoming revenge and of an acceptance of the repetitive needs of the body and the soul—of one's motion and one's motives, one's ecstasies and routines, one's sexuality and one's loves" (ibid.).

But in reading comedy in terms of Nietzsche's vision of the Eternal Recurrence we must not forget that it is for Nietzsche both an affirmative and a melancholy truth. We encounter it in our "loneliest hour," by ourselves in the moonlight, contemplating the coldly glittering circles of the spider's web. The thought of the Eternal Recurrence may offer us, then, the possibility of an ever-repeated affirmation, but it announces itself also as an unbreakable necessity, and such necessity, as we know from the Greeks, is also always the root of tragedy. It is true, Nietzsche writes in his essay *On the Genealogy of Morals*, that a great tragedian will only reach "the final summit of his achievement when he knows how to see himself and his art *beneath* him—and knows how to *laugh* at himself."[8] All the great teachers of purpose, he writes in a similar vein in *The Gay Science*, have, in fact, "in the long run" been vanquished by laughter. "The short tragedy always gave way again and returned into the eternal comedy of existence." Setting himself against the philosophical mainstream—and against the spirit of seriousness of his own earlier writings—Nietzsche in *Gay Science* derides the ever-repeated sentiment that "there is something at which it is absolutely forbidden henceforth to laugh." Instead, he announces the possibility of a new, merry, singing, and dancing consciousness. But Nietzsche admits reluctantly after more thought that "for the present things are still quite different. For the present, the comedy of existence has not yet 'become conscious' of itself. For the present, we still live in the age of tragedy, the age of moralities and religion." And he concludes in a yet more cautiously reflective mood that corresponds to the juncture between Cavell's "Avoidance of Love" and his *Pursuits of Happiness*: "Not only laughter and gay wisdom but the tragic, too, with all its sublime unreason belongs among the means and necessities of the preservation of the species."[9]

CHAPTER ELEVEN

Cordelia's Calculus: Love and Loneliness in Cavell's Reading of *Lear*

Thomas L. Dumm

These old-fashioned contingencies shamed us
but the new had no agenda, no secret plan or past.

—ANN LAUTERBACH, "SEPTEMBER SONG"

Sovereignty and Presence

In studies published over the past several years, some important contemporary thinkers have retraced the path of representational power back to what may have been an originary moment of sovereignty, that is, to a moment when a law of human being may first have been enunciated. If undertaken in earlier eras of scholarship such studies may well have been predominantly theological in character, but such frameworks of understanding are not available to scholars who have learned how important it is to grapple with the consequences of the death of God. It is a mark of their courage that these thinkers write without such authority. Eschewing the doctrinal, their works focus on transitions, liminal spaces, obscure moments, impossibly fragile circumstances on the thresholds of death and birth that shaped and energized sovereign power as it emerged from fields of ancient circumstance and came to shape political experience. Appreciative of the power of theistic faith, they have come to realize that to trace sovereignty in this time requires more exacting and disillusioned methods, for if the death of God has given us the message that all things are possible, it also means that the question of sovereignty is more than ever at issue in the play of human being.

While their points of departure have varied, these thinkers have had similar reasons for tracing sovereignty: they have all sought to provide us with ethical responses to a crisis that is urgently contemporary, and have found in the study of sovereignty and its vicissitudes a key to understanding the depth and breadth of that crisis. As the status of sovereignty becomes a question in late modernity, they see in its genealogy lessons for us, ways that we might be able to move forward as human beings out of the shadow of a politics that has come to risk our existence in its name. For all of these thinkers, the quality of the future of humankind depends upon a common recognition of and attempt to influence the path of sovereignty's (dis)solution.

Following upon and refining a key insight of Carl Schmitt concerning the relationship of sovereignty to law, Giorgio Agamben has recently rehabilitated the figure of *homo sacer*, illuminating the abject power of the untouchable killer who establishes order from outside of the community. For Agamben, the sovereign is uniquely located in a liminal non-place so as to be able to establish law by determining the exception to it. The mysteriousness of exceptional being is the obscurity that covers its closeness to a primordial, bare life. A secret held by no one bars our way from being present in the circumstances that either force or allow a sovereign power to decide. That source of sovereignty cannot be enunciated without the irretrievable loss of the very quality that enables sovereign being to emerge. We may come to know of sovereign power only by imagining the unimaginable—the return to bare life—that accompanies the loss of its ordering force in law, teetering on the edge of an abyss at that infinitely obscure point between life and death.[1]

From a different position, Judith Butler has located another allegiance that emerges from this ancient unnameable place, not yet symbolic, and not quite of the order of kinship against which the state is to constitute itself. In the moment of Antigone's refusal to obey the state and instead to bury her brother, her allegiance to the demands of the forever dead can only overtake the demands of the living state through an impossible performance. And as her sister Ismeme says, "Impossible things should not be tried at all." In response to this impossibility, Antigone still acts. Her action allows her to *speak* an unwritten law in the face of the written law of the state, it invests her with a power to refer the polity back to the not yet symbolic realm of kinship between life and death, transforming kinship's possibilities for both crossing genders and invoking a future. That Antigone is a figment of the poetic imagination of Sophocles need not deter us from understanding the truth of her action: indeed, through Sophocles' tragedy we may come to know her performance better.[2]

From yet another starting point, in their wide-ranging study of globalization and its consequences, Michael Hardt and Antonio Negri have imagined the loss of a centered system of imperial power as having everything to do with the creation of contemporary empire. In the dissipation and pathetic transfiguration of sovereignty they suggest that we can discern a remaking of the world that is to be subordinated to a power without center. Power comes to penetrate the infrastructure of each and every body and the forces that emanate from them through an intensification and radical fragmentation of the symbolic codes of commodification, even as an untraceable source of sovereignty flees from the realm of appearances. Down to the level of the (dis)possessed subject who once met the needs of epochal capital, they picture a transfiguration under way as radical as Antigone's enunciation of an unwritten law, the possibility of a democratic politics emerging through the flesh of a multitudinous being of a humanity yet to come.[3]

All of these thinkers want to understand better an originary moment of sovereignty, not to engage in exercises of conservation or reaction, but to locate some points against which we may begin to reckon sovereign authority's loss and the possible recuperation of human being in the wake of that loss. Variously hazarding accusations of hyperbole, they all see the current moment as one of ontological crisis, as old forms give way to new worlds not yet knowable, and consequently as the very future of human being comes to be in need of rethinking. Joined by others of us, they hope to speak to the urgency of the time, and yet they are chastened by their own audacity, and variously acknowledge that they are not yet able to say to us what is not yet sayable. Moreover, all of these thinkers are concerned with the question of sovereignty, not out of a sense of responsibility to past or future, but out of a sense of responsibility to the present. They struggle to free ethical thinking from the Procrustean bed of the alternative historical narratives of progress and telos.[4]

How we may adequately characterize the present is the unavoidable topic of this essay, written as a reflection on a meditation on the tragedy of the condition of failing to be present in the present, for if a cardinal failure of humans in the twentieth century was a refusal to allow the present to be present, and this failure was a consequence of a concomitant poverty of sympathetic imagination—a claim recently advanced by the political theorist George Kateb—then Cavell's thinking about the idea of being present importantly distinguishes his contribution to the reinstantiation of ethical human being for the twenty-first century.[5] Because the theme of being present and its relationship to the present time was first broached by Cavell as a political matter early in his writings by way of an extended discussion of Shakespeare's *Tragedy of King Lear* in his deeply influential essay "The Avoidance of Love," the most important concerns of these thinkers have been adumbrated by him. Through the critical study of Lear, Cavell has foregrounded questions concerning the relationship of presence to being present, acknowledgment to knowledge, sovereignty to power, shame to self-consciousness, and the particularity of character to national aspiration. At the heart of those different concerns, the relationship of love to loneliness and the import of that relationship to shaping the body—what Cavell calls "the first object of shame"—is the figuring of a body as nation and nation as an impossible presence. In untying this knot of the body's relationship to nation, he thus gives us a critical purchase on the paradox of sovereignty in the age of sovereignty's dissolution.

Cavell introduces "The Avoidance of Love" with a discussion of the role that the analysis of character may play in thinking about tragic drama.[6] He is interested in character not because he is uninterested in language, but because to comprehend the use of words it is necessary to understand the intersection of the words that are used and who it is who uses them. For Cavell, the comprehension of the meaning of an event, as a philosophical matter, cannot be separated from the meaning a particular person attaches to it. When this already complicated connection is further contextualized by various analyses concerning the uncertainty of intention, we are asked to think more deeply about the fate of what we say and do. As he puts it, the word "ordinary" in ordinary language

reminds us that whatever words are said and meant are said and meant by particular [persons], and to understand what they (the words) mean you must understand what they (whoever is using them) mean, and that sometimes [people] do
not see what they mean, that usually they cannot say what they mean, that for various reasons they may not know what they mean, and that when they are forced
to recognize this they feel they do not, and perhaps cannot, mean anything, and
they are struck dumb. (AL, p. 270)

Cavell's hope is that the supposedly finite space of a staged play allows us
a certain permission to explore the issues associated with the claims of ordinary language philosophy. And yet upon reflection he understands that
this supposed finitude does not allow us the certainty we would seek. If
once we humans did, we do not now live in such a world, and Cavell is at
pains to show us not only why this is so, but to share with us a sensibility
that may invite us to think again about how we are to be with each other
in this world.

    As Lear's tragic dilemma becomes ours through the migrations of
sovereignty in the modern era, we may come to feel something akin to his
shame. Caught between twinned impossibilities, which for lack of better terms we might call national identity on the one hand and personal autonomy on the other, we are faced with a great responsibility and a
great opportunity to change our posture toward our common existence.
Yet whether and how Lear's dilemma has become ours still remain to be
seen. For this reason, one import of Cavell's reading of *King Lear* still rests
largely in the claims his reading may allow us to make regarding a recovery
of our selves in the face of a tragedy that somehow has become a defining
limit of our experiential possibilities.

Encompassing Shame

    Cavell suggests that a core motivation of the character Lear in Shake-
speare's tragedy is his wish to avoid the love of his daughters. His claim
is that Lear experiences a deep shame, that the tragedy begins because of
"[his] attempt to avoid recognition, the shame of exposure, the threat of
self-revelation" (p. 286). Lear accepts the counterfeit love of Regan and
Goneril, but he becomes enraged at Cordelia, who refuses to accept his
bribe and instead tells the truth, that she love him truly. His rage at her

honesty is a reaction to his own shame. This shame is complexly social. It is not allowed for Lear to love without the accouterments of sovereignty, and his (failed) abdication, a parceling out of power that frustrates an honest expression of love, redounds as a tragedy, as a great crime to futurity, because there is no solution to his problem—he cannot escape the shame of his need to avoid love by any route save madness, and he cannot recover from his madness through any means other than a reentry into the struggle for self-revelation that results in the death of his children and himself.

It is shame, not guilt, that motivates Lear. Shame is everywhere in the crisis of Lear, moving him, moving Gloucester, moving every character who despite all, loves, even if they are unable to acknowledge the love of those who love them back.[7] Cavell writes:

[Shame] is the most isolating of feelings, the most comprehensible perhaps in idea, but the most incomprehensible or incommunicable in fact. Shame, I've said, is the most primitive, the most private, of emotions; but it is also the most primitive of *social* responses. With the discovery of the individual, whether in Paradise or in the Renaissance, there is the simultaneous discovery of the isolation of the individual; his presence to himself, but simultaneously to *others*. Moreover, shame is felt not only toward one's own actions and one's own being, but toward the actions and the being of those with whom one is identified—fathers, daughters, wives . . . , the beings whose self-revelations reveal oneself. Families, any objects of one's love and commitment, ought to be the places where shame is overcome (hence happy families are all alike); but they are also the place of its deepest manufacture, and one is then hostage to that power, or fugitive. (p. 286)[8]

That the family in this case is the royal family, that the fate of a nation rests on the abdication of Lear, broadens the import of this shame. But the shame is more encompassing than any family, and even may overflow the containment of any nation. How encompassing is the shame of Lear? Cavell's sense of Lear's shame, given his profound sense of the import of Lear's being a sovereign power seeking to abdicate, resists the psychologizing of shame that would go by the name of guilt. This turn toward something other than guilt, a move instead toward what may be called the ontological, is at the heart of the crisis represented by Lear's shame.[9] Thought about politically, shame has a double aspect: primitive and private, yet social. In the crossing of these elements the ontological dimension of shame becomes apparent to those who are subject to its power.

In a discussion of shame that bears directly if implicitly upon the problem of abdication presented by *King Lear*, but explicitly addresses the problem of developing a post-Auschwitzian ethics, Giorgio Agamben suggests that it would be an error to think of the double aspect of shame as being dialectical in character: shame overwhelms the guilty/innocent binary of the tragic figure as read backward into tragedy from Hegel until the middle of the twentieth century.[10] Agamben argues that shame—*aidos*—may connect us to the most fundamental affective condition of existence. In a gloss on Martin Heidegger's reading of the term in his lectures on Parmenides, he suggests that Heidegger understands shame to be "a kind of ontological sentiment that has its characteristic place in the encounter between man and Being." He (controversially) cites Heidegger as saying, "Being itself carries with itself shame, the shame of Being."[11] Noting that Heidegger suggests that we may understand shame better if we were to compare it to disgust (and noting as well that Heidegger fails to develop that point), Agamben guides us to Walter Benjamin's discussion of disgust as being the experience of recognizing oneself in an alterity that cannot be assumed—"that is, he subjectifies himself in an absolute desubjectification."[12] He closes this element of his discussion of shame with a provisional definition: "[Shame] is nothing less than the fundamental sentiment of being a subject, in the two apparently opposed senses of this phrase; to be subjected and to be sovereign. Shame is what is produced in the absolute concomitance of subjectification and desubjectification, self-loss and self-possession, servitude and sovereignty."[13] This recapitulation of the production of shame echoes what would seem to be one of Cavell's most straightforward assertions: "[I]n *King Lear* shame comes first, and brings rage and folly in its train" (AL, p. 287). We can readily imagine Lear's situation within the dynamics that Agamben describes as he attempts to abdicate. But we may wonder if it is the act of abdication that establishes the condition of shame, or if Lear attempts to abdicate because of his shameful condition.

If Agamben's linkage of shame to disgust is plausible, we need to comprehend the blinding of Gloucester, in the subplot that Cavell convincingly links to the main plot of *King Lear* through the vehicle of shame and lack of recognition, to be connected to the main plot through this feeling state of disgust as well (AL, pp. 278–89). The vile jelly gouged from Gloucester's eye; Lear's later desire to wipe his hand that smells of mortality

before Gloucester kisses it: these are disgusting phenomena. The jelly ooz-
es, the hand stinks, in both cases we are repulsed by matter out of place.[14]
They materialize the shame within the individual bodies of Gloucester
and Lear. (And we may also wonder at Lear's first object of rage, Cordelia, as possibly causing him disgust even as she breaks his heart by loving
him truly.[15])

The seat of disgust is the stomach, not the head. If we trace (shame-
lessly? clinically?) the corporeality of the body of Lear, we may find other
ways to express the linkages between the King's body and the nation. Informed not only by Heidegger but by recent neurophysiological research,
William E. Connolly has suggested that disgust is a thought-imbued feeling.[16] Connolly argues that an ethical "politics of becoming" entails a sort
of body work that encourages more explicit connections between feeling
states and abstract reasoning than is possible under the prevailing neo-
Kantian paradigm of thought, with its absolutizing distinctions between
the sensible and the supersensible. As part of a project to develop a political
ethos of pluralization, he seeks to overcome some of the most basic distinctions between these differing states of thought by focusing on the somatics
of thinking. In reference to disgust as a thought-imbued feeling he writes:

> Since multiple brains in each human have a complex social structure, with numer-
> ous sites existing in domestic, foreign, and warlike relations, you work on several
> registers of subjectivity and intersubjectivity in relation to each other. You some-
> times work on corporealized patterns of cultural appraisal, reviewing periodically
> the effects that work upon your explicit articulations. In the light of that review,
> you might renew your previous effort or pursue another strategy, all the while
> keeping one eye on a larger ethical agenda: the expansion of little spaces of joy and
> generosity already there so as to cultivate the spirit needed to respond creatively
> and generously to political movements of identity that cast universal pretensions
> of this or that aspect of your own identity into doubt.[17]

Connolly wants to show us how through living our metaphors we affec-
tively modify the materiality of our mortal selves. The crossing and re-
crossing of thought and action, the play of words and deeds, the active re-
lays between brain, body, and culture are deeply corporeal elements in the
politics of becoming. How we embody our thoughts affects the postures
that we hold not only in regard to the materiality of our psychic states,
but in regard to the metaphors we live through, operating to materialize

those metaphors, in a sense de-metaphorizing and re-metaphorizing our statements in language through our bodies as they enact or perform our statements. In the face of dominant metaphors of political life that fix into place such divisions as public and private, the infrapolitics of embodiment that operates at the level of the infrasensible appears as a haunting of the modern world. This infrapolitics is a primal site of incitement and provocation, surfacing too often in the most contentious and horrifying of visceral reactions, leading to political repressions made in the name of saving us from our selves.

If we were to apply Connolly's analysis of disgust to Lear, we may imagine that Lear's shame leads him through the territory of disgust, and that Lear's working through of his disgust is a way toward reclaiming a sort of sanity out of his madness, however unsuccessful the journey's end is to be. Lear's disgust must focus on the reclamation of his abdicated self as a precondition of his return to sanity. Before that moment, he must go through a severe test of his encompassing shame. Early in the storm scene, after rejecting an offer of shelter, terrified that in the absence of the distraction of the storm his thoughts will dwell on the harm his daughters have inflicted upon him, Lear describes this struggle in somatic terms.

Lear. Thou think'st 'tis much that this contentious storm
Invades us to the skin; so 'tis to thee;
But where the greater malady is fix'd,
the lesser is scarce felt. Thou'dst shun a bear,
But if [thy] flight lay toward the roaring sea,
Thou'dst meet the bear i' th' mouth. When the mind's free,
The body's delicate; [this] tempest in my mind
Doth from my senses take all feeling else,
Save what beats there—filial ingratitude!
Is it not as this mouth should tear this hand
For lifting food to't? But I will punish home.
No, I will weep no more. In such a night
To shut me out? Pour on, I will endure.
In such a night as this? O Regan, Goneril!
Your old kind father, whose frank heart gave all—
O, that way madness lies, let me shun that!
No more of that. (III.iv.6–22)[18]

Lear's body is engaged in a great civil war. His mouth and his hand are as his daughters and him: his body can withstand the storm from the heaven but not the storm from his brain and his gut, the storm that he projects upon his kin, that is begun with his attempted abdication. Good Cartesian in practice, his mind is overwhelming his delicate body; it is taking from his senses all feeling, voiding the affective contents of his body, concentrating the very beat of his heart on the powerful and obsessive beating, the constant thought of what his children have refused him. He struggles with that mind through his body, but he is rent by the struggle—his is the physical enactment of the mind/body split, once writ large upon the King's Two Bodies, now brought down to a shape and scale both familiar and shocking in his diminished state, brought about by the foolishness of abdication. But even as he rages honestly, and suffers with a clarity that communicates a great power, he still lies—if even or only to himself—about what makes his heart beat this way, because while he gave all earthly goods to Regan and Goneril, his heart was not true in the giving. He must undergo the storm and all that follows, and he will still not come to rest even as he recovers his sanity.

The paradox of his (failed) abdication puts Lear in this place of absolute concomitance, this place of shame. Lear in the storm tries to inhabit his shame and dispel it: an animal beneath the sky and above the ground, barely holding onto that narrow strip of human habitation.

Lear. Thou wert better in a grave than to answer
with thy uncover'd body this extremity of the skies. Is
man no more than this? Consider him well. Thou
ow'st the worm no silk, the beast no hide, the sheep no
wool, the cat no perfume. Ha? Here's three on's
are sophisticated. Thou art the thing itself: unaccommodated man is no more but such a poor, bare, fork'd
animal as thou art. Off, off, you lendings! Come,
unbutton here. [*Tearing off his clothes.*]   (III.iv.101–9)

The sovereign stripped to nakedness embodies the limits of existence. Lear has not transcended his corporeal being: the two bodies of this king have imploded into animality. The transfiguration of *zoë* as traced in Agamben's amalgam of Foucault's biopolitics and Arendt's *homo laborans*, the unqualified entry of bare life into political calculus, which Agamben reveals as the foundational event of a modernity we have so far failed to reckon with—this moment is represented in Lear's nakedness as his becoming-animal.[19]

But in the heart of madness Lear still has further to go. "Is man no more than this?" he asks, and yet he is still evading his shame. The grave, the sky, the habitation of that space between. This unaccommodated man, in his animality, is still capable of disgust. Lear's disgust, as an element of his shame, drives him into the wild and prepares him for his return. As audience we know, of course, that Lear's return is to be impossible—there is nowhere to turn to by the end, the kingdom he divided and renounced to begin his madness is in dissolution: the capture of Cordelia and her murder by Edmund's order seals his own death. In the meantime, as he waits for death, Lear's wandering will implicate us all in a failed abdication, as his fall to mortality enlists us in his rage.

Mother

But what is the character of this rage that follows in the train of shame? Cavell is led to his reading of shame—the avoidance of recognition—first through his reading of the climactic moment of Lear's self-recognition and his return from the condition of madness. In both the descent and "recovery" the key to comprehending Lear's character is the fact that this man is a king attempting to abdicate to his children. Abdication puts Lear in an impossible position in reference to filial devotion—he wants to give his children everything, but because he is sovereign he must demand proof of their love in return, he must *dictate* the terms of his *abdication.* Hence, Cavell convincingly argues, he would be happiest if in response to his demand for love, he were to receive, not authentic statements of it, but counterfeit expressions. In this way, he could at least comfort himself with not having to know truly whether his daughters love him or not. When Cordelia fails to comply with his wish, she reveals the falseness of his demand. This revelation sets the tragedy in motion. Out of his shame, Lear becomes enraged, first at Cordelia, for being true, and then, later, at Goneril and Regan, for being truly false. Their true falseness is revealed, by his lights, when they reject him from their homes, the very kingdom that he had bequeathed to them as a result of having divided his own.

To falsely simplify, we might be tempted to say that while on the throne Lear had wanted false love, but now that he is off the throne he wants true love, if only he could find it. Goneril and Regan give him false love while he rules in return for power, but now that they have power, why may they not see his request for shelter as offensive, as a renewed demand for the counterfeit expression they only gave him when he held sovereign power over them? Niceties of etiquette aside, Lear can only represent a threat to them now, and they will deal with him accordingly. Their calculus is straightforward: do unto Lear before he does unto them.

Lear's rage, however, must be reckoned differently than that if we are to get the heart of the matter. Having imagined himself rejected by Goneril, upon his departure from her castle Lear sends his servant, the disguised Kent, ahead to announce his untimely visit to his other favored daughter, Regan. He comes upon his unfortunate emissary in stocks, a result of the fact that Goneril had sent her servant (Oswald) to warn Regan of Lear's coming. Learning of his servant's harsh treatment at the hands of his daughter Regan enrages Lear, who in a moment of transcendent anger warns himself of the madness welling up within him.

Lear. O how this mother swells up toward my heart!
[*Hysterica*] *passio*, down thou climbing sorrow,
Thy element's below.—Where is this daughter? (II.iv.55–58)

This exclamation, the first overt self-acknowledgment by Lear of his madness in the play, is an extraordinary moment in which the various themes of the play find expression—love, loss, (mis)recognition, shame, sovereignty, and nihilism, all circling around that particular word "mother." *The Riverside Shakespeare* comments that in this passage "mother" means hysteria, which connects it to the Greek *husterikos*—of the womb.[20] Tracing the word "mother" through the OED we may observe the metonymic chain at work in a series of definitions that emerge in the late fourteenth century. "Mother" is defined as the womb (definition III.12.a)—and this part of the body serves to define the whole. When the womb becomes disordered, then the word describes the disorder of "*a rising (suffocation, swelling upward) of the mother. Hysteria.*" I think that the hysteria of the mother plays a crucial role in the madness of Lear, linking affective state to metaphorical powers, imagination becoming embodied through the displacements of gender, the whole way up and down. There is a silent metonymical doubling at the heart of this tragedy, in which Lear's abdication—the loss of the Crown—that results in the loss of the King himself, is paralleled by an offstage tragedy in which the loss of the Queen, which may have triggered the abdication, results in the loss of the Queen's daughter, Cordelia. (Cordelia would most likely be this queen's daughter, as the youngest of the three children.)

Love and loss—where *is* the mother in Lear? This play begins with the abdication scene, the crucial scene that sets all events in motion, and yet we do not know why Lear chooses this moment of all moments to abdicate. In the universe of the play, the event of the decision to abdicate occurs off stage. Misrecognition and shame—is Lear the mother of these motherless children, and is this a source of his shame? If Lear's hysteria is an expression of his impossible desire to mother his children, this explanation may supplement Cavell's accounting for Lear's avoidance of love, and his desire to have only its signs. The moment of what may be Lear's most repulsive expressions of hate lends credence to this idea.[21] When Lear meets Gloucester, still mad, immediately after Gloucester is led by Edgar to the false edge of Dover cliff, Lear responds to Gloucester when Gloucester recognizes his voice.

Lear. Ay, every inch a king!
When I do stare, see how the subject quakes.
I pardon that man's life. What was thy cause?
Adultery?
Thou shall not die. Die for adultery? No,
the wren goes to't, and the small gilded fly
Does lecher in my sight.
Let copulation thrive; for Gloucester's bastard son
Was kinder to his father than my daughters
Got 'tween the lawful sheets.
To't, luxury, pell-mell, for I lack soldiers.
Behold, yond simp'ring dame,
Whose face between her forks presages snow;
That minces virtue, and does shake the head
To hear of pleasure's name—
The fitchew nor the soiled horse goes to't
With a more riotous appetite.
Down from the waist they are Centaurs,
Though women all above;

But to the girdle do the gods inherit,
Beneath is all the fiends': there's hell, there's darkness,
There is the sulphorous pit, burning, scalding,
Stench, consumption. Fie, fie, fie! pah, pah!
Give me an ounce of civet, good apothecary,
Sweeten my imagination. There's money for thee.   (IV.vi.107–31)

Lear's kingly consideration of the pardonable adulterer places matters in terrible context: women's sexuality is an expression of great evil in an oblique yet overwhelming comparison to the evil of that fruit of illegitimate if not adulterous love, that bastard son of Gloucester: Edmund, he who is proximately responsible for both his father's blinding and Cordelia's death. Lear begins by suggesting that women are to be considered as animals below the waist, but he concludes, using the Elizabethan slang for women's genitalia, "hell," by suggesting that there is a fiendish corruption emitted from their bodies that is beyond animal, deeply, fetidly, rottenly evil. And it is a torment for Lear to think that from his lawful sheets, from his wife evil bit, come his daughters. In this rant, it all comes together as a misogyny that reduces, if it does not completely eliminate, distinctions, most importantly the distinction that might be made between love and mere lust.

How is Lear to overcome this mad hatred? Bloom suggests that the deepest pathos of this most misogynistic passage is expressed in the line, "Sweeten my imagination," that in this infamous speech Lear is expressing much more than a hatred of women, his misogyny a cover for his fearful rage against mortality itself, the complex interplay of life and death, the very harm of living.[22] Who is to be more acutely aware of the harm of mortality than the King, the one who bears immortality in his office? In the very next lines Lear, in response to Gloucester's request to kiss his hand, responds: "Let me wipe it first, it smells of mortality" (IV.vi.135). Lear seeks to overcome his stench, a stench of death, but here we may also be permitted to think of a stench of birth as well. Of this entire scene, Cavell suggests that Shakespeare hopes to represent Lear's self-understanding that love itself is inherently debased. For Lear, the thought of this debased love " . . . is a maddening thought; but still more comforting than the truth. For some spirits, to be loved knowing you cannot return that love, is the most radical of psychic tortures" (AL, p. 289). This debased love cannot be expressed beyond the relation of one's embodied self to the world one inhabits, and yet Lear's duty is to be somehow beyond this world. It may be that his love—his love of the mother—is beyond this world as well.

Of the meeting of Gloucester and Lear, Cavell says, "In this fusion of plots and identities, we have the great image, the double or mirror image, of everyman who has gone to every length to avoid himself, caught at the moment of coming upon himself face to face" (AL, p. 280). This fusion of plots, more than a chiasmic doubling, but that as well, underscores the struggle of Lear the sovereign to abdicate his very being. His horror is that of the father who has failed, precisely because he could not mother his motherless children, precisely because to allow the mother to rise up would be to succumb to madness. Lear cannot look at himself, for to look at himself he would be forced to stare into an abyss of lovelessness, and this he cannot do. Cast into the storm, stripped naked, he is close to representing bare life, but it is a life in which he must provide a matrix in the face of Being, and he remains ashamed. Debased love is a matrix torn from its moorings, a rising mother. Lear would rather be nothing than to be a mother. And yet Lear may be the mother of us all.[23]

Cordelia's Calculus

Following on Cavell, I believe that it is important to come to terms with these elements of character contained in *King Lear* if we are to use this great play to think productively about the shape of the experience of loneliness at the threshold of modernity, for understanding the play as a depiction of an indiscernible moment when the lonely self slips the confines of exceptional being and furtively assumes a place in the experiential field of ordinary life. From this perspective, Cordelia's calculus may be understood as a reckoning made from the field of modernity back to that of the medieval, a wager that she may be able to recognize what her father cannot, that the death of the mother does not have to mean that the father will fall into nothingness. Though it may be hyperbolic to say it so bluntly, in this sense the bridge to modern experience lies across the body of Cordelia.

But if, as Cavell insists, Cordelia loves Lear completely, does this also mean that she loves his expressions of motherly love? Sovereignty and nihilism—if it is the abdication that leads Lear to the face of nothingness, what is it that leads him to abdicate if not the death of the mother? The sovereignty of the King already places him above the constraints of ordinary mortals, but in abdication he may fall below the threshold of ordinary existence, into a nothingness unlike all others. The struggle he enacts is to be present in the world when he has renounced all claims on those in whose presence he wishes to be. Cordelia offers something else, and Lear's tragedy may be figured as his failure to recognize, not only her love, but the kind of love she offers.

When we return to think about the extraordinary first scene of the play, we may see more clearly how Cordelia's pronouncement of her love so moves us. Her first words are an aside to herself: "What shall Cordelia speak? Love, and be silent" (I.i.63–64). Cavell suggests that Cordelia figures her silence as a way out of a dilemma. "She sees from Goneril's speech and Lear's acceptance of it what it is he wants [an expression of counterfeit love, a love he would not have to return in kind], and she would provide it if she could. But to pretend publicly to love, where you do not love, is easy; to pretend to love, where you really do love, is not obviously possible" (AL, p. 290). So she loves *by being silent*. Her second speech is another aside, a report on her impaired ability to speak!

Cor. [*Aside.*] Then poor Cordelia!
And yet not so, since I am sure my love's
More ponderous than my tongue. (I.i.76–77)

Cordelia responds directly to Lear. This is the famous first part of their exchange.

Lear. . . . —Now, our joy,
Although last and least, to whose young love
The vines of France and milk of Burgundy
Strive to be interress'd, what can you say to draw
A third more opulent than your sisters'? Speak.
Cor. Nothing, my lord.
Lear. Nothing?
Cor. Nothing.
Lear. Nothing will come of nothing, speak again.
Cor. Unhappy that I am, I cannot heave
My heart into my mouth. I love your Majesty
According to my bond, no more nor less. (I.i.82–93)

What is Lear demanding, and why doesn't Cordelia give it to him? Cavell suggests that at this moment the great confusions of the play are set to explode, that Cordelia, in the position of truly loving Lear, cannot summon the ability to *pretend* to love him (which is what he wants in this public setting: "But to pretend publicly to love, where you do not love, is easy; to pretend to love, where you really do love, is not obviously possible" (AL, p. 290)). Instead, Cordelia is forced into a public statement of her love as a public reckoning, a calculation of what she owes the sovereign. This public reckoning humiliates Lear: its coldness, from one who loves him so warmly, reveals the hypocrisy of his demand (p. 292). Yet Cordelia prefaces her statement with a report on her affective condition: "Unhappy that I am, I cannot heave/My heart into my mouth."

Cordelia cannot connect her heart to her words—she cannot put her love into words, and this is a result of her unhappiness. She is frozen, without words to say what she must not say. But why is she unhappy? Is the humiliation of the demand being placed upon her by Lear for a public performance in place of a private assurance an adequate explanation of her response to his demand for a public expression of love? Is there a deeper pity that prevents her from imitating her older sisters? Is her relationship to her hypocritical sisters silencing her? Is her youth contributing to a stage fright? Of course, yes to all of these questions. But here a consideration of the missing mother may help explain more: it is a great absence in this drama. And if Cordelia is motivated purely by love, is it enough to claim that Lear is motivated by his desire to avoid her pure love? We may imagine that *because* Cordelia cannot put her heart into her mouth, Lear cannot restrain the mother rising to his heart. His rage is motherly because Cordelia reminds him that she is a motherless child, and there is nothing he can do to repair that loss. While this tension frames the exchange between Lear and Cordelia, the problem of the mother enables the conflict between love and its avoidance to occur at the level of the motivation of these characters. The problem of the mother thus bears on the national tragedy that moves into the world in the post-Lear era.

In contrast to Cavell's insistence that Cordelia's love is purely one of acceptance, it has been noted that Cordelia's great act appears to be one of refusal, and that she thus joins with other great refusers in the history of Western literature.[24] But Cavell is not blind to the stubbornness of the child in the face of a parental demand. Could it be that her acceptance is a refusal, and her refusal an acceptance, that she confounds us because she combines both? What is she refusing, and in refusing, what is she affirming? What is she affirming, and in affirming, refusing? These are Cavellian questions. They admit no certain answers, but in contrast require a series of acknowledgments—of the force of love, of the madness that love foments, of our insistent demands for answers that true love places on us any time we are touched by it, and of the lack of any adequate answer to our demands.

We may be able to understand Cordelia's position better if we compare her to Antigone, who may be said to have provided a template for subsequent tragic acts of refusal. Judith Butler positions Antigone in such a way to aid in the comparison. Of Antigone's action in reference to the state and kinship, she suggests:

> Her words, understood as deeds, are chiasmically related to the vernacular of sovereign power, speaking in and against it, delivering and defying imperatives at the same time, inhabiting the language of sovereignty at the very moment in which she opposes sovereign power and is excluded from its terms. What this suggests is that she cannot make her claim outside the language of the state, but neither can the claim she wants to make be fully assimilated by the state.[25]

Butler emphasizes both sides of Antigone's problematic status even as she illuminates the challenge to the state her action represents. She notes that in the past, critics of the play have idealized the kinship side of the problem, failing to address the ways in which Antigone's performance deforms kinship as she challenges the state (p. 28). She argues that "Antigone represents neither kinship nor its radical outside but becomes the occasion for a reading of a structurally constrained notion of kinship in terms of its social iterability, the aberrant temporality of the norm" (p. 29). Struggling against those readings that would have Antigone simply asserting a right to kinship against the state, Butler insists that "Antigone refuses to allow her love for her brother to become assimilated to a symbolic order that requires the communicability of the sign . . . [S]he refuses to submit her love to the chain of signification, that life of substitutability that that language inaugurates" (p. 52). Noting that Lacan defines the symbolic as "the curse of the father, . . . That obligation of the progeny to carry on in their own aberrant directions his very words," Butler asks if Antigone's claim is not

instead to assert "an unconscious right, marking a legality prior to codifi-
cation on which the symbolic in its hasty foreclosures must founder, establishing the question of whether there might be new grounds for communicability and for life?" (pp. 54–55).

While it would be a form of blindness to deny that the issue of incest
and the violation of the law are somehow at stake in this question, Butler
emphasizes that there is a multivocality in Antigone's love of her brother
that cannot be reduced to that law and its violation, that there is another
voice that may disrupt law. "Consider," she writes,

> that in the situation of blended families, a child says "mother" and might expect
> more than one individual to respond to the call. Or that, in the case of adoption,
> a child might say "father" and might mean that at once, or sequentially, or in ways
> that are not clearly disarticulated from one another . . . And when there are two
> men or two women who parent, are we to assume that some primary division of
> gendered roles organizes their psychic places within the scene, so that the empirical
> contingency of two same-gendered parents is nevertheless straightened out by the
> presocial psychic place of the Mother and Father into which they enter? (p. 69)

These movements, asserted not as simple kinship claims but as new grounds
of communicability, reshape and refigure the ways in which we live together. Indeed, she concludes, "If kinship is the precondition of the human, then Antigone is the occasion for a new field of the human, achieved
through political catachresis, when gender is displaced, and kinship founders on its own founding laws. She acts, she speaks, she becomes one for
whom the speech act is a fatal crime, but this fatality exceeds her life and
enters the discourse of intelligibility as its own promising fatality, the social
form of its aberrant, unprecedented future" (p. 82).

While Cordelia is not reducible to Antigone, she is similarly situated
in reference to sovereign power and similarly refuses to submit her love to
the chain of signification. The issue is not directly the question of incest.
Bloom is surely correct when he insists that the issue of Lear's outrage is
not reducible to the Father's displaced shame over that terrible crossing.
But the larger love and the larger loneliness Lear experiences as a consequence of love's withdrawal, the themes Cavell emphasizes, must be reckoned in explaining Cordelia's calculus, if not Lear's. In her refusal to subject her love to the chain of signification Cordelia does not appeal to an
unwritten law of kinship—her act of refusal and her act of acceptance has

as its immediate consequence a disinheritance that throws her into a wilderness of politics. It is not a claim to deeper kinship, and it so directs us otherwise. Cordelia overcomes her dumbness, she speaks with a clarity and power, and the abyss opens for her and her father when she does. Her appeal is that of love, love that divides, as it must for the abdication to proceed. When Cordelia insists that she will divide her love, she knows that in dividing her love she will be true to her love of Lear.

Cor. Good my lord,
You have begot me, bred me, lov'd me; I
Return those duties back as are right fit,
Obey you, love you, and most honor you.
Why have my sisters husbands, if they say
They love you all? Happily, when I shall wed,
That lord whose hand must take my plight shall carry
Half my love with him, half my care and duty.
Sure I shall never marry like my sisters,
[To love my father all].
Lear. But goes your heart with this?
Cor. Ay, my good lord.
Lear. So young, and so untender?
Cor. So young, my lord, and true.
Lear. Let it be so: thy truth then be thy dow'r!   (I.i.95–108)

Cavell suggests that this speech is said in suppression, confusion, and abandonment. Lear's curse of Cordelia, a curse that silences all, surely reflects this pain, but Cordelia loves Lear: and her speech shows this because he follows him into the deep split that he himself is enacting: "She is trying to conceal him; and to do that she cuts herself in two" (AL, p. 292). In doing so, she expresses a deep truth of this play, that the divisions we are to enact between head and heart, heart and mouth, mother and heart set us on a path of desolation. Half of Cordelia's love, being true, is worth infinitely more than the love of Regan and Goneril, which is no love at all. But Lear learns this too late, and Cordelia, full of this wisdom from the start, since she knows love as her exclusive quality, casts us into an aberrant, unprecedented future. She speaks a new language, a language of loneliness and longing, for a healing of divisions of self and the social that is to mark the isolated self of the modern era. She speaks this truth: Love is all we need to overcome absence—and loneliness is the absence we cannot overcome. This is the present in which we live.

"Tragedy Has Moved into the World"

The constancy through the arc of Cavell's work of a concern for a world torn by divided love is evident in his recent work when he observes, "I perhaps make more of the rift between the philosophical traditions than other philosophers may find productive, wishing to think, when I can, within the tear in the Western philosophical mind represented, I believe, by the distances between the English-American and the German-French dispensations."[26] Cavell, like Cordelia, is true to his love, and he knows that to think within the tear means, among other things, to try to recreate the experience of Lear as he is torn and to follow him down to the site of his divided existence. Cordelia hopes that the division between Britain and France may be overcome by a love that divides itself, and hence a love that shares in the multiplicity of experience that may become available to it. It may historically be true that the divisions of love begun through a certain genre of abdication were already migrating into the everyday of all of us when Shakespeare presented this tragedy "uppon S. Stephans night at Christmas iast," December 26, 1606.[27] It may also be that the calculus that Cordelia offered in her despaired confusion, repression, and abandonment has indefinitely multiplied our occasions for tragedy as the selves of modern experience have divided and redivided, even as we fail to notice our tragedy in the pains of the everyday. (But it is not as though we now know better of tragedy in the everyday, if only because we still may not know enough of what the everyday is.) The death of Lear, Cavell tells us, marks the end of high tragedy in the sense that tragedy itself bursts its bounds with Lear's exploded heart (AL, p. 343). Writing of these occasions of pain and death, Cavell returns us to our present presence:

We are present at these events, and no one is present without making something happen; everything which is happening is happening to me, and I do not know what is happening. I do not know that my helplessness is limited only by my separateness, because I do not know which fortune is mine and which is yours. The world did not become sad; it was always sad. Tragedy has moved into the world, and with it the world becomes theatrical. (p. 344)

We are present at the place of our absence, lost in the stars, watching each other.

Is this nihilism? Much is rightly made by many now of the nothings of *King Lear*,[28] how nothing comes of nothing, how Cordelia has nothing to say, how the Fool's breaking of the circle (the egg) to make two crowns shadows the dissolution of the King, how the abdication of Lear sets him on the road to nowhere, how any possible recovery is ruined through the death of all players of import, save Edgar, whose import is primarily the fact that only he survives, and secondarily the fact of how he "sullenly," that is, melancholically, survives. These largest questions lead critics like Bloom to deify Shakespeare, hoping that this human encompasses our humanity, and hence giving the gnostic something to worship.

But the demands of philosophy are not those of faith. Cavell will insist to us that there still may be something, and the fact is that we *live* that something. Cavell insists upon something even as a prayer, prayer itself for him being only one thing, prayer for the strength to change, successful prayer itself being the beginning of change, and change being the dying of the self and the ending of the world (p. 351). In his subsequent writing Cavell shares with us how Emerson works this out, clapping his hands in infantine joy, preparing us to live through our skepticism. But we may do well when we make our attempts to re-member the divided self as the subject of tragedy to also remember that Cavell's occasion for thinking of Lear was the national tragedy, ongoing, of that nation that does not exist as a nation, a polity born of revolution that was not a civil war, fighting a civil war that was not a revolution, knowing only its power and fearing only its impotence, at the time of the writing of "The Avoidance of Love" destroying villages to save them, a country killing its young to try to prove to itself that it could live (pp. 344–45). Thirty-odd years from the publication of "The Avoidance of Love," which we may also know as an essay of refusal and acceptance, the dissolution of imperialism has given way to shades of empire, and at the empty heart of globalization, struggling with its absent presence as the first meta-power, is the network power called the United States of America.[29]

Because this essay was drafted before the attack on the World Trade Center in New York City and has been revised in the time afterward, a time when the United States has fought one war to avenge the killings on

American soil, and embarked on another war in a quest for a new empire, somehow linking the two in a larger, metaphysical war on terrorism, this writer is compelled to test this thought of a prayer against the prospect of an ever widening experience of twenty-first–century war. There are claims we make in and of the world unanswered in the void that opened at the tip of the island of Manhattan, a void that has spread to the heart of Baghdad. What we expect of the world is sometimes denied to us by the actions of others. How we respond to that denial, it turns out, may in turn determine questions of war and peace, may, in fact, determine such matters more than the strategies of generals and fanatics, who are always already ready for war, regardless of their reluctance. This is still the claim that philosophy makes on the world.

Our tragedy is ongoing, but there is always a turn to be made. In this sense, a question that Simon Critchley asked of Cavell's philosophical disposition several years ago remains an important one: "What is the relation of Cavell's Emersonian perfectionism to the hybrid ensemble of traditions and inheritances which make up the great rhizome of American cultural identity?"[30] Critchley described Cavell's Emersonianism as a form of romanticism that works to overcome itself, an unworking of romanticism that oscillates between criteria and skepticism, irony and wit . . . work and unworking—to yield a tragic wisdom into the finitude of human being as that which cannot be overcome. Cavell's practice, he suggested, recalls the practice of romantic fragmentism, the work of death.[31] The turn to Emerson may not have come directly from his tears for Cordelia, but I do not know anyone better prepared to read Thoreau and Emerson than he, for having thought through the dilemma of love and loneliness presented in *King Lear* and for having noticed how unlimited the question has become (p. 352).

And yet, again, there is always a turn to be made. The newest name for such a turn, as the divisions of experience further fragment the conditions of self-awareness and multiply the means through which we can challenge the imposed unities of a sovereignty now risking existence in the name of nothing more than itself, may be Hardt and Negri's ontologically romantic category of the multitude.[32] They identify the multitude with the notion of the *posse*, and suggest that the posse is the machine that weaves together knowledge and being in an expansive, constitutive process.[33] The militant communist of the emergent era eschews representation and "makes rebellion into a project of love."[34] This communist is heir to Cordelia as much as she is heir to St. Francis—Hardt and Negri's exemplary hero—a militant who set us on the path of fragmentation through the division of her love as a response to the abdication of the King. That Hardt and Negri are able to conclude this radical study on the crumbling of the modern sovereign order with such an abashed projection of love suggests that they too have come to know what Cavell has been constantly thinking about, the tragedy of love as the tragedy of the modern world—figured as the working and unworking of an ontological romanticism that can only come into play when the insistent demands of our existence are revealed by a gradual unveiling of the ordinary enabled by the great catastrophic event of the abdication of sovereignty.

Here we are, still unable to abdicate, still unable to free the prisoners. What are we waiting for? Tragedy moves into the world as the certainties of sovereignty crumble. Cordelia enables this passage. Cavell's claim as a political theorist—what we may understand as his demand of political theory—is to confront this enormous fact without embarrassment and without shrinking from its philosophical import not only or for the sake of the future, but for the sake of a rethinking of who we are and how we may be present. If we are to avoid the avoidance of love, we must rethink the loneliness that is the consequence of our flight from the ruined scene of love's division. In so doing, do we return to the figure of Cordelia, she who loves by means of division, and ask her, What would it have meant had Lear been able to catch a hint of your breath in his mirror, to live a little longer, his heart not burst? What wishful thinking is entailed in the sentimental rewriting of the tragic that satisfied audiences for several centuries after the initial recoil from the hurt of a death that overwhelmed them? Or, recognizing the fatality of the division of Cordelia's love, can we learn other affective ways of attaching ourselves to the world?

CHAPTER TWELVE

Aesthetics and Receptivity:
Kant, Nietzsche, Cavell, and Astaire

Robert Gooding-Williams

In the *Critique of Pure Reason*, Kant famously writes that "[our] knowledge springs from two fundamental sources of the mind; the first is the capacity of receiving representations . . . the second is the power of knowing an object through these representations. . . . the *receptivity* of our mind . . . is to be entitled sensibility."[1] The present essay is a chapter in the history of post-Kantian philosophy's reception of Kant's concept of receptivity. Specifically, I concentrate on two renderings of receptivity, one gendered and one raced. In *Also Sprach Zarathustra* (hereafter *Zarathustra*), Nietzsche revises Kant's concept of receptivity and, ironically, adapts it to a critique of Kantian and Cartesian notions of the thinking subject.[2] More precisely, he presents a genealogy for these notions that roots them in the male body's estrangement from its power of receptivity, a power he identifies with the mythical Ariadne. Like Nietzsche, Stanley Cavell has also attempted to rethink Kant's concept of receptivity, drawing inspiration from Thoreau, Emerson, Heidegger, and, of course, Nietzsche. In his 1996 presidential address to the American Philosophical Association, and then again in his 1998 Spinoza lectures, Cavell continues this line of thinking by invoking the idea of receptivity to interpret two Fred Astaire routines from the Hollywood film *The Band Wagon*.[3] In the second routine, as

Cavell views it, an aging, melancholic Astaire regains his power of receptivity through his encounter with a black bootblack—a shoeshine man. Part 1 of the present essay explains Nietzsche's revision of Kant and feminizing of receptivity. Part 2 recounts and complicates Cavell's reading of the Astaire routines, which finds Astaire finding receptivity through blackness. Part 3 consists of critical reflections relating to both Nietzsche and Cavell, and to Cavell's sense of Emerson as finding and founding philosophy for America.

Part 1. Sublimity, Beauty, Femininity

In the first chapter of the first *Critique*, Kant writes that "the science of all principles of *a priori* sensibility I call *transcendental aesthetic*." It is well known that Kant follows this remark with a footnote relating to his use of the term *aesthetic*. Specifically, he contrasts Baumgarten's use of that term "to signify what others call the critique of taste" to his own, more traditional use of it to designate "that doctrine of sensibility which is true science."[4] It is equally well known that Kant later adopts Baumgarten's terminology in the *Critique of Judgment*, where he describes the judgment of taste as aesthetic. In the third *Critique*, Kant aims to give beauty its due not by elaborating the first *Critique*'s treatment of the mind's power of receptivity but by explaining the judgment of taste. Here, then, it seems not to occur to him to treat the first *Critique*'s transcendental aesthetic as a contribution to *aesthetics*—e.g., to the theory of beauty—as if the point of such a theory were to explore different ways of bearing, or living, the mind's power of receptivity rather than to justify aesthetic judgments.[5] By subordinating aesthetics to a critique of judgment, Kant forgoes an approach to aesthetics that would treat beauty as a mode of comportment.

In *Zarathustra* Nietzsche develops such an approach and ties it to a power of receptivity that he attributes to the human body.[6] Because I elsewhere analyze that approach in detail, through a section-by-section interpretation of, roughly, the first half of *Zarathustra*, Part 2, I limit myself here to outlining its key elements.[7] Specifically, I concentrate on Zarathustra's analysis of a version of the modern will to truth, his interpretation of that will as a form of self-estrangement, and his suggestion that a body ceases to be sublime and becomes beautiful when it discards its will to truth and acknowledges its power of receptivity.

In Part 2 of *Zarathustra*, Zarathustra argues that the culture of modern Europe is a "sterile" (*unfruchtbare*) affair that, while recognizing all past faiths, celebrates no faith, no passion of its own ("On the Land of Education"). Thus, it takes emasculated, passionless contemplation (*Beschaulichkeit*) to be essential to the perception of beauty ("On Immaculate Perception") and sees the dry, passionless spectator (*Zuschauer*) as the paradigm of scholarly excellence ("On Scholars").[8] Bent on banishing passion and the possibility of experiencing passional chaos from human life, the culture of modern Europe is the repressive, ascetic regime that Zarathustra first describes with the figure of the last man. Building on this earlier portrait of the modern world, Zarathustra now suggests, especially in his treatments of the modern scholar and the modern conception of beauty, that modernity rationalizes repression by representing a more or less Cartesian or, better, Kantian notion of suprasensible, dispassionate subjectivity as characterizing the proper basis of scholarly, moral, and aesthetic judgment.

Zarathustra ties the modern representation of human beings as suprasensible judging and knowing subjects to a quasi-idealist will to truth that reduces reality to what the human subject can know and limits knowledge to what the human subject creates, or "makes." At the beginning of Part 2—and, importantly, before he recognizes that modern representations of the subject rationalize repression—he himself endorses this will to truth, thus envisioning himself as a spontaneous, suprasensible subject who knows no "given" element in experience. Reminiscent, perhaps, of Fichte, who radicalizes Kant's idealism by denying the existence of given intuitions, he views objects of knowledge as effects that the knowers who know those objects have generated.

Starting with "The Night Song," roughly the middle sections of Part 2 mark a turning point in Zarathustra's appraisal of his will to truth. In Part 1, Zarathustra teaches that, the ravages of modern asceticism notwithstanding, human beings can overcome themselves by revaluing the passions that commonly claim their bodies. Moreover, he maintains that these passions constitute the natural furniture of human facticity, a dimension of the human condition that is given and not created and that he calls "the earth" in the prologue with which Part 1 begins. It is ironic, then, that Zarathustra espouses idealism at the beginning of Part 2, for by doing so he tacitly denies that such passions exist and contradicts his earlier teaching. In "The Night Song," Zarathustra expresses and begins to diagnose the suffering caused by this denial. Singing his song, he figures himself as a sun that suffers because it can no more feel the warmth of its own light than it can feel the light of other suns. Estranged from the light of others, Zarathustra is also a self-estranged stranger to his own light. Considered allegorically and in a Kantian idiom, Zarathustra's double estrangement is a form of in-sensibility, a numbness that affects him because he has disowned his power of receptivity. Oblivious to that power, nothing—not even his body's given, uncreated passions—can sensibly affect or move him. Coming in the wake of his turn to idealism, Zarathustra's night song shows that his will to truth, precisely by denying that his passions exist, has alienated him from his ability to sense, feel, and revalue those passions.

In further submitting his will to truth to critical appraisal, Zarathustra relates that will to his image of himself as knowing subject through a revision of Kant's disclosive conception of the dynamical sublime. As Kant analyzes it, the experience of the dynamical sublime has a compensatory quality such that our apprehension of physical incapacity is accompanied by the revelation of a suprasensible ability to resist what we cannot resist physically. We delight in our sublimity, when we discover that, as agents able to act from principles, we are immune to the might to which nature may subject us as physical creatures. For Kant, the dynamical sublime heralds human transcendence by disclosing human beings to be suprasensible, rational subjects who exist independently of nature. Zarathustra revises Kant by proposing that the sense of suprasensible transcendence that the latter associates with the dynamical sublime is an illusion caused by a self-estranging will to truth. In Zarathustra's view, the sublime is a mode of experience that, far from disclosing human beings to be suprasensible subjects, prompts them falsely to picture themselves as such.

Zarathustra sets forth his "theory" of the sublime in "On Those Who Are Sublime" (Part 2, §13), a speech that relies on the figure of the hero to depict the modern will to truth as a heroic will to personal sublimity. Zarathustra's description of this figure has self-critical implications, for it so clearly echoes his previous self-descriptions. Figuring the sublime hero as possessing a "swelled chest [*erhobener Brust*] . . . like one who holds in his breath" and as harboring "knowledge" [*Erkenntniss*] in the manner of "a wild beast" [*ein wildes Thier*], Zarathustra quite explicitly recalls his portrait of himself—his chest heaving and he proclaiming the wisdom of a wild animal—in "The Child with the Mirror": "Violently my chest will expand [*wird sich meine Brust heben*], violently will it blow its storm . . . and thus find relief . . . Indeed, you will be frightened, my friends, by my wild wisdom . . . Would that my lioness, wisdom, might learn how to roar tenderly."[9] Similarly, when Zarathustra suggests that the hero's retreat to the "woods of knowledge" was prompted by nausea and contempt at being close to "the earth," he reminds us of his portrait of his own nausea-fleeing flight to the "cold wells" and "strong winds" of knowledge in "On the Rabble." The sublime hero, Zarathustra says, is one "who withdraw[s]." Repenting an "earthly" life that disgusts him (he is, we are told, a "penitent of the spirit"), he seems to have invented a life—a life of "hunting" for knowledge—that compensates for the life he has renounced. Withdrawing into himself and asserting his heroic will to truth and knowledge, the sublime hero projects the *image* of a deathly and otherworldly life, appearing to be a shadowy phantom whose essence is suprasensible.[10] Standing aloof from the world of appearances, he seems to reside wholly beyond the reach of warm sunlight, and even beyond the touch and warmth of *his own* sunlight, reminiscent of Zarathustra in "The Night Song": "And only when he turns away from himself, will he jump over his shadow—and verily into *his* sun. All too long has he been sitting in the shadow, and the cheeks of the penitent of the spirit have grown pale; he almost starved to death on his expectations."

Personifying a happiness that "smells" of contempt for the earth, yet *not* of the earth itself, the sublime hero disowns and estranges himself from his body's power to be sensibly affected and so to feel the force of its "earthly," physical existence.[11] To reclaim his power of receptivity, he must (like Zarathustra in "The Dancing Song") "discard his heroic will." In fine, he must forsake his will to truth and knowledge, admit that he is a body gripped by passions, and accept that he is not the incorporeal and shadowy phantom he appears to be: "When power becomes gracious [*gnädig*] and descends [*herabkommt*] into the visible—such descent [*Herabkommen*] I call beauty." Beauty, here, entails the repudiation of sublimity: it is a movement—a mode of comportment—by which a once heroic, truth-willing will to power, having renounced the illusion of suprasensible subjectivity, and having ceased to hold aloof from the "visible" world of appearances, graciously condescends to re-value the passions through which that world stirs and moves the human body. For Zarathustra, beauty is the cure that relieves the self-estrangement of the sublime.[12]

"On Those Who Are Sublime" argues that Zarathustra's sense of himself as a spontaneous, suprasensible subject has been the product of an experience of sublime transcendence that is rooted in self-estrangement. And it suggests that this sort of experience generates the image and illusion of a suprasensible subjectivity, the existence of which Kant's disclosive conception of the sublime presupposes. More generally, Zarathustra's speech on the sublime sketches a specifically *aesthetic* genealogy of the modern tendency to view human beings as judging and knowing subjects who (1) exist apart from the world of appearances, and (2) reduce reality to what can be known. Zarathustra's genealogy is "aesthetic" in both the senses that Kant identifies. Revising the first *Critique*'s transcendental aesthetic (Kant's theory of a priori sensibility), it attributes a power of receptivity to the human body and ties the illusion of suprasensible subjectivity to a will to truth that estranges human beings from that power. Revising the third *Critique*'s theory of aesthetic judgment (Kant's theory of the judgments of the beautiful and the sublime), it interprets sublimity as a self-estranged mode of comportment—that is, of bearing, or carrying, the human body's power of receptivity—and beauty as the manifest act of transforming that mode of comportment by openly avowing the body's power of receptivity. For Zarathustra, the individual who envisions himself as a Cartesian or Kantian knowing subject has reified the fantasy that he transcends the world of sensible objects, a fantasy that has been generated by an experience of the sublime that originated in self-estrangement. Through much of Part 2—in "The Night Song," for example—Zarathustra himself indulges this fantasy. In "On Those Who Are Sublime" he revises Kant and tells us how he was able to renounce it.

Zarathustra concludes "On Those Who Are Sublime" with a sentence that genders the truth-willing, heroic subject of knowledge as male and his body's power of receptivity as female: "For this is the soul's secret: only when the hero has abandoned her, she is approached in a dream by the overhero."[13] I have elsewhere argued that the figure of the hero in this passage alludes to Theseus and that of the soul to Ariadne.[14] Within the context of Part 2 and, specifically, in the aftermath of Zarathustra's night song, these allusions have a telling significance, for Nietzsche proclaims in *Ecce Homo* that Ariadne would be "the answer" to Zarathustra's night song.[15] Ariadne is the rejoinder to Zarathustra's lament, because she is a metaphor for the power of receptivity that the night song singing Zarathustra or, indeed, any other sublime, truth-willing subject of knowledge, needs to reclaim in order to end his suffering.[16] Gendering the putatively suprasensible subject of knowledge as the hero Theseus, Zarathustra announces that this subject can regain his ability to sense, feel, revalue his passions only if he repudiates his sublime, heroic will to truth and knowledge and acknowledges his Ariadnean power to be sensibly affected by passion and desire. Put in terms of the myth of Theseus and Ariadne, the modern male, Theseus-like, subject of knowledge must "discard his heroic will" and "abandon" his feminine, Ariadnean soul to a life bereft of that will if, through the medium of his soul, he is to be sensibly affected by the soul-rescuing Dionysian passions he has to revalue to become a beautiful "overhero."

I turn now to Part 2 of this paper, and to Stanley Cavell's treatment of *The Band Wagon*, a film whose depiction of a melancholy song-and-dance man very clearly echoes Nietzsche's portrait of the sublime hero. But where Nietzsche feminizes receptivity to counter sublimity, *The Band Wagon* blackens it to counter melancholy. In Part 3 I criticize both renderings of receptivity, building on Kelly Oliver's Irigaray-inspired discussion of Nietzsche and remonstrating against Cavell's appraisals of the two Astaire routines.

Part 2. Melancholy, Ecstasy, Blackness

Cavell offers his readings of the two Astaire routines as adaptations of Kant's notion of aesthetic judgment. According to Cavell, "Kant's location of the aesthetic judgment . . . makes room for a particular form of criticism, one that supplies the concepts that, after the fact of pleasure, articulate the grounds of that experience in particular objects."[17] Thus criticism, which Cavell sometimes calls "reading," is the critic's rebukable effort to justify and so to show to be acceptable the pleasure she takes in some work of art. It is a subsumption of a work under concepts—hence a judgment that the critic adduces and expounds in order to express her wish and demand that others take pleasure where she has taken it. Proceeding on the assumption that the object of criticism "has yet to have its due effect, that something there, fully open to the senses, has despite that been missed," the critic aspires to find the idea of that object "to which one may pay tribute" and to which others may be moved to pay tribute.[18]

Cavell begins his criticism of the first routine by purporting to describe it "uncontroversially." He notes that a man—Astaire, playing "a song-and-dance man whose star has faded in Hollywood and who is returning nervously to New York to try a comeback on Broadway"[19]—walks along a train platform singing; that throughout his singing the camera leads him with one continuous shot; and that when he stops, the camera stops and watches him leave through the gate. Cavell adds that we then cut to a view within the station, see the man continue his walk toward us, humming the same tune, and that the man then pauses and shifts nervously, looking around, as if expecting someone. The song Astaire has been singing is "By Myself." Cavell remarks that Astaire begins to sing this song with a self-conscious laugh that may be taken as his self-reflective response to the fact that his thinking, manifest in the film as melancholy, is about to become singing.

Cavell's criticism of the first routine considers three of its features. One is the sense of "hovering" that the routine conveys. Cavell attributes this sense to the facts that Astaire's song never reaches to dance and that its opening chord progression, which echoes the opening chord progression of *Tristan and Isolde*, figures Astaire's emotional state as suspended animation. The second feature is that the camera frames Astaire's walk along the train platform—a walk Cavell describes as a "proto-dancing" that is not quite dancing—so that his feet never appear. Cavell relates the second feature to the first when he observes that the camera's screening of Astaire's walk registers "that this man, with those feet, never arrives at unequivocal dancing in this routine." The third feature is Astaire's invisibility—his missability.[20] As he enters the train station, his musical syllabification DA: DA, DA, DA; DA, DA, DA alerts us, Cavell writes,

to the fact, or the convention according to which, the opening delivery of the singing was inaudible and the opening proto-dancing was unnotable, invisible, within its fictional world. Had that crowd of passers-by on the platform been aware of a man doing in their presence what Astaire, or his particular shadow is doing in ours, they would have felt, let us say, a reportable indecorousness . . . I take the unremarkableness . . . together with the remarkableness . . . of Astaire's musical syllabification, and of the routine that renders it so, to emblematize a way of manifesting the ordinary.[21]

By noting three features of the first routine, Cavell presents Astaire as a figure for the skepticism of which "our ordinary lives partake."[22] Unable to transmute his singing into a dancing that finds and feels the ground, Astaire seems a soul in suspension above the earth, a man uncertain and doubtful that he exists (or could *again* exist) as a man with feet—to wit, *as a dancer* (and if this man, this Hollywood "individuality,"[23] cannot exist as a dancer, how can he exist at all?). Embodying and living his skepticism, he personifies a loss of intimacy with existence,[24] an everyday condition that Cavell here, echoing Emerson, calls melancholy. Unnoticed and unheard by passers-by, Astaire's skepticism—in Thoreau's language, his "quiet desperation"—expresses a "sense of invisibility" that Cavell elsewhere ties to the modern experience of privacy.[25] Hovering above the earth, the missable Astaire "haunts" the earth like the ghost that is Cavell's Hamlet. Where the tragedy of Hamlet works out "a scene of skepticism," the comedy of Astaire's comeback will work out a "festive abatement of skepticism"—an event that Cavell will locate in the *second* routine.[26] But before Astaire performs that routine—hence, before he is relieved of his skepticism—he is "by himself," a figure for the lonely, modern subject who ordinarily and invisibly "partakes of tragedy in partaking of skepticism."[27]

Here is Cavell's summary of his criticism and aesthetic judgment of Astaire's first routine:

Now the utterance or delivery of Astaire's song and proto-dance has singled me out for a response of pleasure which I propose to read in terms of the concepts of psychic hovering, of dissociation from the body, within a state of ordinary invisibility . . . In my wish to share this pleasure I judge the scene of walking and of melodic syllabification as appropriate expressions of the ordinary as the missable.[28]

In Part 3 of this paper, I reject Cavell's judgment and offer an alternative aesthetic appraisal of the first routine. Here, however, I wish to amend his description of that routine, and so to lay the grounds for my alternative appraisal. Specifically, I discuss the two pairings of Astaire and Ava Gardner that precede the first routine, as well as the camera's correlation of Astaire's proto-dancing with the mostly black passers-by who appear on the train platform. My aim is to show that and how the first routine *racializes* the ordinary as the missable.

Cavell notes the second, physical pairing of Gardner and Astaire when he mentions her cameo appearance. But he misses, or declines to mention, the first, conversational pairing of the two actors. This first pairing transpires before Astaire leaves the train during the scene in which he first appears. Sitting in the corner of a diner coach, and holding what seems to be a menu to his face, we find Astaire facing the camera (but hiding behind his menu) and flanked on his right and left by two white men engaged in a conversation about Hollywood stars. Precisely as the scene begins, a black waiter appears and begins to attend to the tables of the two men, a white woman sitting at the edge of the scene, and Astaire. While the waiter remains visible, his activity blocks the camera's view of Astaire, leaving the audience to attend to the conversation between the two men, who remain fully in sight. In the course of their exchange, one man expresses his desire to meet Ava Gardner, only to be told by the other that he is too late and that Gardner is married.[29] Just after the waiter leaves the scene, the conversation turns to an actor named Tony Hunter, the song-and-dance man played by Astaire, whose comeback story is in fact modeled on Astaire's career (for Astaire had recently made a comeback from a voluntary retirement).[30] One of the men remarks that Astaire, or Astaire/Hunter (henceforth, I mostly write "Astaire"), was good twelve or fifteen years ago, but that the Hollywood columnists now say that he is through. The scene ends with Astaire revealing himself and exiting the coach, just after the two men recognize him from his picture in a magazine.

I draw attention to the setting of this scene, for it uses racial blackness to establish a difference between Gardner and Astaire. While the black waiter occupies the set and obstructs our view of Astaire, the conversation concentrates on Gardner. But just as soon as the waiter departs, the conversation turns to Astaire—as if to suggest that talk about Gardner requires an apparent reference to black folk, where talk about Astaire will not tolerate it. The dining coach scene figures Hollywood success with the advent of a black waiter and Hollywood failure with his disappearance. By coordinating the scene's dialogue with the quiet movement of the waiter, Minnelli's direction proposes that the important and perhaps critical difference between Gardner's success and Astaire's failure is specifically and essentially a racial difference.

Before turning to the second pairing of Gardner and Astaire, we should recall that just two years before her cameo in *The Band Wagon* (1953), Gardner's appearance in *Showboat* (1951) had transformed her into MGM's number-one female star.[31] Because Gardner played a mulatto in *Showboat*, a character named Julie LaVerne, it can come as no surprise that the dining coach scene attributes her recent success to blackness. Gardner succeeded, we are asked to believe, because she was able to appropriate blackness and to make it her own, at least on screen. This point may seem forced, but the second pairing serves subtly to reinforce it. As Astaire exits the train, he takes the awaiting reporters and photographers to have come to interview him. He quickly discovers, however, that they are awaiting Ava Gardner. As Gardner appears in the door of the next car, the newshounds rush to her. Statuesque in a jet black dress, she poses for a moment until she sees Astaire and comes over to chat with him. Seen close up, it is clear that Gardner has been dressed in detail to produce an array of chiaroscuro contrasts: not only jet black dress against white skin, but whitish, silvery earrings against jet black hair and a white coat streaked with fuzzy lines of black. As she speaks to Astaire, Gardner's black-white color coding prominently stands out against the background of motley clothing worn by the white men behind her and forms a sharp contrast to the sky-blue suit worn by Astaire. Although she has left the role of Julie LaVerne behind her, Gardner remains visually a mulatto, and so visually stained with the blackness that *The Band Wagon* argues has been the key to her cinematic stardom.

A final point relating to the second pairing: before Gardner appears, the film shows us an image of Astaire's former possessions, a top hat and a cane—both of them as black as Gardner's dress—and a pair of white gloves, all of which attend the film's opening credits. As we quickly learn in the scene following the credits, the hat, cane, and gloves were used by Astaire/Hunter during his heyday in Hollywood. Specifically, an auctioneer attempting to sell these effects lets on that Astaire used them in *Swinging Down to Panama*, a fictional film the title of which cleverly plays on the titles of two of his earlier movies: *Flying Down to Rio* (1933), his first film with Ginger Rogers, and *Swingtime* (1936), a movie that includes a blackface "homage" to Bill "Bojangles" Robinson (as we shall see, reference to Robinson recurs in *The Band Wagon*). When Gardner arrives, we are recalled to Astaire/Hunter's former effects—therefore, to his past—for her black dress has the shading of his hat and cane, while her black-white body echoes the image of his hat and gloves. In her cameo appearance, Gardner adorns her body with the blackness that prompted her mulatto, chiaroscuro, success, a blackness that Astaire has lost but must regain to make a comeback.

It is obvious, no doubt, that my reading of the dining coach scene, of Gardner's appearance, and of the image of the hat, cane, and gloves depends for its plausibility on the assumption that Minnelli, as a director, gave careful consideration to scenic composition, to costuming, and to color contrasts. As it turns out, this assumption is true, for in the words of film scholar James Naremore, Minnelli "used set decorations in an almost Brechtian way, to 'narrate' and explicitly comment on the action"; was "unusually attentive to women's dresses, hairstyles, or accessories"; and repeatedly exploited the opportunity to "create patterns of light and color."[32] Due, arguably, to his background as a store-window designer for Marshall Field, Vincent Minnelli brought to his films a "display art" sensibility that lavished attention on visual detail.[33] It is also significant that, even before he directed *The Band Wagon*, Minnelli's work as a director and a set designer had demonstrated a strong and developed interest in specifically black and Africanist racial motifs[34]—still a further reason to suppose that his display of black-white color coding in *The Band Wagon*'s opening scenes was deliberate.

I turn now to the camera's correlation of Astaire's proto-dancing with the mostly black passers-by appearing on the train platform.[35] If the two pairings of Astaire and Gardner establish Astaire's want of blackness, the first routine further articulates that want as the want of a melancholy skeptic for intimacy with existence. Strolling down the train platform, Astaire, as his song lyric testifies, is "all alone in a crowd." With the exception of a couple of white men, the men we see walking along the platform with him are black (we see no women). We *expect* to see mainly blacks now, for as the train pulled into the station we noticed through the window four or five porters—all of them black—mingling on the platform. After the departure of the reporters and paparazzi come to meet Gardner, the platform becomes again what it is *ordinarily*—a place where black men routinely work. As the camera leads Astaire down the platform, mostly black men pass him by (I count six blacks and two whites), one in front and two in back, while those walking in the opposite direction fade away into the ever-widening distance between them and Astaire, whose feet we never see. If Astaire, in this fictional world, is invisible to these men, then they too remain invisible to him. Yet there is an important difference, for what they miss is not what he misses. The missable ordinary that Astaire misses and for which he wants is the intimacy with existence that the largely black passers-by—none of whom sings with suspended animation and a few of whose grounded feet the camera takes care to show us—seem to possess. What the black passers-by miss is precisely *not* this intimacy, but the privately felt melancholy of a skeptic, doubtful of his existence and dissociated from his body "within a state of ordinary invisibility." The blacks miss the skeptic and the skeptic misses the blacks' intimacy with existence. An important corollary to this depiction is that the skeptic *cannot be black*, for then he would not want for the blackness that supplies intimacy and enables comebacks. In the perspective of Astaire's platform routine, which builds on the explanation of the decline of his movie career that the comparisons to Ava Gardner elaborate (again, that he failed—that he ceased to be a success—because he lost the blackness he once possessed), the trials and tribulations of skeptical, modern subjectivity belong exclusively to whites. Produced just a year before the Supreme Court's famous *Brown* decision, Astaire's first routine projects a Jim Crow version of the human capacity for skepticism.

Let me hasten to emphasize here that I attribute a Jim Crow version of the capacity for skepticism to *The Band Wagon*'s screening of the first Astaire routine, *not to Cavell*. We need only look to Cavell's reading of *Othello* to see that he does not deny the experience of skepticism to blacks and that he brilliantly finds Shakespeare intimating that modern black subjects will be tragically prompted to skepticism as a defense against racializing white desire.[36] More generally, Cavell suggests in a number of his writings that skepticism is "an argument internal to the individual, or separate, human creature, as it were an argument of the self with itself (over its finitude)."[37] In short, he proposes that conflicting tendencies—both the affirmation of criteria and the skeptical repudiation of criteria—inhabit the human condition *in general*.[38] There is nothing in Cavell's writing to suggest that lives which partake of skepticism are exclusively white and that blackness is the key to recovering from skepticism. This, however, is precisely the message of the opening scenes of *The Band Wagon*, culminating with the first Astaire routine. According to Cavell, the unwitting "truth" or "moral" of skepticism is that our relation to the existence of the world is not that of knowing, but "one in which it is accepted, that is to say, received."[39] The abatement of skepticism is in part a matter of appreciating this moral—thus of aspiring to receive and acknowledge existence rather than to know it. As depicted by the opening scenes of *The Band Wagon*, the skepticism that Astaire personifies will be abated when he recovers his power to receive and acknowledge his earth-bound, bodily existence. He will recover that power—that is, he will regain his intimacy with that existence—when he repossesses the blackness he has lost. In racializing the skepticism that inhabits the ordinary as white, *The Band Wagon* reductively figures blackness as the supplement that whites require to recover from skepticism—as if the argument of the ordinary were not an argument of the self with itself but an interracial argument, an argument between white and black.

Like Nietzsche, Cavell revises Kant by connecting the concept of receptivity to the turn away from an epistemological orientation that makes the existence of the world a problem of knowledge—an orientation that Nietzsche links to the modern will to truth (which holds that the world exists to the extent that we have knowledge of it) and Cavell to skepticism.[40] As we have seen, Nietzsche figures this turn as from a beautiful to a sublime mode of bearing the body's power of receptivity. Although Cavell seems similarly to figure it in one of his recent books (in terms of the distinction between the unhandsome and the handsome[41]), his reading of the second Astaire routine, echoing his early writing on Thoreau, rather differently casts the recovery of receptivity as an ecstatic release from melancholy.[42] I turn now to that routine.

In his Spinoza lectures, Cavell's presents a different and more complicated account of his aesthetic judgment of the second routine than he presents in his APA address. In the latter, Cavell articulates the grounds of the pleasure he takes in the second routine with the judgment that Astaire's taking a photo of his shod foot is a skepticism-abating "ecstatic attestation of existence."[43] In the Spinoza lectures, he complicates this judgment by relating his criticism of the second routine to Michael Rogin's remarks about it in *Blackface, White Noise*. As Cavell interprets Rogin's book, its "burden . . . is the establishment of America's national identity and culture through the appropriation of black culture . . . a process . . . that has from the beginning to end been accomplished at the price of excluding African Americans from the mix." Rogin dismisses the second routine's "homage to black tap" as a form of domination.[44] Cavell in turn takes Rogin to task for his errors in recounting the second routine and for a view of film that leaves no room for treating it as one of the great arts. Cavell's chief concern, however, is that Rogin's dismissal of Astaire's homage does not permit him to see that Astaire's dance of praise is self-referentially about "[the] painful and potentially deadly irony of the white praise of a black culture whose very terms of praise it has appropriated."[45] In the Spinoza lectures, Cavell aesthetically judges the second routine, offering a reading of its self-referentiality that presents his pleasure and praise as other than vain. More exactly, he presents criticism of the second routine that declares a ground for finding pleasure in it and praising it *notwithstanding* the conditions of injustice (of white America's unjust appropriation of black culture) it depicts. That judgment and ground, he tells us, is that Astaire's dance of praise, because it affords a "glimpse of Utopia" that contests the unjust conditions it depicts, is itself not vain.

Cavell divides the second routine into three sections and an epilogue. Rather than summarize his description of the entire routine before amending it—as I did in the case of the first routine—I shall amend his description as I proceed from section to section. As before, I aim to lay the basis for an aesthetic judgment of the second routine that differs from Cavell's.

The first section begins with Astaire entering a penny Arcade, taking a hot dog from a man behind a counter, passing an exhibit entitled "The Gorillas Bride," and handing the hot dog to a young boy. As Cavell describes this section, Astaire goes on to discover a machine decorated by a question mark; receives two fortune tickets from a mechanical gypsy; plays pin-ball poker that he wins by cheating; is declared to be gorgeous by a machine that measures love appeal; and sees himself in a distorting mirror. Then, says Cavell, "something serious happens. He trips over the outstretched legs of a meditative shoeshine man."[46] According to Cavell,

Astaire's encounters with machines, which seem ever ready to tell him who he is, and which remind him, perhaps, that he has been displaced by the mechanism of film but may be redeemed by it, suggest that his ensuing dance with the shoeshine man (section 2) will be a dance of identity, as if the Arcade were an allegorical version of a movie theater, or a sound stage, in which he is to seek out "new origins."[47]

Before turning to section 2, three amendments to Cavell's description of section 1 are in order. First, that when Astaire enters the Arcade and wanders past "The Gorillas Bride," we see near him a notably tall white woman and the young white boy who will get his hot dog. Second, that "The Gorillas Bride," which shows a gorilla in a cage with two white women (one in his grip and one prostrate), seems an obvious allusion to RKO's *King Kong* (1933). The allusion to *King Kong* is significant, for that movie tells the tale of a monstrous, black gorilla worshiped by a tribe of Hollywood "jungle blacks" said to live somewhere "west of Sumatra"—thus, a gorilla that the movie imagines as embodying, writ-large, the jungle animality that it attributes to blacks in general. After hunters capture Kong and take him to America, he escapes and abducts a white woman. He is killed, of course, in order to save America and the woman from the bestial blackness he epitomizes.[48] My final amendment relates to the second: as Astaire turns from "The Gorillas Bride" and the camera shows him approaching a trash can, we see the shoeshine man for the first time, shining shoes on back of the machine that is decorated with a question mark. Leading Astaire away from the myth that blackness is a monstrous threat to American civilization, Minnelli's direction brings into focus the protagonist of what we shall see is an alternative myth.[49]

In section 2 this protagonist, a shoeshine man played by Leroy Daniels (Daniels shined shoes in downtown Los Angeles and was recruited specifically for the second routine[50]), shines Astaire's shoes after Astaire stumbles over him and begins to sing to him. When Astaire's song turns to the idea of getting a shoeshine, Daniels welcomes Astaire onto his stand and, in Cavell's words, "provides the song a habitation and a new beat with his brushes." With Astaire on the stand, his feet seeming to dance on air, Daniels shines Astaire's shoes, giving him a "fantastic or fantasmatic" shoeshine, as if his object, Cavell writes, were "not alone to transform shoes but to transfigure the creature on earth who wears the shoes."[51]

In describing the second section, Cavell notes that "A Shine on Your Shoes," Astaire's song, puns on the word *shine*, a "derogatory name for a black man." Cavell adds that

You can either understand Astaire . . . to be using the word conformably accepting its derogatory association, or you can understand Astaire to be mentioning this word as part of risking the full sense of what it means for him to be singing this song to this man. It *is* essential that the shoeshine man be black, specifically African-American, for the routine to be the one I have been reading, call it Astaire's comeback song.[52]

Perhaps we should hear Astaire as wishing to revalue the word *shine*, just as Minnelli, I have suggested, wishes to revalue blackness. As we have seen, *The Band Wagon*'s pairings of Astaire and Ava Gardner figure Astaire as lacking the blackness he required to make a comeback. The second section of the second routine shows him acquiring that blackness through the agency of a "shine" who, by shining his shoes, works a sorcery that disseminates his blackness, as if a priapic Daniels had discharged a second, miniature "shine," a sort of black homunculus, onto the surface of Astaire's footwear. If Minnelli has repudiated the myth that blackness is a potency threatening to American civilization, he now gestures in the direction of a different myth—that it is a potency needful to that civilization as an adorning supplement.[53]

Where the second routine's second section shows Astaire absorbing the magic of Daniels's shoeshine, section 3 shows him in the grip of it. Incessantly repeating the words "Shoe shine; shine on my shoes," Astaire is, according to Cavell,

taking in, trying to make out, what has happened to him, how it happens that he has found his feet again, come into his body again, asking what his words mean when he cannot just now know what they mean. He is reacquiring language, reconsidering all his words, pivoting around "shine." It is the moment of comeback. That the discovery of intact existence expresses itself here as ecstasy is linked in my mind to Thoreau's once expressing his recognition of his double existence . . . as a condition of being beside himself—by himself—roughly the dictionary definition of ecstasy . . .[54]

Possessed by blackness and his skepticism abated, Astaire has now retrieved his power to receive and acknowledge his earth-bound, bodily existence.

Like Zarathustra, after he has discarded his will to truth, Astaire has redis-
covered his body, which is to say that he is now *available* to be stirred and
moved by his body, and so can find himself just beside himself, ecstatically
transported. Simply put, the blackening of Astaire's shoes has relieved him
of the melancholic hovering he personifies in the first routine (in Cavell's
phrasing, "hovering has found its landing, melancholy has found its ecstasy"[55]). As we have seen, a sublime Zarathustra beautifully returns himself
to the possibility of revaluing his body's passions by reclaiming his feminine power to be sensibly affected by them. Similarly, a melancholic and
hovering Astaire comes back to, ecstatically returns himself to, the intimacy with existence that he missed in the first routine—specifically, to an
intimacy with his feet that is indispensable to dancing—by regaining an
essentially black power to be gripped and carried away by his body. For
Zarathustra and Astaire alike, some acknowledgment of the power to sense
and accept the claims of the body is essential to self-renewal.

What femininity does for Zarathustra, blackness does for Astaire:
it qualifies his masculinity, thus rendering him susceptible to his body's
promptings (where Ariadne is the answer to Zarathustra's night song, blackness is the answer to Astaire's Wagnerian musical syllabification). That the
Arcade routine imagines the acquisition of blackness as the acquisition of
a homunculus-harboring substance disseminated by a black man is not
my only reason for asserting that it presents the blackness Astaire gets as
qualifying, by augmenting, his masculinity. More pertinent, I think, is
that "a comically withdrawn and awkwardly tall woman screams in terror"
as Astaire, having left the shoeshine stand, moves toward her.[56] As it turns
out, this woman is the white woman we saw with Astaire and a young
white boy in the vicinity of "The Gorillas Bride." When the woman later
sees Astaire coming toward her, manic and deranged by the blackness that
has possessed him, she shrieks and runs away. Because her reaction strikes
us as silly and comical, it serves further to distance *The Band Wagon*'s myth
of blackness from *King Kong*'s. As we have seen, *King Kong*, like *The Birth
of a Nation* (1915) before it, portrays the threat of blackness to civilization
as, among other things, a sexual threat that black men, the putative likes
of Kong, pose to white women. By mocking a white woman's terror of a
white man suddenly become a "White Negro" (Norman Mailer's notorious phrase), the Arcade routine discredits that fear. It attributes a black-

ened masculinity to Astaire but denies that a blackened masculinity endangers white women.

The Arcade routine is also marked by the recurrent appearance of the young white boy. Attracted to Astaire as he turns away from "The Gorillas Bride," the boy takes Astaire's hot dog just after Daniels comes into view behind the question-mark machine. While Astaire gets his shoes shined, we barely notice that the boy has moved to the back of the Arcade, but when the white women Astaire scares runs away, we see the boy again, in the corner, closely watching the train of events. Continuing to haunt Astaire, the boy yet again shows up, a few moments later, trying to shake Astaire's hand, or maybe just to touch him, after Astaire turns the question-mark machine into a flurry of "whistles, flags, and flashing lights."[57] Our last sight of the boy shows him watching Astaire exit the Arcade after he has finished his dance with Daniels. Think of Astaire, then, as the boy's unwitting exemplar: as a wise elder to whom the boy repeatedly attaches himself and whose unwitting vocation is to prompt the boy to attain a better self than he is otherwise likely to attain.[58] In the perspective of the Arcade routine—read now as a scene of instruction—that self will be a black masculine self that is a boon to white men but never a threat to white women. According to Minnelli's alternative myth, blackness can be an adorning supplement to American civilization because blackness can be an adorning supplement to white American manhood.[59] He suggests, in effect, that while the racial myths of *King Kong* belong to America's past, the promise of its future, as personified by the boy, is the promise of a white manhood redeemed through the appropriation of black masculinity, a promise that is as dated as America's antebellum traditions of blackface minstrelsy. As Eric Lott reminds us, "to wear or enjoy blackface was literally, for a time, to become black, to inherit the cool, virility, abandon or *gaité de Coeur* that were the prime components of white ideologies of black manhood."[60]

We may now turn to the second routine's epilogue, which Cavell describes as "an Apollo Theater finale . . . a perfectly recognizable and perfectly executed walk off."[61] Cavell's interpretation of this finale is critical to his claim that his praise of Astaire is not vain, for it explicitly declares a ground for accepting pleasure in and praising the second routine *notwithstanding* the conditions of injustice it depicts.

In declaring my acceptance of [pleasure] I go back to the men's re-encounter of one another for their walk-off and recall that as they reach the entrance, or now the exit, of the Arcade, the marquee from a neighboring theater is visible above their heads that announces THE "PROUD LAND." I take the placement above the center of the entrance/exit to suggest that the Arcade itself is a portrait or allegory of the proud land, call it America, containing not only amusements and occupations and false promises for those with nothing better to do, but a territory of magic or exemption in which such things as the walk-off can form itself. I have called it perfect in recognition and execution. I mean that it demonstrates that these two can dance together—for a while—on an equal basis, equally choreographed, equally standing, equally kneeling, equally happy with the knowledge of their achievement in their joint work, a momentary achievement of the Kingdom of Ends, a traumatic glimpse of Utopia. But it demonstrates at the same time that they cannot leave the scene of entertainment together, and cannot for no good reason. This is against reason, against the scene of mutuality (of mutual legislation you might say) that we have witnessed.[62]

Certainly Cavell is right to insist that the walk-off shows that the two men can dance together on an equal basis, equally choreographed, equally happy, et cetera. Less convincing, however, is his claim that it shows "a momentary achievement of the Kingdom of Ends, a traumatic glimpse of Utopia." What reason is there to attribute this achievement to the walk-off? To be sure, Daniels and Astaire exhibit an image of equality, but it is an equality to which a white man has risen by taking possession of the black masculinity that has possessed him—thus, by learning to express himself, to dance, through the medium of that masculinity. If Astaire and Daniels now appear as equals, it is, according to the Arcade's myths and ideologies of blackness and black manhood, because Astaire's new-found, blackened masculinity has let him find his feet and dance as Daniels, the bootblack, dances, equally standing, equally kneeling, and so on. With his shoes shined, Astaire mirrors Daniels just as Daniels mirrors Astaire, each equally manifesting the black masculinity that joins them, each legislating, let us suppose, *not* as Cavell imagines, for the republic of all rational beings—Kant's Kingdom of Ends—but for a republic of all the white men who crave black manhood.

Cavell is also right to claim that the Arcade is an allegory that sees America as "containing not only amusements and occupations and false promises . . . but a territory of magic or exemption in which such things as that walk-off can form itself." For Cavell, the magic of the walk-off is its glimpse of a Kantian utopia and its implied call for social change. *Pace* Cavell, I have been urging that the walk-off affords us no such glimpse, and that whatever utopia it envisions it envisions in the perspective of white mythologies and ideologies of black manhood. The epilogue to the second routine will seem a genuine utopia—as though its beauty really were a symbol of the moral good—only if we ignore those mythologies and ideologies.[63]

In his Spinoza lectures, Cavell distinguishes between false praise and vain praise. As we have seen, he takes the Astaire routines, especially the second, as raising the question of vain praise. Henry James's story "The Birthplace," he takes as raising the question of false praise, "a traditional concept of . . . [which] is idolatry, freezing allegiance into superstition."[64] One way to summarize my amendments to Cavell's reading of the second routine is to say that it too raises the question of false praise. In *Swing Time*, Astaire pays homage to the tradition and genius of black dance by blackening his face and performing "Bojangles of Harlem." If, in *The Band Wagon*, he gets his shoes rather than his face "blacked up," the substance of the performance remains the same: homage that cannot separate itself from the legacy of blackface minstrelsy's myths and fantasies about black masculinity.[65] *The Band Wagon's* reiteration of these myths and fantasies—specifically its suggestion that blackness and especially black masculinity is a magical force that can bring alienated, melancholic white men to earth[66]—suffuses and saturates its gestures toward homage, thus compromising, fatally, our ability to see in Astaire's "dance of praise" anything more than a form of idolatry that superstitiously mistakes a myth about black manhood for the rich artistic tradition to which Astaire owes his existence as a dancer.[67]

There is no doubt that *The Band Wagon* aspires to acknowledge the roots of the Hollywood musical, and of Astaire's dancing, in black dance.[68] In the scene that follows the second routine, Astaire asks Jeff Cordova (Jack Buchanan), the director who has been solicited to direct his comeback, and whom Astaire has just seen play the role of Oedipus in a sequence from *Oedipus Rex*, whether he really wants to make a musical. Cordova retorts that he is sick of artificial distinctions between the musical and the drama, emphatically insisting that there is "no difference between the magic rhythms of Bill Shakespeare's verse and the magic rhythms of Bill Robinson's feet."[69] Here, then, through a short dialogue, *The Band Wagon* verbally acknowledges what Astaire has performatively acknowledged in the second routine: the musical's roots, thus Astaire's roots, in the tradition of black dance. But because the second routine has failed to distinguish its preoccupations from those of a minstrel show, this later acknowledgment rings hollow. The problem is a difficult one: how, within American culture, pervaded as it is with white counterfeits and caricatures of black cultural productivity, can "white praise of a black culture whose very terms of praise it has appropriated"—Cavell's words—persuade that it is not false praise?[70] Or, to borrow one of Cavell's key critical concepts, how can white praise of a black culture whose terms of praise it has appropriated defeat its perhaps inevitable tendency to a sort of *theatricality* that is pitched to white fantasies and ideologies about blacks?[71]

Part 3. Invisible Femininity, Invisible Blackness

I begin the final part of this paper with a discussion of Kelly Oliver's reading of Luce Irigaray's *Marine Lover of Nietzsche*. Oliver's reading of Irigaray speaks to my purposes, for it raises questions pertaining to Nietzsche's appropriation of femininity that apply, *mutatis mutandis*, to *The Band Wagon*'s appropriation of blackness. In extrapolating those questions to a discussion of *The Band Wagon*, I will explain my rejection of Cavell's appraisals of the two Astaire routines, drawing on my analysis of those routines in part 2 of this paper. I conclude by suggesting that an important implication of the general line of argument I bring against Cavell's aesthetic judgments is a reconsideration of his interpretation of philosophy in American life that perhaps parallels Oliver's Irigaray-inspired aspiration to open philosophy to a dialogue with its feminine and other others.[72]

On Oliver's account, Irigaray's *Marine Lover* is Ariadne's plaint against the appropriation of "the feminine" within the "masculine imaginary." More specifically, it is a plaint against "the desire by a man to be a woman . . . If man becomes woman, then there is no woman/other, there is only man and the woman/other is a mask worn by the selfsame." Irigaray's argument bears directly on Part 2 of *Zarathustra*, for there, we have seen, Nietzsche presents the feminine Ariadne as a dimension, or qualification, of Zarathustra's masculinity. For Oliver's Irigaray, this presentation of the feminine demonstrates a general tendency in Nietzsche's thought to "speak for, and as, the feminine," thus "to represent woman as the mirror whose non reflective surfaces . . . cannot be seen." Miming women, it seems, is "just another strategy to ensure that those surfaces that do not reflect the masculine will not be seen." In fine, it is a recuperation of the other "into the economy of the same."[73]

It is essential to see, I think, that this economy is at once instrumental and reductive. It is instrumental, for it makes femininity an instrument of masculinity. More precisely, it assigns femininity a significance that is dictated by male interests, desires, and fantasies. In *Zarathustra*, for example, the economy of the same attributes to femininity the power of receptivity craved by the male singer of the night song. This economy is reductive, because it reduces the figure of woman to a horizon of possibilities that serve male concerns, thus leaving invisible the innumerable alternative possibilities that Oliver describes as women's "nonreflective surfaces."

The first Astaire routine's recuperation of blackness into an economy of the same lies at the heart of my rejection of Cavell's judgment of that routine. That judgment, again, took "the scene of walking and of melodic syllabification as appropriate expressions of the ordinary as the missable." I demur at Cavell's judgment for two reasons. First, because the first routine, along with the preceding pairings of Astaire and Ava Gardner, presents blackness as the power of receptivity whites require to recover from skepticism. In fine, it presents blackness as an instrument for redeeming melancholic, white subjectivity. My second reason is that the first routine, by making blackness into an instrument for redeeming white subjectivity, contributes to the film's more general tendency to reduce the manifold human possibilities available to blacks to the services they provide whites (Astaire takes money from his pocket thrice in *The Band Wagon*'s opening twenty or so minutes: first to pay the black waiter who has been serving him on the train; second, to tip a black porter in advance for taking his luggage; and third, to pay Daniels for the shine on his shoes—that is, for his newly acquired black masculinity. And, of course, the only blacks we see in these scenes are the waiter, porters, and Daniels).[74] As I suggested in the second part of this paper, one aspect of this reductionist tendency is the odd implication that skepticism's loss of the world is not available to blacks. At once instrumental and reductive in its treatment of blacks, the first routine presents a Jim Crow version of skepticism and racially divides the ordinary. Because it thus distorts the ordinary, I repudiate the judgment that it presents *appropriate* expressions of the ordinary as the missable. Rather than find pleasure in the first routine's portrait of the ordinary, I am dismayed by it. In articulating the grounds of that dismay—that is, in articulating a negative aesthetic judgment—I declare my wish, my demand, that the first Astaire routine prompt dismay in others.

It will be recalled that Cavell judges the second routine to warrant praise on the grounds that its dance of praise contests the very conditions it depicts. Again, I demur at Cavell's judgment, this time for three reasons. One is that the second routine is founded on the first routine's racializing distortion of the ordinary (the second routine shows the racial redemption that the first routine shows the melancholic white subject to require). A second is that I find no glimpse (not even a traumatic one) of Kant's Kingdom of Ends in the second routine's epilogue—Cavell's protestations to the contrary notwithstanding—but simply the jazzy, big-band–accompanied climax of Minnelli's celebration of the minstrel tradition. My third reason is that the second routine invites the suspicion of false praise, for it seems to pertain less to "the transcendent accomplishment of black dancing" than to black idols in the minds of whites.[75] Dismayed by the second routine, as well as by the first, I present these reasons as the grounds of my dismay.

My third reason for rejecting Cavell's judgment returns us to the idea of an economy of the same. Here, the issue is not simply that the two Astaire routines present blackness as an instrument for redeeming melancholic, white subjectivity, but that the presentation of blackness in this fashion is pitched to white fantasies and expectations of black serviceability. For Irigaray and Oliver, of course there is a parallel and general tendency in the West to pitch presentations of femininity to male fantasies and expectations of women's serviceability. Responding to that tendency, Oliver urges that we begin to envision philosophy "as a dialogue of human experiences." Specifically, she invites philosophy to "engage in a dialogue with its feminine other." Feminist philosophy, Oliver argues, "can listen to and speak the excluded feminine(s)."[76] Oliver's point, I take it, is that philosophy should include sensibilities, perspectives, and self-understandings that reflect the unreflective surfaces of the feminine and that have not been sanctioned as serving the demands of a masculinist agenda. I offer a coda to the present paper by briefly pressing a similar point in connection to Cavell's conception of Emerson's finding and founding of philosophy for America.

Consider, then, Cavell's "Emerson's Constitutional Amending: Reading 'Fate.'" In this extended discussion of "Fate," Cavell's central concern is that Emerson's essay, written in 1850 and just a few months after the passage of the Fugitive Slave Law, makes no mention of that law. It is well known that Emerson was "unforgettingly, unforgivingly"[77] horrified by Daniel Webster's support of the "Fugitive Slave Law." Why, then, asks Cavell,

> throughout the distressed, difficult, dense stretches of metaphysical speculation of this essay does Emerson seem mostly, even essentially, to keep silent about the subject of slavery, make nothing special of it? It is a silence that must still encourage his critics, as not long ago his admirer Harold Bloom and his detractor John Updike, to imagine that Emerson gave up hope of democracy. But since I am continuing to follow out the consequences of finding in Emerson the founding of American thinking—the consequence, for example, that his thought is repressed in the culture he founded—the irony of discovering that this repressed thinking has given up on the hope and demand for a nation of the self-governing, would be, so I fear, harder than I could digest.[78]

Cavell answers the question relating to Emerson's silence by insisting that "Fate" was not intended as polemic, but meant by Emerson as an effort "to preserve philosophy in the face of conditions that negate philosophy."[79] More interesting to me than this answer, however, is the role that references to enslaved African Americans play in the unfolding of Cavell's argument. Although Emerson (on Cavell's reading) is mindful of slavery but omits to mention it, Cavell mentions it explicitly, ultimately with an eye to defending Emerson against the likes of Harold Bloom and John Updike. Specifically, Cavell refers to slavery so that he can vindicate Emerson against the charge that he gave up on democracy. Notice, here, the similarity between "Emerson's Constitutional Amending" and Cavell's Spinoza lectures. If, in the former essay, Cavell is intent on vindicating Emerson, in the latter essay he is intent on vindicating Astaire against Michael Rogin's complaints. In both cases Cavell alludes to America's history of racial injustice, mainly in order to acquit the white protagonist of his essay—Astaire in the one case, Emerson in the other—of false charges. Put differently, he invokes that history as an instrument—as something like a legal instrument—for preparing extended briefs on behalf of Astaire and Emerson. Here, then, we have two further cases in which blackness, or the presence of blacks—here, specifically, the fact of blacks' subjection to racial injustice—has proved serviceable for a purpose relating to whites, that purpose being absolution. One question these cases raise, I think, is whether Cavell's effort "to follow out the consequences of finding in Emerson the founding of American thinking" can dispense with narrative economies of the same that, to borrow Toni Morrison's words, speak "of" the African in America, but decline to hearken to a "response from the Africanist persona."[80] As we have seen, Oliver hopes to expand the horizon of philosophy to include feminine voices that have not been constructed, as, for example, Nietzsche constructs them, to serve a masculinist philosophical agenda. What would it mean similarly to expand the horizon of consequences that Cavell follows out to include a hearkening to African American voices in tracing out the significance of Emerson's philosophical legacy?

Although I cannot begin here even to outline an answer to this question, three books—three points of departure—come to mind: Douglass's *My Bondage and My Freedom* (1855); Du Bois's *The Souls of Black Folk* (1903); and Ellison's *Invisible Man* (1952). I mention these books, for each of them may be read as, in part, an African American engagement with Emerson's founding of American thought. In *Bondage*, for example, Douglass presents himself as an Emersonian representative man, as an aversive thinker ("I paced the seven miles . . . thinking much by the solitary way—averse to my condition; but *thinking* was all I could do"[81]), and, I believe, as revising Emerson's thesis that self-reliance is the aversion of conformity. In *Souls*, one likewise hears revisionary echoes of Emerson, not only in Du Bois's much-commented-on analysis of the idea of double consciousness—an idea that Emerson invokes in "Fate" and that Cavell discusses at length—but, and perhaps more significantly, in the final paragraph of "Of the Training of Black Men," where Du Bois, like Emerson near the end of "The American Scholar," finds "company" among "the shades of all the good and great." "I walk with Shakespeare," Du Bois writes, "and he winces not."[82] In *Invisible Man*, finally, Ellison's attempt to think with and against Emerson's founding of thinking is as overt as could be imagined. One obvious example of this effort is the white "trustee" (Norton) who after repeatedly mentioning his "pleasant fate" asks the invisible man whether he has studied Emerson. Learning that he has not, the trustee returns to the theme of fate and advises the invisible man to read him, "for he was important to your people. He had a hand in your destiny."[83]

Cavell remarks that Emerson's thought is repressed in the culture he founded. How do we take the measure of that repression? Could it be that part of the task is to listen to a tradition of philosophical thought—of, precisely, African American philosophical thought—that has intermittently heard and responded to Emerson's call to think, speaking back critically but not deafly? And could it be that this tradition has been less embarrassed to receive Emerson, and so less inclined to repress him, than other American philosophical traditions? It is obvious, I suppose, that these questions raise a host of issues that would better mark the beginning than the end of a proper paper presentation. I conclude, then, by conjecturing that something like the reverse of what the trustee says is true: that Douglass, Du Bois, Ellison, and other African American thinkers have had a hand in Emerson's destiny, and that they have handsomely turned that destiny to the hope of democracy.

CHAPTER THIRTEEN

The Incessance and the Absence of the Political

Stanley Cavell

I suppose it was as some gesture in the effort to keep my responsibility in taking up so rich an array of texts under some illusion of control that I have ordered my responses to the foregoing essays according to the order in which Andrew Norris listed and mailed them to me, with the exception that, on an impulse to juxtapose the two interventions dealing with film, I reversed the order of the last two.

Sandra Laugier's contribution (Chapter 2) sets an admirable tone for beginning to read the collection through. Not only is she at home, among other matters, in the entire history of analytical philosophy (from the time of her doctoral dissertation on Quine two decades ago, she has published work on essentially every major figure in that tradition from Frege and Carnap to Austin and the later Wittgenstein), but she has the touch of getting to and staying with a depth of the concepts involved, none trickier than that of the ordinary, that many, even clearly gifted, philosophers despair of successfully conveying. We all know, I believe—I mean those who have tried to express their sense of the power and richness of the writings of Wittgenstein and of Austin—the frustration in trying to convey this sense and at the same time show the knowledge that the trivial details of words and experiences that our lives at any time turn upon, and are the questionable treasures these writers return to us, may after all leave one struck with the sense that philosophy is itself trivial, that indeed the moral of the work of ordinary language investigations seems to be that the daily round of human life as such, seen as it were from within itself, is for the most part hardly worth the candle of understanding.

Austin and Wittgenstein each have characteristic ways of making explicit, or confessing, this, let's call it, anxiety of the trivial. In "Pretending," Austin says this: "Importance is not important. Truth is." Evidently someone, perhaps Austin himself, has been asking Austin why what he does is important, namely why it isn't as trivial as it may seem, trafficking with unflinching explicitness in exchanges of the obvious. And at §118 of *Philosophical Investigations*, Wittgenstein turns upon himself to ask: "Where does our investigation get its importance from, since it seems only to destroy everything interesting, that is, all that is great and important." His response here is to say: "What we are destroying is nothing but houses of cards [*Luftgebäude*: structures of air]." Each, I think we must grant, knows that these responses are, perhaps must be, as provocative as they may be reassuring. Austin's retort ("Truth is.") is not merely abrupt but apparently impertinent, implying stuffily that questioning the importance of what he does philosophically can only come from an insouciance toward truth. Moreover, the discovery and analysis of importance can be said to be methodologically fundamental to Austin, whose doctrine of illocutionary force undertakes to make clear that, and why, to speak comprehensibly is to speak with comprehensible, let's say, *import*—to say more than you say. (In Emerson's phrase: "Character teaches above our will"; put otherwise, but controversially, our utterance communicates beyond its words. One could add: To philosophy's sometime dismay; to Freud's perpetual interest.) In Wittgenstein's case the "houses of cards" he is destroying include the architectural systems that have dominated the philosophical landscape since the invention of the genre by Plato. Wittgenstein is, I imagine, expressing his sense of permanent destructiveness—or destructiveness relocated—in his denial of a phantasm of the ground covered with rubble as a result of his investigations, which, while indicating that his philosophical words have destroyed no buildings (certainly no more than past philosophical words—one sense of his sometimes-mysterious assertion "Philosophy leaves everything as it is") expresses or confesses his sense of inner devastation. Such is the necessary risk of philosophy's inescapable task of subjecting to assessment, reconsideration, the importance and interest of what we take to be important and interesting.

Such is a way of framing something of the background, or foreground, against which or behind which I think Sandra Laugier's remarks here may be read, perhaps beginning with her greatly valuable caution that "there is nothing obvious or immediate about the ordinary: it is to be discovered, and that is the task that Austin's minute analyses and Wittgenstein's innumerable examples set themselves" (p. 23). Take it as a moral of the human prompting (refined explosively in philosophy) to leap to—or take on the posture of—importance that, in the visions of Wittgenstein and Austin, we wander through the world as strangers to it and to ourselves: they perceive (in Austin rather by implication than description) our ordinary lives to be as filled with illusion, trance, confusion, caprice, self-defeat, and intellectual or spiritual violence as they are seen to be in Plato or Hume or Rousseau or Kant or Nietzsche or Marx. In such a state of estrangement it must seem a miracle that we can speak for ourselves, let alone speak for others. But so long as this is mysterious, how can we trust any solution to the debate between, for example, libertarians and communitarians, who take sides on the prior and darker question of whom we speak for, and with what right? Laugier perceives this as a cause of their debate's being "tired." I should regard measures that allow us to speak together, about matters of common importance, with increased vividness and interest, to be a distinct contribution to political life.

The proposal, and practice, of the ordinary language philosophers is to find the means for moving away from tired, indeed exhausted, human self-entanglements within the very power of the language, the language we call ours, that philosophy, throughout its history, has so chronically distrusted and on the whole wished to exile. I sometimes say this expresses a human wish for the inhuman. What the source is, or what the forms are, of this wish is an issue for philosophical investigation, or should be. I should simply say here that Sandra Laugier's emphasizing of the significance I attach to the idea of our language as natural (to the same extent that it is asserted to be conventional) is something I am particularly grateful for. (She addresses the issue as part of what she calls philosophy's anthropology.) Of course nothing might seem less promising, or more philosophically retrograde, than an appeal to the naturalness of our language at a time when for many it remains part of philosophy's avant-garde to consider naturalism in philosophy a program for inscribing, in Quine's phrase, philosophy as a chapter of (natural) science (meaning, I take it, experimentally and mathematically driven science, not, for example, geology or paleontology). Yet here Wittgenstein's proposals, mentioned in Laugier's text, about the natural history of the human perhaps request a perspective still insufficiently followed out as an address to his work. An element of philosophy as natural history is expressed in Wittgenstein's description of his task in his *Investigations* as one requiring us to "turn our whole examination round . . . but about the fixed point of our real need" (§108). (I hope it will not seem to cheapen, or harden, the idea if I note that this speaks to the observation about the discourse of the presidential campaign we are now (i.e. in 2004) living through in the United States, that the effort to bring the cruelly generalized idea of "values" to the center of discussion serves to distract the citizenry from consulting its real need.)

I allow myself to single out one instance of the sort of subtlety, or compression, of which Sandra Laugier is able to avail herself, as, in effect, a marker of a location from which further work is to be done. When she writes, "the adequacy of language to reality—the truth of language—is not to be constructed or to be proven: it is to be shown in language and its uses" (p. 22), "adequacy," as naming the relation of language to reality, takes over the more literal Latin form for the idea of "correspondence" as the assurance of the connection between word and thing. I understand her claim, accordingly, to be that this assurance is not to be expected from constructions revealing that individual words refer to individual things, but from, as Wittgenstein puts the matter, the way "grammar tells us what anything is." That natural language reveals the world is no more in need of, or open to, philosophical explanation than the circumstance, so to speak, that there is something rather than nothing, and speech rather than calls. Neither, however, are these ideas to be *assumed* (any more than I can undertake to assume, to adapt another formulation of Wittgenstein's, that he—some other—has a soul). How we come to experience such a need, imagine such an omission, confirms the reality of the threat of skepticism.

Piergiorgio Donatelli's reading of J. S. Mill's perfectionist texts under the title "Bringing Truth Home" (Chapter 3) speaks directly to the issue of philosophical debate becoming "tired," exhausting itself where apparently opposite sides are unable to free themselves of each other because they share a common, unarticulated supposition—in the case in question, the supposition that speaking for oneself and speaking for others are philosophically transparent and separate matters. The issue of language as becoming formulaic, "incrusting and petrifying" the mind (cf. p. 44), of thoughts expressed, or rather unexpressed, in "cram" versions (p. 41)— various efforts to avoid thinking for oneself, avoid moving "to the active from the passive mind" (p. 42)—will come up in later discussions. A way of epitomizing a philosophical issue at stake here, of particular interest to me, is to note a kind of ambiguity in something Mill says about understanding proverbs: "The full meaning *cannot* be realized until personal experience has brought it home" (quoted on p. 45). Donatelli glosses this, among other ways, as follows: "The way in which proverbs can be striking is disclosed by their capacity to show us a sense in which we can take their words, a sense which destroys the previous illusion of having meant anything at all, and which is connected to, and is the expression of, our experience." What I called a "kind of ambiguity" is as between understanding the "illusion of having meant anything at all" as a state in which the sense of words has become encrusted, formulaic, dead ("salvation is not through works but through faith"), and a state in which there is an attempt to force a sense upon words (as, for example, in the *Investigations*, §253: "I have seen a person in a discussion on this subject strike himself on the breast and say: 'But surely another person can't have THIS pain!'"). Is one of these states the more fundamental, or the more revelatory of what human speech is?

Putting such questions together with Sandra Laugier's questions concerning the right to speak, we are asked to reach to the level of Aristotle's vision of the human city, say of political existence, as made possible, and necessary, by the condition of the human possession of language. Mill in 1832, as Emerson later in that decade, as Austin and Wittgenstein a century later, is questioning the sense in which that condition, the condition or capacity of meaningful, useful exchange, of judging our shared lives, is any longer reliably fulfilled. They are questioning accordingly what, or whether anything, now counts as political existence. (In my graduate student days, it was common to accept the idea that politics, or say visible politics, is power. Today I imagine not a few would feel that such a simultaneous underestimation and overestimation of power understands human existence as conducting itself largely in the absence of the political. David Owen's discussion of Foucault [in Chapter 7] is obviously pertinent here.)

Donatelli's focus on Mill's perception of the deadening of our understanding asks us, as *On Liberty* so passionately and repeatedly asks us, to consider how we speak to one another—what our lives together look like, what our ordinary is, what, let's say, we ratify each other in taking for granted—as if that is the primary evidence of the state of our politics, or of our lack of it. Mill's answer is that our society is one in which our speech exists as a medium in which we are intimidated, policed, by each other. This might be compared with Marx's perception that in capitalist society we have contempt for each other. Emerson confesses, in a moment that I have found chilling in "Self-Reliance," that every word his countrymen say chagrins him. I have stressed in Rawls's theory of justice an essential dependence upon what I have called the conversation of justice. In expressing my reservations about how the conversation seems sometimes to be imagined by Rawls, I have not hitherto raised the question of how one assesses the judgments of one's fellow citizens' state of society's compliance with the principles of justice. Take, for example, what are called "focus groups," supposedly representative small collections of people whose responses, when they are interviewed by a television personality, are sampled to presidential addresses, or debates, or issues before congress. One finds in these responses, I believe, mostly nothing but phrases repeated more or less accurately from the speeches in question, or from remembered criticisms of former speeches. The air of the formulaic or encrusted is itself deadening. (Proust, as I recall, describes this reduction of speech as using "public words," attributing to them power enough to keep his own order of words incognito.) I mean to speak uncynically, namely in fear of the cynicism of taking such reactions for granted.

Donatelli's portrait of Mill, showing the persistence of signature ideas of his from the time of "On Genius," in 1832, one of the early works signaling his recovery from the depression that overcame him in his twentieth year, to the relatively late *On Liberty* twenty-five years later, enriches the received portrait of Mill in professional philosophy on this side of the Atlantic, according to which, after a brush with romanticism in recovering from his collapse, Mill essentially reverted to the utilitarian views that had disheartened him, modifying them, or say softening them, but through means that will lead him into supposedly well-known argumentative lapses. The thought, implicit in Donatelli's discussion, that Mill's unswerving project had consistently become that of reconciling social utility with personal perfectionism seems to me distinctly more promising.

Joseph Lima and Tracy B. Strong (Chapter 4)—after a whirlwind yet valuable rehearsal of some decades in which the work initiated in Austin and the later Wittgenstein had been sought and largely missed in its pertinence to political theory—refigure the political significance of the loss and recovery of our ordinary and its words (emphasizing this recovery in its connection with skepticism and its character as uncanny, thus as internal to Wittgenstein's signature idea and practices of "returning words from their metaphysical to their everyday use") to be a movement, inspired by Rousseau, from an ordinary characterized by our non-presence to our words, to an ordinary in which, returning us to each other (each to each and each to our words), we find our political present (p. 79), say the capacity to "speak as a 'we'" (p. 77). They adduce, fascinatingly, the case of Louis XVI, who inadvertently provided the scene for a new claim to "the authority of the political voice" (p. 76), discounting the past, recounting the present, as raising "the possibility that the time of the political is always now" (p. 77); and they go on to propose an articulation of this break in history ("a transformation or transfiguration of the world" [ibid.]) in terms of Austin's idea of the performativity of speech, modified by my proposal of two directions in Wittgenstein's appeal to "forms of life."

These formulations bind together a cluster of ideas—the presence of the political, the claim of authority, the loss of institutional force, the consequent break in history shown by a rediscovery of speech—so forcibly putting me in mind of a project of mine on Austin that has preoccupied me on and off in recent years (the development of what I call passionate utterance out of, as an extension of, Austin's work on performative utterance) that I cannot forbear from concentrating my remarks here on the role Lima and Strong assign in their discussion to their (and my) readings of Austin and Wittgenstein as the founders of ordinary language philosophy. (This project on Austin was adumbrated in an address to the American Philosophical Association, "Something out of the Ordinary," in 1996, and circulated in its *Proceedings* the following year; a full, or fuller, version is due to appear in 2005 in a collection of mine entitled *Philosophy the Day After Tomorrow.*) My response to Lima and Strong can accordingly be taken as focused on the following pair of their questions: "The political question here is then which performative is to be efficacious, what one might call the ethnological, social convention (that of the King), or the biological, that is the claim to life advanced by the would-be Assembly. Is it too much to see the contrast this way?" I agree with the importance they attach to the first question, and I would like to account for the accuracy of the hesitation ("Is it too much to see . . . ") in the second. The gist of my summary account which follows is that Austin has not, without perhaps an extension of his theory of the performativity of speech, provided an understanding of what may be marked out by the idea of a "biological performative," or "claim to life," that allows for an unhesitant (non-exclusive and non-evasive) answer.

I had for a long time not been particularly interested in Austin's theory of the performative utterance (I once referred to it as his most exoteric work). Something that annoyed me about its fame in academic literary circles was the consequent neglect of his other work, as, for example, represented in his texts "Other Minds" and "Excuses," which had been decisive for me in coming to recognize the depth and originality of his mind. But when in the early 1990s I became drawn into thinking about opera and, in looking for what can be said about the conditions of its passionate utterance, turned for help to rereading Austin's *How to Do Things with Words*, I was puzzled to find that, while Austin kept coming upon questions of passion (as well as action) in speech, he invariably, quite consciously, turned away from pursuing these questions. The most obvious avoidance of the issue of passion, to my mind, is revealed when, having reached a workable characterization of illocutionary force, locating it between locutionary and perlocutionary acts, Austin drops the consideration of the perlocutionary almost as soon as he distinguishes it. He illuminatingly ties the illocutionary to the locutionary, asserting that every act of speech is as such ("*eo ipso,*" Austin says more than once, stressing the point) an illocutionary act, and he uses this discovery to conclude his discussion by producing a list of illocutionary verbs extensive and various enough to give an idea of the radiation of these forces throughout human speech (e.g., warning, promising, betting, informing, notifying, conceding, naming, nominating, swearing allegiance, etc., which one may think of in each case as naming the point of the utterance). But while Austin has insisted that that every locutionary act has at the same time, in addition to illocutionary force, a perlocutionary effect (e.g., alarming, threatening, intimidating, astonishing, inciting, convincing, dissuading, amusing, amazing, distracting, seducing, ingratiating yourself, showing allegiance, revealing affection or respect or contempt, etc., which may or may not be taken as the point of the utterance), instead of going on to specify a list of perlocutionary effects to range along with those of illocutionary force, he departs from the topic with the observation, or impression, that "almost any sentence may have, in special circumstances, any perlocutionary effect." (My lists, incorporating instances of Austin's, are principally based on Austin's criteria that performative utterances occur in first person singular present indicative active, and [characteristically] name what they do, that is, name their illocutionary force.) To say "I promise" is (under accepted circumstances) to promise. Perlocutionary effects are not thus named: By saying "I convince (or seduce, or astonish) you" I do not convince or seduce or astonish you. (Barring, perhaps, accompanying my words with hypnosis or drugs.) Austin notices, but makes nothing in particular of the fact, that one cannot say (it is not English to say) "I convince you," just like that. But compare: "I convince you, I hear"; "I astonish you, it would appear." And consider the unexceptionable "You convince me"; "You astonish me." Austin says: In a performative utterance the "I" comes essentially into the picture. I will add: In a passionate utterance, the "you" comes essentially into the picture.

It is worth noting, in the present volume, in which Austin's name is recurrently invoked in connection with the political, that Austin never gets around (as I recall), in the lecture notes from which the text of *How to Do Things with Words* was made, to questioning the necessity of the first person singular in his articulation of the performative utterance. Surely "We hold these truths to be self-evident . . . ," while first person plural, is performative. "Surely"? At least under certain circumstances. Not when they were first written (on what?). When they were first adopted (by whom?)?

If Austin is opening the way to a characterization of passionate utterance (hence to an essential register of political speech), it must lie in the region of perlocutionary effect, so it occurred to me to begin a characterization of this region by fastening on its differences from illocutionary force, which Austin takes as the hallmark of the performative utterance. Austin gives a list of six necessary (and sufficient) conditions (he sometimes calls them rules) for the successful, or as Austin likes to put matters, for the felicitous, issuing of a performative utterance. The first condition is that there must exist a conventional procedure for uttering certain words in certain contexts; the second is that the particular persons and circumstances must be appropriate for the invocation of the procedure. Now instead of taking the absence of convention as a lack in the condition of an utterance, let's take it as the first condition of a passionate utterance. But then Austin's second condition, establishing the appropriateness of persons and circumstances in which the performative words are uttered, is at the same time absent for passionate utterance. Then it becomes open to question, or argument, how I establish the standing to single you out as the object of my passion. Call *establishing standing* and *singling out* the second compound condition of passionate utterance. Austin's third and fourth conditions for the performative utterance are that the conventional procedure must be executed correctly and completely. These requirements again obviously have no pertinence to passionate utterance, given the absence of an established procedure, and indeed are contradicted by the new (the second compound) condition that in passionate utterance it is open to question in the individual case how appropriateness of procedure is established. Austin's fifth condition is that where the procedure requires certain thoughts or feelings the parties must have those feelings or thoughts, and the sixth condition is that where intentions are required to inaugurate consequential conduct, the parties must actually so conduct themselves subsequently (e.g., actually keep the promise, pay the bet, hand over the expected gift). The fifth condition obviously goes over directly to passionate utterance: the one declaring the passion must actually have the passion, must, let's say, be *moved* to declare it. But the sixth condition consequently undergoes significant elaboration. Instead of a demand for *subsequent conduct*, a passionate utterance is a demand for a response *now*, and moreover a response *in kind*, namely one that responds to the passion. Unlike the performative case, it is open to the one addressed to *resist the demand*. Either acceptance or resistance satisfies the condition. What is at stake is the question whether a "we" is or is not in effect now.

I have summarized these differences this way: A performative utterance is an offer of participation in the order of law. A passionate utterance is an invitation to improvisation in the disorders of desire ("Something out of the Ordinary," pp. 30–31). Both seem registers of political life. Contemplating, on the basis of the short lists I have given of illocutionary and perlocutionary acts—actions, or interactions, that occur multitudinously every day (Austin, after doing some serious counting, estimates that there are many thousands of illocutionary acts; I judge, on the basis of some random pages, that there are a comparable number of perlocutionary acts distinguished in English)—the impression I get is of our interactions as constituting an incessant formation and deformation of the public realm, or say a continuous affirmation or denial of its existence. I suppose this is patently true only with the downfall of royal or tyrannical rule (or as the precursor of the visible downfall). (This complexity of the ordinary—its nervous and cardiovascular and endocrine systems as it were—is not invisible to, as it were, the naked eye. But practically we must learn oblivion to most of it as we cut our swaths through it—putting our skeletal and muscular systems most patently in play—according to seemingly simple plans of life.)

Passionate utterance, as I imagine it, does not exhaust the region of perlocutionary effect (or, if it is taken so, then there are distinct species of such utterance). I have been thinking of it as comprising instances in which one person claims standing and singles out another for a response. In hate speech, the other, the you in question, is a group and the aim is precisely not to elicit a response in kind but to dictate or to stifle response, to make "we" impossible. Political utterance might be conceived as the case in which one or more persons seek to establish a group by recommending or urging or rashly declaring its separation, in the case of the social contract, by separating it from nature and from strangers (separating "we" from "it" and from "they").

It had not, I think, occurred to me, before reading the present text of Lima and Strong's, that the difference between performative and passionate utterance might be articulated in conjunction with the difference I draw between the ethnological and biological directions of Wittgenstein's idea of forms of life. The case they invoke of Louis XVI might provide a test.

Since there is no established procedure conferring authority by which the legitimacy is established for "the Third Estate [to declare] itself to *be* the National Assembly of France" (p. 75), we have to understand its words to be perlocutionary in effect. (I wish I knew precisely what its, and the others', words actually were.) What the Third Estate is doing is declaring a standing for itself, and singling out three others (two estates and, primarily, the crown) as the objects of their announced desire or perception. The effort did not elicit a response in kind, one that responded to (the justice of) the passion expressed and thereby created a new now between the parties (calling the cops generally serves to keep the current now in place). The perlocutionary effect failed, the passionate utterance was unhappy (its demand was resisted). Without contesting Lima and Strong's suggestion that the question of sovereignty is in question, we may ask with what hope the declaration exclusively to be the National Assembly was taken. The Third Estate could hardly think of itself as capable of annulling the divinity that hedges a King. But it could think of the earthly conceptual point that a ruler without obedience rules nothing, and recognize that the capacity for disobedience is in principle theirs. Here is where I see (at the moment) the distinction in the understanding of two energies or directions of forms of life coming into play. Lima and Strong perceive that the "would-be Assembly" has advanced "the claim to life" (p. 76). My question then is with what hope, or vision, it advanced this claim in the face of the actual (the now, the ordinary) conventions within which the rule of the King existed. What sense could they make to themselves?

I have sometimes put an idea pertinent here by claiming that no set of what are sometimes called subject-positions (call them ethnological descriptions) of itself exhausts a subject's (biological, psychobiological) possibilities. Heidegger can be understood to be grounding this idea in declaring from the outset (of *Being and Time*) that predicates do not attach to human existence as properties attach, as it were, to an object. The claim to life (at something like the level of Locke's "appeal to God" when earthly legitimacy is at stake) implies that a "we" is no longer in effect, that the actual, the ordinary, the now, with its customary legitimacies, is no longer what it has been taken to be. When Shakespeare imagines a King to say in reply to the flirtatious objection of a foreign Princess, "We are the makers of custom, Kate," he instructs her, and us, in the perception of custom, of legitimacy, as responsive to desire. So an Assembly might eventually find it in itself to say, in reply to conventional power: We are the re-makers of custom, reformers in a transformed, reforming present, instructing you in the rights of desire, of the need for a voice in our common history. But now it looks as if my suggestion that there might be an unhesitant ("non-exclusive and non-evasive," cf. above, p. 270) understanding of such claims, by an appeal even to an extension of Austin's theory of performativity, was too optimistic. Unless the appeal could locate the issue in such a way as to show why, and where, hesitancy is an essential mark of a situation in which a "break in history" seems its accurate characterization. Since what is at issue is precisely the contesting of convention, so at stake is the contesting of a given disposition of authority or standing, hence the clear distinction between illocutionary force and perlocutionary effect. I am inclined to say (not quite unhesitatingly) that it follows that the illocutionary is out of joint and that we are in the realm of the perlocutionary, where the political and the passionate necessarily intersect. The only place I recall at which Austin faces what must have seemed to him the irrationality of speech (not merely of argument) is in his hesitancy over whether to call "I insult you" illocutionary or perlocutionary. Suppose we try to locate the act here as somewhere between saying "I defy you" and "I forbid you" (where convention is, if not broken, at least tested), and then explicitly ask for the result of the complexity in moving to "We defy you" or "We forbid you." That the you comes essentially into the picture is still clear (it is you who determine whether our act is felicitous). But the added complexity is that there are two plurals (the other being either the King's "We" or the President's "we"). It is I who speak, but my authority can be challenged by those for whom I speak as well as by those to whom I speak. It made sense to say that in such a circumstance history is broken; it makes equal sense to say that here history is made.

The most grating of the ironies in the struggles over the reception of ordinary language philosophy has, for me, been the persisting weight of insistence in taking Wittgenstein and Austin as defenders (perhaps in the line of G. E. Moore) of ordinary beliefs, and implicitly therewith of the current arrangement of institutions, whereas their vision of the (actual, as opposed to the eventual) ordinary is, on the contrary, as a place, or cave, of illusion, confusion, chaos, of, in a word, the unexamined life—a life calling out for, as it resists, transformation. Lima and Strong are kind enough to describe efforts of mine as extensions of Wittgenstein's and of Austin's thought in unanticipated directions, and I think there is a reason for my continuing motivation in this (as an ambition, whatever the achievement).

Of course my extensions begin with my sense of liberation by the originality of Wittgenstein's and of Austin's work, especially in my sense of it as a development (if one that implies discontinuities) of philosophy, in which their appeal to ordinary language (turning back from philosophy's millennia of predominantly fleeing the ordinary, as well as from the ordinary person's fleeing from philosophy) replaces philosophical system with a more powerful system of illumination, using ordinary language against its betrayals of itself (in metaphysics, in skepticism, in politics), giving it the power to exist, as Nietzsche, essentially following Emerson, required of the philosopher's life, "in opposition to today" (Emerson had demanded, "in aversion to conformity"). (It is the nature of custom, as of law, perpetually to seek to overcome, or violently shape, the disruptions of desire. According to Freud, not even Kings wholly enjoy civilization.) And the motivation continued in my sense that both Wittgenstein and Austin had drastically under-described their understandings of the ordinary itself. Austin is mostly content often just to accuse philosophers of being lazy or drunk with false profundity. When Wittgenstein speaks of requiring a "turn" in our investigations, he is still, I believe, most often taken as suggesting, in speaking of going up against the limits of language, that we are infringing a priori rules, which suits oddly with his also saying that there are not rules for every occasion, unless this is taken to suggest that language is in this regard defective. And while he says philosophy is to "return" words to their everyday use, it is not clear that when we use his methods for getting words "back," we have come to a consciousness of things we had ever had before. Without asking now why Austin and Wittgenstein were content, or compelled, to leave such matters open, I say merely that my sense of their break with the dispensation of analytical philosophy that they inherited is radical beyond any measure in currency (they distrust system; they distrust the impulse to translate ordinary words into the language of logic; they even distrust the impulse to replace one set of ordinary words by others— which is to distrust "analysis" as such—such as statements about objects into statements about sense experience). My sense, in brief, was that the conditions of their discoveries (and of the passions they aroused, arouse, positive and negative) were so elusive, or so unfamiliar and contrary to professional philosophical taste and practice, that to articulate them would require tracking a hint of method or a momentum of habit or a gag of taste in their writing that it is unclear they themselves would always have attached significance to. Often this looks, I believe, as if I am concerned with the literary conditions of their philosophizing. Very well. How, or where, does this differ from being concerned with the philosophical implications of their manners of writing?

I realize that I must try to be briefer as I proceed. Having read through all the papers before composing my individual responses, I was inevitably guided from the beginning of my writing by the sense of the range of interests to come. I accordingly knew, as I turn to the next paper, that Andrew Norris (Chapter 5) had something distinctive to say about just about every topic touched on so far. For example, following out the importance Aristotle attaches to shared language, call it the human power of judgment, as the condition of the realm of the political, from which I drew a moment ago the suggestion that compromise in our common speech indicates compromise in the formation of the political, Norris adds a striking image: "The deliberation between citizens that Aristotle presents as taking place within the polis [taking it that Aristotle pictures our speech 'as already full and present to us, the polis as achieved'] is on Cavell's account one that takes place, as it were, at the city's gates" (p. 87–88). This allows Norris to open the thought that the limits of a polis, what is within it and what is beyond it, are not determined by what is inside and outside the gates but by what you determine in entering the gates. And the thought that the city, so far as it invites the democratic aspiration, is always in the process of forming and reforming itself, the biological direction in the human life form challenging the ethnological direction (some might say, the idea of natural law challenging the finality of history), is in effect invoked in Norris's description of Socrates' position as one in which he is "not able to divorce himself from the city he condemns," but "cleaves to it and treats it as a city to which he owes his loyalty because he recognizes it to be something it has not yet become. Socrates as citizen must precede the eventual city in which he will be at home" (p. 82–83). Here is the classical case of perlocutionary confrontation, claiming standing before one whom you single out for your passion (rebuke or affection). (This will require a certain adjustment in view of the fact that Socrates is pictured not as the one to speak first in philosophizing, but as being confronted, for example, stopped in the public street.)

But now Norris introduces a complication in the *Republic* that he finds my account "glosses over," namely "the distinction . . . between the Socratic conversation and the education in compulsion the future philosopher-kings will suffer and undertake. He begins his account by singling out the conversational aspect of the *Republic* and infers from that the conversion, as if the conversion were not the topic but the effect of the conversation" (p. 96). I don't know about glossing over this distinction, but I confess that I remain unclear what I think about it. It is true that (for the purpose of characterizing perfectionism) I concentrate on the mighty fact of conversation and treat the "other philosopher," the philosopher-king, as belonging to the same fictional space as the cave and the chains and the sun (ladders perhaps to be thrown away after climbing them).

I take as obviously pertinent that after setting the opening situation of the prisoners in the myth of the cave—its life-long inhabitants in fetters, their heads fixed straight ahead of them, perceiving moving shadows of human and animal figurines, et cetera, and receiving Glaucon's observation, "This is a strange picture, and strange prisoners"—Socrates reports himself to say: "They are like us".[1] How are they like? Well, the myth describes the origin of and the capacity for human education as such (518b), and the fact that since we remain all our lives, however alleviated or punctuated, in the realm of the visible, we never wholly escape the shades of the prison dwelling (517b). But take "like us" to mean "like us now, at this stage of our (or your) education," namely with a capacity for conversation. Then I understand that to mark a particular moment within the myth of the cave, namely the point at which a "man trie[s] to free [us] and lead [us] upward" (517). This is contrasted with the first imagination of our being freed, namely by its "naturally happening" (515c). The contrast between the natural happening and the idea of our being led, suggests to me that the new (non-natural) element, brought by the "man," the liberating philosopher, is that of conventional communication, I suppose speech. I add that "being led" also contrasts with the earlier picture, when the freeing naturally happened, and the one freed is "dragged by force up the rough and steep path" (516e). "Being led," namely by speech, suggests that education is not purely or inevitably managed through "compulsion." (Compulsion is, on the contrary, always required to make the philosopher *return* to the cave.) But if we can speak with the philosopher, then we are past (or have sublimated) our murderous rage against our liberator, and our education is well under way—perhaps it will continue until we present ourselves to see the sun for ourselves. Which means that the conversion can indeed be seen as the effect, not alone the topic, of the conversation. (Taking the light of the sun not as the cause but as the sign or seal of conversion.)

But this must be conversation not among those in fetters (which, Norris insists, accurately, Socrates takes to be "quite insufficient"), but between those in that condition and the philosopher returned from the upward journey. Can we avoid the question how the journey was first (naturally) made, say how philosophy originates, since evidently we all begin as prisoners, trusting our senses, unapproachable, uneducable, by those in our condition? Shall we reconsider Socrates' description of "what deliverance from their bonds and the curing of their ignorance would be if something like this naturally happened to them"? He answers: "Whenever one of them was freed, had to stand up suddenly, turn his head, walk, and look up toward the light, doing all that would give him pain, the flash of the fire would make it impossible for him to see the objects of which he had earlier seen the shadows." We need, accordingly, to consider what instinct or insight or surmise we must imagine in order that it cause us to stand up suddenly (as with some realization), turn our head (as if searching for something suddenly felt lacking, to be desired), walk and look (in the search) upward to the light, all causing us pain.

I shall propose that this is a little sub-myth of the origin of (the impulse to) philosophy, perhaps we can say, of the origin of wonder, as follows. I am, one or another day, like any other, brought to my feet suddenly, torn from my ordinary, with some instinct of consciousness that the way we are living partakes of irreality, unnecessary necessaries, an insight that we are, in our distraction by shows and echoes of what seem shadows, lost, out of place, filled with the sense that reality is, as it were, behind us or above us. That I am drawn, in my quest to transform my existence, to walk and look for reality despite the quest's causing me pain, is the sign that I was already in greater pain, without realizing it; I had learned, grown ac-

customed, to consider the constrictions of pain as the normal condition of
the ordinary human dispensation. As this realization becomes articulated
as my being drawn, or dragged, dragging myself, to a state of illumination,
or perspicuity, concerning my fate, I recognize that I now have news that
I am compelled to convey. It is a story, however, the members of the audience for which I will have to create—paradoxically, since the story is precisely theirs. So I return to my old home from my new home, leaving the
new, as I left the old, in pain. One could say I am at home nowhere or everywhere.

If one accepts this as a characterization of the voices of the philosopher in *Philosophical Investigations*, then one has a candidate for what Norris phrases as "a commonality between the political and the philosophical"
(p. 83).

I share, and welcome, Richard Flathman's sense of ample agreement
between us (Chapter 6). His adducing Montaigne, in the second half of
his essay, is certainly to the point, and I mean to let the care in his reading of that corpus of work send me back to it. In the meantime, I note
a moment that strikes me in a citation Flathman gives from Montaigne's
"On Experience": "I, who operate close to the ground, hate that inhuman
wisdom that would make us disdainful enemies of the cultivation of the
body" (p. 123). It has been important to me in distinguishing Montaigne's
skepticism from that associated with Descartes to characterize the latter,
modern skepticism as a craving for the inhuman, the infinite. Whereas
in Montaigne, following the classical view, a disdain for the human condition, even a certain horror of it (as Montaigne describes this in "Some
Verses of Virgil"), can be lived with by cultivating a certain self-humor and
worldly wisdom, a relief from modern skepticism can come about only, if
not through rescue by internalizing an idea of God (as in Descartes), then
by massive distraction (of a Pascalian or of a Humean kind), or by transformation into outright nihilism or (if this is different) indifference. This
is important to me in explaining something about the Shakespearean intervention in Western culture, which I propose as an anticipation, or realization, of modern skepticism, relating its unappeasable threat to a new
perception of tragedy.

And this difference bears directly on the other main issue (in addition to enriching the concept of perfectionism by focusing on Montaigne's

writing) that Flathman has intended to raise in the opening half of his essay, namely "concerning [moral and political perfectionism's] implications for the good and the better life" (p. 99). He concludes his opening half by asking: "Would it be wrong to say that one of the risks [moral and political perfectionism] runs is making the better life the enemy of the good life, of the life that is desired by some?" (p. 109). Montaigne and the topic of (the politics of?) conversation come together in Flathman's closing paragraph:

[Montaigne] has experienced first-hand the dull, repetitive, stupefying banality of much familiar discourse and talk. But he has also experienced its quieting, supportive, reassuring qualities, the ways in which it diminishes the incidence of destructive hatred and conflict and allows of moments of tranquility. His advice . . . to accommodate to it externally, to conform to established customs, conventions and laws . . . is not given out of admiration for their content but in the hope that by following it he and his . . . fellow citizens can be comfortable with one another, can enter into true friendships with one another. . . . (p. 126)

I ask myself, with some apprehensiveness, whether anything I have argued for over the years has suggested that I desire that one should refuse to accommodate to much familiar discourse, as if I approve without reservation (whatever combination of sympathy and impatience I may secretly greet it with) Moliere's Alceste's demand for pure sincerity in every utterance, sharing a physiological intolerance of any grain of hypocrisy. In a little piece I wrote about Alceste some years ago (in *Themes out of School*) I thought I was clear that the value of sociability was under reasonable conditions (conditions under which reason could realistically be hoped to prevail) important enough to trump an unleashed call for truth-telling and till-counting.

It is true that I evidently allow myself to identify with Nora in her claim at the close of *A Doll's House* that she and her husband have never had a serious conversation and that this charge, or observation, is understandably important enough that Nora can be accepted as rational, as justified, in her claim that it allows her to, in some sense demands that she, leave her house and home. But this is not a case of social accommodation to temporary and shifting conditions of familiar open discourse. It is said in deepest privacy to her husband of some eight years, and about a condition that has been constant, to which she sees no possibility of change from within, and which is stifling her. It is arguable that she is wrong about this, hasty in arriving at this judgment, but that side of the argument is thoroughly represented by that husband, who asks not merely that she accommodate to these conditions externally, but that she embrace and internalize them as the sign of her fulfillment as a morally serious woman.

And it is true that I claim to understand what Emerson is getting at when he cries out hyperbolically, "Every word they say chagrins us." But I also claim to understand Emerson's call for the scholar, we might say the intellectual, to raise and cheer, which has forever grated on the nerves of many of his readers. I see it as Emerson's recognizing the capacity to encourage his or her fellows to participation, in act and judgment, in communal affairs, as a precious democratic emotion and virtue.

I see two philosophical issues immediately at stake in the question of serious or productive conversation—"philosophical" as shaped by the practices, as I understand them, of philosophy as I care about it most. First, I have described what I call Wittgenstein's fantasy of a private language as expressing complementary fears about one's relation to one's language, either that it leaves one inexpressive to the point of suffocation, or exposed to the point of defenselessness. These are marks of conversation that has become insupportable. Second, the danger of suppressing what is genuinely good, found genuinely valuable, in favor of a possibility of something theoretically superior is mitigated, I would say obviated, by a fundamental point of philosophical tact displayed most consistently, or unmistakably, by Socrates and Thoreau and Wittgenstein (in the *Investigations*), namely, as I have phrased the idea, that philosophy does not speak first. I have no idea of rushing in upon what I regard as a boring exchange or monologue and demanding that its participants satisfy my desire for sense and depth. As Thoreau puts the matter at its best: "I would not run amok against society; I would prefer that it run amok against me." Not every time is a time for philosophy, or for that conversation that is an intersection of the philosophical and the political. But when the time comes, nothing else will fill it. (I should recall here that my own interest in the power of conversation grew from Milton's revolutionary justification of divorce by appealing to the justification of marriage, namely, interpreting the Genesis story of the creation of Eve as the intended provision of a "meet and happy conversation," as correcting the wrong, recognized by God, of the man's being alone. A genuine conversation is the state in which one is no longer alone in the world. It can thus be taken as a candidate for the cure of skepticism. That there is conversation that disguises and perpetuates loneliness is perhaps better known.)

I feel I have not been responsive to the range of what Flathman means by the good exchange that is in danger from the better encounter—the quieting, supportive, reassuring, exchanges that clear the ground for whatever is the basis of higher encounter. I recall my asking, in response to Donatelli's invoking of Mill's perception of deadening discourse, how we think of our ordinary ways of speaking together as members of a (an aspiring) democracy. I think here of a remark that impressed me (by the historian Gordon Wood) to the effect that a mark of the fact that the American Revolution really was a revolution (something I realized that in my ignorance, or as compared with the more famous events of the French and Russian revolutions, and of the American Civil War, I had somehow doubted—without doubting that it made way for a political revolution) was that after the fighting settled the issue of the separation from royalty, the people spoke differently to one another. Here is where, perhaps, Flathman's approving reference comes into Oakeshott's description of conversation as having the sole objective of mutual "delighting" (see chap. 6, n. 6). I do not know the Oakeshott piece, but it seems to me that such a perlocutionary objective requires a talent or gift as unfairly distributed as perfect pitch or a beautiful voice or the ability to clown or to sprint, anyway as rare as that person whose charm of chatter brings an involuntary smile to the glummest face, a capacity to elicit interest by the sheer fact of saying a thing that interests them, something that said by anyone else would fall like a shot bird. Every lucky anniversary party or town meeting or playground may have one or two present with such a talent. (An English friend of notable charm once described to me what it was he missed about England, during a year in which he had been living in the States, as "the social mud." I can understand that yearning without thinking of it as missing delight. Familiar intricacy, as of one's own language, has its depth of pleasures.) I have friends with whom conversation is sometimes difficult, but I would rather have it than anything else then in my world. Shall I think of the delight as in the line of country of Emerson's cheerfulness? I think this goes beyond the warmth of pub talk, which I do not mean to discount. When I ask how we conceive of our obligations to raise and cheer one another I am looking for something like a tropism of responsibility toward social integrity, something within the capacity of the ordinary citizen.

The idea of conversation, from Aristotle to Dante and Castiglione, elicits ideas of the creation and maintenance of civility and justice and friendship. The responsibility is most exposed in a democracy, where the ability to speak well is at once admired and held in suspicion. The genre of the novel is made for the effect of conversation, but, as with other registers of human complexity, Shakespeare can have it when he wants it. At the opening of *Hamlet*, "For this relief, much thanks" conveys a moment of peace and friendship in an anxious watch. A similar provision of momentary quiet and reassurance is given, in *Henry V*, by "a little touch of Harry in the night." A sense of familiarity, standing apart from, and commenting on ceremony, is afforded in the opening lines of *King Lear*, between courtiers, touching upon concepts whose lethal powers are not yet envisioned: "I thought the King had more affected the Duke of Albany than of Cornwell." "It did seem so to us. . . . " But these do not represent goods of exchange that my encounters think better of and seek to replace. What is someone who cannot or will not provide these moments of public, passing intimacy? A snob? The figure of melancholy whom comedy must overcome? Do I risk this?

A word for the moment about Flathman's finding himself "unsettled" (in n. 12) by my assertion that a sense of compromise is the sign of being implicated by the actions of my society. Flathman is concerned that this may "make it too easy for the authorities to claim the skulkers have consented," which is, I agree, no small matter. Here I would like to appeal to a distinction (I do not know how real it may be under various conditions) between my sense of formative consent to a society and forming part of a consensus on its present actions. What I am focusing on is the necessity, given that I am compromised (precisely by my sense of consent, of being spoken for, acted in the name of), of claiming my right to speak in (loyal) opposition, the thing those who are part of the consensus may call my skulking. Isn't the capacity to feel and exhibit shame at the actions of one's society an inescapable sign, or price, of democracy?

I think I can accept with gratitude the pertinence of essentially everything David Owen offers as elucidation of my work in bringing to bear on it the writing of Foucault (Chapter 7). I would at the same time like to be able to demonstrate this gratitude by taking further what Owen calls the "productive dialogue" (p. 154) he has hoped to have begun to sketch, but here I feel hampered by having worked with Foucault's writing so much less closely and responsibly than Owen has. The intuition he describes himself as setting out to explore, which he found initially expressed by Arnold Davidson, concerning my interest in ethics as a mode of being as well as a map of good conduct, is something Davidson had also expressed to me about my work some years ago, and he and I went so far as to offer an exploratory seminar together at Chicago in the spring of 2000 on the concept of the ordinary which featured a reading of Foucault's work (especially that on the care of the self) in conjunction with the work of Freud (featuring *The Psychopathology of Everyday Life*) and of J. L. Austin (featuring "Excuses"). I got to the point then of recognizing painfully my belatedness in getting into the richness of the material Foucault deploys, but not to the point of confidence in putting it into practice in what I do. Maybe I can say a useful word about that here.

I do not hesitate to express appreciation for the pertinence of Owen's adducing the figure of the risky truth-teller as furthering the picture of the perfectionist friend, as for example manifested in Cary Grant's realization of Dexter Haven in relation to Tracy Lord, in *The Philadelphia Story*. But until I can spend some time with, I gather, Foucault's *Fearless Speech*, I can say nothing about Owen's instruction that Foucault distinguishes the *parrhesiastes* from the sage, in response to my remark that Dexter is "a kind of sage" (p. 145). Something in my descriptions of Dexter will have now to be considered further. If "integrity and steadiness of mind" (p. 144) is a criterion of the truth-teller, the characters played by (staying with our example) Cary Grant in the companion films of remarriage, in which his role of perfectionist friend remains quite visible, are questionable candidates for the title. In *His Girl Friday*, his relation to the Rosalind Russell character is that of a trickster. In *The Awful Truth*, his relation to Irene Dunne is changeable to the point of mystery; the woman characterizes him as "crazy," or doing crazy things, and it turns out this is why she cannot deny that she loves him. What characteristics can be assigned to these figures that suit them as credible sources of truth about oneself? And now thinking of Dexter more suspiciously, it strikes me how strangely removed his position is from the world. This aura of distance is what, perhaps, gave him in my eyes a sense of a sage's steady perception of the world, a scene in which he takes no active part, except in relation to Tracy, otherwise reading books and building a boat designed to carry exactly two people away from the things of man. He has acquired the self-mastery that is the condition and the consequence of conquering an addiction. But has he been honest with Tracy about that? Not only was she not a "helpmeet" there, as he tells her; but the implication of his lecture to her about her "coldness" is that she was the cause of his deepening attachment to his "gorgeous thirst." And in service of what way of "being useful in the world" (as Tracy longingly calls what she seeks) does this mastery prepare him? His steadiness is dependent on his being useful to her, but to manage this he seems to have put mastery aside and have achieved the power in a complete passiveness. It suggests itself that what fits the friend to convey the truth to a given other, to hold up the mirror of objectivity credibly, is to be chosen by that other for that role. There is no criterion of pertinence apart from that. The risk required then seems to reside in the very relinquishment of mastery itself, the bearing of separateness. This does not seem foreign to the moving passage Owen quotes from Foucault in which he accounts for "the demand of responsiveness" (p. 152), finding this not to require that one "be in solidarity with them [tellers of truth]. . . . It is sufficient that they exist. . . . "

My sense of affinity and difficulty with Foucault is captured in the paragraph Owen cites (p. 135) in which Foucault speaks of conversion, changing one's life, as "essential to philosophical parrhesiatic practices" (I rather take it for granted that Foucault is declaring his work to be doing something more than merely describing such practices), where this is not completely different from asking "his fellow citizens to wake up" in such a way as to change "one's style of life, one's relation to others, and one's relation to oneself." This passage compresses issues that I cannot fail to recognize every time I deal with the work of Emerson (where "aversion" is his active concept for conversion), or Wittgenstein's *Investigations* (where the ideas of "turning" his investigations around and "returning" words from their metaphysical to their everyday use are to be seen as modes of conversion, even aversion), matters I expressed recently and concentratedly in undertaking (in an essay collected in my *Philosophy the Day After Tomor-*

row) to compare Thoreau and Heidegger on demanding of their country-men that they "wake up" (Thoreau's epigraph to *Walden* declares this ex-plicitly, and Heidegger invokes the idea around another body of water, a segment of the Danube, in Hölderlin's Ister hymn). But these undeniable intimacies precisely pose the obstacle I feel. Since I am not confident that I grasp the mode of Foucault's philosophical practices in relation to those he describes, I do not see how to attempt to continue them in some touch of afterlife, however small, in what I do, as I seem to see in the case of the other philosophical writers I cite (where I have some trust in my sense, for example, of the work to be done in carrying out the return of words from metaphysical to ordinary registers, or in capturing the conversions in an Emersonian sentence).

But from the little I have just been saying I am prepared to predict that if I find the touch, it will concern immediately two matters. One of them—prompted by Foucault's allusion to changing one's "style of life" (I am trusting the translation)—will raise the question of how the concept of "biopower" relates to the issue that came up in my response to Lima and Strong's essay, namely the two directions, social and biological, that I un-derstand as internal to Wittgenstein's idea of a form of life (or life form). The other matter concerns learning how better to describe what appears in my work as the claim that the ordinary (what I call the actual, or unevent-ful, ordinary as opposed to the eventual, or returned, ordinary) is inher-ently violent, that when Wittgenstein says "philosophy leaves everything as it is" what he is pointing to is that, in philosophy's bottomless powerless-ness, it cannot alter the fact that our relations to ourselves and others are ordered, kept in order, to an unfathomable extent, by ordinary conditions, visible and invisible, that leave no certain time or place in which our lives may find themselves, detect and declare themselves, that the peace philoso-phy seeks vanishes the moment after it is glimpsed.

I cannot forbear adding a word about Owen's suggestion of a tension within my project between my "rejection of the idea of a true self and [my] recourse to Freudian psychoanalysis" (p. 142) (since Freudian psychoanaly-sis requires such an idea). Since my relation to Freud remains in process, and the process is one of recognizing his intervention as a continuation, or discontinuation, of philosophy, I feel I am in a position to declare myself free of supporting it as a science involved in the "modern medical management of sexuality" (ibid.). The vision of desire as sexual and as essentially, and incessantly, characterizing, in transfigured ways, anything we can recognize as a human self does not strike me as positing a true or deepest self. The picture of a human life, of my life, as patterns of struggles or detours away from painful and ineffective reparations and from pleasures that are fractured, investments or necessities that are as foreign as they are familiar to me, toward a discovery and acceptance of the reality of my own death, strikes me as intuitively incompatible with such a thing.

I accept, and I am grateful for, Espen Hammer's (Chapter 9) double perception, not unrelated to perceptions expressed in other texts in this volume, that "even when its distance from the political appears to be considerable," most of "[Cavell's] thinking . . . actually is inseparable from some form of socio-political articulation" (p. 164). So a fair account of the work I do will have, probably simultaneously, to account for the appearance as well as the actuality of this matter. I think my sense of the simultaneous here comes from a memory of my response some years ago to Santayana's concluding an essay on Shakespeare by saying that the writer known for considering more aspects of human existence than any other failed to consider the topic of religion, to which I responded with the thought that the topic may be invisible in Shakespeare because it is everywhere there. (I was at the time writing about *The Winter's Tale*, whose concluding scene of "resurrection" I wished to understand as the declaration of a competition of Shakespeare's theater with religion.) I shall assume it makes sense—sense enough to begin exploring—to suggest that my concern with the political, from the time at least of my essay on *King Lear* in my first book, and my succeeding little book on *Walden*, may be hard to see for roughly the same reason, because of the way its presence, or perhaps its absence, is obvious.

This would help explain my thought, in reaction to Hammer's concern that I am subject to the charge of aestheticizing the political, that it is not I but politics itself that has done the aestheticizing. (I can imagine that this will have any number of connections with Hammer's proposal that the aesthetics I should invoke further is not that of beauty but of the sublime.) In some form this is as familiar a perception as Machiavelli's that the Prince only exists as a Prince, in his own eyes, in relation to the eyes of his audience, that is, his subjects. (I think I owe this way of putting things to an essay of Merleau-Ponty's; I know it is a thought from the so-called General Education course I taught on moving back to teach at Harvard some forty years ago.) It is a topic burlesqued, political authority shockingly theatricalized, in by-play between Shakespeare's Richard III and his minion Buckingham; it is a defensive fantasy of Lear's in his delirium, remembering his kingly authority as something that can make a subject "quake." It is encoded in the role played by Jacques-Louis David's great painting of the death of Marat in a ceremony of authority staged on behalf of the Revolution (described in T. J. Clark's recent *Farewell to an Idea*). It is one of the implications of Kenneth Burke's text "Anthony on Behalf of the Play," in which Burke identifies the power of Shakespeare's language over his audience (that is, over us, represented by Anthony's depicted audience at Caesar's funeral) as the language of a tyrant. Such events, real and fictional, challenge the idea Hammer attributes to Hegel and Schmitt of "the political [as having become] an autonomous domain," something which did not happen, for example, when Napoleon placed the imperial crown upon his own head.

I do not suppose romanticism would have been able to challenge the autonomy of the political without a re-conception of art, or rather of the realm of the arts as a whole, claiming a new autonomy for itself. (I think I would not have adduced David's painting as challenging the autonomy of the political unless I had been moved to call it "great," that is, to take it as inspired to universal expression, in this case, by the movement of the political.) Hammer relates such a development within the arts to Hegel's speaking of "a general subjectivization of the arts" (p. 172) and to Hegel's and Schmitt's "view that the political romanticist advocates a withdrawal to the private sphere" (p. 177). Something of the sort was said, in accusation, of Emerson's promotion, in the generation following that of Hegel, of the individual over the social in evaluating the worth of human existence. But it is no easier to comprehend the relation of the individual and the collective in Emerson's thinking than to articulate the relation of the private and the conventional in *Philosophical Investigations*. The issue of finding the right, or the conditions under which, to say "we" keeps coming up. In both Emerson and Wittgenstein it makes sense to say that we live (in an unexamined ordinary) in the absence of the discovery of either the private or the public. From which it follows for Emerson that we live in the absence of the discovery of America.

Hammer finds that in my fascination with the figure of the prophet I fail to thematize the realms of right and of value "crucial to contemporary neo-Kantian theory" and the "collective aspiration toward the good life." I have no quarrel with Rawls's thematization that takes justice as primary; indeed I assume that some such thematization must be in view in the way I dispute what happens to what I call (and treasure in Rawls's account) "the conversation of justice." In order that this not be dismissed as another instance of Schmitt's idea of a "depoliticized liberal social order [in which] political debate [is transformed] into an endless conversation" (p. 173), I merely repeat here my thought that philosophy participates in two conversations essential to the formation of a reforming polity, namely the argument of the ordinary, which I say must never be won (since in retrieving words from their exile—of fixity, encrustation, capture, illusory or empty purity—no one has a privileged authority), as well as the conversation of justice, which I say must never be lost (specifically by being closed in citing the rules of a current institution, as in the practice of Nora's husband). My invocation of the prophetic voice was principally meant to warn against false prophets.

True prophets are desperate not to have to talk, and what they say is always: "Turn." To the extent that philosophy inherits their role, it tunes itself, in Heidegger's image, in a negative key: what Emerson calls living in aversion to conformity; what Nietzsche translates as living "in opposition to today."

I sense that I will want at the end of my collection of comments to return to the role of philosophy in political life, and to what I call philosophy's powerlessness, its perpetual questioning of power, as seen in Emerson. For the moment I add a thought about how I begin to understand Hammer's proposal to emphasize, in accounting for the aestheticization of the political, the idea of sublimity rather than that of beauty. The impression I get from Hammer's strong words of conclusion (e.g., as he invokes Garbo's "sublime transcendence of our powers of acknowledgment," on p. 184) is of an appeal not to our powers of judgment and an articulation of common ground (as in Kant's understanding of the claim to perceive beauty, a power of articulation also essential, I trust, to political reformation) but before that of our capacity for suffering or passiveness in the face of a renewed exposure to the existence of others. I have a number of times pointed in this regard to the opening paragraph of Emerson's "Self-Reliance," where Emerson reports the experience of recognizing that, in consequence of chronically suppressing one's own voice, one finds "in every work of genius one's rejected words returning to us with an alienated majesty"—an implicit characterization of our ordinary lives as ones of inexpressiveness, suffering not experienced as such. It is in the idea of "alienated majesty" that I have sensed the idea of the sublime, a transference (in Freud's sense) of recognition (beyond "our ordinary powers of acknowledgment"?) to the other's intact powers of expressiveness. If I say that this should remind us of romanticism's emphasis on the sublime, and also of Levinas's portrayal of our relation to the other (among many other ways) as to an elevation, I also note its presence, in a climactic moment of J. S. Mill's perception of happiness in society, as he speaks of what marriage may be as a mutual "looking up" to each other (Donatelli quotes the passage). We do not, except as exiles or immigrants, choose our fellow citizens, any more than (proverbially) we choose our family, but I do not think it beyond rational aspiration that we shall learn better to acknowledge the existence of human others in such a way that we remind each other of the possession of conscience (instead of contributing to the illusions of "leadership").

Ted Cohen's isolating and throwing back in my lap my outburst about being "convinced that those who wish to oppose [abortion] legally are tyrannical and sentimental hypocrites" (in Chapter 8, p. 159) makes me wish I had controlled myself more effectively and thought better of expressing myself so. I suppose I hoped it was clear enough that I was deliberately going a bit overboard, expressing the sense that one cannot readily avoid becoming somewhat irrational in this region, as evidenced, for example, by my providing this negative hyperbole after having just confessed, as Cohen mentions, my own feeling of abhorrence at the prospect of abortion. Something simpler I should have made clear was that what produced my phrase "sentimental hypocrites" was not, as Cohen apparently, and understandably, takes it, that I doubted "that some people are appalled by abortion," doubted "the fact of their feeling" (ibid.); or not simply or primarily that. The slur was motivated, rather on the contrary, more specifically by witnessing displays of this stark feeling (I pass a vivid picket line of protesters at an abortion clinic on my not-infrequent Saturday morning trips to my local post office), fueled by poster-sized photographs of fetuses captioned with right-to-life slogans, but expressed in, from my point of view, the equally stark absence of poster-sized pictures of capital punishments and of neglected children and abandoned mothers, instances in which credible feelings of the right to life should equally and simultaneously produce abhorrence and make us appalled. It was a sense of the scrupulous isolating of one expression of social tragedy in a sea of suffering— about which something could and should be done, and which these picket lines were, I felt, worsening—that was getting me down.

As for questioning the feeling itself of, let's say, being appalled, a recent incident brings to mind my sense of the importance in questioning the meaningfulness of the assertion that a human fetus is from the beginning a human being. The scene, on the evening television news, was one of those outbreaks and aftermaths in which a man with a gun had fired at random into a crowd. A detective interviewed on the scene said: "One of the victims was pregnant and the bullet went through the baby. There's life out there!" (The first sentence may not have the exact words. I'm quite certain the second does.) That there is something particularly terrible in contemplating children getting caught up in murderous events that they have no conceivable part in causing or understanding, I do not question. But being faced with the knowledge that, in the presence of multiple corpses on the ground, the idea that life lost in violence does not come home to a competent adult until a fetus is imagined and announced as a victim alarms me; I feel unsafe. The feeling expressed is not natural but selective, violent, metaphysical. This is what caused my calling opponents of abortion who want to make it illegal not only sentimental but tyrannical, wishing to legislate metaphysics.

Selective hypocrisy is something different from the hypocrisy of insincerity. In neither case do I want to outlaw or in general shun all acquaintance with any person fitting these descriptions. Indeed, a democracy, let alone a royal court, could scarcely function without a healthy tolerance toward insincerity or the capacity to compartmentalize passions. When a senator from one party speaks of a member of the opposed party as "My good friend senator so-and-so from the great state of such-and-such," I am perhaps momentarily shocked by the sense of falseness, but quickly enough relieved that, since I know how high feeling runs over the issue on which they disagree, the magic words of formal courtesy acknowledge that there is between them something, a tomorrow, that transcends this disagreement. Civil institutions rely on a measure of civility, say forbearance. (We had occasion earlier to note that Moliere's Alceste ruled himself out of such civilization.) While the measure must not be pushed too far, there are no a priori limits. Lines are to be drawn in each case. The conversation of justice must not be lost.

Another word about the idea of sharing the world; or appreciating, not merely grudgingly accepting, the existence of the other; and the scary idea of writing others off, consigning them to some other world (p. 160). I have involved myself in two consequential crossroads at which a philosopher has appealed to the idea of ruling out others as incompetent or deviant participants in a community. The earlier concerns Rawls's comparing a crossroads in the moral life to one in the life of games, comparing someone's casualness about breaking a promise with someone's asking, "Can I have a fourth strike?"; Rawls responds to this as either a joke or a sign of ignorance of or incompetence at the game, or say life, of baseball. This is a recognizable kind of episode, variously generalizable to instruction in other games. My claim, however, in "Rawls on Rules," chapter 11 of *The Claim of Reason*, is that there is precisely no equivalent in the moral life of the defining rules of games. ("Precisely." It is definitive of the moral life that there are no such rules, no citing of some accepted promulgation that is the flat or objectively determinable end of an argument. I might now qualify this rejection, or say prove it, by taking into consideration ethical rules and regulations, or codes of conduct, promulgated for particular professions, for example for lawyers or doctors or teachers. In such cases the state declares its interest in stylizing moral judgment for the purpose of identifying and preventing or requiring certain specific actions of members of certain publicly sensitive professions.) To imagine another who is, say, about to break a promise because of a change of mind about the importance of his own wishes, or who refuses to help a friend when the cost of doing so is some slight inconvenience, or who dismisses a person's assertion that he cannot live on the current minimum wage, as if there is some rule the person did not know, is to imagine him as morally incompetent. Put otherwise: Instruction in morality is instruction about the moral life itself, about, say, the seriousness of promising, the worth of friendship, the importance of fairness, the separate and equal existence of others and of oneself (one's desires as well as duties). Citing a defining rule of baseball tells you about baseball only if you already know what the life of a game is. The importance of this matter is that the picture of defining rules is taken over into *A Theory of Justice*, where Rawls regards institutions as defined by rules and imagines one who complains of injustice as incompetent or irrelevant (e.g., envious) unless he can show that a rule of a, let's say, just enough institution has been broken or is systematically infringed.

The second crossroads of the claim of incompetence concerns Kripke's reading of Wittgenstein's scene of instruction: "If my justifications have come to an end my spade has hit bedrock. Then I am inclined to say: 'This is simply what I do.'" Kripke takes the response as strong: Do it my way or suffer the consequences. ("The child [who cannot follow a rule as we do, that is, to our satisfaction] is separated out and treated as a lunatic.") I take the response as weak: I had better listen to, or await, the other, and (re)consider what it is I do, or suffer the consequences.

The place I deal most specifically with the epistemological framework (call it) of such matters is in chapters 7 and 8 of *The Claim of Reason*, on Wittgenstein's vision of language and the sense in which (agreement in) language is groundless, or looked at otherwise, in which I am, we each are, the ground there is. Here ideas arise of our not being able, or having, to talk to everyone about everything, while at the same time there are some things about which we have to talk to someone if we are to have anything to say to that one. How far we can demand of ourselves to make ourselves intelligible, or of others to understand our leaps and sallies of communication, is essentially unpredictable. The argument of the ordinary must not be won.

(By the way, I would have liked to respond to the important issues Cohen raises about using forms or styles of music as, let's say, touchstones of intimacy. But I am hampered by the instances he cites, of Wagner and Beethoven; they seem somehow to loom too large to serve in this way. I cannot think I am alone in this sense. For instance, suppose one thinks of Beethoven as a culmination of the establishment of music as part of human culture as such, on a par with literature and painting and theater, not something separately accompanying occasions in church or the court or the populace at play. It is part of why one thinks of Beethoven as inherently revolutionary. One may date the beginnings of this, as it were, advancement or cultural inheritance of music variously far back, but the first undeniable, for me, achievement is the decade of the great Mozart operas (coeval with Kant's three *Critiques* and his book on religion, with which major philosophy becomes something producible in the university, the culture of educated society at large), in which the passions of servants, or as Proust would insist, peasants, are as magnificently telling and acknowledged as those of nobility. So not to accept the achievement of Beethoven can feel like not accepting the cultural pertinence of music—a possible position to occupy but not closely an individual test of intimacy. Wagner, in his totalitarian greediness of passion, is at the other end of this revolution, where his taking cultural Paris by storm in 1860 (evidence here is the sumptuousness of the review of *Lohengrin* and *Tannhäuser* produced by a signature poet [Baudelaire]) seems just meant to divide audiences, as the audience for the modern has been divided since. If we take such division as a mark of the modern, then the fact that Wagner inspires sensibilities to champion differences all of which one can, in some sense must, accept as plausible is not a test of tolerance but a recognition of some deeper compulsion of the human to intimacy. And, I suppose, a sign that we had better not count on art to heal injustice. (Not counting on it is not the same as giving up on it.)

Hans Sluga (Chapter 10) describes my work as having "an implicit commitment to the idea that the great politics of the public sphere ['the large-scale politics of government and the state . . . of the Platonic-Aristotelian model'] is (historically, ontologically, and conceptually) based on the politics of the ordinary and can therefore be understood only in its terms and by means of its characteristic notions" (p. 193). Sluga goes on to say that in this work I am "thereby reviving, perhaps without realizing it, an understanding of politics first advanced by the sophist Protagoras—a conception explicitly denied in the Platonic-Aristotelian model." I find these proposals attractive, including the implied thought, since the term "sophist" seems not in Sluga's description to be tuned in a negative key, that this figure has not been awarded a fair legacy in the Platonic portrait of one who debases philosophy by, let's say, professionalizing it, by turning what is called knowledge and good conduct into salable commodities. Whether I have revived such an understanding of politics "without realizing it" is not clear to me (unless that fact of unclarity proves it). Sluga's articulation of Protagoras' sense of politics as a "care of the common" that is "not merely the precondition of politics but constitutes its content and essence" sounds a congenial Wittgensteinian note, suggesting that the attempt to get beyond the surface of ordinary concepts to their essence precisely avoids their essence, namely as expressed in the grammar in which the concept has its life. And when Sluga goes on to characterize the Protagorean conception of politics "not as rule or *arché* but as *paideia*" (p. 194) and further glosses this in saying "we are all and constantly teachers of each other," I have to think of the concluding paragraph of my essay on Wittgenstein in *This New Yet Unapproachable America*, "Declining Decline," which begins, almost, as follows: "In the culture depicted in the *Investigations* we are all teachers, and all students—talkers, hearers, overhearers, hearsayers, believers, explainers; we learn and teach incessantly, indiscriminately; we are all elders and all children, wanting a hearing, for our injustices, for our justices." (This seems a reasonable expansion of Foucault's formula, reported in David Owen's essay, that in political thinking we have yet "to cut off the head of the king," that is, to uncover the biopower of ordinary life. I might have gone on to say that this seems to suggest an exceptionalism in American life, in which there was no king within its reach at the time of its revolution. But in Gordon Woods's account of that period, the act of regicide proves not to have been necessary in order to effect a radical change in ordinary life on these shores amounting to the collapse of the hierarchy flowing from monarchy. Can this not be connected with the fact, remarked by Hannah Arendt, that the American Revolution was less bloody, and its aftermath incomparably more peaceable (within its citizenry), than those of somewhat greater fame? In any case, our Civil War made up for the want of violence.)

But that essay of mine is relatively late, from 1989. In an essay on Beckett's *Endgame*, in *Must We Mean What We Say?*, twenty-five years before that, I express what I believe is my first essential consciousness of the incessance and absence of what may be called the political in any ordinary hour of one's life: "The question is whether enough men can afford the knowledge that the way the world is comes down in the end to what each son is doing now, sitting within his ordinary walls, making his everyday demands" (p. 141). I wonder, at this distance, to what extent I *meant* the male pronoun in this sentence from another era. Its immediate context is a recaptured immediacy of the curse of slavery (this was the Freedom Summer of 1964 and I had just returned from some time in Mississippi that summer). But the implication is that this context is only the most lurid manifestation of the fact that, in a society of democratic or republican aspiration, the presence of injustice compromises the life of each of its citizens.

This necessary register of compromise is another direction to the thought that for a society of such aspiration, shame is its honest price, or the price of honesty; and hence to the thought that, since justice in any actual society is going to be at best partial—we are, in Rawls's measure, at best in partial compliance with the principle(s) of justice—we are, or at any hour may become, aware of the reality of what it means to say that our consent is demanded, and that it is given, what it means that my society is mine, that I am the judge of the case whether our partial justice is good enough to participate in whole-heartedly. The remarriage comedies I have brought into political evidence judge the answer to be that consent is warranted, meaning that reform is rationally to be expected to continue, if discontinuously. I think they were right. Whether they are still right depends upon what we are doing and what we go on to do. Yet here is a connection between politics and tragedy. Can this mean, thinking of Sluga's adducing of a glamorous case of this conjunction, that we are each to think of ourselves as a diminished, or faithless, Antigone, allowing the state to slight the rights of our brother (whom all men are, and all women, each equal, each irreplaceable, so we came to teach ourselves)?

Let's have before us the sort of passage Sluga will be going on in speaking of Protagoras, in Plato's dialogue that bears his name, as the discoverer of a new politics, an essential politics of the ordinary. Socrates has just arrived in his narration at the point at which Protagoras continues the discussion of education in virtue by reference to a poem (a poem of praise, raising the question of who has the knowledge, the right, to praise). Socrates after a while reports his rebelling against this practice:

The talk about the poets seems to me like a commonplace entertainment to which a vulgar company have recourse; who, because they are not able to converse or amuse one another, while they are drinking, with the sound of their own voices and conversation, by reason of their stupidity, raise the price of flute-girls in the market, hiring . . . the voice of a flute instead of their own breath, to be the medium of intercourse among them; but where the company are real gentleman and men of education, you will see no flute-girls . . . ; and they have no nonsense or games, but are contented with one another's conversation, of which their own voices are the medium, and which they carry on by turns and in an orderly manner, even though they are very liberal in their potations. [Drink makes them amiable, not disorderly. It is, I suppose a sign that political relationship is not "natural." It needs stimulation, an awareness of, let's say, one's body in relation to the presence of another's, but without distraction.] And a company like this of ours, and men such as we profess to be, do not require the help of another's voice, or of the poets whom you cannot interrogate about the meaning of what they are saying. . . . This sort of entertainment they decline, and prefer to talk with one another, and put one another to the proof in conversation. . . . Leaving the poets, and keeping to ourselves, let us try the mettle of one another and make proof of the truth in conversation. (Passage nos. 347–48)

I note particularly here the emphasis on establishing "one's own voice," on not needing "another's" voice, matters of high importance to what I understand as the procedures of Wittgenstein and of Austin (in which I have taken the idea of the ordinary to come to the discovery, for each of us, of our own language). But explicitly in the *Protagoras* the other is a voice (of a flute, or a poet, or a stranger) other than *ours*. Putting one another "to the proof in conversation" seems, before all, to be the proof that, as it were, conversation in fact takes place between us, that we have discovered a "we," that we are the source of contentment and entertainment for one another, without the need for distraction from the medium of our own breath. I read "contentment and entertainment for one another" to capture, or epitomize, what I have meant by saying that in Wittgenstein's vision of language (the title of chapter 7 of *The Claim of Reason*), human communication depends upon—is grounded on nothing more nor less than—sharing interests and cares and commitments and senses of humor and of outrage and of shame, et cetera. This is the condition of possibility of both the argument of the ordinary (losing and seeking specific control of the limits of our expression) and the conversation of justice (losing and seeking specific grasp of the limits of our moral and political authority).

Sluga's appreciation of the pertinence of the remarriage comedies (in conjunction with what I have proposed about Shakespearean tragedy) ensures that his reservation about them is something I want to take with utmost seriousness, if here only very briefly. He writes: "The more general problem is that these comedies know only one model for the union and re-union of human beings and that is the union of man and woman as con-ceived at one moment in American history" (p. 202). Something is obvi-ously right about this, but there is an unclarity or ambiguity in the idea of a "model," about the level at which it is to be understood. Take first of all the fact that these films, like their companion melodramas of the unknown woman, are seen by me as critiques of marriage as it stands, not as celebra-tions of it ("critique" in Kant's sense, a determination of its conditions of possibility). In one sense of model, the model of marriage in remarriage comedy is one that proposes a mode of conversation—of exchange in word and gesture—that is morally serious and emotionally and intellectually playful, exploratory, hence risky, one that initially so absorbs the man and woman of the principal pair in each other's attention that they periodically become opaque to the members of their larger society, and they postpone the idea of producing children (keeping themselves free, as it were, to oc-cupy childish positions as required in their mutual and joint explorations) until this medium, this fact of marriage, is established between them. The conditions of this conversation seem to require the absence of the woman's mother, and if her father is present he is on the side of his daughter's de-sire not, as in classical comedy, on that of the law, and the narrative moves from a city to a forest setting, et cetera. These conditions are shown to be compensated for in successive instances of the genre—for example, if the couple do not move to a place outside the city, they are shown to be "on the move," on the road (*It Happened One Night*), or in some further form of adventure (*The Philadelphia Story*). And so on.

Now where does the requirement of a man and a woman fit in? This is a feature of the comedies, call it a realization of the remarriage model of marriage, that, at the moment of American history at which the genre was established, was never breached and, in my lingo, compensated for. But nothing shows that this requirement is generically fixed. It is worth not-ing that George Cukor's last film, *Rich and Famous*, from 1981, uses the sig-nature remarriage setting of a surprising reunion at midnight in pastoral Connecticut as occurring between two women (played by Candice Ber-gen and Jacqueline Bisset). And there is intuitively no reason why the pair should not be realized by two men or by an interracial pair, et cetera. We will not know what compensations will or will not be required until it is tried and pondered and screened in various economies. The question is at issue in a different form not infrequently pressed upon me: Are remarriage comedies still made? And if not, why not?

There are various answers here, among them that there are many good films with a remarriage "feel" to them, as well as an overall structure in which a pair get together again after a breakup. But it is clear enough that these films do not occupy the cultural role of the classical remarriage comedies, which I have claimed are among the principal and enduring successes of what is called Hollywood's Golden Age in its sound period. Neither does American film continue to occupy its former role (nor, for that matter, does marriage), but at the same time, the *history* of film (present on videos, etc.) is a fact of cultural consciousness as never before. But as long as marriage continues to be problematized in movies, what I specified as the model or set of conditions of marriage as specified in remarriage comedy may be expected to persist, in forms that may be unheard of. For example, the degree and intersection of intimacy and psychic freedom or zaniness featured in classical remarriage comedy may now be found in a recent group of interesting films exploring the limits and desire for what may be understood as an improvised family, which includes the *philia* of friendship and of marriage within it (an improvisation of relationship rendering its principals hard to understand from outside—except by us). Examples here (confined by my increasingly impoverished knowledge of recent movies) are *About a Boy* (with Hugh Grant), *My First Mister* (with Albert Brooks, Leelee Sobieski, and John Goodman), *Flawless* (with Robert de Niro and Philip Seymour Hoffman), and *Daddy and Them* (written, directed by, and starring Billy Bob Thornton). A clear source of embedding a marriage within a family that is itself eccentric in the degree of its toleration of difference and eccentricity is *You Can't Take It with You*, from the stage play by Kaufman and Hart (winning the Pulitzer Prize in 1937), which early in the play (I have not checked the play) cites Ralph Waldo Emerson as the guide to the pursuit of happiness.

The conjunction of the medium of film with Plato's *Protagoras*, which invokes the difficulty of praise as a topic waiting to upset conversation, brings me to Robert Gooding-Williams's response to my reading of the opening Astaire routines from the film *The Band Wagon* (Chapter 12).

Gooding-Williams's absolute rejection of my wish to find the praiseworthiness, philosophical and political, of the routines opens with a discussion of Kant and Nietzsche that is clearly part of a larger project whose richness I would not touch without more knowledge of it and thought about it than are feasible here. The discussion closes with a proposal that what I call the repression of Emerson's legacy in the culture Emerson helped, or wished, to found should be measured by "[listening] to African American philosophical thought," a "tradition [that] has been less embarrassed to receive Emerson, and so less inclined to repress him" (p. 262). That is a gloriously pertinent suggestion, which I hope to have the years to participate in following. I have no defense against my having not tried to listen and to respond to it before now, other than (to take the case of gender that Gooding-Williams links with that of race), as with feminism, I seem to have needed an invitation to feel entitled to take it up—to go beyond autobiographical responses to isolated events.

About Gooding-Williams's discussions of my reading of the two routines, I say at once and in general that I do not feel well perceived in them. But I do not want to defend to him the specific words, or the ways I have used them, in which I have so far said things in the essay of mine he takes up. His rejection of them seems so complete that at least for the moment I regard them as out of order between us. I shall accordingly try now to arrive again at a fresh articulation of my response to my sense (and memory) of the routines. Gooding-Williams exempts me from the charge of sharing the idea, which he sees in Vincente Minnelli's film, of "a Jim Crow version of the capacity for skepticism" (p. 248). But it is still bad enough if I have failed to perceive it there.

My reflections about the treacherous difficulties of false and of hollow praise, of blasphemy and idolatry, were to set the stage for a discussion of a dance (I take the second routine initially), or rather say a quasi-dance (I explicitly say it is not a tap dance, and most of this dancing is not any obvious other kind either), something like a chain of proto-dance movements of twirling and weaving, unlike any other routine of Astaire's I remember, like his proto-words "Da: *da*, da da; da, da *da*." I call attention here to Astaire's uttering to himself at the end of the first routine, as analogous in their self-absorption to the seventy-plus repetitions of the phrase, or fragments of the phrase, "I've got a shoe shine" in the second routine, a (quasi-)dance which is precisely one that questions his right to dance. It is a dance of open frenzy, of madness, of the threat of the loss of language, of incomprehension and incomprehensibility. If he cannot dance this dance, he cannot dance at all, since what he does would not exist without the relation this routine declares to the heritage of black dancing; and since to dance as he does is his life, if he cannot dance such a dance he cannot exist. Then because I find I want him to exist, want him to want to exist, to claim his existence, and find that the America with him dancing in it was better than it would have been without him, the question arises for me how he asserts, or may assert, the right to exist.

I say in my original essay that in Astaire's claiming an inheritance, his way, from black dancing, "nobody does what Astaire does better than Astaire," I suppose taking encouragement from remembering, from the same period of the 1950s, Miles Davis's taking to himself songs from *Porgy and Bess*, as if he were prepared to hear: Nobody does what George Gershwin does better than Gershwin. But hear it when? After the 1950s comes the 1960s. And hear it from whom? In claiming the right, or standing, of Astaire to praise here, I am claiming my right, or standing, to praise Astaire on this ground. I recognize no established convention as grounding me; the utterance is not performative but passionate, its act irreducibly perlocutionary. Its acceptability is exposed to the other. And here I am not in a position to single out the other to whom I address myself. Why take so stacked a risk? I suppose because I have already taken it, I have in my life taken Astaire to heart as part of my education by film and by music. It is understandable that another may claim the standing to contest it.

Astaire's mad incorporation of the entranced dervish is brought to an end by his making explicit the answer to the question mark of America— the mysterious box that is present early in the routine when it resists his probing but is reencountered later and bursts open for him, precipitating the routine's close as he recoils from its mechanical, flag-waving ballyhoo as an answer of belonging, of overcoming loneliness. As he reels away from this declaration, luck intervenes and he and the black man reencounter each other and for the first time satisfy the conditions for dancing together equally on level ground. But what they dance is only and precisely the conclusion of a dance, of a dance of equality that they have not danced, that does not (yet?) exist; all they can dance is farewell, since what they have realized cannot be taken outside, beyond the America of the Arcade. I call this a glimpse of Utopia and I want to see the glimpse expressed in Astaire's final gesture, reciprocally holding his arms out to the black man as he himself is drawn away by the crowd in which, as his first routine explicitly declares—the song without exactly a dance—he is all alone, going his way by himself. It is the concluding gesture of a tragic dance, an expression of pain and non-existence. (I am thinking of my speaking of Emerson's "Fate"— the paradoxical title of an essay about Freedom, a continuous expression, on my reading, of the pain in recognizing that one cannot solve a state of radical injustice alone—as a tragic essay.) In the film we cut from that final gesture of Astaire's incompletion and longing to a rehearsal of a Greek tragedy. It is up to us what we miss, or choose to miss, or deplore as vulgar or as cute, in this conjunction; perhaps it is not a tip to consider the tragedy in what we have just seen, but it is rather or only meant to encourage the suggestion that film is the latest discoverer of some register of homogeneous entertainment in which the history of human theatricality in all its forms takes part.

But Gooding-Williams will not have it. He says:

> If, in *The Band Wagon,* he gets his shoes rather than his face "blacked up," the substance of the performance remains the same: homage that cannot separate itself from the legacy of blackface minstrelsy's myth and fantasies about black masculinity. *The Band Wagon*'s reiteration of these myths and fantasies—specifically its suggestion that blackness and especially black masculinity is a magical force that can bring alienated, melancholic white men to earth—suffuses and saturates its gestures toward homage, thus compromising, fatally, our ability to see in Astaire's "dance of praise" anything more than a form of idolatry that superstitiously mistakes a myth about black manhood for the rich artistic tradition to which Astaire owes his existence as a dancer. (p. 256)

(Gooding-Williams had spelled out the mythical force as a fantasy a few pages earlier: "[Astaire is shown] acquiring that blackness through the agency of a 'shine' who, by shining his shoes, works a sorcery that disseminates his blackness, as if a priapic Daniels had discharged a second, miniature 'shine,' a sort of black homunculus, onto the surface of Astaire's footwear" [p. 252].) This is strong material, and if it must be accepted then I can see that "the substance of the performance remains the same: homage that cannot separate itself from the legacy of blackface minstrelsy's myth and fantasies about black masculinity." The claim that it must be accepted is evidently the same necessity as claimed in "homage that cannot separate itself from the legacy of blackface. . . . " Then the question is: Why *must* it be accepted? Why *cannot* the homage separate itself from insupportable legacies?

What we actually are shown is a "shoeshine" in which the polishing cloth never (maybe once) touches the shoes, and in which it is waved over Astaire's hands as well as feet, equating the power of "polishing" his nails with polishing his shoes. Astaire's ecstatic cry "Wonderful!" on the shoe stand only makes explicit what can hardly in any case be missed, that this is no ordinary shoeshine; something of breakthrough magic is in evidence. But I am suggesting that what we are invited to attribute the magic to is left open. Gooding-Williams finds that an older myth and accompanying fantasies are in force. I am proposing an alternative interpretation, or perception. ("Interpretation" may already be prejudicial. I understand the concept virtually to imply that an alternative is possible. I am prepared, if that is thought prejudicial, to stay with the idea of perception.)

I take up the idea that presides over my reading, or perception, of the closing moments of the routine—namely the absent, longed-for, dance of equality, of reciprocity, on the level ground, what I called a glimpse of Utopia, of the Kingdom of Ends, from which Astaire (alone, unequally) tears himself away. Here is where I see the sense of compromise entering. Not in an inability to achieve the ecstatic reciprocity of the dance, but—precisely because that has been momentarily achieved—in an inability to sustain the dance outside the Arcade, out in what a marquee announces as "The Proud Land," which is, accordingly, ironically designated to be shameful. Justice cannot be attained privately, neither in vengeance nor in magnanimity; how much injustice we are willing to absorb, or judge ourselves as having to absorb, is up to each of us to know.

So here is my alternative understanding of the source of magic. I do not take Astaire to attribute his offcenteredness, ungroundedness, to a lack of infusion. He still has his rare talent (his initial walk, in the first routine, down the platform proves that, no other [white] man walks like that); but he has lost the sense of a place for it, the point of it, his right to his possession of it. In his song, alone in a crowd, he says further that he is under a cloud, facing the unknown, needing to build a home of his own. None of the entertainments for sale in the arcade seriously attract him, no for-tune-telling machines nor cardboard myths of black men as marauding apes, nor distorting mirrors. What stops his roaming is stumbling over the outstretched legs of the black shoeshine man. What starts his song is the effort to cheer him (the black man, the other), not to be cheered by him. The song could be seen as intrusive, motivated by a mere assumption of the black man's melancholy. But that man shows interest in the interest being offered him; perhaps it is not all he wants, or needs, but it evident-ly goes beyond anything he expects to come along in an ordinary hour in this place.

From the time of this initial encounter, Astaire (I should by now use, anyway mention, the name of the character he plays in this film, Tony Hunter, one who shares certain biographical details with Astaire, but level is everything here) is no longer alone in a crowd or walking under a cloud. His old friends, who met him at the train station but from whom he has managed to take a break, had not broken into his isolation. In the Arcade he has begun recovering the home he vows to build of his own, using what he has made so far of his everyday. No one can predict (any more than it was at once predictable when God found that it is not good that the first man be alone) who or what will be apt for him, end his being alone. It is anything but accidental to Astaire that his isolation is ended by this man's being black. But it is not that fact that produces the magic, as if magic is a transportable object. It is critical that Astaire take this fact of beginning recovery as ordinary, as a return home, a reminder of the self to which he aspires, which he has misplaced, not a self to be appropriated (anyway, no more than any self is a matter of appropriation), but one to be inspired to attain, or regain, from within his attained self. This black man cannot teach him how to inherit and modify black dancing, any more than Astaire can teach the black man how to inherit and modify the remainder of white American culture. But their futures depend upon the learning that they have done, and perhaps that they will still do.

The song and shine we are now given to see—like the song Astaire sang on the train platform—are, I am bound to assume, not what is seen in that depicted world. There what is visible is a white man climbing on a stand and getting a somewhat exaggerated shoe shine from a black man, with extra waves of the rag and clicks of the brushes. Nothing has happened to that ordinary to draw a crowd. The fantastic events on and around the shoe shine stand, revealed to us privileged viewers, open to the judgment of our judgment, are the responses of these two men to the ordinary fact that they have reciprocated each other's interest and acknowledgment, itself of no more than passing interest, alas, as yet, to those beyond in their world. One bio-ethnological form of life has reciprocally interpenetrated another, producing an everyday miracle, namely one human being's recognition of and by another, a defeat of self-absorption, the creation of a small "we." They would still need, if occasion arose, to find how to acknowledge each other outside, beyond the enclosure and privacy of the Arcade, in which the black man will visibly do more than accompany and encourage Astaire's mood with his brushes. As for the black man's consciousness of the event, the man played, we are told, by a real bootblack named Leroy Daniels, I picture it as somewhat amused, not unhappy about the diversion provided on a dull day by this rather over-excited, not badly dressed visitor, who talked a lot and moved pretty well, seemingly well-intentioned, though maybe trying too hard to prove something, but not as left with the sense that anything superbly good, or bad, has happened to him, or been asked of him, nothing much given to him nor taken from him, just possibly an encounter worth a remark to friends or family.

I should emphasize that evidence against this reading would not, from my point of view, come from adducing expectations based on anything that Vincente Minnelli and his colleagues have achieved elsewhere, nor from trying to unify the opening routines with the rest of the film. My sense is that this is breakthrough material, that work is being here produced (I don't know about elsewhere, each case needs its own attention) that may well be beyond the intention and grasp of those then and there at work. I have recurrently emphasized this fact about serious writing, that one writes (with luck, call it) beyond oneself, better than oneself. Emerson puts the matter by saying "Character teaches above our wills." Otherwise criticism is fated to be a limited, monitoring thing.

Of course I can understand that what I have been saying is variously controversial. But I have to say that I still do not see that my reading of the first, companion routine is fairly thought of as controversial, as far as it goes. That Astaire misses something in others other than they miss in him is surely right, and important, and that there may be a Jim Crow version of skepticism (pp. 248, 259), in which one race excludes another from the complexities of skepticism, seems to me a startling and fascinating idea. (The closest I have come to it, I believe, is my recording the thought, in *The World Viewed*, that Scarlett O'Hara's rage and abuse of her personal slave [played in the film of *Gone With the Wind* by Butterfly McQueen] is produced by Scarlett's "natural" assumption that, being black, this inexperienced young woman *must* be familiar with the intimate business of the earth, such as giving birth.) There are bound to be, if this is right, many examples of it (it is perhaps endemic in colonialist contexts, and it occurs to me that Iago may not think of Othello as capable of skepticism, but only of superstition, which ironically does the trick, for Othello's own reasons), but I do not see it in the present Astaire case. Gooding-Williams's counting "mostly black men" on the train platform, four among a total of six men, does not establish an opposed world. And the thing that the members of that depicted world miss is not what we ordinarily miss every day—call this the mortality of the others passing to their oblivion—but specifically they miss what it is *we*, the viewers of that world, are shown: those passers-by see an unremarkable man silently walking down a platform (or quietly da-da-da-ing), walking as they are walking; whereas we are shown the state of mind of this walking man, whose manifestation of this way of walking and singing reveals him to be cheering himself up with an effort of swaying, even swaggering good humor, and whose absence of feet goes to explain his sense of psychic suspension. That no one I have spoken with about the film had noticed that Astaire's feet were excluded from the framing of that routine throughout the walk, that it had to dawn on us as things proceed that this fact is telling, is something I am counting on to get us to see the standing possibility of film to reveal our blindness to the ordinary, and to bring to consciousness the fact that these Astaire routines are both of them about what is ordinarily visible and invisible, and how this is challenged (e.g., in Plato, in Wittgenstein). (I have not been able to check the initial invisibility of Astaire's feet on a 35-mm print. If the video reproduction has caused this then the initial cinematography missed a bet here.)

When I praise I do not ask others to praise, to imitate me, but to see or hear. When I condemn, or shun, I do, it seems, ask them to condemn; I provide an example for others to follow. The stakes have changed. Perhaps they should. I do not think Kant helps when the question is a matter of what Proust calls "aesthetic sacrilege" (in the preface to his translation of Ruskin's *The Bible of Amiens*). But spelling things out this way, while it has increased my conviction in my views, has at the same time shown me more clearly their fundamental vulnerability. Just as I feel that my discussion of the material begins after Gooding-Williams's considerations have been advanced—that Astaire's dancing already explicitly incorporates, and enacts, such doubts—so I see more starkly that he may feel comparably that his views begin after mine have been considered. He would be in effect claiming that the film's incorporation of blindness masks its blindness to itself. I cannot deny the possibility. For the moment that is where I would hope to leave things, namely with a possibility, or say with a grave risk.

Thomas Dumm's (Chapter 11) understanding and expansions of ways I have followed into *King Lear* may be taken as translating, however else, into arguably its expressively most extreme case, a theme that has been developing in various of my responses over the course of the essays of this volume. In that theme, what I have called the two directions, or axes (whatever others may be posited), of the life form called the human, the vertical and the horizontal, or the biological and the ethnological (a duplicity unshared with life forms lacking, or to the extent that they lack, language) are put in motion and internalized, as pictured, for example, in my elaboration of the distinction between performative and passionate utterance (or better between the illocutionary and the perlocutionary implications and conspiracies of speech), so that in any utterance a struggle between, let's call them, nature and convention, or natural law and common law, may come into play. These struggles are no longer well thought, as classically in Kant and Mill, to occur between homogeneous and separate realms, say between that of inclination or desire and that of reason or order, but as forces perpetually incorporating and calling each other to account, within each breast, constituting our present, our ordinary. Emerson called the forces intuition and tuition, or power and form, Nietzsche followed with the figures of the Dionysian and the Apollonian. (I invoke Nietzsche's too-famous distinction to suggest that from my point of view the judgment of a political present, as with the case of judgment in general, is in part—or has in part become—irreducibly aesthetic, marking a point at which the sensible and the intellectual must cross. This point recurs in principle with every utterance, every human expression. An underlying thought here is

Freud's discussion of negation in his essay "Negation," as the condition of possibility of judgment in general, in which, among the most primitive of human instincts, the oral, there is the choice between expressing yes and expressing no, between incorporation and rejection, swallowing and spitting out. Here is a reason that I hope not to ignore Dumm's calling upon the concept of disgust, a perturbation in our taste for human existence.)

We have in effect witnessed this economy of forces in Mill's picture of the withered or crippled mass of humanity forgetting their right to their individual eccentricities; of the Third Estate claiming to speak for the General Assembly; of a prisoner in Plato's cave violently resisting the thrust, or say his and her own sense, of the real, the present, of the beyond projected by every ordinary; of Astaire's frenzy or madness in recognizing the comparative impotence of his isolated talent to rectify the horror in the suppression of those who have invented the medium of expression of that talent; of the opposition between sovereignty and bare life. And now we have Cordelia, isolated and exposed in her love and pity for her father, by her father's making his absolute power meaningless, commanding speech and silence simultaneously, hence making her feelings inexpressible. (To say "Nothing," her first public word, is precisely to speak by saying nothing. It may be taken as an allegory of a particular political state of affairs.) I add that the perpetual interaction of the horizontal and the vertical, or the performative and the passionate, is essential to Wittgenstein's idea that we are, in thinking, led to speak "outside language games," hence to the idea of a longing for the transcendent (cf. *Culture and Value*, p. 15). I think of the interaction as essential to the concept of expression, of its distortion and its suppression, of the difficulty of saying what we mean, of incessantly saying more and saying less than we mean. The *Investigations* seems to sketch a vision of the human being, following Schopenhauer and Nietzsche and Freud, as what I sometimes call a perpetual expression machine, unappeasably desirous (even if all that is left to desire is, as in Nietzsche, nothing). It seems to picture us as born with one foot in hell.

My reading of *King Lear* was criticized quite fervently, in a recent round table on the essay, along the following lines (I include I think most of the words used): "How can you claim to know so much about what Cordelia means since we know nothing about her, nothing about her childhood, her relation with her mother and sisters, let alone her life with her father?" My reply was to propose that the opening of *Lear* is precisely about the essentially nothing we are apt to know about the immediate, or visible, embodiments of power. No one knows why Lear has ordered this mysterious ritual of abdication which is no abdication. The play's first words are, as familiar elsewhere in Shakespeare, heard (or overheard?) between relatively subordinate figures who will turn out to be brushing against concepts that will emerge as focal in the events to follow. I had occasion to cite a while ago, "I thought the King had more affected the Duke of Albany than of Cornwall." "It did seem so to us, but. . . . " But, Gloucester goes on to say to Kent, this affection isn't evident in the way Lear is drawing his map of political division. And we know about Cordelia that her first expression is an aside, namely a form of speech which is unheard in her world and, as it were, overheard in ours—suggesting an allegory of a political state of affairs, one in which each of us senses our language as simultaneously and perpetually unheard and overheard, ourselves as unresponded to, and exposed.

Of the countless matters I will have to postpone in responding to Dumm's remarkable and poignant text (the time is past in which I can for this occasion cure my ignorance of Heidegger's *Parmenides*, in part the cause of my postponement in reading Agamben's discussion of the *homo sacer*), I say at once that, given Dumm's insistence on forcing us to look at and to question the glaring fact of the absence of the mother, and his sense of a particular association of that fact with abdication and with the figure of Cordelia in her radical expression of loneliness, I have no quarrel with Dumm's sense of the importance of the question nor with his major associations with it, which are now part of how I have to think about these matters, but I also have no sense that I have come to rest with them. Perhaps I can say a word or two about that absence of sense, or sense of absence.

By the way, is it too obvious to mention that the image of Agamben's "abject power of the untouchable killer who establishes order from outside of the community" (p. 213) has a version, or versions, that is studied in the Hollywood genre of the western, providing an unguarded chance to observe the elaboration of the communal fantasy of the bringing of law to a land, having to serve at the same time as the veiling of the fact that the land was not previously void of human order, but that the new bringers or supplicants of law have voided that order. This reordering, or rediscovery, requires not an Athena or a Moses but a figure nevertheless whose deed of settlement will become touched with the mythic, and will contribute to myth. In two of the most famous and celebrated westerns, *The Man Who Shot Liberty Valance* and *Shane*, a (now) peaceable community, of a small city or of a set of farms, can be perpetuated only with the removal of a killer whom only a killer can remove. In the former, the rescuer is a member of the community but his outsideness to its confidence is established by his concealing from it the fact that it is his shot that kills the anarchic villain—he transfers the identity of "the man who shot Liberty Valance" to the man, studying the law, whom he is instrumental also in electing to serve in Congress as the first representative of a territory becoming a state. In the latter, Shane explicitly comes from outside and leaves, wounded, after killing the villain in a duel, despite its being rigged against him. In both cases the community is spared having to identify correctly the one who makes the reign of law possible with anyone who profits from the peace. In both, the one subject to inner or outer exile is shown to be in love with the wife of the man who, but for him, would have taken on the villain and surely been killed. The woman is either in fact a mother (in *Shane*) or notably maternal, and is evidently one too pure to have to bear the violence of the bringer of law. In *My Darling Clementine* the good sheriff, Wyatt Earp, leaves at the end to bring the news to his mother of the murder of his brother, her youngest son; the villain, the murderer of that son and brother, is a father who had sired male children only, all of whom he had seen killed in the concluding gunfight. The implication is that the violence, hence inevitable complicity in crime (as Freud saw), in establishing the coherence of a group governed by law—now that we do not expect an Athena to visit us from outside—has to be forgiven, the ground cleared accepted as a place of habitation and future, by a mother, as if the deed of the domestic was done for her. In her absence, justice goes unjudged.

But I was about to say something further about the more general sense of absence in the mother's absence, invoking mysterious absences circling the Shakespearean corpus at large, a repeated insistence on a lack of general resolution. Think of Lady Macbeth and the famous issue of her absent child or children; of Gertrude, in whom legitimacy is lodged and dislodged in lethal connection with her desire; of Hermione, the mother actually shown marvelously in exchange with a young child, who loses, as far as she knows, both of her children and is herself dead, as it were, throughout the bulk of the play, her resurrection being the issue of the play; of Cleopatra, whose manner of death she chooses, with other elements of her being, as becoming a mother dying by nursing; and of the absence of Miranda's mother. The virtually total absence of women in *Timon of Athens* seems to go with the absoluteness of Timon's wish for the destruction of humanity, of the future, posing as it were the question: If human existence is so full of pain, what attaches us to it?

In this spirit of irresolution, I would turn (Dumm says there is always another turn) to several questions underlying the pressure on the question of what happened to Lear's wife and (we suppose) Cordelia's mother, namely how we picture specifically her among Shakespearean mothers; and what particular role her absence plays in the play's events; and why she is not the subject of exchange among the members of her family or her subjects, as if her existence and (presumed) death are, as topics, taboo. Concretely, her absence establishes two conditions of the play. First, the absence is the condition under which this mysterious ritual of abdication can take place: in his wife's presence, it is hard to imagine Lear implying his ungovernable need and fear of love by demanding public declarations, indeed contests, of love for himself from his daughters, receiving from Cordelia virtually the declaration of a marriage vow ("obey you, love you, and most honor you"). Second, in her absence, in a play about speech, about the demand for and the danger of speech, of the easy falsification of speech, of its hollowness, of its inhabitation by hysteria, there is no one to speak in equal exchange, or say in confidence, with the king; everyone else can be banished or cursed for saying what the king does not want to hear without changing the play and its drift to Lear and Cordelia at the end isolated but together. We want to imagine that in the mother's presence her daughters would have seen the path to powerful, beneficent womanly nurturance, but what evidence is there for this idea in Shakespeare?

Let me follow out a little the suggestion in what I have been led to say in considering Dumm's text, that idea that the absence of the mother signals another absence pervading the play (but which of Shakespeare's tragedies and romances does not?), namely that of a nurturant political dispensation. The first remark I recall made to me (apart from conversation with friends) after my essay on *Lear* appeared, as the closing and longest segment of my first book, was that it neglects the politics of the play. I was not able to answer then much beyond declaring my sense that the question of, say, whether Lear's dividing his kingdom in three parts was politically wise or foolish, is swamped by the mad declaration that he is dividing it in response to, in part proportioned by, declarations of love that are themselves as dark as whatever he means by speaking of his "darker purpose." Now I want to answer that it is the play itself that incorporates the neglect of politics, that the vanishing of the political is its subject.

I don't know that I can yet supply sufficient tuition for this intuition, but it will have to do with my sense that Shakespeare's extremity and juxtaposition of moods, or his sense of absolute isolation, for example, revealing the propinquity of respect to the absolute abjection of having your eyes put out, throws in question the perpetuation of the communal, as if Shakespeare's very supremacy (might we say sovereignty?) of expressiveness can create the impression that, falling considerably short of supremacy, here as elsewhere, we may cease to understand each other, or to believe we do, that we may become unable to express ourselves. Here is a further suggestion that Aristotle's trust in the possession of language, and its provision of judgment, is a rougher ground for commonality than Aristotle had reason to consider (unless ruling out barbarians and slaves already sufficiently hedged who counted as having language in common). As if not the mere possession of language (if that is a comprehensible idea) but the assumption of reasons for speaking, a willingness to intervene, if only to affirm obedience, recognizing the point of expressing oneself, is what the polis requires or inspires. As if Cordelia's opening aside about the possibility of speech marks a question for the entire play, recoiling from, interpreting, Goneril's ironic invocation of "A love that makes breath poor, and speech unable," and reaching to the concluding scene in which Regan imagines an appropriate answer to Goneril would be to vomit words ("answer/From a full-flowing stomach"), links together speaking with conditions that prevent speaking, namely the conditions of a difficulty in breathing and of an advent of nausea (disgust).

A difficulty in breathing is revealed, to my mind, in a way of understanding Lear's familiarity with the storm. I have elsewhere taken his refusal to accept Goneril's and Regan's grudging hospitality and instead, with the approaching storm, to "abjure all roofs, and choose/To wage against the enmity o' th' air," to prompt the thought of this enmity not as directed (alone) from a disturbed sky but as leveled against the living mortal's condition of having to live, under whatever sky, in the medium of air, having to breath. I said about this (in an essay in *Shakespeare Studies* 27 [1999]) that this waging/wager reveals the persistence of Lear's hysteria, his sense of suffocation ("Hysterica passio" occurs earlier in this long scene), and in a form that, to my ear, is preserved in a passage from Emerson's "Fate" that I have more than once stopped over, in which Emerson is asking how we can withstand, or understand, bear up under, the weight of ideas in the air, especially that of slavery, which mars, fractions, our body politic, our constitution: "We should be crushed by the atmosphere, but for the reaction of the air within the body." I emphasize again that a fear of inexpressiveness, as a kind of death in life, in conjunction with a fear of over-expressiveness, of exposure to the human element, is recurrent in my reading, in *The Claim of Reason* (e.g., p. 351), of Wittgenstein's passages on the idea of a private language, passages not answered by an appeal to the effect that language "is" "public," since the point of those passages of Wittgenstein's is that we do not know what the distinction between public and something else, call it private, is. (Dumm's idea of a new loneliness seems to speak to this metaphysical uncertainty.) But now we are back at the opening essays of this volume, and I shall take the hint that it is time to wind up these remarks.

I said in my response to Espen Hammer's intervention that I would not want to close without returning to the question of the role of philosophy in political life, in particular to how I see the idea of philosophy's powerlessness, or passiveness, as articulated in Emerson. What was on my mind was a well-attended celebration in 2003 of the bicentennial of Emerson's birth, at the time the invasion of Iraq was just under way. I closed my contribution to a round table discussion by invoking the opening sentence of the last paragraph of Emerson's "Experience": "I know that the world I converse with in the city and in the farms is not the world I *think*," a piece of knowledge that, for any who claim to have it, sets the task (moral and political more than aesthetic and religious?) of bringing that further world (one beyond conversation, but evidently implied in that conversation, in its very sense of limitation, of horizontality), into existence. These two worlds of Emerson's form a fair version of a dominant image from Kant's

Groundwork of the Metaphysics of Morals—the image of the human being as having "two standpoints" from which to regard himself, "first, insofar as he belongs to the world of sense, under laws of nature (heteronomy); second, as belonging to the intelligible world, under laws which, being independent of nature, are not empirical but grounded merely in reason" (Ak. 452). Since what Emerson means by "standing" is expressing ourselves autonomously, and by "leaning" or "skulking," expressing ourselves heteronomously (not now however in accordance with the laws of nature but rather in accordance with the dictates of social conformity), I take Emerson's distinction to be homologous with Kant's, and moreover to be a plausible revision of Kant's insight invoking the proposal of different standpoints upon the self. Emerson's revision is at least as strong philosophically as John Stuart Mill's similar perception the following decade in *On Liberty*.

This connection now seems to me to call out for an assessment of different economies in play in the intersection of the biological and the ethnological dimensions of the human life form, Mill finding the ethnological to swamp the biological, Kant finding something like the reverse, but more accurately requiring a third axis or dimension (something I suggested we might have to consider) that supervenes into the play between the biological and the social, a law beyond, or before, law, a passion beyond passion. Emerson too requires the intervention of a beyond, but the idea of a further axis intersecting the intersection of the biological and the social does not picture his familiar, early claim that "the deeper [the scholar] dives into his privatest, secretest presentiment, to his wonder he finds this is the most acceptable, most public, and universally true." This seems to be, in its sense that the human is all of one substance, an interpretation of what it means to possess language, to have the capacity to speak together, to confront each other, which allows the double creature to reflect, to turn upon itself in aversion to its conduct and its impulses and its words.

The remainder of the concluding paragraph of "Experience" goes on to develop a response to the problem that Kant, at the end of the *Groundwork*, declares unsolvable, namely to explain *how pure reason can be practical* (Ak. 461). The unanswerable question for Kant is "how *the mere principle of validity of all its maxims as laws* [namely the Categorical Imperative] . . . without any matter (object) of the will in which one could take some interest in advance, can of itself furnish an incentive and produce an interest that would be called purely *moral*" (emphases in original). The form Kant's question (concerning how pure reason can be practical) takes at the close of "Experience" is as one that Emerson imagines others will direct to *him*: "Why not realize your world?"—a form Emerson characterizes as inviting a polemical answer, as though he is claiming to converse with and to think worlds other than those everyone else also knows, or may know.

The complex answer Emerson sketches goes this way: He deflects the question by replying that he has "not found that much was gained by manipular attempts to realize the world of thought" and formulates the goal of bringing about "victory for all justice" as a matter of "the transformation of genius into practical power" (a version of Plato's idea, that Plato calls paradoxical, of the mutual transformation of philosophers and kings—with the difference that Emersonian genius is possessed by each of us). In "Experience," the transformation we require is effected by our "always returning" to the solitude in which we find passage to what Emerson calls "new worlds"—expressing Emerson's tireless effort to discover America, that is, to discern what is, or what may be, new in this locale—a returning in the sanity and revelation of which we learn that the realization of justice, namely of the world of reason, is "the true romance which the world exists to realize." That is to say, there is a false romance in which it is manipular assaults on the world that are the objects of faith. The true romance is to see that the world of thought (a few pages earlier he has identified "this realm of thought" with his discovery of a new yet unapproachable America) is, as it were, awaiting realization, a world now within our world as it stands, one which we must learn to let approach us, to change us (as if it were no less immediate than news of our child's death, the pervasive subtext of "Experience"). It is neither a large nor a small thing that he asks us to learn, but it is asked of each of us.

Now realization, thinking, as that final paragraph repeatedly emphasizes, takes time. If there is no time for thought, we remain in, or relapse into, a world of what in "The American Scholar" Emerson calls "refractory fact," a world that is unresponsive to the transfigurations of thought, unmanageable by it. It is a world without truth or falsity, of human significance only in its production of need and relief ("as when, being thirsty, I drink water"), of life and death. In such a case, as the opening sentence of "Experience" asks, "Where do we find ourselves?" Here and now (that is, first aloud on March 28, 2003), I will answer as follows: First, we find ourselves aggrieved at being spoken for while being unspoken for; second, manipulated by assurances of our moral purity, and that of our standing America's; third, asked to think of everything but of how to assess our partiality (for example, the partiality of our society's realization of the principles of justice) and to change ourselves; fourth, unconvinced by our own voices unless they are raised polemically, etymologically meaning taking sides in a war, which is to say, unphilosophically.

In a further word of that final paragraph of "Experience," philosophy under these conditions is made *ridiculous*. Emerson's advice is: "Never mind the defeat; up again, old heart! . . . We shall win at the last. . . . Patience, patience." This may strike one as tame testimony. But what it says is that faith in philosophy—to have its turn, its time, at realization—must outlast, bear up under, hence confront with another possibility, every other form of human fervor or mask of skepticism.

It remains for me to say that I am as sensible of, and grateful for, the honor of being the object of the care in preparing the papers constituting the occasion of this volume, as I am of the pleasure, despite the pain of encountering my insufficiencies, in working on my replies.

Notes

CHAPTER I

1. I am grateful to Jane Bennett, Stanley Cavell, Tom Dumm, Richard Eldridge, Espen Hammer, Yasemin Ok, Tracy Strong, and Eric Wilson for their
helpful comments on earlier drafts of this essay.

2. *Stanley Cavell*, ed. R. Eldridge (Cambridge: Cambridge University Press,
2003), p. 11. Eldridge's own essay, "Cavell on American Philosophy and the Idea of
America," does provide a sensitive and thoughtful discussion of some of the political implications of Cavell's conception of the philosophical meaning and place
of America and of the roots of Cavell's perfectionism in Emerson and Thoreau.
But, as we shall see, Cavell's contribution to and importance for political philosophy is not limited to American philosophy and the idea of America. That said, although it does not focus on political questions, Eldridge's essay "The Normal and
the Normative: Wittgenstein's Legacy, Kripke, and Cavell" gives a nuanced and
perceptive account of Cavell's conception of the claim to community to which I
am here indebted (*Philosophy and Phenomenological Research* 46, no. 4 [June 1986]:
555–57).

3. As of October 1, 2004. A survey of titles is hardly definitive, of course, and
Cavell has been drawn upon more subtly by a number of political theorists, particularly those concerned with delineating the political implications and resources
of the later Wittgenstein. See in this regard Cressida Heyes's characterization of
Cavell's contribution as amounting to a sea change in the study of this question in
her introduction to *The Grammar of Politics: Wittgenstein and Political Philosophy*,
ed. C. Heyes (Ithaca: Cornell University Press, 2003), p. 8; and see the numerous
references to Cavell throughout the collection. There are also helpful discussions
of political matters in both of the two books that survey and introduce Cavell's
work as a whole, Stephen Mulhall's *Stanley Cavell: Philosophy's Recounting of the
Ordinary* (Oxford: Clarendon Press, 1994); and Espen Hammer's *Stanley Cavell:
Skepticism, Subjectivity, and the Ordinary* (Malden, Mass.: Polity Press, 2002). But
the general point remains.

4. Sheldon Wolin, *Politics and Vision: Continuity and Innovation in Western
Political Thought*, expanded ed. (Princeton: Princeton University Press, 2004), p.

10; cf. Christian Meier, *Die Entstehung des Politischen bei den Griechen* (Frankfurt/ Main: Suhrkamp, 1980), pp. 15f.

5. Leo Strauss, *The City and Man* (Chicago: University of Chicago Press, 1978), p. 52. Compare Cavell: "the good city we would inhabit . . . exists only in our intelligible encounters with each other" (Cavell, *Cities of Words: Pedagogical Letters on a Register of the Moral Life* [Cambridge, Mass.: Belknap, 2004], p. 5 [hereafter *CW*]).

6. See Anne Norton, *Leo Strauss and the Politics of American Empire* (New Haven: Yale University Press, 2004).

7. Cited in Elaine Tyler May, "Echoes of the Cold War: The Aftermath of September 11 at Home," in *September 11 in History: A Watershed Moment?*, ed. Mary Dudziak (London: Duke University Press, 2003), p. 49. This is representative of the Bush-Cheney administration's attempt to identify patriotism with obedience to the executive.

8. I turn to Hobbes here rather than Plato, who is regularly attacked as one of the founding father of the politics of unity, because, though the *Republic* emphasizes unity at the expense of much of what moderns like Mill most prize, it also emphasizes that this unity is maintained and governed by *philosophers*. Stability, unity, and order alone are not sufficient for a legitimate polity.

9. Hobbes, *Leviathan*, ed. C. B. Macpherson (New York: Penguin, 1968), p. 227; cf. p. 220. James Conant argues, with repeated reference to Cavell, that a "defense of America" such as that proposed by Bush and Ashcroft is at best a deep misunderstanding of the meaning of America in his "The Concept of America," *Society* 41, no. 1 (November–December 2003).

10. For Hobbes's views on the stark limitations of private judgment and deliberation, see *Leviathan*, p. 111. For the awkward status of a founding document of political science that succumbs to those limitations, consider Hobbes's turn in his Introduction from deduction to hermeneutics: "He that is to govern a whole Nation, must read in himself, not this, or that particular man; but Man-kind: which though it be hard to do, harder to learn than Language, or Science; yet, when I shall have set down my own reading orderly, and perspicuously, the pains left another, will be only to consider, if he also find not the same in himself. For this kind of Doctrine, admitteth no other Demonstration" (p. 83).

11. Carl Schmitt, *The Concept of the Political*, trans. George Schwab (Chicago: University of Chicago Press, 1996), p. 30.

12. A similar point is made by Richard Fleming in *The State of Philosophy: An Invitation to a Reading in Three Parts of Stanley Cavell's The Claim of Reason* (Cranbury, N.J.: Associated, 1993), pp. 162–63.

13. Cavell, "What Is the Emersonian Event?: A Comment on Kateb's Emerson," *Emerson's Transcendental Etudes* (Stanford: Stanford University Press, 2003), pp. 184 and 189.

14. The texts devoted to the delineation of a form of community that avoids aping the unity of the early Christian church or the Platonic republic are too numerous to list here, but a few of the best-known and most significant examples follow: Judith Butler, Ernesto Laclau, and Slavoj Zizek, *Contingency, Hegemony, Universality: Contemporary Dialogues on the Left* (London: Verso, 2000); Bill Connolly, *Identity/Difference: Democratic Negotiations of Political Paradox* (Ithaca: Cornell University Press, 1991); William Corlett, *Community Without Unity* (Durham, N.C.: Duke University Press, 1989); Drucilla Cornell, *The Philosophy of the Limit* (London: Routledge, 1992); Jean-Francois Lyotard, *The Differend: Phrases in Dispute*, trans. G. Van Den Abbeelle (Minneapolis: University of Minnesota Press, 1988); Chantal Mouffe, *The Democratic Paradox* (London: Verso, 2000); and Jean-Luc Nancy, *The Inoperative Community*, trans. Peter Connor et. al. (Minneapolis: University of Minnesota Press, 1991). That these texts contest similar assumptions about politics hardly implies that they do so in the same way. As is clear from the remarks above concerning polemics, though Cavell shares Mouffe's and Laclau's resistance to a politics of unity and identity, he is much more wary than they of moving from this to a celebration of (violent) conflict and antagonism. I discuss the striking limitations of Laclau's account of the latter in "Against Antagonism: On Ernesto Laclau's Political Thought," *Constellations* 9, no. 4 (December 2002): 554–73.

15. Wittgenstein, *Philosophical Investigations*, trans. G. E. M. Anscombe (New York: Macmillan, 1958), I:242 (hereafter *PI*).

16. The language of attunement is Cavell's: "The idea of agreement here is not that of coming to or arriving at an agreement on a given occasion, but of being in agreement throughout, being in harmony, like pitches or tones, or clocks, or weighing scales, or columns of figures. That a group of human beings *stimmen* in their language *überein* says, so to speak, that they are mutually voiced with respect to it, mutually *attuned* from top to bottom" (Cavell, *The Claim of Reason: Wittgenstein, Skepticism, Morality, and Tragedy* [New York: Oxford University Press, 1979], p. 32). The analogy with pitch is a central feature of his volume *The Pitch of Philosophy*, as the title suggests.

17. What it is to follow a rule and what Wittgenstein is driving at in his discussion of the question are enormously complicated matters, and what follows here is only intended to orient those unfamiliar with Cavell's own take on the matter. For other important interpretations, see Saul Kripke, *Wittgenstein on Rules and Private Language* (Cambridge, Mass.: Harvard University Press, 1982); *Wittgenstein: To Follow a Rule*, ed. S. Holtzman and C. Leich (London: Routledge & Kegan Paul, 1982); and G. P. Baker and P.M.S. Hacker, *Wittgenstein: Rules, Grammar and Necessity* (New York: Oxford University Press, 1985).

18. Winch, *The Idea of a Social Science and Its Relation to Philosophy* (London: Routledge & Kegan Paul, 1963), p. 52. The third, 1963, impression of the book

contained some corrections of the 1958 original.

19. In his fine introduction to Cavell's work, Espen Hammer perceptively observes that in 1958's "Must We Mean What We Say?," Cavell advances a position
on the relative priority and status of rules and judgment that is surprisingly close
to the one he attacks four years later in "On the Availability of Wittgenstein's Later
Philosophy." It is striking that the earlier piece focuses on Austin rather than Wittgenstein. As I have discussed elsewhere, in *The Claim of Reason* Cavell indicates
that though Austin puts the question of the voice back into (philosophical) play
for him, it is Wittgenstein who puts that voice into *conversation*. Though Cavell
often honors Austin by speaking of him as his "teacher," the notion of the human
voice is only revealed in its true significance for Cavell in conversation with another. We can briefly indicate the reasons for this by noting that it is only in such a
context that one can sensibly make *claims* and ask for and give *acknowledgment*—
two of Cavell's pivotal concepts. (This is not, of course, to foreclose the question
of whether and to what extent I at any juncture might stand as other to myself.)
See Hammer, *Stanley Cavell*, pp. 8–9 and 21; Norris, "Political Revisions: Stanley
Cavell and Political Philosophy," *Political Theory* 30, no. 6 (December 2002): 832;
and *CR*, pp. xi–xii and xiii.

20. Winch also argues that rule-following is a practice, and he emphasizes
that declarations of one's competence to represent one's community are not based
upon a disinterested knowledge available apart from one's membership in the
community—say, to an anthropologist—but are an existential matter of who one
is and how one lives. As Winch puts it, it is not a matter of my "ability to formulate statistical laws which would enable us to predict with fair accuracy what
people would be likely to do in any given circumstances[, as] we might be able
to make predictions of great accuracy and still not be able to claim any real understanding of what [people in our community] were doing" (*The Idea of a Social
Science*, p. 115). Real understanding is demonstrated by actual participation in the
form of life. But Winch's reliance on rules and on the idea that rules require interpretation (p. 92) makes it difficult for him to cast much light upon the notion of
practice. If meaningful behavior is "*ipso facto* rule-governed," how meaningful is
the interpretation of any rule? If the interpretation is also rule-governed, doesn't
this produce the regress identified by Wittgenstein? Here as there it would seem
that the practice of interpretation underlies any rules, rather than rules providing
a foundation for and condition of the intelligibility of any given practice—a view
Winch ultimately adopts in a wonderful late essay that explicitly criticizes his earlier assumptions (Winch, "Judgment: Propositions and Practices," *Philosophical
Investigations* 21, no. 3 [July 1988]: 189–202). (See as well Winch's comments on his
earlier characterization of rules in the Foreword to the 1990 Second Edition of the
book.) Even here, however, Winch's vision of the practice of language is not one
that highlights personal and existential responsibility in the manner of Cavell.

21. Cavell, "The Availability of Wittgenstein's Later Philosophy," *Must We Mean What We Say?* (Cambridge: Cambridge University Press, 1969), p. 50 (hereafter AWLP). It would indeed be impossible to say once and for all how we follow rules or follow the many rules that weave through our lives: "I cannot *say* what following rules is *überhaupt*, nor say how to obey a rule in a way that doesn't presuppose that you already know what it is to follow them" (*CR*, p. 184).

22. John McDowell, "Non-Cognitivism and Rule-Following," *Mind, Value, and Reality* (Cambridge, Mass.: Harvard University Press, 1998), p. 207.

23. P. M. S. Hacker, *Insight and Illusion: Themes in the Philosophy of Wittgenstein* (Bristol: Thoemmes Press, 1977), pp. 208 and 174.

24. Aristotle, *Nicomachean Ethics*, trans. T. Irwin (Indianapolis: Hackett, 1985), p. 1094b. Compare Arendt's account of the role of modern science and Cartesian philosophy in the undermining of "common sense" and the development of "world alienation" in chapter 6 of Arendt, *The Human Condition* (Chicago: University of Chicago Press, 1958); Charles Taylor's turn to hermeneutics in "Interpretation and the Sciences of Man," *Philosophy and the Human Sciences: Philosophical Papers 2* (Cambridge: Cambridge University Press, 1985); Gadamer's account of "the hermeneutic relevance of Aristotle" in *Truth and Method*, trans. J. Weinsheimer and D. Marshall (New York: Continuum, 1999), pp. 312ff; and the general accounts in Richard Bernstein, *Beyond Objectivism and Relativism: Science, Hermeneutics, and Praxis* (Philadelphia: University of Pennsylvania Press, 1983); and Ronald Beiner, *Political Judgment* (Chicago: University of Chicago Press, 1983). Gerald Bruns argues that the kinship between Gadamer and Cavell is closer than I allow here in his essay, "Stanley Cavell's Shakespeare," *Critical Inquiry* 16, no. 3 (Spring 1989): 612–32. Bruns is right to emphasize the strong similarities between the two; though he does not cite it, Gadamer's claim that "understanding is, primarily, agreement" (p. 180) is particularly suggestive in this regard. Nonetheless, I think Bruns does not take seriously enough the importance of the disagreement between the two concerning the significance of modern skepticism.

25. It is this claim to which Richard Rorty objects in his critical review of *The Claim of Reason* ("Cavell on Skepticism," *Consequences of Pragmatism* [Minneapolis: University of Minnesota Press, 1982]). On Rorty's account, modern philosophy is best left behind, there is little or no sense of speaking (ahistorically) about "the human self," and Cavell's arguments to the contrary rest upon an illicit assumption that dry-as-dust epistemologists in the Anglo-American tradition are raising and grappling with the profound existential questions we associate with Sartre and the existentialists. How justified these charges strike us will depend in part upon who we find to be a more sensitive reader of the relevant texts, Cavell or Rorty. It will also depend on whether we identify (and to what extent we identify with) modernity as *progress* and how we conceive of the radical self-reflection of modernity. In a more recent exchange with Cavell's former student James Conant,

Rorty writes: "If there were something like what Cavell calls 'the Ordinary' . . . I doubt I should have any interest in dwelling within it. I see the desire for ever-new, revisionary, extraordinary, paradoxical languages as the manic eros which gave us the Platonic dialogues, *The Phenomenology of Mind, Concluding Unscientific Postscript*, 'Empiricism and the Philosophy of Mind,' 'A Nice Derangement of Epithets,' and *The Postcard*" (Rorty, "Response to James Conant," in *Rorty and His Critics*, ed. R. Brandom [Oxford: Blackwell, 2000], p. 349).

26. Ludwig Wittgenstein, *Tractatus Logico-Philosophicus*, trans. C. K. Ogden (London: Routledge & Kegan Paul, 1982), 6:51.

27. I am speaking loosely here. Sebastian Gardner argues persuasively that what the analytic tradition has identified as a transcendental argument is not consistent with central features of the Kantian project. For this and his alternative account of Kant's approach to skepticism, see Gardner, *Kant and the Critique of Pure Reason* (London: Routledge, 1999), pp. 188–96. Gardner follows Barry Stroud, who concludes his own consideration of Kant's appeal to transcendental conditions by rejecting it as too skeptical a solution to skepticism: "If I understand the transcendental at all, I find it difficult to distinguish transcendental idealism, in its explanatory power, from the kind of scepticism that seemed so inevitable on Descartes' argument in the *First Meditation*" (Stroud, *The Significance of Philosophical Scepticism* [Oxford: Clarendon, 1987], p. 166).

28. Norman Malcolm, "Wittgenstein's *Philosophical Investigations*," in his *Knowledge and Certainty: Essays and Lectures* (Ithaca: Cornell University Press, 1963), pp. 116–17. Compare Han-Johann Glock's *Wittgenstein Dictionary* (Oxford: Blackwell, 1996), which provides a concise version of the standard "Wittgenstein as anti-skeptic" argument, an argument that relies upon the notion that "doubt and the allaying of doubt (justification) make sense only within a language-game [that] itself can be neither justified nor doubted" (p. 339). Alice Crary gives a subtle and nuanced critique of this line of thought, paying particular attention to Rorty's reading, in "Wittgenstein's Philosophy in Relation to Political Thought," in *The New Wittgenstein*, ed. A. Crary and R. Read (New York: Routledge, 2000), pp. 118–45. She acknowledges her debt to Cavell's discussion of the complex relation between the natural and the conventional in note 59.

29. Cavell's formulation here invites comparison with Arendt's notion of world alienation (note 24 above). This is but one of many points at which Arendt and Cavell approach one another, if only so as to emphasize the distance between them. Their shared debt to Heidegger is obviously crucial to any consideration of these matters. I discuss this further in my manuscript "Ordinary Politics."

30. Cavell thus distinguishes himself sharply from those who argue that the skeptical philosopher's statements are, strictly speaking, nonsensical. The *words* are meaningful, not just what *you* are saying. The difference here is, if I understand Cavell correctly, what he is pointing to in the wonderfully elliptical title, "Must We Mean What We Say?"

31. To the frustration of many, Cavell has resisted reading Wittgenstein's *On Certainty* (*CR*, p. xiv), but a joke of Wittgenstein's there makes this point well: "I am," Wittgenstein writes, "sitting with a philosopher in the garden; he says again and again, 'I know that's a tree,' pointing to a tree that is near us. Someone else arrives and hears this, and I tell him, 'This fellow isn't insane. We are only doing philosophy'" (*On Certainty*, trans. G. E. M. Anscombe and D. Paul [New York: Harper, 1969], p. 467).

32. Cavell, "Declining Decline: Wittgenstein as a Philosopher of Culture," *This New Yet Unapproachable America: Lectures After Emerson After Wittgenstein* (Albuquerque: Living Batch Press, 1989), p. 57 (hereafter DD).

33. "I do not . . . confine the term [*skepticism*] to philosophers who wind up denying that we can ever know; I apply it to any view which takes the existence of the world to be a problem of knowledge" (*CR*, p. 46). It is an especial strength of Hammer's book that it foregrounds this aspect of Cavell's work.

34. In an earlier formulation, Cavell writes, "what skepticism suggests is that since we cannot know the world exists, its presentness to us cannot be a function of knowing. The world is to be accepted; as the presentness of other minds is not to be known, but acknowledged" ("The Avoidance of Love: A Reading of King Lear," in *Must We Mean What We Say?* [Cambridge: Cambridge University Press, 1976] [hereafter AL], p. 324).

35. Cavell, "The Philosopher in American Life (Toward Thoreau and Emerson)," in *In Quest of the Ordinary* (Chicago: University of Chicago Press, 1988), p. 8.

36. Robert Paul Wolff argues that there are at least three "selves" at work in the Critical Philosophy, an empirical, a noumenal, and a transcendental, the relations between whom defy explication. In addition, there is, he further argues, a moral self that cannot be mapped onto any of the other three without incoherent results. In each case it is impossible to account for the plurality of epistemic and moral agents on the basis of an non-individuated, single, synthesizing, transcendental ego. Wolff concludes, in terms that speak directly to the discussion at hand, "Despite his overriding concern for moral matters, Kant never seems to have asked himself the fundamental question, What is it for one man to stand in a real relation to another man?" (*The Autonomy of Reason: A Commentary on Kant's Groundwork of the Metaphysic of Morals* [New York: Harper & Row, 1973], p. 15).

37. Compare Arendt, "What Is Freedom?" in *Between Past and Future* (Middlesex: Penguin, 1968).

38. Cavell, "Work in Progress: An Introductory Report," *This New Yet Unapproachable America: Lectures After Emerson After Wittgenstein*, p. 23.

39. This brings Cavell into conversation with a great deal of recent work in political theory. Compare Stephen White's review and analysis in *Sustaining Affirmation: The Strengths of Weak Ontology in Political Theory* (Princeton: Prince-

ton University Press, 2000). See in particular White's discussion of "critical responsiveness" as a virtue requiring "a greater attentiveness to the difficulties and suffering that occur as a relatively inchoate force of becoming struggles toward the threshold of establishment as a movement" (p. 124), a discussion that recalls Cavell's analysis (in "The Conversation of Justice: Rawls and the Drama of Consent") of Nora's struggle to find her own voice in Ibsen's *A Doll's House*.

40. The third chapter of Stephen Mulhall's *Stanley Cavell: Philosophy's Recounting of the Ordinary* gives a very helpful account of Cavell's use of the idea of the social contract. If it requires amendment, that is a function of Mulhall's broader resistance to Cavell's radical recasting of the relationship between our use of rules and our responsibility as speakers. To accurately gauge what Cavell is getting at in his account of what it means to speak for one another, we need to appreciate what he thinks it means for us to speak for ourselves, and this in turn requires an appreciation of the priority of individual commitment over any appeal to rules. Stephen Affeldt has argued persuasively that Mulhall's own sense of this is quite different from that found in Cavell. Compare Affeldt, "The Ground of Mutuality: Criteria, Judgment, and Intelligibility in Stephen Mulhall and Stanley Cavell," *The European Journal of Philosophy* 6 (1998): 1–31; and Mulhall, "Stanley Cavell's Vision of the Normativity of Language: Grammar, Criteria, and Rules," in Eldridge, *Stanley Cavell*.

41. Rousseau thus cuts across Michael Sandel's distinction between the "cognitive" and the "voluntarist" dimensions of agency: The central question is the "cognitive" one, "Who am I?"; but the answer is a voluntarist one: "I am what we will." Compare Sandel, *Liberalism and the Limits of Justice* (Cambridge: Cambridge University Press, 1982), pp. 58–59.

42. Jean Jacques Rousseau, *The Social Contract*, trans. M. Cranston (New York: Penguin, 1968), p. 153; *Du Contrat Social* (Paris: Garnier-Flammarion, 1966), p. 149.

43. *The Social Contract*, III, ii. As I argue in "Political Revisions," Rousseau also downplays the role of speech and deliberation and is misled by the model of epistemology in ways that set him at odds with Cavell. In this light, it is not surprising that though Cavell makes extensive use of Rousseau in *The Claim of Reason*, he has made very little reference to him since, and in his 2004 *City of Words* includes chapters on Locke and Mill, but none on Rousseau. One might say that Cavell's concern with psychoanalysis is the true development of his concerns here.

44. This obviously hearkens back to the manner in which Cavell reinterprets Kant's identification of subjectivity with the activity of judgment. On the relation between Rousseau and Kant, see Richard Velkley, *Freedom and the Ends of Reason: On the Moral Foundation of Kant's Critical Philosophy* (Chicago: University of Chicago Press, 1989).

45. Eldridge, "The Normal and the Normative," p. 571, emphasis his.

46. Cavell's own account of the latter aligns itself with and draws upon recent work in feminism in ways that have yet to be properly appreciated. Cavell has engaged sporadically with feminist arguments, and he has indicated more broadly that his own political education in the last thirty years has been decisively marked by the emergence of such arguments (e.g., Cavell, *Disowning Knowledge in Seven Plays of Shakespeare*, updated edition [Cambridge: Cambridge University Press, 2003], p. xii). The effects are readily observed in a comparison with Janet Flammang's inventory of the ways feminist political science contrasts with the conventional political science it disputes. On Flammang's account, "there are important differences in what the two camps find empirically interesting, or worth knowing about: state vs. community, government vs. politics, military state vs. welfare state, stability vs. change, powerful vs. powerless, insiders vs. outsiders, elite vs. mass, interest groups vs. social movements, electoral politics vs. familial politics, political parties vs. voluntary associations, opinions vs. consciousness, power over vs. power to, force vs. empowerment, rights vs. responsibilities, public-private separation vs. public-private integration, and the separation of politics and morality vs. the integration of politics and morality" (Janet A. Flammang, *Women's Political Voice: How Women are Transforming the Practice and Study of Politics* [Philadelphia, Pa.: Temple University Press, 1997], p. 4). The vast majority of the terms aligned here with feminism are Cavell's, and the few exceptions—elite vs. mass, for instance—are places where Cavell seeks to further complicate an overly simple opposition. The same can be said of Flammang's later appeal to "the politics of everyday life" (p. 20) and "the need for members of oppressed groups to find their 'voice'" (p. 31, citing Martha Ackelsberg and Irene Diamond). For a sensitive discussion of Cavell's engagement with feminism itself, see Hammer, pp. 84f. For criticism of his use of gendered categories, see Tania Modelski, *Feminism Without Women* (New York: Routledge, 1991), pp. 8ff.

47. That it is Wittgenstein in particular who makes it possible for us to really see what Emerson and Thoreau are doing is indicated in the very title of Cavell's *This New Yet Unapproachable America: Lectures After Emerson After Wittgenstein*.

48. Cavell, "The Politics of Interpretation (Politics as Opposed to What?)," *Themes out of School* (Chicago: University of Chicago Press, 1984), pp. 32–33.

49. Cavell, "The Conversation of Justice: Rawls and the Drama of Consent," in *Conditions Handsome and Unhandsome* (Chicago: University of Chicago Press, 1990), p. 125. Compare Cavell's comments on partiality and the desire it makes possible in "Old and New in Emerson and Nietzsche," *Emerson's Transcendental Etudes*.

CHAPTER 2

1. Stanley Cavell, *Must We Mean What We Say?* (Cambridge: Cambridge University Press, 1976), p. 1.

2. Ibid., p. 52.

3. Cavell, *The Claim of Reason* (New York: Oxford University Press, 1979) (hereafter *CR*), p. 20.

4. Ibid.

5. Ludwig Wittgenstein, *Philosophical Investigations*, 2d ed., trans. G. E. M. Anscombe (Oxford: Blackwell, 1978), §§241–42.

6. *CR*, p. 31.

7. Cavell, *Must We Mean What We Say?*, p. 42.

8. *CR*, p. 125.

9. Alasdair MacIntyre, *After Virtue* (South Bend, Ind.: Notre Dame University Press, 1981) (hereafter *AV*), p. 6.

10. Emerson, *Essays and Lectures* (New York: Library of America, 1983), p. 264.

11. J. C. Nyíri, *Tradition and Individuality: Essays* (Dordrecht: Kluwer Academic Publishers, 1992).

12. Brian McGuinness, ed., *Wittgenstein and the Vienna Circle: Conversations Recorded by Friedrich Waismann*, trans. Joachim Schulte and Brian McGuiness (Oxford: Basil Blackwell, 1979), p. 115.

13. *CR*, p. 30.

14. Cavell, *This New Yet Unapproachable America: Lectures After Emerson After Wittgenstein* (Albuquerque, N.M.: Living Batch Press, 1989), p. 44.

15. *CR*, p. 32.

16. Ibid., p. 22.

17. Ibid., p. 18.

18. Ibid., p. 25.

19. Ibid., p. 19.

20. John McDowell, "Non-Cognitivism and Rule-Following," in his *Mind, Value, and Reality* (Cambridge, Mass.: Harvard University Press, 1998), p. 207.

21. John R. Searle, *The Construction of Social Reality* (New York: Free Press, 1995), chap. 6.

22. E.g., "The Availability of Wittgenstein's Later Philosophy," in his *Must We Mean What We Say?*, p. 52.

23. G. H. von Wright and Heikki Nyman, eds., *Remarks on the Philosophy of Psychology*, vol. 2, trans. C. G. Luckhardt and M.A.E. Aue (Chicago: University of Chicago Press, 1980), §§624–25 and 629.

CHAPTER 3

1. Stanley Cavell, *Conditions Handsome and Unhandsome: The Constitution of Emersonian Perfectionism* (Chicago: University of Chicago Press, 1990), p. 4.

2. Ibid., p. 46.

3. Ibid., p. 54.

4. Ibid., p. 8.

5. Ibid., p. xxxiv. See also pp. 59–60: "The idea of the self as always to be furthered is not expressed by familiar fantasies of a noumenal self, nor of the self as entelechy, either final or initial."

6. Ibid., pp. 54, 57.

7. What sort of dissatisfaction? We should say that they are both moral—that is, connected to finding one's way in life practically—and theoretical—in that they touch on our understanding of things. But it is important here to realize that what sort of dissatisfaction will count as the one which invites the perfectionist response can be seen only at the end of the perfectionist journey. Only of those dissatisfactions which are seen at the end of the journey as expressions of a self that has not yet reached clarity with itself can we say that they are the proper kind of dissatisfaction. This point is also connected to the famous remark of Cavell's according to which the investigation that authors like Wittgenstein and Heidegger were pursuing, though "it may express itself as a moral or religious demand," "is not the subject of a *separate* study within it, call it Ethics" ("Declining Decline," in *This New Yet Unapproachable America: Lectures After Emerson After Wittgenstein* [Albuquerque, N.M.: Living Batch Press, 1989], pp. 29–75: also see p. 40); see also *Conditions*, pp. 2, 7, 61–62.

8. *Conditions*, p. xxx.

9. Ibid., p. 57.

10. Ibid., p. xxxii.

11. Ibid.

12. Ibid., p. 5.

13. I cannot here do any justice to this thesis. See Mill himself on this: J. S. Mill, "Autobiography," in *Autobiography and Literary Essays*, ed. J. M. Robson and J. Stillinger, *Collected Works* (Toronto: University of Toronto Press, 1981), I:253. The importance of the romantic line in Mill's philosophy is stressed by R. J. Halliday, in *John Stuart Mill* (London: Allen & Unwin, 1976), but it finds expression in a reading of Mill as an eclectic author. What is missed is precisely the project of furnishing certain (romantic) ideas with a new philosophical context, where this operation radically transforms both those ideas and the context in which they are supposed to be received and made room for.

14. "On Genius," in *Collected Works*, I:332.

15. Ibid.

16. Ibid., I:337.

17. Ibid.

18. J. S. Mill, *Collected Works*, vol. XII, *The Earlier Letters*, ed. F. E. Mineka (Toronto: University of Toronto Press, 1963), p. 49.

19. "On Genius," p. 334.

20. Ibid., p. 335. For a reading of this issue connected to what I am trying to do here, see R. H. Haraldsson, "'This All but Universal Illusion . . .': Remarks on the Question: Why Did Mill Write *On Liberty?*," *Sats—Nordic Journal of Philosophy* 5 (2004): 83–109.

21. *On Liberty*, in *Collected Works*, vol. 18, *Essays on Politics and Society*, ed. J. M. Robson (Toronto: University of Toronto Press, 1977), p. 248.

22. Ibid., p. 248.

23. Ibid., p. 247.

24. Ibid.

25. Ibid., p. 249.

26. Ibid., p. 250.

27. Ibid.

28. C. L. Ten, *Mill on Liberty* (Oxford: Clarendon Press, 1980), p. 128, distinguishes "knowing truth" from "having true opinions" in order to connect the value of truth in Mill's thought to the importance of the progress of the individual mind. The tension here is also connected to a tension, internal to Mill's text, between a positivist and a perfectionist understanding of truth. I cannot explore this here.

29. Cavell, "Aesthetic Problems of Modern Philosophy," in *Must We Mean What We Say? A Book of Essays* (Cambridge: Cambridge University Press, 1976), pp. 73–96; see p. 96: "philosophy concerns those necessities we cannot, being human, fail to know. Except that nothing is more human than to deny them."

30. *On Liberty*, p. 248.

31. Ibid., p. 250.

32. Ibid., p. 224.

33. *Conditions*, p. 62.

34. "Philosophy," in *Philosophical Occasions*, ed. J. C. Klagge and A. Nordmann (Indianapolis: Hackett, 1993), pp. 158–199; see pp. 161–63.

35. Ibid., p. 161.

36. *Tractatus Logico-Philosophicus*, trans. C. K. Ogden (London: Routledge & Kegan Paul, 1922), 6:521.

37. *Philosophical Investigations*, ed. G.E.M. Anscombe and R. Rhees, trans. G.E.M. Anscombe (Oxford: Blackwell, 1958), §133.

38. "Aesthetic Problems of Modern Philosophy," p. 85.

39. I draw here from a reading of the *Tractatus* which was explored and made familiar by the works of Cora Diamond and James Conant. See, e.g., C. Diamond, *The Realistic Spirit* (Cambridge, Mass.; MIT Press, 1991); J. Conant, "The Method of the Tractatus," in *From Frege to Wittgenstein*, ed. E. H. Reck (Oxford: Oxford University Press, 2002), pp. 374–462. See also P. Donatelli, *Wittgenstein e l'etica* (Roma-Bari: Laterza, 1998); idem, "The Problem of 'the Higher' in Wittgenstein's *Tractatus*," in *Religion and Wittgenstein's Legacy*, ed. D. Z. Phillips (Aldershot: Ashgate, 2004).

40. Wittgenstein, "Philosophy," p. 161.

41. Stanley Cavell, *The Claim of Reason: Wittgenstein, Skepticism, Morality, and Tragedy* (Oxford: Oxford University Press, 1979), pp. 354–55.

42. It is important to recall that I am not furnishing this description of such cases as an analysis of the nature of proverbs, etc. On the contrary, a proverb might count as such a Millian case of truth only insofar as it bears this special relationship with the self. See on this note 7 above. See also Cavell on a related issue: "The *Investigations'* Everyday Aesthetics of Itself," in *Wittgenstein in America*, ed. T. G. McCarthy and S. C. Stidd (Oxford: Clarendon Press, 2001), p. 264. Cavell distinguishes here between "adages, or maxims of practical wisdom," which "present standing, sociable responses to life's recurrences" from what appear as "new, eccentric, personal responses, to some present crossroads of culture." Mill says that a true understanding of a certain maxim requires such eccentric and personal response. (This leaves open the question of language and style, which is also important to Cavell's thought.)

43. Wittgenstein was interested in this phenomenon of the opening up of possibilities for us, and what I am doing could be read as the broaching of one possible reading of this. Cavell mentions a different one with his comparison with seeing-as. There are other readings: see for example Cora Diamond's treatment of this topic in her "Riddles and Anselm's Riddle," in *The Realistic Spirit*, pp. 267–89; and her "What if x isn't the number of sheep? Wittgenstein and Thought-Experiments in Ethics," *Philosophical Papers* 31 (2002): 227–50. They all show different ways of approaching Wittgenstein's interest in this, but they are also all connected to his notion (various notions) of philosophy.

44. *On Liberty*, pp. 101, 103.

45. G.E.M. Anscombe, "Modern Moral Philosophy," in *Ethics, Religion and Politics: The Collected Philosophical Papers*, vol. 3 (Minneapolis: University of Minnesota Press, 1981), pp. 26–42. See on this J. Conant, "Nietzsche, Kierkegaard and Anscombe on Moral Unintelligibility," in *Religion and Morality*, ed. D. Z. Phillips (New York: St. Martin's Press, 1996), pp. 250–98; see also C. Diamond, "Losing Your Concepts," *Ethics* 98 (1988): 255–77.

46. For one example of this kind of approach see A. I. Davidson, *The Emergence of Sexuality: Historical Epistemology and the Formation of Concepts* (Cambridge, Mass: Harvard University Press, 2001).

47. Cavell, "Aesthetic Problems of Modern Philosophy," p. 85.

48. In this connection Cavell speaks of the power of philosophy to free us from "false necessities and false ideas of the necessary" ("The Fantastic of Philosophy," in *In Quest of the Ordinary: Lines of Skepticism and Romanticism* (Chicago: University of Chicago Press, 1988), p. 184), or, as he writes elsewhere, from "a spiritual paralysis, as it were a hallucination of necessity, of some necessary meaning" ("The *Investigations'* Everyday Aesthetics of Itself," p. 255). In this latter context

Cavell introduces an illuminating difference between different forms of words accomplishing this liberation. One is the constructing of language-games; another is signaled by those special moments in Wittgenstein's *Investigations* when a special form of words is created, "words that epitomize, separate a thought, with finish permanence (one might say it is with beauty), from the general range of experience"—a form of words to which Cavell gives "the working name of the aphoristic" ("The *Investigations*' Everyday Aesthetics of Itself," p. 260). There is a connection between these special moments in Wittgenstein's philosophy and the sort of case I am interested in in my reading of Mill.

49. I am indebted for what follows to a fruitful conversation with James Conant.

50. *Conditions*, pp. 57–58.

51. "The Fantastic of Philosophy," in *In Quest of the Ordinary: Lines of Skepticism and Romanticism* (Chicago: University of Chicago Press, 1988), pp. 181–88; see p. 188. I have also touched on this topic in my "The Problem of the Higher in Wittgenstein's *Tractatus*," §6.

52. A general discussion of the issue can be found in E. Hammer, *Stanley Cavell: Skepticism, Subjectivity, and the Ordinary* (Cambridge: Polity Press, 2002), pp. 128–42. See also S. Mulhall, *Stanley Cavell: Philosophy's Recounting of the Ordinary* (Oxford: Clarendon Press, 1994), pp. 263–82; S. Bates, "Stanley Cavell and Ethics," in *Stanley Cavell*, ed. R. Eldridge (Cambridge: Cambridge University Press, 2003), pp. 15–47.

53. *Conditions*, p. 125.

54. There is a perfectionist preoccupation with the corruption of the citizen to which Mill responds. See, e.g., Tocqueville as quoted by Mill in "De Tocqueville on Democracy in America [I]" (1835), in *Collected Works*, XVIII:47–90. See pp. 52–53: "It is not by the exercise of power or by the habit of obedience that men are debased; it is by the exercise of a power which they believe to be illegitimate, and by obedience to a rule which they consider to be usurped and unjust." The issue is complicated also by Mill's changes on this from the 1830s to mature writings such as *On Liberty* and *Considerations on Representative Government*.

55. I briefly touch on this topic in my "Hate Speech and Speech Acts: A Reply to Professor Hornsby," in *Normatività Fatti Valori*, ed. R. Egidi, M. Dell'Utri, and M. De Caro (Macerata: Quodlibet, 2003), pp. 311–16, a response to J. Hornsby, "Free Speech and Hate Speech: Language and Rights," ibid., pp. 297–316. For a different treatment from that of Hornsby see J. Butler, *Excitable Speech: A Politics of the Performative* (New York: Routledge, 1997), chap. 2. The phenomenon also includes more than language, that is, anything which is expressive. See for example J. M. Coetzee's *Disgrace* (New York: Viking, 1999), on how the fact of being white in South Africa already expresses a whole history of discrimination and violence that defeats one's conscious and intentional assertion against it.

56. *Conditions*, p. 112.

57. Ibid., p. 115.

58. I wish to thank Arnold Davidson for helpful comments and suggestions on an earlier version of this essay.

CHAPTER 4

1. See James Conant, "Must We Show What We Cannot Say," in *The Senses of Stanley Cavell*, ed. Paul Guyer and Hilary Putnam (Lewisburg, Pa.: Bucknell University Press, 1989), esp. pp. 252–53.

2. See the discussion in Stanley Cavell, *Themes out of School* (Chicago: University of Chicago Press, 1984), p. 36.

3. And the matter was broader: the term "social construction," as in Berger and Luckman's 1966 book, *The Social Construction of Reality*, stood in for or rather with Kuhn in the social sciences. Citations were at fifty to sixty a year in the early 1970s, jumped to 120 in 1974, and then ranged between 140 and 160 a year until the early 1990s. See Andrew Abbott, *Chaos of Disciplines* (Chicago: University of Chicago Press, 2001), chap. 3, and esp. pp. 89ff. Were one to add such books as Burkhart Holzner's *Reality Construction in Society*, the count would go much higher.

4. Ludwig Wittgenstein, *Philosophical Investigations* (Oxford: Basil Blackwell, 1958) (hereafter *PI*), §115.

5. The term was originally Gustav Bergman's. See the discussion in the introduction to Richard Rorty, ed., *The Linguistic Turn* (Chicago: University of Chicago Press, [1967] 1992).

6. We believe that Graham Allison gave this expression currency, generalizing a maxim of Douglas Price's. See Graham Allison, *Essence of Decision* (Boston: Little, Brown, 1971).

7. For some discussion see Gaile Pohlhaus and John R. Wright, "Using Wittgenstein Critically: A Political Approach to Philosophy," *Political Theory* 30, no. 6 (December 2002): 800–827.

8. It is also a matter of historical record that Kuhn and Cavell were colleagues at the University of California, Berkeley, in the early 1960s and that each man's work found its place in the other's. There is a little discussion of the influence of Cavell and ordinary language philosophy in Stephen Fuller, *Thomas Kuhn: A Philosophical History for Our Times* (Chicago: University of Chicago Press, 2000), pp. 8, 54, 68.

9. For Saul Kripke, see his *Wittgenstein on Rules and Private Language* (Cambridge: Cambridge University Press, 1982).

10. Cavell's argument about criteria (too simply: that they serve to establish what something is, but not that it is) on pp. 3–48 of *The Claim of Reason*, 2d ed.

(Oxford: Oxford University Press, 1999) (hereafter *CR*), is aimed most directly at this interpretation. We believe that it has its ancestor in Kant's argument against the ontological proof for the existence of God.

11. In German the terms means either (in biology) "life form," or "way of life."

12. One thinks here of the work of Michael Sandel or Charles Taylor.

13. Stanley Cavell, "Declining Decline: Wittgenstein as a Philosopher of Culture," in his *This New Yet Unapproachable America: Lectures After Emerson After Wittgenstein* (Albuquerque, N.M.: Living Batch Press, 1989), p. 41. (Hereafter DD in the text.) Our discussion in the present section is heavily indebted to this essay.

14. For an examination and rejection of the idea that Wittgenstein's thought is conservative, see David Cerbone, "The Limits of Conservatism," in *Wittgenstein and Political Philosophy*, ed. Cressida J. Heyes (Ithaca and London: Cornell University Press, 2003), 43–62; and Allen Janik, "Notes on the Natural History of Politics" in the same volume, p. 61.

15. See Ernest Gellner, *Words and Things: A Critical Account of Linguistic Philosophy and a Study in Ideology* (London: Gollancz, 1959), with a foreword by Bertrand Russell. This book was the object of critique in one of Cavell's early essays, "Austin at Criticism," in *Must We Mean What We Say?* (New York: Scribners, 1969).

16. See also *PI*, p. 56n: "What we have to mention in order to explain the significance, I mean the importance, of a concept, are often extremely general facts of nature: such facts as are hardly ever mentioned because of their great generality."

17. Thus Wittgenstein will exhort: "Don't think! But look!" (*PI*, §66). Something like this requirement is repeated several times in Wittgenstein. See for instance *Notebooks, 1914–1916* (Oxford: B. Blackwell, 1961), p. 11; *Remarks on the Foundations of Mathematics* (Cambridge, Mass.: MIT Press, 1978), p. 43; *PI*, §578.

18. *PI*, §133. Wittgenstein himself speaks here of "being capable of stopping doing philosophy when I want to"—which seems rather to sketch a picture (perhaps it is a utopia?) of philosophy fully responsive to desire.

19. See the interesting discussion in David Owen, "Cultural Diversity and the Conversation of Justice," *Political Theory*, 27, no. 5 (October 1999): 579–96.

20. This passage has gone mostly uncommented on to our knowledge. For an exception, see the important article by Andrew Norris, "Political Revisions: Stanley Cavell and Political Philosophy," *Political Theory* 30, no. 6 (December 2002): 828–51. See also Thomas Dumm, *A Political Theory of the Ordinary.*

21. The relation of Wittgenstein to Aristotle remains unexplored. And could one see here a way to begin a fruitful dialogue with defenders of "animal rights" such as Peter Singer?

22. See also *CR*, pp. 109–11, 118–25.

23. Friedrich Nietzsche, *Werke Kritische Gesamtausgabe* (Berlin: Gruyter, 1967ff), volume IV-1, p. 190. See Nietzsche's *Schopenhauer as Educator* and the discussion in Cavell's *Conditions Handsome and Unhandsome*, pp. 49ff. Cavell's discussion here has been seized on by several others as an entry into political philosophy. To some degree it is, although it is much more an entry into a critique of Rawls, and a lot depends on whether one thinks Rawls is doing political philosophy or political theory or moral philosophy, and what the difference is between them. See here for instance Stephen Mulhall, *Stanley Cavell: Philosophy's Recounting of the Ordinary* (Oxford: Clarendon, 1999); Stephen Mulhall, "Promising, Consent, and Citizenship: Rawls and Cavell on Morality and Politics," *Political Theory* 25, no. 2 (April 1997): 171–92; Richard Shusterman, "Putnam and Cavell on the Ethics of Democracy," *Political Theory* 25, no. 2 (April 1997): 193–214; Dan Conway, *Nietzsche and the Political* (London: Routledge, 1996); James Conant, "'Emerson as Educator' (from 'Nietzsche's Perfectionism: A Reading of Schopenhauer as Educator')," *Emerson Studies Quarterly* 43, nos. 1–4 (1997); Tracy B. Strong, "The Song in the Self," *New Nietzsche Studies* 1, no. 1/2. As important an entry to political theory is Cavell's essay "The Politics of Interpretation," in *Themes out of School* (Chicago: University of Chicago Press, 1984); and the essay on Coriolanus in the same volume.

24. It is fair to say that some of the problems in Kuhn come from his being overly influenced by N. R. Hanson's adoption of Gestalt psychology (of which the duck-rabbit is the classic example). He pays far too little attention to the *activity* of change: for Kuhn, paradigm "switches" acquire an almost magical quality. See the discussion in *PI*, §§194–95; and discussion of those passages in Tracy B. Strong, *The Idea of Political Theory* (Notre Dame: Notre Dame Press, 1991), chap. 3.

25. See, in this connection, the excellent essay of Adam Phillips, "A Stab at Hinting," in his *The Beast in the Nursery: On Curiosity and Other Appetites* (Pantheon: New York, 1998).

26. To teach in a manner that does not privilege the teacher and yet is still teaching is very difficult for both the teacher and the student, as any teacher who has had students who have not (yet?) found their own voice will attest. See the end of Rousseau's *Emile* for a locus classicus about students.

27. For an excellent examination of what the incompatibilities are, see James Tully, "Wittgenstein and Political Philosophy," in *Wittgenstein and Political Philosophy*, esp. pp. 23–36.

28. For an extended discussion of Kripke, see Stanley Cavell, *Conditions Handsome and Unhandsome* (Chicago: University of Chicago Press, 1990), pp. 44–100.

29. We draw here on Conant, "Must We Show What We Cannot Say?," in *The Senses of Stanley Cavell*.

30. See the discussion in DD, p. 46; and in Hanna F. Pitkin, *Wittgenstein and*

Justice (Berkeley and Los Angeles: University of California Press, 1972).

31. See Hannah Arendt, "What Is Authority?" in *Between Past and Future* (New York: Viking, 1968), p. 101.

32. For an alternative understanding, see David Owen and Tracy B. Strong, "Introduction," to Max Weber, *The Vocation Lectures* (Indianapolis: Hackett Publishing, 2004).

33. Pitkin, *Wittgenstein and Justice*, pp. 21–22.

34. For Cavell, see chap. 9 ("Knowing and Acknowledging") of *Must We Mean What We Say?*; and for Wittgenstein, see his *On Certainty*, §378 ("Knowledge is in the end based on acknowledgment"). Cavell wrote his essay without knowledge of the then-unpublished Wittgenstein passage. Although we cannot go into it here, this move in Cavell constitutes a radicalization of various aspects of Kantian epistemology, specifically the relation between the noumenal and the phenomenal. See his discussion of Heidegger in the later part of *The Senses of Walden*.

35. See however her dismantling of that word.

36. For an example see Ted Miller and Tracy B. Strong, "Meaning and Contexts: Mr. Skinner's Hobbes and the English Mode of Political Theory," *Inquiry* (Fall 1997).

37. For a critique of a contemporary appropriation of this claim, see Ted Miller and Tracy B. Strong, "Meanings and Contexts: Mr. Skinner's Hobbes and the English Mode of Political Theory," *Inquiry* (Fall 1997).

38. The literature on performatives is enormous. See the work of Stanley Fish, John Searle, Jacques Derrida, and many, many others. See the discussion below.

39. "Counter-Philosophy and the Pawn of Voice," in Stanley Cavell, *A Pitch of Philosophy* (Cambridge: Harvard University Press, 1994).

40. Hannah Pitkin, *Wittgenstein and Justice*, p. 39.

41. Judith Butler, *Gender Trouble* (New York: Routledge, 1989); idem, *Bodies That Matter* (New York: Routledge, 1993); idem, *Excitable Speech: A Politics of the Performative* (New York: Routledge, 1997); Bonnie Honig, "Declarations of Independence: Arendt and Derrida on the Problem of Founding a Republic," *American Political Science Review* 85, no. 1 (March 1991): 97–113; Jacques Derrida, "Signature Event Context," in his *Margins of Philosophy* (Chicago: University of Chicago Press, 1982), §§3 and 4; and idem, *Limited Inc* (reprint ed., Evanston, Ill.: Northwestern University Press, 1988).

42. Cavell, *Pitch of Philosophy*, second essay.

43. The titles of two of the essays in Austin's *Philosophical Papers* (New York: Oxford University Press, 1979).

44. Butler, while conceding what she takes to be Pierre Bourdieu's criticism of deconstruction's sometime view that "the speech act, by virtue of its internal powers, breaks with every context from which it emerges," nevertheless insists that "the possibility for the speech act to take on a non-ordinary meaning, to function

in contexts where it has not belonged, is precisely the political promise of the performative." See Butler, *Excitable Speech*, p. 161.

45. J. L. Austin, *How to Do Things with Words* (Cambridge, Mass.: Harvard University Press, [1961] 1975); and an immense literature including especially Shoshana Felman, *The Literary Speech Act: Don Juan with J. L. Austin, or Seduction in Two Languages* (Ithaca: Cornell University Press, 1983); and Judith Butler, *Excitable Speech* (New York: Routledge, 1997). The following section draws upon Tracy Strong, "Politics and Time" (forthcoming).

46. Monique Wittig is pointing to the realm of performativity when she asserts that gender introduces the "division of Being" into language, such that "gender must then be destroyed." She holds that contests over naming become contests over Being: "The possibility of [gender's] destruction is given through the very exercise of language. For each time I say 'I,' I reorganize the world from my point of view and through abstraction I lay claim to universality. This fact holds true for every locutor" (Monique Wittig, "The Mark of Gender," in *The Straight Mind and Other Essays* [Boston: Beacon Press, 1985], p. 81). See again Judith Butler's *Gender Trouble* (New York: Routledge, 1989); *Bodies That Matter* (New York: Routledge, 1993); and *Excitable Speech* (New York: Routledge, 1997); as well as a number of other theorists on the politics of gender performativity. See Judith Butler and Joan W. Scott, eds. *Feminists Theorize the Political* (New York: Routledge, 1992).

47. We are indebted for the example (though our discussion is different) to Josiah Ober, *The Athenian Revolution* (Princeton: Princeton University Press, 1996), pp. 46ff. He draws upon Sandy Petrey, *Realism and Revolution* (Ithaca: Cornell University Press, 1988).

48. For a parallel investigation of how one ordinary might replace another, see the penetrating essay by Linda Zerilli, "Doing Without Knowing: Feminism's Politics of the Ordinary," *Political Theory* 26, no. 4 (1998): 435–58, reprinted in Cressida Heyes, ed., *Wittgenstein and Political Philosophy*, pp. 129–48.

49. Slavoj Zizek, "A Leftist Plea for 'Eurocentrism,'" *Critical Inquiry* 24, no. 4 (Summer 1998). Zizek's reflections are worth quoting at length: "The political struggle proper is therefore never simply a rational debate between multiple interests but, simultaneously, the struggle for one's voice to be heard. . . . When the excluded, from the Greek demos to Polish workers, protested against the ruling elite (the aristocracy or nomenklatura), the true stakes were not only their explicit demands (for higher wages, better working conditions, and so forth) but their very right to be heard. . . . In this precise sense, politics and democracy are synonymous: the basic aim of antidemocratic politics always and by definition is and was depoliticization." See the discussion in Marcel Hénaff and Tracy B. Strong, "Conclusion: Public Space, Virtual Space and Democracy," in *Public Space and Democracy* (Minneapolis: University of Minnesota Press, 2001). See also Marcel

Detienne, "Public Space and the Autonomy of the First Greek Cities," in *Public Space and Democracy.*

50. J. J. Rousseau, *Social Contract*, bk. 3, chap. 10. After which Rousseau remarks, they "fall back into the most perfect Hobbism."

51. See his notion of an "evanescent homogeneity" of interests and of democracy as a "fugitive" or unstable political mode that nevertheless embodies the essence of the political way of being in the world (Sheldon S. Wolin, "Fugitive Democracy," in *Democracy and Difference*, ed. Seyla Benhabib [Princeton: Princeton University Press, 1996]). See also the seven new chapters in the new edition of his *Politics and Vision*, forthcoming from Princeton University Press.

52. *Fragments politiques*, in *Oeuvres complètes*, vol. 3, p. 485.

53. *Social Contract*, iii, 11, in *Oeuvres complètes*, vol. 3, p. 424.

54. For a discussion of representation in Rousseau, see C. Nathan Dugan and Tracy B. Strong, "'A Language More Vital than Speech': Rousseau on Music, Representation and Language," in *Cambridge Companion to Rousseau*, ed. Patrick Riley (Cambridge: Cambridge University Press, 2000).

55. See Cavell's demolition of Paul Deman's too thin understanding of this famous line from Yeats's "Among School Children" (Cavell, "The Politics of Interpretation," in *Themes out of School* [Chicago: University of Chicago Press, 1984], pp. 45–47).

56. Cavell, "Finding as Founding: Taking Steps in Emerson's 'Experience,'" in *This New Yet Unapproachable America*, p. 94.

57. See DD, pp. 56–57: "I must empty out *my* contribution to words, so that language itself, as if beyond me, exclusively takes over responsibility for meaning." Among the many passages that might be adduced from the *Claim of Reason* to give a sense of how this theme resonates throughout Cavell's reading of Wittgenstein's response to skepticism by way of the ordinary, two will have to suffice:

"What is left out of an expression if it is used 'outside its ordinary language game' is not necessarily what the *words* mean . . . but what we mean in using them when and where we do" (*CR*, 207).

"What is disappointing about [Wittgenstein's grammatical, that is to say, our ordinary] criteria? There is something they do not do; it can seem the essential. I have to know what they are for; I have to accept them, use them" (*CR*, 83).

58. Sheldon S. Wolin, "Paradigms and Political Theories," in *Politics and Experience: Essays Presented to Michael Oakeshott*, ed. Preston King and B. C. Parekh (Cambridge: Cambridge University Press, 1968), pp. 125–52.

CHAPTER 5

1. From "The Man with a Blue Guitar," in Wallace Stevens, *The Palm at the End of the Mind: Selected Poems and a Play*, ed. Holly Stevens (New York: Vintage, 1972), p. 133.

2. This for instance is the tack taken by David Owen in "Cultural Diversity and the Conversation of Justice," *Political Theory* 27, no. 5 (October 1999): 579–96.

3. On contract theory, see Cavell, *The Claim of Reason* (New York: Oxford University Press, 1979), pp. 22ff (hereafter *CR*); Cavell, "The Conversation of Justice: Rawls and the Drama of Consent," in *Conditions Handsome and Unhandsome* (Chicago: University of Chicago Press, 1990); and chap. 3 of Stephen Mulhall, *Stanley Cavell: Philosophy's Recounting of the Ordinary* (Oxford: Clarendon Press, 1994). On the universal voice, compare the Preface to *Conditions Handsome and Unhandsome*, pp. xxvi–xxvii; and "Aesthetic Problems of Modern Philosophy," in *Must We Mean What We Say?* (Cambridge: Cambridge University Press, 1969).

4. For the role, such that it is, of language in Rousseau's contract theory, see *The Social Contract*, trans. M. Cranston (New York: Penguin, 1968), pp. 86, 137, 148–49, 151; and the discussion of fables in the Fourth Walk of the *Reveries of a Solitary Walker*, trans. P. France (New York: Penguin, 1979). On knowing and acknowledgment, see the essay of that name in *Must We Mean What We Say?* For a provisional definition of Cavell's central concept of skepticism, see his *CR*, pp. 46 and 493; and "The Philosopher in American Life," in *In Quest of the Ordinary* (Chicago: University of Chicago Press, 1988).

5. For Pitkin's "unusual" reliance upon Cavell's published and unpublished work, see *Wittgenstein and Justice* (Berkeley: University of California Press, 1972), pp. viii and xiii and the footnotes citing him throughout the text. Perhaps in part because Cavell's discussion of contract theory had not yet been published, Pitkin does not discuss it.

6. Cavell notes that "moral discourse is not singly an order of public debate on issues known and taken to be of moment, but is a form of intimate examination, you might say private, by one soul of another. It teaches us to ask not alone, What is to be done?, but as well, What am I to do? And not just, Is what the other does acceptable?, but as well, How am I prepared to confront that other?" (*CR*, p. xii). What is too easily overlooked here is the qualifying *singly* and the fact that Cavell is describing not two fields of activity but two aspects of the same activity: talking. Contrast Pitkin, who writes, in strikingly similar language: "The central question of moral discourse might be characterized as 'what was done?' [while] the central question in politics would have to be . . . 'what shall we do?'" (pp. 206–7), and who argues that "there is no such thing as private politics, intimate politics" (p. 204).

7. See in this regard Arendt's admission that she herself asks what is left of political questions when their "social" content is removed in *Hannah Arendt: The Recovery of the Public World*, ed. M. Hill (New York: St. Martin's, 1979), pp. 315ff. It is striking that Arendt avoids making the political empty and irrelevant insofar as she deemphasizes the categorical distinctions between the public and the private,

and emphasizes the notion of politics as action in speech as opposed to social administration.

8. Plato, *Gorgias*, trans. W. D. Woodhead, in *The Collected Dialogues of Plato*, ed. E. Hamilton and H. Cairns (Princeton: Princeton University Press, 1961), 521d.

9. Plato, *Republic*, trans. A. Bloom (New York: Basic Books, 1991), 414d. (Further references to the *Republic* will be given in the text.) This example may seem overly prejudicial, focusing as it does upon a notorious attempt to eliminate distinctions between the public and the private. But this will hinge on how seriously one takes Socrates' claim that this is the elimination of a misunderstanding. Compare the discussion of myths (with an example from the *Republic*) in *CR*, p. 365.

10. Wittgenstein, *Philosophical Investigations*, 3rd ed., trans. G.E.M. Anscombe (New York: Macmillan, 1968), part I:123 (hereafter *PI*); and Cavell, "Declining Decline: Wittgenstein as a Philosopher of Culture," in *This New Yet Unapproachable America* (Albuquerque: Living Batch Press, 1989), pp. 36 and 39–40. Compare p. 172 of "Kierkegaard's *On Authority and Revelation*," in *Must We Mean What We Say?*, where Cavell pairs the same passage from Kierkegaard with the passage from the *Investigations* (p. 223) that describes our finding others enigmatic as one in which a knowledge of the language of a people without familiarity with their traditions leaves us unable to find ourselves in them (*Wir können uns nicht in sie finden*).

11. *CR*, p. 179. And compare Cavell's characterization of the wish of self-effacement that underlies skepticism on pp. 351–52 of *CR*, a characterization that explicitly compares this problem to that of the legitimacy of the state.

12. Though it should be noted, first, that Cavell describes Wittgenstein as doing the work of the Socratic gadfly in "Existentialism and Analytic Philosophy" (in *Themes out of School* [Chicago: University of Chicago Press, 1984], p. 199; but cf. p. 230) and, second, that Cavell's teacher Austin claims Socrates as a predecessor when he addresses the status of what he prefers to call "linguistic phenomenology" in "A Plea for Excuses" (*Philosophical Papers*, ed. J. O. Urmson and G. J. Warnock [Oxford: Oxford University Press, 1961], pp. 130–31). On Socrates as therapist, see Jonathan Lear, *Open Minded: Working Out the Logic of the Soul* (London: Harvard University Press, 1998), particularly the fourth and seventh essays.

13. *CR*, p. 3.

14. Rosen, *Nihilism: A Philosophical Essay* (London: Yale University Press, 1969), p. 12n12.

15. Compare Sheldon Wolin's classic *Politics and Vision*: "political philosophy constitutes a form of 'seeing' political phenomena" (Wolin, *Politics and Vision: Continuity and Innovation in Western Political Thought*, expanded ed. [Princeton: Princeton University Press, 2004], p. 17). And, in a more direct line of influence for Cavell, Wittgenstein: "I wanted to put this picture before your eyes, and your

acceptance of this picture consists in your being inclined to regard a given case differently; that is, to compare it with *this* set of pictures. I have changed your *way of seeing [Anschauungsweise]*" (Wittgenstein, *Zettel*, ed. G.E.M. Anscombe and G. H. von Wright, trans. G.E.M. Anscombe [Berkeley: University of California Press, 1970], p. 461); and see Wittgenstein, *PI*, §144. For unusually concrete examples of Cavell's attempt to effect such a change, see his discussion of what it means "to speak sensibly of seeing or treating or taking persons as persons," in *CR*, pp. 372ff.

16. *CR*, pp. xi–xii; compare p. 58 of *A Pitch of Philosophy* (London: Harvard University Press, 1994), where the same is said of the book that (parts of) that dissertation eventually became.

17. Cavell will draw a number of connections between narcissism and Wittgenstein's "private language argument"; see for example Cavell, *Pursuits of Happiness: The Hollywood Comedy of Remarriage* (Cambridge, Mass., and London: Harvard University Press, 1981), p. 74; and note the political echoes in the title of the latter.

18. *CR*, p. xii.

19. I wrote and published this essay a few years before the appearance of Cavell's *Cities of Words: Pedagogical Letters on a Register of the Moral Life* (Cambridge, Mass.: Belknap, 2004), in which Cavell foregrounds both the political in general and the significance of Aristotle in particular much more than he had in earlier writings. He does so, however, in ways that are, I think, fully consonant with what I say here.

20. "*Coriolanus* and Interpretations of Politics," in *Themes out of School*, p. 84.

21. Aristotle, *Politics*, trans. E. Barker and R. F. Stalley (New York: Oxford University Press, 1998), p. 1253a. Further references to the *Politics* will be given in the text.

22. On the interminable nature of "the conversation of justice," see *Conditions Handsome and Unhandsome*, p. xxv.

23. Emerson, "The American Scholar," in *Selected Essays* (New York: Penguin, 1982), p. 84.

24. *A Pitch of Philosophy*, pp. 46 and 76.

25. The example of the feast here recalls the *Coriolanus* essay's interest in cannibalism, in particular the connection Cavell makes there between the common feast and the common language (pp. 83f).

26. It may be for this reason that when he writes of Emerson's "reversing . . . Plato's allegory of the soul by the social," he focuses upon Plato and not Aristotle: In what is perhaps already nostalgia, Aristotle celebrates a *polis* life that, though quickly vanishing, is found in cities other than those made of words (*Luftgebäude*). That said, Aristotle's connection of the body with democracy is an im-

portant one for Cavell's purposes. See *Conditions Handsome and Unhandsome*, p. xxx; and compare one of Cavell's few references to Aristotle in "Aversive Thinking," p. 56 in the same volume, where Aristotle's perfectionist emphasis upon the cultural preconditions of "a democratic existence" is compared with that of Plato and Nietzsche.

27. "*Coriolanus* and Interpretations of Politics," pp. 88, 83–84, and 86. If this seems to cast the majority of us into too passive a role, we should recall *CR*, p. 58: "who makes sure that the singing is on pitch, the singer or the sung to?"; and Emerson, whose question in "Self-Reliance" makes sense of Cavell's: "If you can hear what these patriarchs say, surely you can reply to them in the same pitch of voice?" (*Selected Essays*, p. 199). To gauge the wider significance of this back and forth, consider the title of Cavell's recent *A Pitch of Philosophy*.

28. *CR*, p. 5.

29. Gadamer's account is the more relevant here, focusing as it does on the threat of skepticism: Gadamer argues that, in the Aristotelian, humanist tradition, "what gives the human will its direction is not the abstract universality of reason but the concrete universality represented by the community of a group, a people, a nation, or the whole human race. Hence developing this communal sense is of decisive importance for living" (*Truth and Method*, 2d ed., trans. J. Weinsheimer and D. Marshall [New York: Continuum, 1999], p. 21). But such a sense cannot meet the epistemological demands of modernity. Kant "solves" this problem by grounding aesthetics on taste understood as the free play of the cognitive faculties. This grounding "does justice to both aspects of the phenomenon: its empirical non-universality and its *a priori* claim to universality. But the price that he pays for this legitimation of critique in the area of taste is that he denies that taste has any *significance as knowledge*. He reduces *sensus communis* to a subjective principle" (p. 43). Hence the Kantian *sensus communis aestheticus* is only a subjectivized form of the common sense that for republicans such as Vico and Shaftesbury made possible free civic culture. Kant himself hints at the political origins of the *sensus communis* when he distinguishes judgment (*Urteilskraft*) from the understanding and Reason by writing that though judgment has a "territory," unlike the other two "it has not a field of objects appropriate to it as its realm" over which it might have the authority to prescribe laws (Kant, *Critique of Judgment*, trans. J. C. Meredith [Oxford: Clarendon, 1989], p. 15). This field was precisely the free republic, the "public thing" that is now found only in the reflective judgments of aesthetics. Whether this displacement is the result of the threat of skepticism is less clear. Kant says that "we assume a common sense as the necessary condition of the universal communicability of our knowledge, which is presupposed in every logic and every principle of knowledge that is not one of skepticism" (*Critique of Judgment*, p. 84). But does this mean that in assuming the *sensus communis* Kant is assuming that skepticism is false, or that in assuming that logic and principles of knowledge

are answerable to skepticism he is making the *sensus communis* other and less than it would otherwise be, other than it was?

30. *CR*, p. 20. Mulhall for instance sees this discussion as beginning two pages later than it does, and hence passes over this connection. See Mulhall, *Stanley Cavell*, p. 55.

31. Though the distinguished Aristotle scholar Jonathan Lear suggests that some of this confidence is a performative front for Aristotle's own sense that this life is unfounded. See Lear, *Happiness, Death, and the Remainder of Life* (Cambridge, Mass.: Harvard University Press, 2000), pp. 6ff.

32. Consider in this regard the etymological roots of *decision*—or of *Entscheidung*. As a counter to the perhaps overly existentialist note I strike here, see Cavell's discussion of the concept of decision throughout *CR* and in "The Availability of Wittgenstein's Later Philosophy," particularly the note on p. 54. For a good discussion of *krisis* see Ron Polansky's "The Unity of Plato's *Crito*," *Scholia: Natal Studies in Classical Antiquity* 6 (1997).

33. *The Senses of Walden*, expanded ed. (San Francisco: North Point Press, 1981), p. 85. Jay Bernstein is thus off the mark when, in his generally excellent *The Fate of Art* (University Park: Pennsylvania State University Press, 1992), he suggests that Cavell's account of the *sensus communis* is "an image of given community, of a passive *sensus communis*, of like-mindedness without history, of like-mindedness that is given rather than created" (p. 102).

34. *CR*, p. 23; and compare p. 25.

35. *The Ethics of Authenticity* (Canadian Broadcast Corporation, 1991), p. 27; compare Taylor's "The Politics of Recognition," in *Multiculturalism: A Critical Reader*, ed. D. Goldberg (Cambridge: Blackwell, 1994), pp. 75–106, which without acknowledgment repeats this as well as most of the earlier book's main points almost word for word.

36. Rousseau, *Reveries of a Solitary Walker*, p. 89.

37. It follows that Stephen Mulhall is if nothing else overly hasty when he writes that Cavell's work "confirms[s] the accuracy and perceptiveness of Taylor's analysis of modernity" (Mulhall, *Stanley Cavell*, p. 305).

38. *Reveries of a Solitary Walker*, p. 27. In the *Discourse on the Origins of Inequality*, Rousseau notes that people today have a different "sentiment of existence" than they once did. The soul of the "savage . . . is given over to the sole sentiment of its present existence [*seul sentiment de son existence actuelle*] without any idea of the future" (*The First and Second Discourses*, trans. R. and J. Masters [New York: St. Martin's, 1964], p. 117). It is also oblivious to others of its type: "the savage lives within himself; the sociable man, always outside himself, knows only how to live in the opinion of others; and it is, so to speak, from their judgment alone that he draws the sentiment of his own existence [*le sentiment de sa propre existence*]" (p. 179). Clearly the former fits Taylor's model better. But reading this as a

description of Rousseau in the fifth Reverie would require seeing him as a savage, and would violate Rousseau's insistence that such anachronism or atavism is foolishness (p. 201). Instead he should be seen as he sees himself: as a character at the margins of society, one who writes to others of what he feels in their absence.

39. Aristotle, *Nicomachean Ethics*, trans. T. Irwin (Cambridge: Hackett, 1985), p. 1177b. Further references to the *Ethics* will be given in the text.

40. He makes a rather feeble attempt to in the *Politics*, when he concludes a discussion of the relative merits of the political and the philosophical lives with a somewhat bizarre account of a contemplative city (pp. 1324a–25b). Because my identification of Aristotle as symptomatic or exemplary of the split between these ideals or ideas of the human does not take him to be identifying *himself* as such, the analysis I propose here differs considerably from that advanced by Martha Nussbaum in *The Fragility of Goodness* (New York: Cambridge University Press, 1986). Nussbaum argues that Aristotle's "philosophy of appearances" should be seen as a therapeutic attempt to return us to the ordinary comparable to that of Wittgenstein (260 and 261), though with the caveat that Aristotle's work is less destructive in intent, aimed as it is at "removing imposture" (which she earlier identifies as "bad philosophy") so as to make it possible for the average person to begin to get, and appreciate, the positive *paideia* which he or she desires (p. 262). Contrasting Aristotle with Empedocles, Parmenides, and Plato's Socrates, who all associated philosophy with the divine, Nussbaum describes him as "the professional human being" (p. 261). She is of course aware of the imagery of divinity that characterizes book ten of the *Ethics*, and argues persuasively that this Platonism is at odds with the bulk of Aristotle's work (p. 377). But what she does not do is to show how Aristotle *incorporates* this rejected Platonism into his own work. Indeed, not only does Aristotle not try to resolve the conflict between the tenth book and the views that precede it; he does not even *acknowledge* the conflict. What we have is a series of contradictions, rather than conversational exchanges—and this in itself does not constitute a dialectical consideration of an opposing view. Least of all does it constitute therapy for one who is bewitched by the Platonic position. Given these profound differences it is somewhat ironic that Nussbaum may have been influenced by Cavell; see in this regard her acknowledgments and p. 442n78.

41. For a contrary reading of Aristotle that emphasizes the continuity between "ordinary life" (*gewöhnliches Leben*) and the philosopher's onto-theological experience of the divine, see Joachim Ritter, "Die Lehre vom Ursprung und Sinn der Theorie bei Aristoteles," *Metaphysik und Politik: Studien zu Aristoteles und Hegel*, expanded ed. (Baden-Baden: Suhrkamp, 2003).

42. *CR*, p. 79.

43. *The Senses of Walden*, p. 55.

44. Thomas McCarthy, "Critique of Impure Reason," *Political Theory* 18, no. 3 (August 1990): 440. When I wrote this essay David Owen's "Genealogy as Perspic-

uous Representation" was not yet published, and I was unfamiliar with his helpful distinction between "ideological captivity," in which our beliefs are false, and
"aspectual captivity," in which a picture holds us captive and limits the possible
beliefs we might have in a manner open only to indirect therapy that brings us to
see ourselves in a new way (Owen, "Genealogy as Perspicuous Representation," in
The Grammar of Politics: Wittgenstein and Political Philosophy, ed. C. Heyes [Itha-
ca: Cornell University Press, 2003]). The latter is clearly Cavell's concern, as it is
Wittgenstein's. Though Owen does not cite it, the following passage from *Culture
and Value* sums up his point nicely: "The effect of making men think in accordance with dogmas, perhaps in the form of certain graphic propositions, will be
very peculiar: I am not thinking of these dogmas as determining men's opinions
but rather as completely controlling the *expression* of all opinions. People will live
under an absolute, palpable tyranny, though without being able to say that they
are not free" (Wittgenstein, *Culture and Value*, ed. G. H. von Wright [Chicago:
University of Chicago Press, 1984], p. 28e).

45. *CR*, p. 44. On common sense and the hegemonic, see Ian Lustick, *Unsettled States, Disputed Lands* (London: Cornell University Press, 1993), pp. 43, 53–56,
and 60.

46. Cavell, "Declining Decline," pp. 43–44; compare *CR*, p. 125. In an interview with James Conant, Cavell says that he has with time "become more confident in understanding the turn to ordinary language philosophy, indeed to a certain sort of modern philosophizing altogether, as an experience of conversion";
and he describes his own experience of Austin's work in precisely these terms. Of
Austin's painstaking analysis of the way native English speakers carefully but utterly unself-consciously use the expressions "I know" and "I believe" quite differently, and say, for instance, "How do you know?" and "Why do you believe?" but
not "Why do you know?" or "How do you believe?," Cavell says, "You may feel
that these grammatical forms are arbitrary, or anyway that they cannot possibly
carry very great significance. But I can testify that there is a mood in which that
simple set of observations can itself (well, almost itself) effect something like a
philosophical conversion. You feel that your whole life you have discounted your
experience of the daily events of language, taken them for inherently trivial matters, then all of a sudden you feel: it is myself, the events of my daily existence, my
life in language, that I have taken as inherently trivial" ("James Conant: Interview
with Cavell," *The Senses of Stanley Cavell*, ed. R. Fleming and M. Payne [Lewis-
burg, Pa.: Bucknell University Press, 1989], pp. 45 and 44). Compare *CR*, p. xvii,
where Cavell writes of Wittgenstein's destruction of houses of air, "What feels like
destruction, what expresses itself here in the idea of destruction, is really a shift in
what we are asked to let interest us, in the tumbling of our ideas of the great and
the important, as in conversion."

47. The conservative and the transfigurative are said by Cavell to be differ-

ent ways of understanding Wittgenstein's notion of forms of life (*Lebensformen*), where the conservative reading emphasizes the idea that our language and hence our (vocabulary of) need is a set of historical conventions, conventions that might be the subject of a decision or a contract; and the challenge to that reading empha-sizes the notion that such conventions and contracts and choices are based upon "biological" and natural needs that they can themselves misinterpret, or misrep-resent: "The biological interpretation of form of life is not merely another avail-able interpretation to that of the ethnographical, but contests its sense of politi-cal or social conservatism" (*This New Yet Unapproachable America*, p. 44). This raises issues that Cavell does not here pursue. In the introduction to the volume within which "Declining Decline" is found, he notes that he has recently begun but not yet finished Nancy and Lacoue-Labarthe's *Literary Absolute* (pp. 2, 11, and 20). What primarily interests him here in this text are the interwoven (Romantic) notions of the fragment as a form of work, of *Ausbildung* as the completion and perfection of nature, and of that education's centrally requiring a uniting of poet-ry and philosophy. He moves from noting this to considering these favorite lines from Emerson's "The American Scholar": "This revolution [in human aspiration] is to be wrought by the gradual domestication of the idea of Culture. The main enterprise of the world for splendor, for extent, is the upbuilding of a man. Here are materials strewn along the ground." Cavell reads this last line in potentially political terms, as referring to "the men and women that are scattered (that is, as yet unsocial)," and in turn characterizes this lack of sociality as a lack (perhaps it-self incomplete) of humanity: "To go further with these thoughts is, for me, to take on the issues of what I conceive as moral perfectionism . . . attracting the hu-man . . . to the work of becoming human" (pp. 9 and 10). (Given that, as we have seen, Emerson depicts "the social state" as one in which we are dismembered, we might better speak of "unpolitical" here.) Cavell indicates that one of his differ-ences with deconstruction concerns the latter's distrust or denial of "a certain soci-ality." I do not know if that sociality is the same one Cavell hears called for in Em-erson, and I would not want to be the one to give precise reference to the troubled term *deconstruction*. But I imagine that most would see Nancy and Lacoue-Lab-arthe as being covered by it, if only because of the nature of their relation to the work of Derrida. Hence it may be important to note that *The Literary Absolute*'s depiction of the themes that interest Cavell is much more critical and disturbed than his; in particular that its picture of the fantasy of *autopoeisis* incorporated in these themes is part and parcel of what its authors elsewhere term the logic of fas-cism. Corresponding to the *subject-work* of Romanticism ("the becoming-artist of the work or absolute auto-production itself: man as the work of art creating itself, art henceforth identified with the being-artist") is the vision of the *Volk* as the re-ciprocation between and production of nature and culture and as such the most human form of humanity; as the natural culture it is nothing other than the "autoimagining or autofictioning of nature." Totalitarian movements defy all utilitarian considerations because the natural totality has to be constantly reasserted, and this requires unceasing movement, the continual production and elimination of the unnatural. Terror as the free defiance of all laws can never settle into a way of life of a nation-state; instead, it must endlessly purify itself and the outer world. This is the impossible logic of the *autopoiesis* of the absolute subject. No doubt this is long ways from Emerson's call for a gathering of our scattered parts; but, if the authors of *The Literary Absolute* are right, the passage here is not impassable. I discuss this argument at length elsewhere ("Jean-Luc Nancy and the Myth of the Common," *Constellations* 7, no. 2 [June 2000]) and raise these claims here only to indicate that if there is a distrust of sociality here, it is not wholly unsupported. And considering it may prove necessary for an Emersonian moral perfectionist. If we say that we are yet to become human, are we saying that we are not yet human? And if we are, what status (and rights) do these as yet inhuman creatures have? Such questions are most forcefully raised in the recent work of Giorgio Agamben, which I discuss in "Giorgio Agamben and the Politics of the Living Dead," *Diacritics* 30, no. 4 (Winter 2002); Cavell begins to address them in *Conditions Handsome and Unhandsome*, pp. xvi–xvii, and in the closing pages of "Emerson's Constitutional Amending," *Philosophical Passages* (Oxford: Blackwell, 1995).

48. *This New Yet Unapproachable America: Lectures After Emerson After Wittgenstein* (Albuquerque: Living Batch Press, 1989), p. 44.

49. For evidence of this simply contrast the above discussions of *The Social Contract* and of the *Reveries*.

50. It is true that the language of revolution will reappear in *Conditions Handsome and Unhandsome*, but always, I think, in the sense indicated above. So for instance Cavell will use the verb *revolutionize* rather than *revolt* (pp. 6–7).

51. *This New Yet Unapproachable America*, p. 43; and see "The Argument of the Ordinary," p. 83. Compare Emerson: "The ruin or the blank that we see when we look at nature, is in our own eye. The axis of vision is not coincident with the axis of things, and so they appear not transparent but opaque" (*Selected Essays*, p. 79).

52. Friedrich Nietzsche, *The Genealogy of Morals*, trans. R. J. Hollingdale and W. Kaufmann (New York: Vintage, 1989), III:12.

53. Likewise, the more concrete the image is made, the more our weight rests upon and is supported by our need.

54. One might invoke as well Kierkegaard's enigmatic description of the "essential author": he "has his own perspective, he constantly comes behind himself in his individual productions; he strives forward indeed, but within the totality, not after it; he never raises more doubt than he can explain . . . " ("Introduction," *On Authority and Revelation: The Book on Adler*, trans. Walter Lowie [New York: Everyman's Library, 1994], p. 117). In his essay on *The Book on Adler*, Cavell proposes that speaking religiously is "to speak from a particular perspective, as it were

to mean anything you say in a special way" ("Kierkegaard's *On Authority and Revelation*," p. 172). All of this is to be contrasted I think with the idea that the surmounting of our problems puts us in the position to see the world rightly (Wittgenstein, *Tractatus Logico-Philosophicus*, trans. C. K. Ogden [London: Routledge & Kegan Paul, 1982], VI:65).

55. "The Conversation of Justice: Rawls and the Drama of Consent," p. 109.

56. *A Pitch of Philosophy*, p. 60. Cavell thus calls for a more radical change than does Stuart Hampshire, who also uses the language of conversion, though in a less personally involved sense: "To follow through the ethical implications of these propositions about the normality of conflict, these Heracleitean truths, a kind of moral conversion is needed, a new way of looking at all the virtues, including the virtue of justice. We need to turn around the mirror of theory, so that we see ourselves both as we are and as we have been" (*Justice Is Conflict* [Princeton: Princeton University Press, 2000], pp. 33–34).

57. Augustine, *The City of God*, bk. XII, chap. 6, in Augustine, *Political Writings*, trans. M. Tkacz and D. Kries (Indianapolis: Hackett, 1994), p. 87 (emphasis added).

58. Cavell's discussion of voice in Ibsen's play invites comparison with his discussions of personal style and of Emerson's comment, "Character teaches above our will. Men imagine that they communicate their virtue or vice only by overt actions, and do not see that virtue or vice emits a breath at every moment." See Cavell, "The *Investigations*' Everyday Aesthetics of Itself," *Wittgenstein in America*, ed. T. McCarthy and S. Stidd (Oxford: Clarendon Press, 2001), pp. 264–65 and 251.

59. "The Conversation of Justice," p. 109.

60. Ibsen, *A Doll's House and Other Plays*, trans. P. Watts (New York: Penguin, 1963), p. 228.

61. Brian Johnston, *Text and Supertext in Ibsen's Drama* (University Park and London: Pennsylvania State Press, 1989), p. 145. The comparison with Marx is one Cavell does "not quite wish" to make ("The Conversation of Justice," p. 110).

62. Consider in this regard Socrates' characterization of the noble dogs that defend the feverish city and from whom the ruling class of philosophers will emerge as being philosophical because they are angry when confronted with those they don't know, and gentle with those whom they know, "even if (they) never had a good experience with him" (p. 376a). Is this a loving pursuit of either wisdom or the happy life?

63. "Obvious candidate features are its ideas of (1) a mode of conversation, (2) between (older and younger) friends, (3) one of whom is intellectually authoritative because (4) his life is somehow exemplary or representative of a life the other(s) are attracted to, and (5) *in the attraction of which* the soul recognizes itself as enchained, fixated, and (6) feels itself removed from reality, *whereupon* (7) the

self finds that it can turn (convert, revolutionize) . . . " (*Conditions Handsome and Unhandsome*, pp. 6–7; emphasis added).

64. This can, of course, only go so far, as what will count as "my" reason will be experienced by me in a wholly passive way. Consider in this regard Lewis Mumford's remarks, cited in W.K.C. Guthrie, *A History of Greek Philosophy*, vol. 4 (New York: Cambridge University Press, 1975), p. 469, on the manner in which most residents of the city are ruled and in being ruled infantilized, deprived of the possibility of making the decisions that the conversation of justice will call for and rest upon.

65. Socrates pretends to respond to the objections of Glaucon that he is making the philosopher miserable by degrading him and forcing him to return to the city by reminding Glaucon that "it's not the concern of the law that any one class in the city fare exceptionally well, but that it contrives to bring this about in the city as a whole" (519e). But the point is that the philosopher is not really part of the whole. Is he alone only a part of what he could be because he lacks an intelligence that others can supply? Or because he, who is a warrior first, needs the spirit of others? Or are we meant to believe that he needs their lower desires? On this point contrast George Kateb's "compromise" between Emersonian perfectionism and democratic politics in "Democratic Individuality and the Claims of Politics," *Political Theory* 12, no. 3 (August 1984): 358.

66. In "The Conversation of Justice" Cavell slips from speaking of Nora's violation to speaking of "the philosopher's violation" (pp. 109–10); I think at this point we can begin to see why.

67. "The Philosopher in American Life," *In Quest of the Ordinary*, p. 9.

68. Nietzsche, *Twilight of the Idols*, trans. R. J. Hollingdale (Harmondsworth: Penguin, 1968), p. 41. Compare "Declining Decline," p. 46, and the discussions of Plato in *Conditions Handsome and Unhandsome*, pp. 6–10, and *Philosophical Passages*, p. 94.

69. *CR*, p. 21.

70. Ibid., p. 120.

71. I am indebted to Stanley Cavell, Tom Dumm, Richard Eldridge, Yasemin Ok, Rogers Smith, Tracy Strong, Stephen White, Eric Wilson, and an anonymous reviewer for *Political Theory* for their help on earlier drafts of this essay.

CHAPTER 6

1. In his recent *Cities of Words: Pedagogical Letters On A Register Of The Moral Life* (Cambridge, Mass.: Belknap Press of the Harvard University Press, 2004) (hereafter *CW*), Cavell has done an excellent job of gathering and extending reflections of a lifetime concerning these and many other topics. I respond primarily to this work, turning to earlier writings primarily where they develop thoughts

not expressed in or in some respects altered by *CW*.

2. See his *Conditions Handsome and Unhandsome* (Chicago: University of Chicago Press, 1990), pp. xviii–xix (hereafter *CHH*).

3. "I do not . . . regard the perfectionism I . . . follow out as requiring an imagination of some ultimate human perfection. Emersonian perfectionism . . . specifically sets itself against any idea of ultimate perfection" (*CHH*, p. 3; see also p. 12).

4. It is evidently important to Cavell that Mill was not an academic. I regularly teach *On Liberty* and *The Subjection of Women*. I will not do so again without also assigning Cavell's chapter on Mill.

5. It emerges that, depending on how we take "coming to rest," Cavell is, and leads us to be, more than a little interested in whether and how conversations arrive, if only temporarily, at this condition.

6. I am inclined to object that Cavell could give more recognition to the fact that conversation is sometimes for its own sake, for the sheer pleasure that it provides. He does, however, discuss this aspect of conversation in his chapter on Aristotle (chap. 19). In this regard, compare the following passage from Oakeshott"s "The Voice of Poetry in the Conversation of Mankind": "In a conversation the participants are not engaged in an inquiry or a debate, there is no 'truth' to be discovered. . . . no conclusion is sought. . . . Thoughts of different species take wing and play around one another, responding to each other's movements and provoking one another to exertions. . . . [I]t is impossible in the absence of a diversity of voices: in it different universes of discourse meet, acknowledge each other and enjoy an oblique relationship which neither requires nor forecasts their being assimilated to one another." The only objective of conversation is mutual "delighting" (*Rationalism in Politics* [Indianapolis: Liberty Press, 1991], p. 489).

7. Conversation and argumentation are not mutually exclusive. But do the two of them jointly exhaust the possibilities?

8. Generalizing, we can say that MPP has two things to explain. The first is why so many human lives are dismal, disappointing, lived in desperation. The second is how this melancholy condition can, at least intermittently, be improved.

9. It is striking that he finds ponderous and portentous issues in films that are conventionally regarded as light, frothy entertainments suitable for "collapsing at the flics" (which, unfortunately, was how the films he discusses were regarded in *my* days at Berkeley).

10. The phrases the "pair becomes incomprehensible to (most) of the rest of the world" and "in the case of our couples, to each other," connect directly and importantly to the question of friendship. I take up this connection in Part Two.

11. Cavell argues, however, that this estrangement of the couple from the world and it from them can be revealing, even enhancing, for both the couple and the larger society. The couple's estrangement from the world may help them

to understand that, though it is unworthy of them in many ways, they consent to it and offer the example of their relationship to it. "Thus is their [now] meet and happy conversation meant for [the rest of] us, a sign of their consent to a world in which [despite its injustices and violations] such a life can be adventured on, can be justified by being adventured, can be justified only by being ventured on, not denying happiness, not accepting it either." These are "instances of democratic art, in exemplifying change, imagining departures from our lives as constituted . . . " (*CHH*, p. 126). The essay is titled "The Conversation Of Justice" and presents the fullest development of this theme.

12. I am unsettled by one of Cavell's remarks in this connection. "You may or may not take an explicit side in some particular conflict, but unless you find some way to show that this society is not yours, it is; your being compromised by its actions expresses the necessity of your being implicated in them. That you nevertheless avoid express participation or express disavowal is what creates that ghost-state of conformity Emerson articulates endlessly, as our being inane, timid, ashamed, skulkers, leaners, apologetic, noncommittal; a gag, a masquerade, pinched in a corner, cowed, cowards, fleeing before a revolution" (Cavell, "What Is the Emersonian Event?," *New Literary History* 25 [1994]: 957). Although hardly a recommendation for non-participation, does this make it too easy for the authorities to claim that the skulkers have consented? As noted above, however, refusing conversation may be one way, in some circumstances perhaps the only way, of initiating or stirring it.

13. As with all our criteria "for all their necessity [they] are open to our repudiation, or dissatisfaction (hence lead to, as well as lead from skepticism)" (Cavell, *In Quest of the Ordinary: Lines of Skepticism and Romanticism* [Chicago: University of Chicago Press, 1988], p. 5).

14. I say "almost" because Cavell speaks of "scoundrels" and "villains" with whom conversation is impossible and who must be "punched out" (*CHH*, pp. xxxiii–xiv; *CW*, p. 207).

15. The senses are the "sovereign masters" of our knowledge, "but they are uncertain and deceivable in all circumstances." Thus we must appeal from our senses to our reason. But the latter is no more reliable than the former. "To judge the appearances that we receive of objects, we would need a judicatory instrument; to verify this instrument, we need a demonstration; to verify the demonstration, an instrument; there we are in a circle." Again, "Since the senses cannot decide our dispute . . . it must be reason that does so. [But because no] reason can be established without another reason; there we go retreating back to infinity" (Michel de Montaigne, *The Complete Essays of Montaigne*, trans. Donald M. Frame [Stanford: Stanford University Press, 1948], p. 447 [hereafter *M*]). The passages are from Essay II, p. 12, "Apology for Raymond Sebond." I have discussed Montaigne in my *Freedom and Its Conditions: Discipline, Autonomy and Resistance* (New York: Rout-

ledge, 2003), and I draw on that work in what follows.

16. To "retreat to the Inner Citadel," as Isaiah Berlin has scornfully described Stoic doctrine.

17. See "Of Custom, and Not Easily Changing an Accepted Law," I:23, esp. pp. 83–86.

18. See esp. II:7. Friendship in the highest sense is an exception which I discuss below.

19. I argue below that on this view Montaigne's perfectionism does not qualify as Emersonian. He places high but not absolute value on friendship.

20. Montaigne says that Aristotle's definition of friendship, "there relationship being that of one soul in two bodies," is "apt," speaks of his friendship with La Boetie as "the complete fusion or our wills," and says that "just as the friendship I feel for myself receives no increase from the help I give myself . . . so the union of such friends, being truly perfect, makes them lose the sense of such duties, and hate and banish from between them these words of separation and distinction: benefit, obligation, gratitude, request, thanks, and the like" ("Of Friendship," p. 141). No such remarks appear elsewhere in *The Essays* and it is tempting to treat them less as among Montaigne's settled convictions than as expressions of sorrow at La Boetie's early death. Below I suggest what I think is a better explanation for their place in Montaigne's thinking.

21. This does not make Montaigne's perfectionism into a form of PP. He identifies qualities of character and relationship that are essential to friendship but their content will vary from person to person and from one friendship to another. Just as the value of friendship is incommensurable with all other relationships, so every friendship is incommensurable with all others. This becomes clear when Montaigne describes the other examples of true friendship that he recognizes.

22. What are we to make of Montaigne's reference to "the friendship I feel for myself"? We might say that I can be a friend to myself only if I see myself in my friend; that is, I can be a friend to myself only if have a friend other than myself. Cavell does not discuss this remark, but it corresponds to his own view. See his *Disowning Knowledge*, updated ed. (Cambridge: Cambridge University Press, 2003), p. 79, where he quotes Montaigne's statement, "We are, I know not how, double in ourselves, so that we believe what we disbelieve, and cannot rid ourselves of what we condemn." (The passage is from "Of Glory," II, 16, p. 469.) An alternative but not incompatible reading would emphasize what I am calling the self for and against itself. The self makes itself intelligible to itself (or not), makes it a friend to itself (or not) by seeing in itself things that it condemns and things that it admires. This seems to posit a third self or a third dimension of the self, one that stands back from the doubled self and makes judgments concerning them. To my knowledge Montaigne never explicitly posits this third self, but I think it consistent with and perhaps implicit in much that he does say.

23. The workability of this practical ethic, of course, depends on the good fortune of living in a time and a place in which there are no significant conflicts among the customs, conventions, and laws to which one is expected to conform (in which, in Cavell's terms, there is justice that is "good enough" to allow us to continue to consent to it). In assessing Montaigne's endorsement of such a practical ethic, we must bear in mind not only his explicit qualifications to and of it, but also the background circumstance that he lived in a time and a place riven with disagreement and brutal conflicts. It was clearly his view that in this situation external conformity was necessary to make tranquillity and more estimable relationships possible. He might have thought differently if he lived in a society that sustained a good enough justice.

24. This is particularly true of what was arguably the most important locus of authority in Montaigne's time, that is, the authority of the Pope and the Catholic Church. Montaigne vigorously defended suicide and can readily be interpreted to defend abortion. He was called to Rome to defend his essays and, later, his book was put on the Index.

CHAPTER 7

1. A. Davidson, "Ethics as Ascetics," in *The Cambridge Companion to Foucault*, ed. G. Gutting (Cambridge: Cambridge University Press, 1994), p. 131.

2. Cavell, *Cities of Words* (Chicago: Belknap Press, 2004), p. 11.

3. See M. Foucault, "On the Genealogy of Ethics," in *The Foucault Reader*, ed. P. Rabinow (Harmondsworth: Penguin Books, 1984), pp. 340–72, where he endorses the Nietzschean view expressed in §290 of *The Gay Science* against the contrasting position of Sartre.

4. J. Tully, "Michel Foucault," in *Encyclopedia of Ethics*, ed. L. C. Becker, 2 vols. (Chicago: St. James Press, 1992), I:384.

5. M. Foucault, *Ethics: The Essential Works* (Harmondsworth: Penguin Books, 1997), I:284.

6. Foucault, *The Use of Pleasure* (Harmondsworth: Penguin Books, 1992), p. 26.

7. Ibid., pp. 26–27.

8. Ibid., p. 27.

9. Ibid.

10. Ibid., p. 28.

11. Ibid.

12. Ibid., p. 29.

13. Ibid., pp. 29–30.

14. Ibid., p. 30.

15. Foucault, *The Foucault Reader*, p. 366.

16. Foucault, *Ethics*, p. 317.

17. "Biopower" refers to a distinct modality of power/knowledge relations which emerges at the end of the eighteenth century: "One might say that the ancient right to *take* life or *let* live was replaced by a power to *foster* life or *disallow* it to the point of death" (Foucault, *The History of Sexuality*, vol. 1 [Harmondsworth: Penguin, 1979], p. 138). What is significant about this form of power is that it unites two poles which emerged in the Classical period: "One of these poles—the first to be formed, it seems—centered on the body as a machine: its disciplining, the optimization of its capabilities, the extortion of its forces, the parallel increase of its usefulness and its docility, its integration into systems of efficient and economic controls, all this was ensured by the procedures of power that characterized the *disciplines*: an *anatomo-politics of the human body*. The second, formed somewhat later, focused on the species body, the body imbued with the mechanics of life and serving as the basis of biological processes: propagation, births and mortality, the level of health, life expectancy and longevity, with all the conditions that can cause these to vary. Their supervision was effected through an entire series of interventions and *regulatory controls*: *a bio-politics of the population*" (p. 139).

In *Discipline and Punish* (Harmondsworth: Penguin, 1977) and *The History of Sexuality* (1979), Foucault seeks to show that these poles are united in particular *diagrams* of power—the panopticon and the confessional—which render intelligible the objectifying and subjectifying practices that provide the conditions of possibility of the human sciences.

18. H. Dreyfus and P. Rabinow, *Michel Foucault: Beyond Structuralism and Hermeneutics* (Chicago: University of Chicago Press, 1982), p. 196.

19. See Tully, "Michel Foucault," p. 384.

20. Foucault, *The Foucault Reader*, p. 343.

21. For a good treatment of this issue, see C. Heyes, *Line Drawings* (Ithaca: Cornell University Press, 2000).

22. This is nicely dealt with in L. McWhorter, *Bodies and Pleasures* (Bloomington: Indiana University Press, 1999).

23. Foucault, *The Foucault Reader*, p. 356.

24. Ibid., p. 336.

25. Ibid., p. 356.

26. R. Flathman, *Freedom and Its Conditions* (London: Routledge, 2003), p. 19.

27. Ibid., p. 21.

28. Ibid.

29. Foucault, *The Use of Pleasure*, p. 62.

30. Ibid.

31. Flathman, *Freedom and Its Conditions*, p. 29.

32. Foucault, *Ethics*, p. 288.

33. Foucault takes up this notion in relation to his own existence as a gay person in a number of interviews; see ibid., pp. 135–62.

34. Foucault, *Fearless Speech* (Los Angeles: Semiotext[e], 2001), p. 97.

35. "The role is characterized in the text as that of a '*basanos*'. . . which *tests* the degree of accord between a person's life and its principle of intelligibility or *logos*. . . . The Greek word *basanos* refers to a 'touchstone,' i.e., a black stone which is used to test the genuineness of gold by examining the streak left on the stone when 'touched' by the gold in question" (ibid., p. 97).

36. Ibid., pp. 97–98.

37. Ibid., p. 106.

38. Ibid.

39. The centrality of friendship to this theme is one stressed by Foucault in his discussion of Plutarch, where the true friend who can act as a *parrhesiates* is distinguished by (1) integrity—the harmony of his words and deeds (which is why Laches identifies Socrates as able to play this role) and (2) steadiness of mind (in contrast to that inconstancy that betrays too much reliance on the views of current interlocutors or fashions in social opinion). This latter issue of steadiness of mind has been subject to a brilliant analysis and discussion by Bernard Williams, *Truth and Truthfulness* (Princeton: Princeton University Press, 2002), pp. 172–205.

40. Foucault, *Ethics*, p. 315.

41. Ibid., p. 319.

42. Ibid.

43. Cavell, *Cities of Words*, p. 11.

44. Cavell, *Conditions Handsome and Unhandsome* (Chicago: University of Chicago Press, 1990), p. 2.

45. Foucault, *The Use of Pleasure*, p. 28.

46. Cavell, *Conditions Handsome and Unhandsome*, p. xxxi.

47. See ibid., p. xxxii; and Foucault, *Fearless Speech*, pp. 135–37.

48. Cavell, *Conditions Handsome and Unhandsome*, p. 26.

49. Ibid., p. xxxiv.

50. Foucault, *Ethics*, p. 317.

51. Cavell, *Conditions Handsome and Unhandsome*, p. 5.

52. Foucault, *Discipline and Punish*, p. 304.

53. Ibid.

54. See, for example, A. Honneth, "Foucault's Theory of Society," in *Critique and Power*, ed. M. Kelly (Cambridge, Mass.: MIT Press, 1994), pp. 157–84, although I should add that Honneth has since rejected this view. I should also add that the interpretation of Adorno appealed to in this contrast has also been powerfully challenged by Bert van den Brink ("Gesellschaftstheorie und Übertreibungskunst: Für eine Alternative Lesart der 'Dialektik der Aufklärung'," *Neue Rundschau* 108, no. 1 [1997]: 37–59).

55. Cavell, *Cities of Words*, p. 96.

56. Cited in ibid., pp. 96–97.

57. Ibid., p. 97.

58. Ibid.

59. F. Nietzsche, "Expeditions of an Untimely Man," in *Twilight of the Idols*, trans. R. J. Hollingdale (London: Penguin Books 1968), p. 38.

60. A. Ridley, "Nietzsche on Art and Freedom," unpublished manuscript (2004), p. 8.

61. Ibid.

62. Ibid., p. 9.

63. Ibid.

64. Ibid., p. 10.

65. See D. Owen and A. Ridley, "On Fate," *International Studies in Philosophy* 35, no. 3 (2003): 63–78.

66. Cavell, *Conditions Handsome and Unhandsome*, p. xxxv.

67. Foucault, *Ethics*, pp. 315–16.

68. Cavell, *Conditions Handsome and Unhandsome*, p. xxxiv; and Foucault, *Ethics*, p. 312.

69. J. Bernauer and M. Mahon, "The Ethics of Michel Foucault," in *The Cambridge Companion to Foucault*, ed. G. Gutting (Cambridge: Cambridge University Press, 1994), p. 150.

70. Cf. S. Mulhall, *Stanley Cavell: Philosophy's Recounting of the Ordinary* (Oxford: Clarendon Press, 1994), pp. 313–43.

71. Cavell, *The Claim of Reason* (Oxford: Oxford University Press, 1979), p. 352.

72. Mulhall, *Stanley Cavell*, pp. 293–94.

73. Cavell, *Cities of Words*, p. 10.

74. Ibid., p. 15.

75. Cavell, *Pursuits of Happiness* (Cambridge, Mass.: Harvard University Press, 1981), p. 146.

76. Foucault, *Fearless Speech*, pp. 134–37.

77. Jim Tully has pointed out to me that one should note the pivotal role played by Mike is bringing Tracy to experience herself as a creature of spontaneity and desire and so to become receptive to Dexter's teaching (and he also raises the issue of class, which deserves a treatment that I cannot provide here), while my wife, Caroline Wintersgill, has noted the Shakespearean character of the relationship of the two couples, Dexter/Tracy and Liz/Mike, in that both are characterized by the relationship mature/immature (in Kant's sense) and yet they are mirror images of each other with respect to gender (Dexter and Liz are mature), to the forms of immaturity (Tracy is resistant to spontaneity and desire, Mike has an excess of these features) and to forms of education appropriate to the immature

partner (Dexter's strategy is active, seeking to arrange events to bring about Tracy's advent into maturity; Liz's pedagogy is passive, letting the world act on Mike to engender maturity).

78. Cavell, *Pursuits of Happiness*, pp. 139 and 150, respectively.

79. Ibid., p. 139.

80. Ibid., p. 150.

81. Ibid., pp. 145–46.

82. Cavell, *Cities of Words*, p. 40; see also p. 79.

83. See P. Rabinow, "Modern and Countermodern: Ethos and Epoch in Heidegger and Foucault," in *The Cambridge Companion to Foucault*, ed. G. Gutting (Cambridge: Cambridge University Press, 1994), p. 205.

84. Cavell, *Pursuits of Happiness*, p. 157.

85. Cavell, *Cities of Words*, p. 53.

86. Cavell, *Pursuits of Happiness*, p. 147.

87. J. Conant, "Nietzsche's Perfectionism," in *Nietzsche's Postmoralism*, ed. R. Schacht (Cambridge: Cambridge University Press, 2001), pp. 227–28.

88. Foucault, *Discipline and Punish*, pp. 88–89.

89. This paragraph draws on D. Owen, "Cultural Diversity and the Conversation of Justice," *Political Theory* 27, no. 5 (1999): 579–96.

90. J. Rawls, *A Theory of Justice* (Oxford: Oxford University Press, 1972), p. 246.

91. Mulhall, *Stanley Cavell*, p. 272.

92. Cavell, *Conditions Handsome and Unhandsome*, p. xxv.

93. Ibid., p. xxv.

94. Ibid., pp. xxv–xxvi.

95. Ibid., p. xxvi.

96. Ibid.

97. Ibid., p. xxv.

98. Ibid., p. 109.

99. Ibid., p. 110.

100. Ibid., p. xxvi.

101. Ibid., p. 110.

102. Ibid., p. 115.

103. Ibid., pp. xxxvii–xxxviii.

104. S. Mulhall, "Promising Consent and Citizenship," *Political Theory* 25, no. 2 (1997): 186.

105. M. Foucault, "Sexual Choice, Sexual Act," in his *Politics, Philosophy, Culture: Interviews and Other Writings 1977–84*, ed. L. D. Kritzman (London: Routledge, 1988), p. 294.

106. Foucault, "Is It Useless to Revolt?," *Philosophy and Social Criticism* 8, no. 1 (1981): 8.

1. This idea first appeared, I think, in "Knowing and Acknowledging," reprinted in Cavell's *Must We Mean What We Say?* (New York: Scribner's, 1969), pp. 238–66, and reprinted again in later editions of that book. In that essay Cavell makes use of the idea in dealing with skepticism—particularly "the problem of other minds." His use of it in *The Claim of Reason* (hereafter *CR*) is a later development, and its deployment in aesthetics is my own idea, for which Cavell bears no responsibility but deserves whatever credit may come.

2. Thomas Mann, *Pro and Contra Wagner*, trans. Allen Blunden, intro. by Erich Heller (Chicago: University of Chicago Press, 1985), pp. 201f.

3. Ibid.

4. W. H. Auden, "The Greatest of the Monsters," reprinted in Auden, *Forewords and Afterwords*, ed. Edward Mendelson (New York: Vintage Books [Random House], 1974), p. 255. The editor reports that this essay first appeared as Auden's review of Robert Gutman's *Richard Wagner: The Man, His Mind, and His Music*, in *The New Yorker*, January 4, 1969.

5. Quoted by Michael Kimmelman in his "Music, Maestro, Please!," a review of books about Toscanini, in *The New York Review of Books* 49, no. 17 (November 7, 2002), p. 20.

6. This is a topic reminiscent of a question about Kant's moral theory. Kant's most appealing formulation of the categorical imperative is the second: "Act always so as to treat humanity, including oneself, never as a means only, but also as an end." There are very difficult questions regarding what argument Kant, or anyone, might give for this injunction, but the formulation itself has a genuine appeal, and it leads immediately to this question: If I am forbidden to treat others as means (only), then does that prohibition still stand when the person I'm dealing with does not himself obey the injunction? That is, if you customarily treat others only as means to your ends, then am I still obliged to treat you as an end, or have you forfeited your right to be treated with respect?

Most lovers of Kant, and other scholars as well, think that this obligation to humanity is owed universally, including to those who do not themselves acknowledge it in their actions. This may be the best understanding of Kant, if Kant takes the obligatory feeling of respect to be owed to all those who are capable of genuine action, that is, all those who are rational and thus able to act properly, whether or not they do. It seems to me difficult to square this understanding of Kant with Kant's own approval of capital punishment, but Kant interpretation is not an aim of this exercise.

7. For instance, see "Identifying with Metaphor: Metaphors of Personal Identification," *The Journal of Aesthetics and Art Criticism* 57, no. 4 (Fall 1999): 399–409.

CHAPTER 9

1. Stanley Cavell, *The Claim of Reason: Wittgenstein, Skepticism, Morality, and Tragedy* (New York and Oxford: Oxford University Press, 1979), p. 23.

2. This is the approach taken by Stephen Mulhall in "Promising, Consent, and Citizenship: Rawls and Cavell on Morality and Politics," *Political Theory* 25, no. 2 (1997): 171–92. See also David Owen, "Cultural Diversity and the Conversation of Justice," *Political Theory* 27, no. 5 (1999): 579–96.

3. See Andrew Norris, "Political Revisions: Stanley Cavell and Political Philosophy," *Political Theory* 30, no. 6 (2002): 828–29.

4. See Philippe Lacoue-Labarthe and Jean-Luc Nancy, *The Literary Absolute: The Theory of Literature in German Romanticism*, trans. Philip Barnard and Cheryl Lester (Albany: State University of New York Press, 1988), p. 17. The authors speak of romanticism as a "repetitive compulsion" (ibid.) and suggest that it is better to become aware of its necessity than to brush it off as an error. For Cavell's response to this book, see the opening essay of *This New Yet Unapproachable America: Lectures After Emerson After Wittgenstein* (Albuquerque, N.M.: Living Batch Press, 1989), pp. 2–6.

5. Richard Eldridge, *The Persistence of Romanticism: Essays in Philosophy and Literature* (Cambridge: Cambridge University Press, 2001). See also my review of Eldridge in *The European Journal of Philosophy* 10, no. 1 (2002): 129–33.

6. For an interesting attempt to relate Cavell's work to romanticism in general, see William Desmond, "A Second *Primavera*: Cavell, German Philosophy, and Romanticism," in *Stanley Cavell*, ed. Richard Eldridge (Cambridge: Cambridge University Press, 2003), pp. 143–71.

7. See Ernesto Laclau, *Emancipation(s)* (New York: Verso, 1996), p. 15, where he argues that the universal cannot be fixed because it "does not have a concrete content of its own but is an always preceding horizon resulting from an indefinite expansion of equivalential demands."

8. *The Claim of Reason*, p. 27.

9. For a recent volume containing important discussions of the political and methodological implications of Wittgenstein's thinking, see Cressida Hayes, ed., *Wittgenstein and Political Philosophy* (Ithaca: Cornell University Press, 2003).

10. Hannah Pitkin, *Wittgenstein and Justice* (Berkeley: University of California Press, 1972). For Pitkin's explicit comments on Cavell, see pp. viii and xiii.

11. Sabina Lovibond, *Realism and Imagination in Ethics* (Minneapolis: University of Minnesota Press, 1983), esp. §§14–15.

12. For an important debate concerning this issue with reference to Cavell, see Steven Affeldt, "The Ground of Mutuality: Criteria, Judgment, and Intelligibility in Stephen Mulhall and Stanley Cavell," *European Journal of Philosophy* 6, no. 2 (1998): 1–31; and Stephen Mulhall, "The Givenness of Grammar: A Reply to Ste-

ven Affeldt," *European Journal of Philosophy* 6, no. 2 (1998): 32–44.

13. Stanley Cavell, *Must We Mean What We Say? A Book of Essays* (Cambridge: Cambridge University Press, 1976), p. 52.

14. It is tempting to compare this view with Nancy's notion of *la communauté désoevrée* or Lyotard's community of sublime non-representability. See Jean-Luc Nancy, *The Inoperative Community* (Minneapolis: University of Minnesota Press, 1991), pp. 1–42; and Jean-François Lyotard, *The Differend: Phrases in Dispute* (Minneapolis: University of Minnesota Press, 1988), pp. 165–69. The real difference is that, unlike Cavell, both Nancy and Lyotard dismiss any talk of universality and seek to interpret the notion of community in terms of the notion of singularities or intensities.

15. See Richard Rorty, *Contingency, Irony, and Solidarity* (Cambridge: Cambridge University Press, 1989).

16. G.W.F. Hegel, *The Phenomenology of Spirit*, trans. A. V. Miller (Oxford: Oxford University Press, 1977), §§632–71.

17. Hegel, *Aesthetics: Lectures on Fine Art*, vol. 1, trans. T. M. Knox (Oxford: Clarendon Press, 1975), pp. 64–69.

18. Ibid., p. 66.

19. Ibid.

20. For Schmitt's assessment of political romanticism, see his *Political Romanticism*, trans. Guy Oakes (Cambridge, Mass.: MIT Press, 1986).

21. Ibid., p. 160.

22. Ibid., pp. 84–85.

23. With regard to the objection someone might raise that Thoreau cannot be counted a romantic but is rather a transcendentalist, and that romanticism and transcendentalism must not be confused with one another (as if these are clear and well-defined terms), it should be noted that I do not intend to argue independently for Thoreau's writing to be a continuation of romanticism. It is sufficient for my purposes to adduce that Cavell (in *This New Yet Unapproachable America*, pp. 4–5) *understands* Thoreau (together with Coleridge, Wordsworth, Emerson, Heidegger, and Wittgenstein) as a romantic, that is, as having produced work that for Cavell "defines romanticism."

24. For an account of how mythical thought may influence conceptions of statehood, see Ernst Cassirer, *The Myth of the State* (New Haven: Yale University Press, 1946).

25. *The Senses of Walden*, p. 9.

26. Ibid., pp. 85–86.

27. For a discussion of this evidently paradoxical thinking of the absolute, see Lacoue-Labarthe and Nancy, *The Literary Absolute*, p. 92. For Cavell's own discussion of Schlegel, see "The *Investigations'* Everyday Aesthetics of Itself," *The Cavell Reader*, ed. Stephen Mulhall (Oxford: Blackwell, 1996), pp. 369–89.

28. Ludwig Wittgenstein, *Philosophical Investigations*, trans. G.E.M. Anscombe (New York: Basil Blackwell, 1958), p. 178.

29. Cavell, "The *Investigations'* Everyday Aesthetics of Itself," p. 385. For a discussion of Cavell's interpretation of Wittgenstein's notion of perspicuous representation, see Espen Hammer, "Verwandlung des Alltäglichen," *Deutsche Zeitschrift für Philosophie* 46, no. 2 (1998): 267–81. See also Hammer, *Stanley Cavell: Skepticism, Subjectivity, and the Ordinary* (Oxford: Polity Press, 2002), pp. 164–67.

30. Cavell, *This New Yet Unapproachable America*, p. 23.

31. Cavell, *The Claim of Reason*, p. 36.

32. Cavell, *The Senses of Walden*, p. 80.

33. For Cavell's acknowledgment of this debt, see *Conditions Handsome and Unhandsome: The Constitution of Emersonian Perfectionism* (Chicago and London: University of Chicago Press, 1990), pp. 5–9. See also *The Senses of Walden*, p. 87.

34. Cavell, *The Claim of Reason*, p. 376.

35. See Theodor W. Adorno, *Aesthetic Theory*, trans. C. Lenhardt (London and New York: Routledge, 1984), p. 151: "The dialectic of modern art to a large extent is such that it seeks to shake off its illusory character, as an animal sometimes seems to want to shake off its antlers. . . . In the aftermath of that rebellion, however, art is now at the point of falling back into mere materiality, as though it were being punished for its arrogant desire to be more than art."

36. For an attempt to examine this line of thought, see Jay Bernstein, *The Fate of Art: Aesthetic Alienation from Kant to Derrida and Adorno* (College Park: Pennsylvania State University Press), esp. pp. 55–63.

37. The term "sublime" does not appear often in Cavell. However, see *This New Yet Unapproachable America*, p. 105: "To feel small for the moment, wordless, abashed, say crushed, before certain writing seems to me a sign of reading its claim correctly. Emerson produces such (prophetic) writing. It is evidently a form of the sublime."

38. Cavell, *Conditions Handsome and Unhandsome*, pp. 108–15.

39. Cavell finds (ibid., p. 109) Emerson expressing a similar sentiment in his totalizing remark, "Every word they say chagrins us."

40. John Rawls, *A Theory of Justice* (Cambridge, Mass.: Harvard University Press, 1971), p. 533.

41. Cavell, *Conditions Handsome and Unhandsome*, p. 112.

42. See Cavell, *Contesting Tears: The Hollywood Melodrama of the Unknown Woman* (Chicago: University of Chicago Press, 1996), pp. 106–7.

43. Ibid.

CHAPTER 10

1. Cavell, *Pursuits of Happiness: The Hollywood Comedy of Remarriage* (Cam-

bridge, Mass.: Harvard University Press, 1981). All page references without further identification are to this text.

2. Hannah Arendt, "Philosophy and Politics," *Social Research* 57 (1990).

3. George Steiner, "Tragedy, Pure and Simple," in *Tragedy and the Tragic: Greek Theatre and Beyond,*" ed. M. S. Silk (Oxford: Clarendon Press, 1996), p. 534.

4. Cavell, "The Avoidance of Love: A Reading of King Lear," in *Must We Mean What We Say?* (Cambridge: Cambridge University Press, 1976), p. 294 (hereafter AL).

5. Plato, *Protagoras,* translated by W.K.C. Guthrie (Baltimore, Md.: Penguin Books, 1956).

6. Hereafter "PV" refers to Max Weber, "Politics as a Vocation," in his *Essays in Sociology,* trans. H. H. Gerth and C. Wright Mills (Oxford: Oxford University Press, 1958).

7. Sophocles, *Antigone,* trans. Robert Fagles (Harmondsworth: Penguin Books, 1984, lines 1468–70.

8. Friedrich Nietzsche, *On the Genealogy of Morals,* trans. Carol Diethe (Cambridge: Cambridge University Press, 1994), essay 3, §4, p. 74.

9. Friedrich Nietzsche, *The Gay Science,* ed. and trans. W. Kaufmann (New York: Random House, 1974), bk. 1, §1. Nietzsche's words remind one here, as so often, of his great antagonist Plato, who wrote in the *Philebus* about how "not only on stage but also in all of life's tragedies and comedies, pleasures are mixed with pains" (p. 50b), I owe this reference to Sophia Leahy (Berkeley), who has helped me with her perceptive comments on an earlier version of this paper. I also owe thanks to Martin Hartmann (Frankfurt) for impressing on me the need to read "The Avoidance of Love" together with *Pursuits of Happiness.*

CHAPTER 11

1. See Giorgio Agamben, *Homo Sacer: Sovereign Power and Bare Life,* trans. Daniel Heller-Roazen (Stanford: Stanford University Press, 1998); for a trenchant commentary on *Homo Sacer* see Peter Fitzpatrick, "Bare Sovereignty: *Homo Sacer* and the Insistence of Law," *Theory & Event* 5, no. 2 (Spring 2001), http://muse. jhu.edu/journals/tae/toc/archive.html#5.2.

2. Judith Butler, *Antigone's Claim: Kinship Between Life and Death* (New York: Columbia University Press, 2000). This point is worth considering when taking serious the tragedy of *King Lear* as well.

3. Michael Hardt and Antonio Negri, *Empire* (Cambridge: Harvard University Press, 2000).

4. On the waning of historical narratives in relationship to political ethics, see Wendy Brown, *Politics out of History* (Princeton: Princeton University Press, 2001).

5. George Kateb, "The Adequacy of the Canon of Political Theory," unpublished manuscript, presented as a symposium paper at the American Political Science Association annual meeting, San Francisco, California, September 1, 2001.

6. See Stanley Cavell, "The Avoidance of Love: A Reading of *King Lear*," in *Must We Mean What We Say? A Book of Essays*, (Cambridge: Cambridge University Press), 1976 (originally published by Charles Scribner's Sons, 1969). Subsequent references to page numbers appear in the text as AL.

7. The lovableness of Lear is commented on at length by Harold Bloom in his chapter on the play in *Shakespeare: The Invention of the Human* (New York: Riverhead Books, 1998). He writes, on p. 479: "When I teach *King Lear*, [I] have to begin by reminding my students that Lear, however unlovable in the first two acts, is very much loved by Cordelia, the Fool, Albany, Kent, Gloucester, and Edgar—that is to say, by every benign character in the play—just as he is hated and feared by Goneril, Regan, Cornwall, and Oswald, the play's lesser villains."

8. Harry Berger, in *Making Trifles of Terrors* (Stanford: Stanford University Press, 1997), pp. xi–xiv, suggests that Cavell's emphasis on shame is slightly misplaced, and finds textual evidence of guilt, understood as an internalization of the judgment of others, as a motive for Lear as well as shame, finding more guilt in the play than Cavell allows. While this qualification of Cavell is important, for the purposes of understanding what Cavell identifies as the larger themes of *King Lear*—how abdication and sovereignty connect to shame, and shame to loneliness and love, Berger's distinction between guilt and shame may not be *so* important. In other words, it may be that Cavellian shame explains that what is most fundamentally at stake in the process by which self-recognition occurs is the moment of the recognition of others, when one is in the *presence* of others. The primitive character of shame—its initial simplicity—does become more complex as the play moves on. Does it transform into something drastically distinguishable from shame called guilt, or is guilt in *King Lear* an extension of shame? Perhaps the question has different answers for different characters, at different moments in the play, as they are present and absent to each other and themselves. Does Lear descend into madness from shame and emerge from madness guilty? One of Cavell's points about the structure of the play is that our presence in Lear's present puts him in the continued presence of others, even when he is most alone, in soliloquy with the Fool. Moreover, the question of guilt as the internalization of conscience psychologizes thinly what may need to remain external to individual subjects. See the comments of Heidegger, below.

9. Cavell could thus be understood as anticipating the recent move by some important political theorists toward an embrace of ontological themes in order to think politically about the contingencies of late modernity. Stephen White has identified several such thinkers—George Kateb, Charles Taylor, Judith Butler, and William E. Connolly; see White, *Sustaining Affirmation: The Strengths of Weak*

Ontology in Political Theory (Princeton: Princeton University Press, 2000).

10. For a comment on Hegel's influence on the interpretation of tragedy, see Agamben, *Remnants of Auschwitz: The Witness and the Archive*, trans. Daniel Heller-Roazen (New York: ZONE Books, 1999), p. 96. A fuller treatment would compare Agamben's refusal of the Hegelian formulation with Butler's analysis of Antigone, and Hardt and Negri's attempt to deform and recuperate Hegel. Cavell's response is embedded in his thinking about Emerson and the possibilities of constitutional amendment, for me especially in "Emerson's Constitutional Amending," in *Philosophical Passages: Wittgenstein, Emerson, Austin, Derrida* (New York: Blackwell Publishers, 1995). For a gloss, see Thomas L. Dumm, "A Politics of the Ordinary," in *A Politics of the Ordinary* (New York: NYU Press, 1999).

11. Agamben, *Remnants of Auschwitz*, p. 106. The reason that I suggest that Agamben's citation of Heidegger here is controversial is in reference to the translation: Agamben translates the Greek term as "shame," whereas the American translators of *Parmenides* translate it as "awe." See Martin Heidegger, *Parmenides*, trans. André Schuwer and Richard Rojcewicz (Bloomington: University of Indiana Press, 1992), pp. 74–75. Awe and shame are very close: are they close enough?

12. Agamben, *Remnants of Auschwitz*, p. 107.

13. Ibid.

14. On this social dimension of disgust, see William E. Connolly's discussion of snot in "A Critique of Pure Politics," in *Why I Am Not a Secularist* (Minneapolis: University of Minnesota Press, 1999), pp. 163–64. When Lear is wiping his hand that smells of mortality, is it possible that he is wiping his hand that wiped his ass? The connection of mortality to compost and the seat to consideration is developed most thoroughly by Thoreau in *Walden*. For a gloss on Thoreau's understanding of shit, see Dumm, "Compensation," in *Politics of the Ordinary*, pp. 88–89. Cavell discusses the King's hand as mortal in regard to the absence of rings on it, a function of his abdication.

15. The question of Lear's incestuous love is at least as old as Freud's observations. For a gloss, see Bloom, *Shakespeare*, pp. 491–92.

16. White, *Sustaining Affirmations*, pp. 107–8, distinguishes Connolly for his efforts on the aesthetic-affective dimension of an ontological politics. (I would wish to emphasize a congruence of the idea concerning the development of *character* in Cavell's "The Avoidance of Love," with Connolly's cultivation, Foucault's care of self, and Butler's political catachresis.)

17. Connolly, "Critique of Pure Politics," pp. 176–77.

18. All citations of *The Tragedy of King Lear* and other plays by William Shakespeare are from *The Riverside Shakespeare* (Boston: Houghton Mifflin Company, 1974).

19. Agamben, *Homo Sacer*, p. 4. Hannah Arendt, *The Human Condition* (Chicago: University of Chicago Press, 1958); Michel Foucault, *The History of Sexual-*

ity, vol. 1, trans. Robert Hurley (New York: Pantheon, 1978), p. 143: "For millennia, man remained what he was for Aristotle: a living animal with the additional capacity for a political existence; modern man is an animal whose politics places his existence as a living being in question."

On becoming animal, see Gilles Deleuze and Felix Guatarri, *A Thousand Plateaus*, trans. Brian Massumi (Minneapolis: University of Minnesota Press, 1987), pp. 243–55. For a comparison on these terms of Lear to Captain Ahab of Melville's *Moby-Dick*, see Dumm, "A Politics of the Ordinary."

20. My thanks to Ann Lauterbach on this point.

21. Bloom cites this next passage to make a point related to my claim below, namely, that the great power of Lear's voice in this passage (as in others) "stems from Lear's usurpation of everyone's experience of ambivalence toward the father, or toward fatherhood" (*Shakespeare*, p. 513). Bloom suggests that the larger shame of Lear is a result of the embrace of the great metaphor of God the Father. He asks, "What can fatherhood be in the *kenoma*?" (p. 515). That is, what can fatherhood know of emptiness, of nothingness? But we may think through this question in gendered terms to the end: a mother may know emptiness as a result of birth, and a sister as a result of the law of state that cuts her off from her kin. (Again, see Butler, *Antigone's Claim*.)

22. Bloom, *Shakespeare*, p. 514.

23. Bloom derides the idea of thinking about the question of the mother. "What would Shakespeare have done with Queen Lear? Would she, like Job's laconic wife, have advised her outraged husband: 'Curse God and die?' Wisely, she is deceased, before the play opens, and receives only one mention by Lear, to add panache to one of his frequent curses against his daughters" (ibid., p. 510). Obviously, I disagree with Bloom, and think that the question of Queen Lear is pertinent. Bloom himself seems blinded by his contempt for what he terms the School of Resentment criticisms of Shakespeare. His self-description as a gnomic school of one hardly covers the anxiety of influence he suffers in regard to these ghostly opponents.

24. In this sense, she is closely associated with Antigone. For a fascinating essay concerned with many of the themes raised in this one (and associated with the problems raised by Cavell and Butler concerning tragedy), see Timothy Gould, "The Unhappy Performative," in *Performativity and Performance*, ed. Andrew Parker and Eve Kosofsky Sedgwick (New York: Routledge, 1995). Gould notes: "Antigone is the principle [sic] character in our culture—equalled perhaps only by Cordelia, Coriolanus, and Bartelby the Scrivener—who is defined, and defines herself, in a speech-act of refusal" (p. 34).

25. Butler, *Antigone's Claim*, p. 28. (Subsequent page references in the text are to this work.) In a note appended to this passage, Butler distinguishes her reading from that of commentators such as Jean Elshtain, who suggest that Antigone

represents civil society. Butler, in contrast, says, "My view is that there is no un-contaminated voice with which Antigone speaks." (p. 88n1). I think this view is consistent with the central claims that Cavell wishes to make concerning ordinary language.

26. Cavell, *A Pitch of Philosophy* (Cambridge: Harvard University Press, 1994), p. 4.

27. Frank Kermode, Introduction to *King Lear*, in *The Riverside Shakespeare*, p. 1249.

28. For helpful references on this field of critical contention, I thank David Sofield.

29. This is partly the point of Hardt and Negri's *Empire*, but it is not clear that we can hear them.

30. Simon Critchley, *Very Little, Almost Nothing: Death, Philosophy, Literature* (New York: Routledge, 1997), p. 127.

31. Ibid., p. 137.

32. Hardt and Negri, *Empire*, 393–413.

33. Ibid., p. 407.

34. Ibid., p. 413.

CHAPTER 12

1. Immanuel Kant, *Critique of Pure Reason*, trans. Norman Kemp Smith (New York: St. Martin's, 1965), pp. 92–93.

2. For references to *Zarathustra* in English translation, I rely on *The Portable Nietzsche*, ed. and trans. Walter Kaufmann (New York: Viking, 1954) (hereafter cited as *Z*). For references to *Zarathustra* in German, I use the *Sämtliche Werke: Kritische Studien Ausgabe in 15 Bänden*, ed. Giorgio Colli and Mazino Montinari (Berlin and Munich: de Gruyter and Deutscher Tauschenbuch Verlag, 1980), hereafter cited as *KSA*, followed by volume and page numbers.

3. For the APA address, see Cavell, "Something Out of the Ordinary," *Proceedings and Addresses of the APA* 71, no. 2 (hereafter cited as SO). My discussion of the Spinoza lectures is based on a typescript that Stanley Cavell has generously made available to me. It is entitled "Praise as Identification: At Moments of Henry James and Fred Astaire" (hereafter cited as PI).

4. Kant, *Critique of Pure Reason*, p. 66.

5. Here, of course, it should not be forgotten (as I have been reminded by Gary Banham) that Kant, in order to emphasize his concern with *pure* aesthetic judgments, describes the project of the third *Critique* as a "transcendental aesthetic of judgment." But *this* transcendental aesthetic is not to be identified with the first *Critique*'s doctrine of a priori sensibility. See Immanuel Kant, *Critique of Judgment*, trans. Werner Pluhar (Indianapolis: Hackett, 1987), p. 130.

6. Peter Fenves has argued that Walter Benjamin "develops the concept of spirit in his *Farbenlehre* by radicalizing the 'Critique of Aesthetic Judgment' of the third *Critique* to the point where it revises the 'Transcendental Aesthetic' of the first." Nietzsche, I am arguing, moves in roughly the opposite direction, transforming the transcendental aesthetic to the point where it revises "The Critique of Aesthetic Judgment." See Peter Fenves, *Arresting Language: From Leibniz to Benjamin* (Stanford: Stanford University Press, 2001), pp. 183–84.

7. Much of the discussion of *Zarathustra* that follows here is an abbreviated version of an argument I make at length in chapter 4 of Robert Gooding-Williams, *Zarathustra's Dionysian Modernism* (Stanford: Stanford University Press, 2001).

8. *Z*, pp. 231–38; *KSA*, 4:153–62.

9. For the quotations in this paragraph from "On the Child with the Mirror," see *Z*, pp. 196–97; *KSA*, 4:107. For the quotations in this paragraph deriving from "On Those Who Are Sublime," see *Z*, pp. 228–31; *KSA*, 4:150–52.

10. Zarathustra rejects Cartesian dualism. He also rejects two theses associated with Kant: (1) that there exist noumenal subjects and (2) that the subject does not belong to—is not a piece of—the world, what Quassim Cassam has called "the exclusion thesis" (see Quassim Cassam, *Self and World* [Oxford: Oxford University Press, 1999], pp. 9–21). Zarathustra seems to be claiming, however, that self-estrangement in the domain of bodies and appearances can produce appearances that give the (false) impression of being appearances *of* otherworldly, suprasensible subjects.

11. For the quoted material in this paragraph, see *Z*, 228–31; *KSA*, 4:15–52.

12. Nietzsche's portrait of the sublime hero as someone who stands aloof from the world of appearances may owe something to Wagner's depiction of Beethoven's sublime genius in Wagner's *Beethoven* (a book to which Nietzsche alludes in *The Birth of Tragedy*'s "Preface to Richard Wagner"). See Richard Wagner, *Beethoven*, trans. Edward Dannreuther (London: Wm. Reeves, 1903), pp. 20, 54, 56, 102–3. I thank John Sallis for pointing out the relevance of Wagner's book to my interpretation of "On Those Who Are Sublime."

13. *Z*, 231; *KSA*, 4:152.

14. Cf. Gooding-Williams, *Zarathustra's Dionysian Modernism*, pp. 180–82.

15. See the discussion of "The Night Song" in the *Zarathustra* section of *Ecce Homo*.

16. Cf. Gooding-Williams, *Zarathustra's Dionysian Modernism*, pp. 180–82 and 264–67, where I defend and develop the thesis that Ariadne is a figure for the body's power of receptivity.

17. SO, p. 25. Cavell's reading of Kant suggests that aesthetic judgment is a response to and an attempt to justify aesthetic pleasure through the articulation of concepts. Although this is not the place to pursue in any detail the niceties of Kant

interpretation, it should be noted that Kant may plausibly be taken to have argued otherwise: that aesthetic pleasure *results* from the articulation and application of concepts in the testing of interpretations (for a convincing reading of Kant along these lines, see Samuel Fleischaker, *A Third Concept of Liberty: Judgment and Freedom in Kant and Adam Smith* [Princeton: Princeton University Press, 1999], chap. 2). As I read Cavell, his view has substantial affinities to that of his former student Paul Guyer, who attributes to Kant a distinction between the pleasure-producing estimation of an object and the judging of a pleasure (see Paul Guyer, *Kant and the Claims of Taste*, 2d ed. [Cambridge: Cambridge University Press, 1997], pp. 97–106). For the purposes of the present paper, I do not take issue with Cavell's and Guyer's reading of Kant.

18. SO, p. 25; PI, p. 10.

19. SO, pp. 33.

20. In PI, Cavell speaks specifically of three features; see pp. 13–16. Cf. SO, pp. 34–36.

21. SO, p. 34.

22. Stanley Cavell, *In Quest of the Ordinary: Lines of Skepticism and Romanticism* (Chicago: University of Chicago Press, 1988), p. 9.

23. Cavell uses the concept of an individuality to refer to the "inflections of disposition and demeanor" that project particular ways of inhabiting a social role. See Stanley Cavell, *The World Viewed*, enlarged ed. (Cambridge: Harvard University Press, 1979), pp. 33, 35.

24. On the theme of "intimacy" with existence, see Cavell, *In Quest of the Ordinary*, pp. 3–9.

25. See Cavell, *The World Viewed*, pp. 40–41.

26. SO, pp. 36–37. The discussion of *Hamlet* in these pages echoes the more detailed analysis Cavell presents in Stanley Cavell, *Disowning Knowledge In Six Plays of Shakespeare* (Cambridge: Cambridge University Press, 1987), pp. 179–91.

27. Cavell, *In Quest of the Ordinary*, p. 9.

28. SO, p. 36.

29. In 1953, the year *The Band Wagon* appeared, Gardner was in fact married to Frank Sinatra.

30. On this point, see John Mueller, *Astaire Dancing: The Musical Films* (New York: Alfred A. Knopf, 1985), p. 351. See also Hugh Fordin, *The World of Entertainment! Hollywood's Greatest Musicals* (New York: Doubleday, 1975), p. 400.

31. For the impact of *Showboat* on Gardner's career, see Roland Flamini, *Ava* (New York: Coward, McCann and Geoghegan, 1983), p. 153; and Karin J. Fowler, *Ava Gardner: A Bio-Bibliography* (New York: Greenwood Press, 1990), p. 11.

32. See James Naremore, *The Films of Vincent Minnelli* (Cambridge: Cambridge University Press, 1993), pp. 34–35.

33. Ibid., p. 33.

34. See below, n. 49.

35. My thinking about the significance of the ways American films correlate images of blacks and whites "in a larger schema of semiotic valuation" has been inspired by James Snead's writing on Hollywood film. See James Snead, *White Screen/Black Images: Hollywood from the Dark Side* (New York: Routledge, 1994), pp. 4–5.

36. See Cavell, *Disowning Knowledge in Six Plays of Shakespeare*, pp. 136–37.

37. Cavell, *In Quest of the Ordinary*, p. 5.

38. Here, my formulation owes a debt to Richard Eldridge. See Eldridge's introduction to his *Stanley Cavell* (Cambridge: Cambridge University Press, 2003), p. 5. See too Eldridge's "Wittgenstein and the Conversation of Justice," in *The Grammar of Politics: Wittgenstein and Political Philosophy*, ed. Cressida J. Heyes (Ithaca: Cornell University Press, 2003), pp. 124–25.

39. Stanley Cavell, *The Senses of Walden*, expanded ed. (Chicago: University of Chicago Press, 1981), p. 133. See also Stanley Cavell, *The Claim of Reason* (Oxford: Oxford University Press, 1979), pp. 241–42. For useful clarification of Cavell's view that it is a mistake to think of the concept of knowing as applying to the existence of the world as a whole, or as such, see James Conant, "On Bruns, On Cavell," *Critical Inquiry* 17 (Spring 1991): 627. See also, on this point, Stephan Mulhall, *Stanley Cavell: Philosophy's Recounting of the Ordinary* (Oxford: Oxford University Press, pp. 77–85.

40. Cf. Cavell, *The Claim of Reason*, p. 46, Conant, "On Bruns, On Cavell," p. 621.

41. See Stanley Cavell, *Conditions Handsome and Unhandsome* (Chicago: University of Chicago Press, 1990), pp. 38–39, 92. In the first of these passages, Cavell links the handsome to receptivity (specifically, to a conception of thinking as receptivity that is evident in Emerson and Heidegger, and that Cavell presents as a revision of Kant) and the unhandsome to "the sublimized violence" of Western conceptualizing. In the second, he links sublimity to the skeptic's "disappointment with criteria."

42. See Cavell, *The Senses of Walden*, pp. 55–56, 104ff.

43. SO, p. 36.

44. Michael Rogin, *Blackface, White Noise: Jewish Immigrants in the Hollywood Melting Pot* (Berkeley: University of California Press, 1996), p. 204.

45. PI, p. 17.

46. Ibid., p. 22.

47. Ibid., pp. 22–23.

48. My summary discussion of *King Kong* owes much to James Snead's reading. See Snead, *White Screens/Black Images*, pp. 1–27. For another useful discussion of the film, see Thomas E. Wartenberg, *Unlikely Couples: Movie Romance as Social Criticism* (Westview Press: Boulder, Colo., 1999), pp. 9–18.

49. Vincent Minnelli's direction (which Cavell, focusing on Astaire, ignores) is crucial, I think, to making sense of the semiotics of race in *The Band Wagon*. As I have suggested, this is no less true of the Astaire-Gardner pairings and the first routine than it is of the second routine. Minnelli was the director of the all-black *Cabin in the Sky* (1943), and in 1939 was already producing set designs that both figured blacks as primitive and promoted an urbane, sophisticated idea of primitivism, an idea according to which primitivism was not a threat to, but could be reconciled with, civilization (see James Naremore, *The Films of Vincent Minnelli*, chap. 2). As will become evident, I believe that the treatment of blacks and blackness in *The Band Wagon* follows along similar lines.

50. For a brief account of the effort to recruit Daniels, and of his performance, leavened with some interesting personal reflections, see Stuart Klawans, "Shined Shoes," in *O.K. You Mugs: Writers on Movie Actors*, ed. Luc Sante and Melissa Holbrook Pierson (New York: Vintage, 2000), pp. 117–30.

51. PI, pp. 23–24.

52. Ibid.

53. As Robin James pointed out in her brilliant response to this paper at a conference at DePaul University, "While Astaire sings throughout the whole number, the only musical contribution the shoeshine man makes is *rhythmic*: he's basically a multifunction percussive instrument, using his shinecloth, buffers, hands and feet to beat out patterns to accompany and educate Astaire." Building on James's insight, I am inclined to add that in essence Daniels the shoeshine man teaches Astaire to "swing." For the relationship between rhythm, the distribution of rhythmic values, and the jazz-critical notion of swing, see Gunther Schuller, *Early Jazz: Its Roots and Musical Development* (New York: Oxford University Press, 1968), pp. 6–26.

54. PI, p. 25.

55. Ibid., p. 27.

56. Ibid., p. 26.

57. Ibid., p. 24.

58. For Cavell on the Nietzschean/Emersonian notion of the exemplar, see Cavell, *Conditions Handsome and Unhandsome*, pp. 6ff, 50ff. For further analysis of this notion, which draws inspiration from Cavell, see James Conant, "Nietzsche's Perfectionism: A Reading of Schopenhauer as Educator" in *Nietzsche's Postmoralism*, ed. Richard Schacht (Cambridge: Cambridge University Press, 2001), pp. 191–96.

59. For my discussion of some related themes in connection to the figure of the black cupid, see Robert Gooding-Williams, "Black Cupids, White Desires: Reading the Representation of Racial Difference in 'Ghost' and 'Casablanca,'" in *Philosophy and Film*, ed. Cynthia A. Freeland and Thomas A. Wartenberg (New York: Routledge, 1995), pp. 143–60.

60. Eric Lott, *Love and Theft: Blackface Minstrelsy and the American Working Class* (New York: Oxford University Press, 1995), p. 52.

61. PI, p. 26.

62. Ibid., p. 29. With respect to the marquee announcement of "The 'Proud Land,'" there is perhaps more to say than Cavell acknowledges. It is significant, for example, that the title recurs in "The Girl Hunt" episode of *The Band Wagon*, and that it is also the name of the film that ruins Jonathan Shields's career in *The Bad and the Beautiful* (the film Minnelli made just before he made *The Band Wagon*). I owe these insights to Arturo Silva's unpublished paper on the "Girl Hunt" episode of *Band Wagon*, and to Stephen Harvey's book, *Directed by Vincente Minnelli* (New York: Museum of Modern Art, 1989), on which Silva relies.

63. For Kant's idea that beauty is a symbol of the moral good, see his *Critique of Judgment*, §59.

64. PI, p. 10.

65. In an e-mail correspondence, Arturo Silva has suggested to me that one of the most astonishing things about the second routine is that it shows Astaire dancing a duet with a man who is black, thus "that there is a biracial gay subtext here." While I am wholly sympathetic to this suggestion, I also believe that it raises as many questions as it answers: for if we have not assumed in advance, and without reference to context, the significance of a depiction of a biracial, gay transaction (that is, if we have not assumed that there is a significance that attaches *essentially* to the depiction of biracial gay transactions), then we must ask, *what work is the depiction of such a transaction doing in this particular filmic context?* My answer to this question—or, at least, the beginning of my answer—is that here a biracial gay transaction serves as the medium for a white man's appropriation of a black male sexuality. But I am reluctant to assert that the sexuality thus appropriated is exclusively "gay," as, arguably, it becomes functional, subsequently, in Astaire's heterosexual involvement with Gabrielle Girard (played in the movie by Cyd Charisse).

66. Cf. Gooding-Williams, "Black Cupids, White Desires: Reading the Representation of Racial Difference in 'Ghost' and 'Casablanca,'" pp. 155–56.

67. Interestingly, Cavell himself touches on the theme of the minstrel show in connection to the first section of the second routine: "Astaire hands the hot dog to a young boy, as if to separate himself from childish things, even from things associated with the wrong kind of entertainment, e.g., food concessions in the lobby of movie theaters (or, for all I know, of minstrel shows" (see PI, p. 21). My view, of course, is that the hot dog hand-off is the beginning of the boy's apprenticeship to Astaire, and that what Astaire has to teach him is precisely the benefits available to white manhood through minstrelsy.

68. In the early 1950s, the Freed unit of Hollywood musicals production seems to have been more than a little preoccupied with the musical's roots in black dance. It is significant, for example, that the theme is also evident in *Singin' in the*

Rain (1951). See, on this point, Carol Clover, "Dancin' in the Rain," *Critical Inquiry* 21 (Summer 1995): 722–47.

69. Here, I suspect that there is a connection between the incest theme in *Oedipus Rex* and Cordova's remarks relating Bill Robinson and Bill Shakespeare. The key point is that denying putatively "artificial" distinctions, e.g., the distinction between a man's mother and his wife that Oedipus overrides, is the very essence of the impurity that incest courts. Thus *The Band Wagon* may be read as an extended critique of Cordova's denial of the putatively artificial distinction between musicals and dramas: when he pretentiously attempts to marry the two forms, by producing a musical version of Faust, he badly fails. Astaire, of course, saves the day, by taking control of the show and leading the cast in the production of a musical revue. I should like to thank Stanley Cavell for drawing my attention (in an e-mail communication) to *The Band Wagon*'s incest motif, and thus for prompting me to think seriously about it.

70. PI, p. 17. For a discussion of minstrelsy as counterfeit, see Lott, *Love and Theft*, pp. 100–105.

71. For Cavell on theatricality, see, e.g., Stanley Cavell, *Must We Mean What We Say?* (Cambridge: Cambridge University Press, 1976), pp. 332–34, and especially 333n16. For a related discussion, see also Cavell, *The World Viewed*, 108–18. For Michael Fried's development of the notion of theatricality, which is relevantly similar to Cavell's—as Cavell acknowledges in the above-mentioned footnote—see Michael Fried, "Art and Objecthood," in his *Art and Objecthood: Essays and Reviews* (Chicago: University of Chicago Press, 1998), pp. 148–72; and Michael Fried, *Absorption and Theatricality: Painting and the Beholder in the Age of Diderot* (Chicago: University of Chicago Press, 1980), passim.

72. In this paper, I do not pursue a reading of *The Band Wagon* beyond the film's first fifteen or twenty minutes (the part of the film on which Cavell concentrates). But I am happy to have been encouraged by two readers of earlier drafts of this essay to believe that a fruitful reading of the remainder of the film could be pursued in the terms I establish through my engagement with Cavell's interpretation. E.g., both Steven Shaviro and Robin James have suggested that the racial motifs established in the film's opening sequences might be usefully brought to bear in an interpretation of the movie's "Girl Hunt" film noir parody.

73. All the material quoted in this paragraph derives from Kelly Oliver, *Womanizing Nietzsche: Philosophy's Relation to the Feminine* (New York: Routledge, 1995), pp. 83–91.

74. James Snead makes a similar point in connection to the Shirley Temple vehicles *The Littlest Rebel* and *The Little Colonel*: "we never see black families or significant relationships between black men and women. Blacks are not here for themselves, clearly, but mainly for others, and more precisely, *for whites*." See Snead, *White Screen/Black Images*, p. 58.

75. PI, p. 30.

76. All material quoted in this paragraph derives from Kelly Oliver, *Womanizing Nietzsche*, p. 200.

77. Stanley Cavell, *Philosophical Passages: Wittgenstein, Emerson, Austin, Derrida* (Oxford: Blackwell, 1995), p. 15.

78. Ibid.

79. Ibid., p. 39.

80. Toni Morrison, *Playing in the Dark: Whiteness and the Literary Imagination* (Cambridge: Harvard University Press, 1992), p. 50.

81. Frederick Douglass, *My Bondage and My Freedom*, ed. and intro. William L. Andrews (Urbana: University of Illinois Press, 1987), p. 128. For Cavell's interpretation of Emerson as an aversive thinker see Cavell, *Conditions Handsome and Unhandsome*, chap. 1.

82. Cavell neither mentions nor uses the expression "double consciousness," but he devotes much of his essay on Emerson's constitutional amending to an analysis of the distinction (between riding on the horse of one's private nature and riding on that of one's public nature) to which Emerson alludes with that expression. See Ralph Waldo Emerson, "Fate," in *Selections from Ralph Waldo Emerson*, ed. Stephen Whicher (Boston: Houghton Mifflin, 1957), p. 351. In the same volume, see "The American Scholar," pp. 79–80. For Du Bois's remarks near the end of "Of the Training of Black Men," see W. E. B. Du Bois, *The Souls of Black Folk*, ed. and intro. David W. Blight and Robert Gooding-Williams (Boston: Beford Books, 1997), p. 102. For an insightful discussion of Emerson and Du Bois in connection to the theme of grief for the loss of a child, see Thomas Dumm, "Political Theory for Losers," in *Vocations of Political Theory*, ed. Jason A. Frank and John Tambornino (Minneapolis: University of Minnesota Press, 2000), pp. 145–65.

83. Ralph Ellison, *Invisible Man* (New York: Vintage, 1995), p. 41.

CHAPTER 13

1. Plato, *Republic*, trans. G.M.A. Grube (Indianapolis: Hackett Pub., 1974), 515.

Contributors

Stanley Cavell is Walter M. Cabot Professor of Aesthetics and the General Theory of Value, Emeritus at Harvard University. He is the author of numerous books, including *Must We Mean What We Say?* (Cambridge, 1969), *The Claim of Reason: Wittgenstein, Skepticism, Morality, and Tragedy* (Oxford, 1979), *Emerson's Transcendental Etudes* (Stanford, 2003), and *Cities of Words: Pedagogical Letters on a Register of the Moral Life* (Belknap, 2004).

Ted Cohen is Professor of Philosophy at the University of Chicago. He is the author of *Jokes: Philosophical Thoughts on Joking Matters* (Chicago, 2001) and the co-editor of *Essays in Kant's Aesthetics* (Chicago, 1985) and *Pursuits of Reason: Essays in Honor of Stanley Cavell* (Texas Tech, 1993).

Piergiorgio Donatelli is Associate Professor of Philosophy at the University of Rome, La Sapienza. He is the author of *Wittgenstein e l'etica* (Laterza, 1998) and *La filosofia morale* (Laterza, 2001).

Thomas L. Dumm is Professor of Political Science at Amherst College. He is the author of numerous books, including *A Politics of the Ordinary* (New York University, 1999) and *Democracy and Punishment: Disciplinary Origins of the United States* (Wisconsin, 1987).

Richard Flathman is the George Armstrong Kelly Memorial Professor of Political Science at the Johns Hopkins University. He is the author of numerous books, including *Thomas Hobbes: Skepticism, Individuality, and Chastened Politics* (Rowman & Littlefield, 2002) and *The Philosophy and Politics of Freedom* (Chicago, 1987).

Robert Gooding-Williams is Professor of Philosophy and African American Studies at Northwestern University. He is the author of *Zarathustra's Dionysian Modernism* (Stanford, 2001) and the editor of *Reading Rodney King, Reading Urban Uprising* (Routledge, 1993).

Espen Hammer is Professor of Philosophy at the University of Oslo and Lecturer in Philosophy at the University of Essex. He is the author of *Stanley Cavell: Skepticism, Subjectivity, and the Ordinary* (Polity Press, 2002) and *Adorno* (Gyldendal, 2002), and the co-editor of *Stanley Cavell: Die Unheimlichkeit des Gewöhnlichen* (Fischer, 2002).

Sandra Laugier is Professor of Philosophy at the Université de Picardie Jules Verne (Amiens) and Junior Fellow of the Institut Universitaire de France. She is the author of *Wittgenstein: Métaphysique et jeu de langage* (PUF, 2001), *Du réel à l'ordinaire* (Vrin, 1999), and *L'anthropologie logique de Quine* (Vrin, 1992), and the French translator of a number of Cavell's books and essays.

Joseph Lima studied political theory at the Graduate Faculty of Political and Social Science, New School University, and at the University of California, San Diego. He is currently Director of Product Development at a technology firm in San Diego.

Andrew Norris is Assistant Professor of Political Science at the University of Pennsylvania. He is the editor of *Politics, Metaphysics, and Death: Essays on Giorgio Agamben's Homo Sacer* (Duke, 2005).

David Owen is Reader in Political Philosophy and Deputy Director, Centre for Post-Analytical Philosophy, University of Southampton. His books include *Maturity and Modernity* (Routledge, 1994) and *Nietzsche, Politics and Modernity* (Sage, 1995).

Hans Sluga is Professor of Philosophy at the University of California at Berkeley. He is the author of *Heidegger's Crisis: Philosophy and Politics in Nazi Germany* (Harvard, 1993) and *Gottlob Frege* (Routledge & Kegan Paul, 1980), and the co-editor of *The Cambridge Companion to Wittgenstein* (Cambridge, 1996).

Tracy B. Strong is Professor of Political Science at the University of California, San Diego. He is the author of numerous books, including *Friedrich Nietzsche and the Politics of Transfiguration* (California, 1988) and *Jean Jacques Rousseau and the Politics of the Ordinary* (Rowman & Littlefield, 2002).

Index